ON
PRODUCING
SHAKESPEARE

To
MY WIFE

ON PRODUCING
SHAKESPEARE

BY RONALD WATKINS

with drawings by

MAURICE PERCIVAL

London
MICHAEL JOSEPH

First published by
MICHAEL JOSEPH LTD.
26 Bloomsbury Street
London, W.C.1
1950

Set and printed in Great Britain by Tonbridge Printers Ltd.,
Peach Hall Works, Tonbridge, in Baskerville ten on eleven
point, on paper made by John Dickinson at Croxley, and bound
by James Burn at Esher

Preface

NO ONE who writes about Shakespeare can hope to acknowledge all that he owes to his predecessors. The names of many to whom I am indebted are recorded in the text or the footnotes of this book: but three I would like to mention here with special gratitude. It was the *Prefaces* of Harley Granville-Barker that first led me to study the Elizabethan presentation of Shakespeare's plays. John Cranford Adams, by his *The Globe Playhouse: Its Design and Equipment*, made clear to me what the material conditions of such a presentation were, and I am glad of the opportunity to thank him for his kindly personal interest in my researches and for his generous permission to make use of his plans and models. Thirdly, I owe much to T. W. Baldwin's *The Organization and Personnel of the Shakespearean Company*, and for leave to reproduce some of the conjectural cast-lists which appear in that book.

My thanks are also due to the Governors of Dulwich College for permission to reproduce the portraits of Richard Burbadge and William Sly from their Gallery; to the Keeper of the Ashmolean Museum for the portrait of John Lowin; and to the Delegates of the Clarendon Press for leave to print E. K. Chambers' chronological list of the plays.

The theory of production put forward in my book would perhaps carry less weight if it had not been possible to test it in practice by continuous and progressive experiment. For this opportunity I am first and foremost indebted to the Governors of Harrow School and to two Head Masters; as also to the enthusiastic co-operation of all who have taken part whether on or off the platform in Speech Room since 1941; especially to Mr. Maurice Percival and the Reverend H. L. Harris, who have collaborated in these productions; to Mr. Henry Havergal and Mr. Hector McCurrach for their help with the music, and to the latter in particular for his advice on the section of my book which deals with the musical accompaniment of the play. Not least is my debt to Mr. E. V. C. Plumptre, who both as official chronicler and unofficial critic of the series has constantly encouraged me to persevere in my attempts to convince others beside myself that there is a right way to produce Shakespeare.

Finally, I take this opportunity of thanking Mrs. Judith Thorp for drawing some of the plans and diagrams, Miss E. Stein and Mrs. M. Blundell for preparing the typescript for the press, and Mr. Douglas Wilson for his meticulous care in checking the quotations and references, and in constructing the indices.

R. W.

Contents

Illustrations

Drawings in the text by MAURICE PERCIVAL

INTRODUCTION

THE history of the production of Shakespeare's plays in this country is an interesting but melancholy study,[1] reflecting little credit on his own profession and excusing, if not justifying, the habitual apathy of those scholars and critics and other admirers of the poet who prefer to experience his plays in imagination rather than in the theatre. Amid a bewildering variety of experiments in new methods of presentation, one fact emerges with unmistakable clarity—that never since the closing of the theatres in 1642 has a play of his been performed in the conditions for which he devised it. The story of divergence begins with a positive and quite sincere attack, on critical principles: D'Avenant, learning in the school of Ben Jonson and in the French tradition, honestly believed that Shakespeare's artless genius needed refinement, and re-wrote *Macbeth* so that it should preserve harmony of style and balance of plot. Yet it was uncritical fashion and the demands of popular taste that, as soon as the theatres were again licensed, made two radical changes in the tradition of performance. The substance of a complaint by the old King's Men (the survivors of Shakespeare's own company) in a petition of October 13th, 1660, was that Killigrew had suppressed them till they agreed to act with women in a new theatre and with stage scenery. Already in the early 1660's Pepys was admiring the painted scenery in a performance of *Hamlet* and approving of the employment of actresses in Shakespearian adaptations; and Dryden's version of *The Tempest* (another "refinement", prompted no doubt by D'Avenant) provided two pairs of lovers, a sister for Caliban, and a lady spirit to dance with Ariel in the finale. The curtained inset that housed the painted scenery inevitably came to acquire more and more importance, but it was not till the eighteenth century that, to make the pit bigger, the fore-stage was reduced: thereafter the main acting arena lay behind the proscenium, and the space in front was no more than an annexe to it. This structural change, together with the previous importation of actresses and painted scenery, and the introduction of lighting effects—in which Garrick had a hand—created a quite new technique in production and (in the words of Harold Child) "henceforth there was a continuous series of attempts (culminating in the theatre of Beerbohm Tree) to fit Shakespeare not (as Dryden, D'Avenant and their like had) into new critical rules, but into a stage for which his plays were not written".[2]

---

[1] It is clearly and concisely set forth by Harold Child in the last chapter of *A Companion to Shakespeare Studies* (Cambridge), 325–46.　　　　[2] *op. cit.*, 335.

To-day we think we are in a position to smile at the misconceptions of D'Avenant and Dryden, to laugh outright at the outrages of Nahum Tate who provided *King Lear* with a happy ending, and to show but qualified approval of the influence of Garrick himself. For we have learnt some respect for the text of the poet. But we still have an inconsistent readiness to alter it when it crosses our purpose, and this it seems to do surprisingly often. Yet we should not be surprised, for the most frequent reason is plain enough—that we are trying the impossible, to fit the square peg into the round hole, to make the plays effective on a stage for which they were not designed. We are not without prophets who have denounced the absurdity of this procedure; William Poel's performances for the Elizabethan Stage Society are now almost legendary, and few in this generation will have been fortunate enough to see them; but Nugent Monck at Norwich still continues his long tradition which can boast the production of all Shakespeare's plays in an Elizabethan style; and Granville-Barker in his *Prefaces* and other essays never ceased to urge, with the sweet reasonableness characteristic of all his advocacy, that Shakespeare's stagecraft cannot be understood apart from the stage for which it was intended. Yet even these prophets of common sense have made concessions to convention and custom and the supposition that the twentieth century has little capacity for make-believe; lighting effects, for instance, are deemed necessary in spite of the Elizabethan daylight tradition, and a boy Cleopatra is still unthinkable. And though these concessions seem trivial, they are not so; for (to take but one example) a dramatist will not write a night scene the same way for a daylight performance as he will for an artificially darkened stage—not if he knows his job, still less if he is a poetic dramatist of genius. The strange thing is that though we acknowledge Shakespeare as the greatest of poets, his own profession, one and all, suppose that they can teach him a thing or two about stagecraft; and if we may judge by the current performances of the London theatre, none realise the truth that he is one of the select few—have there been as many as a dozen in the western hemisphere? —who have known how to create poetic drama.

It is not uncommon nowadays to hear lip-service paid to the memory of William Poel: it is said, for instance, that his soul goes marching on, that his spirit survives in the Shakespearian productions of to-day. Would it were so! The claim would seem to be based largely on such facts as that permanent sets are used in many productions to give speed to the continuity; that the scenic effects are often simple and stylised; that sometimes a kind of apron-annexe is employed to bring the actors nearer to their audience; that in comparison with our predecessors we are much less squeamish in the expurgation of the text. But if these are straws in the wind pointing in Poel's direction, the wind itself has long since lost its force, and with Granville-Barker's late lamented death is in danger of blowing itself out altogether: soon we shall forget what even these straws portend. More sinister even than the delusion that we are following Poel's lead is the belief often expressed by our leading dramatic critics and producers, and even sometimes by scholars, that there are many different ways of presenting Shakespeare and every single one of them right; that all the methods of the Shakespearian producers are valuable, if sincerely, efficiently handled; that each man will bring out his own points; that a production is bound to be successful if it "has an idea behind it"; that (the most insidious form of the doctrine) Shakespeare wrote for all time in writing for his own, and so his universality makes it possible for his work to be produced in a dozen different ways.

Such statements as these ignore the significant fact, one of the few undisputed in Shakespeare's life, that during the busiest years of his career as dramatist he was a working member of the most successful theatrical company in London; and it is not rash to infer from contemporary evidence that he was one of the chief causes of their success. He was indeed a practical man of the theatre and, whatever his skill as an actor, he knew the ropes. He was writing for the immediate needs of his theatre (a theatre fundamentally different from the modern picture stage), and for a particular repertory company of players, whose tradition of acting was by necessity more imaginative and versatile than that needed by our actors. It is with a disloyalty unusual in the profession that their descendants of today allow them to be represented as a sort of crude and incompetent barn-stormers.

Why is it so hard to believe that Shakespeare was a dramatist of genius as well as a poet of genius? Indeed he is perhaps the only writer in our language who was both, and who discovered the elusive art of poetic drama. And if a dramatist of genius, does that not mean that he evolved from the conditions of his playhouse his own method of presenting a story—which must be the *best*, if we can discover it? We do not go to the other side of idolatry in our appreciation if we suggest that it is a reasonable and becoming humility for a producer, in approaching one or other of the plays, to assume that Shakespeare knew more about stagecraft than he does himself. His is the best method—if we can discover it. It is the purpose of this book to show that we can, with the help of modern scholarship, go a long way towards discovering it. If a perusal of this argument brings

actors and scholars closer together in a unity of purpose to interpret
Shakespeare, it will have achieved something: but it is addressed not
only to the experts of the theatre and the study, but also to the
ordinary playgoer. Its ambition is a far-reaching one, nothing short,
indeed, of realising the plays of Shakespeare as they have never been
realised since the destruction of the second Globe. This ambition
cannot, of course, be fulfilled by the mere writing and reading of a
book. The text of a play does not come to life until it is performed,
and the theory of a play's production has even less life than the play's
text until that theory is put into practice. We cannot be sure what a
performance at the Globe would be like till we have built the Globe
and trained a repertory company in the special acting tradition of
the Chamberlain's Men. Much, therefore, of what follows is tentative and conjectural, waiting upon such performance for the ultimate
test: but the theory would not, and could not, have been put forward
if it had not already received some practical testing in a series of
experimental performances in a makeshift Globe; on such a series [3]
the argument of the following pages is largely built.

It should be generally known that in the last decade American
scholarship has provided the practical basis for constructing a replica
of the Globe theatre. In 1942 John Cranford Adams published his
comprehensive study of *The Globe Playhouse: Its Design and Equipment*,
resolving the doubts and problems of previous investigations into a
clear-cut factual account, both practically and æsthetically satisfying,
of that famous structure. His work, while not unchallenged in points
of detail, proceeds on firm critical principles to many positive conclusions, and is summarised in diagrams of the playhouse at all
levels, from which it is possible to draw architect's plans, to construct
a model, and to erect the playhouse itself.

An illustrated description of the Globe, based upon Dr. Adams'
diagrams, is therefore the substance of the first chapter of this book,
so that the reader may quickly feel at home in the familiar surroundings of Shakespeare's daily life. There follows a brief exhortation to
approach the plays afresh by using nothing but the Quarto and
Folio texts, some of which at least are very close to the poet's own
manuscript or to the prompt-book from which the actors worked.
Chapter III takes leave to suppose that a performance at the Globe
would be plotted and rehearsed under the guidance of one leading

---

[3] In Harrow School Speech Room the following plays have been produced in
Elizabethan conditions: *Twelfth Night* (1941), *Henry V* (1942), *Macbeth* (1943), *A
Midsummer Night's Dream* (1945), *Julius Caesar* (1946), 1 *Henry IV* (1947); *Macbeth*
was repeated in 1949, with the addition for the first time of an upper stage; and
Twelfth Night was repeated in 1950.

member of the company, and for the immediate purpose that member is identified with the book-keeper. We look over his shoulder as he sets about preparing his prompt-book for performance: his province would include the distributing of the scene-rotation on the seven different acting areas of the multiple stage; the furnishing and properties; the use of the permanent stage features; the costumes; the music; the effects; the plotting of entries. Certain sequences we shall find recurring as especially well adapted to this playhouse—the street sequences, the battle sequences, and some others—and we shall take note of that characteristic quality of the Elizabethan stage (to the book-keeper and the players a commonplace) of seeming nowhere, of being for the moment unlocalised.

Chapter IV turns the attention of the reader from the book-keeper to his colleagues and discusses the peculiarities of their acting tradition—first, their mastery of the art of speech, involving accomplishments of whose existence all but a few of to-day's actors seem to be unaware; then their creative mimicry; the opportunities for variety of grouping afforded by the shape, dimensions and central position of the platform, and the consequent relation between actor and audience; the unusual quality of their characterisation. In a digression we make personal acquaintance with some of the players and discuss the important issue of the boy-actors playing the feminine rôles. The acting tradition is summarised in an example from *Julius Caesar*, which develops a typical train of reasoning to infer how the Chamberlain's Men would have played the scene of Caesar's murder.

The reader is now in a position to guess at the plotting of any of Shakespeare's plays upon the Globe stage, and to form some idea of how the players would render it. But the investigation would be of little value if it could not be shown that such an imaginative reconstruction of a Globe performance reveals the poet's stagecraft more clearly than ever before. Chapter V therefore sets the poet in his most natural surroundings, not at Court in the train of Essex and Southampton, but among his colleagues and collaborators in the playhouse. The attempt is made to show that the highest flights of his inspiration take wing from the firm ground of the multiple Globe stage, and the hardly changing personnel of a fixed repertory, and that they soar with no less lofty freedom for that reason; that with his genius for turning necessity into opportunity, he found the seeming limitations of his stage and its equipment the perfect vehicle for his poetic drama. The guess may be hazarded that if he had been born in a later age, more mechanically skilled than his own, he might have found the elaborate machinery a stricter curb upon the freedom of his inspiration; and indeed that the growing popular interest in spectacle and masque may have had something to do with his willingness to break his rod at the early age of forty-six.

The argument is rounded off in Chapter VI with an extended example of his mature and sustained stagecraft. Some salient features of a performance of *Macbeth* at the Globe are described in the form of producer's notes. It will be observed that by the choice of this example (and by the drawing of most of the illustrations in the previous chapters from plays written before it) the field of investigation is deliberately limited to a time before the acquisition of the Blackfriars, before the influence of the private theatres and of the masque had begun to affect Shakespeare's style, before—can one say it?—the strain of decadence had crept in, which perhaps was one of the contributory causes of Shakespeare's giving up his association with the theatre. The last period—the period of the so-called romances—examined from this point of view, is worth a separate study. Meanwhile *Macbeth* is chosen to represent a summit of Shakespeare's stagecraft, mature and sustained and as yet unaffected by the decadence of fashion.

The book is by implication a plea for the rebuilding now, after three hundred years, of the Globe—in London, preferably, in Stratford too, if possible, and wherever an audience will meet to support a Shakespearian repertory. This is not the place to discuss the economics of such a venture, but it is worth whispering that, once the theatre was built, equipped and endowed, the expenses of production would be small compared with those current in our London theatres, and that the cost of building and endowment would perhaps be not much more than has been spent in making a film of one single play. It is likely that we shall be obliged to wait a number of years before we are allowed to pace the yard of the twentieth-century Globe. An interim policy is therefore urged in an Epilogue, which sets forth in recapitulation the bare essentials of the Elizabethan circumstances of performance. If a sufficient number of repertories, whether professional or amateur, believe in and practise the right method—Shakespeare's method—we can perhaps look forward to a time when we shall wonder how it was that anything else was ever thought tolerable. In conclusion, the suggestion is put forward that Shakespeare himself, in spite of an occasional disarming apology, was far from dissatisfied with the "Woodden O" in whose planning he is known to have taken a hand; and that poets of to-day might not be the last to welcome a new Globe in which to set free the wings of their inspiration now cramped behind the cage-door of the proscenium arch.

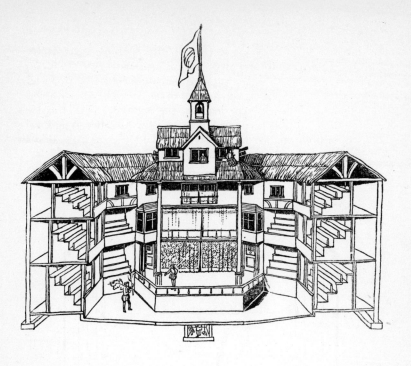

I

THE PLAYHOUSE[1]

SHAKESPEARE had good cause to be satisfied with the
"Woodden O": he had a hand in planning it. The new playhouse, built on the Bankside with materials carried over the
river from the old Theatre, was made to suit the wishes of a syndicate
of seven men, among them Burbadge, Heminges, and Shakespeare.

[1] The account of the playhouse given in this chapter is based upon John Cranford Adams' *The Globe Playhouse: Its Design and Equipment* (Harvard University
Press, 1942). The three sketch-plans are made from the diagrams in his book, and
the diagonal view is based on a model made under his direction at Illinois
University. The details of Adams' reconstruction (and even the octagonal shape)
have not gone unchallenged since the publication of his book, but its completeness,
the practical good sense of its reasoning, and the artistic "rightness" of the resultant
plans, make it the most satisfactory blue-print available for the rebuilding of the
Globe, whether in fact or in imagination, and thereby create the opportunity to
recapture the atmosphere of the Elizabethan playhouse and the essential conditions
of performance.

To this extent the design has the imprimatur of the poet himself. His
familiarity with the idea of architectural projects finds expression in
a play of 1597–8 [2]. We may suppose that the Globe was a development of the plan of its predecessor, but that it included improvements
suggested by the daily experience of the actors.[3] It is not rash to
assume that most of the plays Shakespeare wrote after 1599 [4] were
devised for performance in this playhouse, and it seems likely that all
his plays were at one time or another performed there.

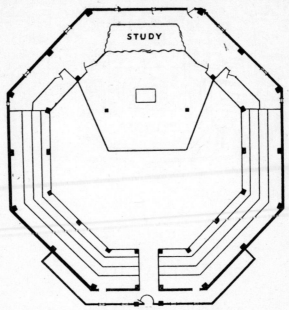

The Playhouse—ground plan

A glance at the ground-plan is the best introduction to this building. The octagonal frame is about 84 feet in outside diameter—
hardly more than the length of a lawn-tennis court. A concentric
octagon within the frame bounds the Yard, which is open to the sky.
Between the two octagons the space is roofed and the building rises
to three storeys. Nearly five of the eight sides of the octagonal frame
are occupied by galleries from which the eyes of the spectators con-
verge upon the stage. The Yard will hold 600 standing close-packed

---

[2] *2 Henry IV*, I. iii. 41 ff. The image is developed for some twenty lines.
[3] See Cranford Adams' diagram, *op. cit.*, 172.
[4] Though the possibility that after 1608 he was writing for the Blackfriars must
be taken into account. See *Shakespeare Survey*, I, p. 47.

(the groundlings); the three galleries about 1,400. At the first
performance of a new play by Shakespeare, there would be as many
as 2,000 "within the Girdle of these walls". The first impression of
the playgoer in this theatre is that of being one of a great crowd, the
next of being in intimate touch with the players. This combination
of community and intimacy is a peculiar characteristic of the
Elizabethan playhouse, hardly known in the modern theatre except
perhaps when the comedian in a music-hall comes down to the foot-

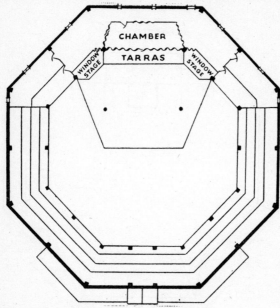

The Playhouse—Tarras level

lights to take his audience into his confidence. Intimacy is possible at
the Globe because of the position of the platform. The middle point
of the front edge is the exact centre of the octagon. The actor in
soliloquy can have his audience on three sides of him. There is real
distance in the depth of the stage, and an actor in the Study will
seem remote while another in front seems close at hand: this contrast
in their relation to the audience is often used for dramatic purpose.

The Platform is the main field of action for the players: it can
never be hidden from view and, except for the curtained recess on
all three levels, it will present the same architectural features
throughout the play. It tapers towards the front, stands probably
between 4 and 5 feet from the floor of the Yard, and is protected

from the groundlings by low rails: the front edge is 24 feet wide, at its widest it is 41 feet; its depth from front to Study-curtain is 29 feet; and the Study itself, when open, adds a further 7 or 8 feet. Conspicuous towards the front of the Platform stand the two Pillars supporting the overhanging canopy of the Heavens: these are probably made of masts from the shipping of the neighbouring Thames, and are boxed in at the bottom to a height of about 3 feet.

The Tiring-House is the permanent background to the Platform:

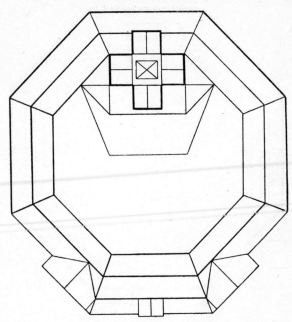

The Playhouse—roof level

its back is turned to the afternoon sun, so that no freaks of light and shade distract from the illusion; at the same time the canopy of the Heavens and the Huts above it protect the spectators from the glare of the sun in their eyes. On the Platform level the curtained inset usually called the Study is flanked by the two Doors, set forward at an angle corresponding to the shape of the octagonal structure. These are the two main entries for the players, and are always in view undisguised: they have the appearance of the street-door of an Elizabethan town-house, with substantial doorposts on either side of them, supporting the bay-windows which overhang the lintel: the streets of Tewkesbury or Gloucester provide examples of the

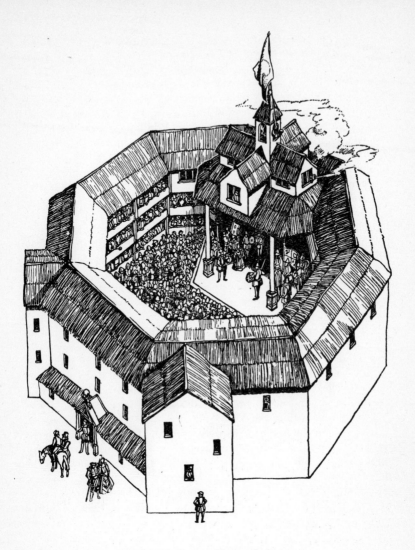

The Playhouse—diagonal view

architectural style. There is a knocker, and a wicket in the upper part for the use of the prompter or sometimes of a character in the play. On the second level the curtained inset, known as the Chamber, is flanked by the Window-Stages which overhang the Doors: these Windows are also used by the actors when the need arises. An important feature of the second level is the Tarras (or terrace), an overhanging balcony connecting the two Window-Stages; the Tarras can be used independently, when the drawn curtain is concealing the Chamber; but since its railing is made of slender balusters, it is no longer noticed when the Chamber is revealed. On either side then of the central face of the Tiring-House, there is a permanent architectural unit modelled on the façade of an Elizabethan town-house.

The appearance of this façade would perhaps be modified by the hangings of different colours chosen to suit the type of play.[5]

The central face is made up of curtained insets at all three levels. On the ground floor is the Study, 23 feet wide, 7 or 8 feet deep, 12 feet high. The appearance of this inner stage can be altered by hangings, furniture and properties, but it too has certain permanent features which can be used or concealed according to the needs of the moment. On the actors' left of the rear wall is a door which when opened reveals behind it the foot of a flight of stairs running up towards the right. On the actors' right is a window. Between door and window is a curtained recess for hiding or disclosing. On the second level the Chamber (23 feet wide, 11 feet deep with the Tarras, 11 feet high) has the same features as the Study, except that the door and window are on opposite sides of the recess: the logical reason for this difference is that the staircase which rises from the Study door on the left leads straight up to the Chamber door on the right. On the third level, a narrower gallery is mainly reserved for the musicians, but this too is sometimes used by the actors when the play demands an appearance at a lofty height.

Above the third level the canopy of the Heavens overhangs most of the Platform, painted blue and adorned with the signs of the zodiac, providing some cover for the actors and serving, it seems, as a sounding-board for their voices. Above the Heavens stand the Huts which contain the thunder (appropriately situated), the artillery and many other devices for creating effects of sound. There is also a winch and pulley operating through a trap-door in the

---

[5] The reader's attention is drawn to an article in *Theatre Notebook*, Vol. I, No. 8, for July, 1947, by C. Walter Hodges, who suggests an elaborate Italianate facade for the Tiring-House. A lively reconstruction of the Globe, which differs in many respects from that of Cranford Adams, appears in Hodges' *Shakespeare and the Players* (1948).

Heavens to allow sprites and other apparitions to descend by a cable on to the Platform. Other machinery and other trap-doors in all three floors of the Tiring-House can be brought into play both during performance and in the process of moving furniture and properties from the storerooms in preparation for the day's play.

The Chamber

Above the Huts rises the Bell-Tower, and, surmounting all, a flag-pole from which streams the flag (of a colour fitting to the occasion) announcing to the citizens of London that the actors are presenting a play.

Under the Platform lies the capacious region of Hell, excavated to allow of a height of perhaps 8 feet, and approached by the big main Trap (8 feet by 4 feet) and other subsidiary traps on the Plat-form itself, and by the "grave-trap" in the Study. From this source arise apparitions, smoke and fog, and into its depths descend those who would go underground, whether into the cellar, the hold of a ship, or the tomb.

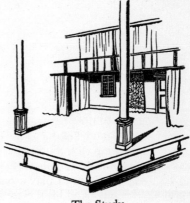

The Study

It will become more and more apparent as we study the plays in the setting of this playhouse how admirably equipped it is for all the needs of the dramatist, and especially how it suits the *poetic* dramatist and stirs him to

The audience from the Platform

his happiest invention. But it should be stressed at once that the conventional picture of the Elizabethan theatre as a simple and primitive structure, a handicap to those who had to work in it, is wide of the mark. As a medium of expression it compares favourably with the modern picture-stage enclosed in its proscenium arch. It has seven separate acting areas—the Platform, the Study, the Chamber, the Tarras, the two Window-Stages, and the Music Gallery—and it has dimensions both of height and depth beyond anything the modern stage can show. The sight-lines from the audience are such as to make the action three-dimensional instead of pictorial. The Platform itself is a vast area and dominates the playhouse. Standing between the Heavens above and Hell beneath, it is indeed a model of the whole world, the great Globe itself, and it is not surprising that Shakespeare was so fond of pointing the likeness in his familiar metaphor. If to him all the world's a stage, a stage where every man must play a part, the poet finds it no less easy to think of his stage and his theatre as all the world.

2

THE PROMPT BOOK

IF we are to study the methods of the Chamberlain's Men, we must first try to come by a copy of their prompt-book. Facsimiles of the early Quartos and the first Folio are now available, and there is no reason why the twentieth-century producer should not be put in touch thus far with the practice of the Globe company. The relation of the Quarto and Folio texts to Shakespeare's manuscript and the players' prompt-copy varies from play to play, and can be studied in Chapters IV, V and IX of the first volume of E. K. Chambers' *William Shakespeare*; for those plays which are already published in the New Cambridge Edition there is further and more elaborate speculation in Dover Wilson's "Notes on the Copy". Pollard, McKerrow and Greg all allow us to think that many of these printed texts may be derived from the theatrical prompt-books; and it is surprising how little the theatre of to-day has profited from this probability.

The value of studying the early printed texts is partly a negative one: by so doing we can ignore the misleading additions of later editors. We shall no longer try to give a geographical locality to scenes which Shakespeare was not at pains to define: we shall no longer be concerned with the division of act and scene, which disturbs the flow and rhythm of Shakespeare's continuity: we shall no longer regularise the metre and impose logic on the punctuation. But there are also positive advantages which, as this argument proceeds, will become clearer in detail. Some of these may well be suggested here in advance.

In the first place, we are helped at once by the feeling of being in and about the Tiring-House of the Globe at rehearsal time. Occasionally the names of the players pop out at us—quite famous actors like Kemp and Cowley, or obscurer "supers" like Sinklo and Humfrey who are bidden to enter *with Crosse-bowes in their hands;* or a singer, when in *Much Ado About Nothing, Enter prince, Leonato, Claudio, and Jacke Wilson;* or a mere musician, when the rustic comedians in *A Midsummer Night's Dream* are preceded by *Tawyer with a trumpet before them.* In an earlier scene of the same play *Enter Piramus with the ass head* has a true whiff of the overworked property stores. As we read in *The Taming of the Shrew, Enter Biondello, Lucentio and Bianca, Gremio is out before,* we seem to hear the spoken explanations of the directing prompter.

.Stage-directions—though few in number, and abrupt in tone, especially while the author is in active association with his players— are nevertheless sometimes revealing of the players' practice. A selected list from quartos and folios is given by W. W. Greg in *The Editorial Problem in Shakespeare.*[1] The most cursory glance at his list evokes a series of vivid pictures in the mind's eye. Particularly rich in description are those plays written before the poet had a major hand in their presentation, and, at the other end of the series, those of the period when Shakespeare was already severing his connection with the playhouse. But whether the directions reproduce the author's descriptive imagination or the book-keeper's practical play-house experience or a reporter's view of what he saw, they often give the hint of the practice of the players in interpreting Shakespeare's sure dramatic instinct. A Messenger enters with news of the Duke of York's death: *Enter one blowing,* reads the Folio. When the Prince of Morocco woos Portia, *Enter Morochus a tawnie Moore all in white, and three or foure followers accordingly:* no doubt the white robe throws his dark face—and Portia's involuntary revulsion—into relief; yet a recent Morocco at Stratford wore black and had a comely almond face. "Sweare," says the old mole in *Hamlet: Ghost cries under the Stage,* we are told; but mostly we must be content with a muffled outcry in the wings. The spellbound lovers in *A Midsummer Night's Dream* are roused by the hunt on May-morning: *Hornes and they wake. Shout within, they all start up:* this is a clear indication of the action on the stage. There is vivid drama in *Enter Cassandra with her haire about her eares.*

Sometimes the characterisation is made clear through the stage-directions of the text: it is thanks to the Folio that we know that Princess Katherine's attendant, Alice, is *an old Gentlewoman; Enter young Osricke* has the appropriate touch of patronage due to that "waterflie"; *Enter the King and his poore Soldiers* hits off to perfection the dangerous crisis of Henry V's invasion of France. Other evidence of this kind appears in the occasional cast-lists printed at beginning or end of the plays, where the persons of the play are sometimes further described by the characteristics of their part, as from *Othello: Iago, a Villaine; Rodorigo, a gull'd Gentleman.* We may feel very close to the prompt-book and indeed to Shakespeare's own composition

---

[1] pp. 158 ff.

when we come across the variation of speech-headings: *Capulet,* for instance, alternates with *Father, Lady Capulet* with *Mother; Armado* becomes *Braggart, Pedant* also stands for *Holofernes.* In discussing this phenomenon, McKerrow says: ". . . it seems to me highly probable that all plays in which we find this peculiar uncertainty as to speech-headings were printed either from the author's original manuscript or from a close transcript of this. I believe that, although Shakespeare generally fixed upon a name for each of his characters on his or her first introduction, in the heat of composition their qualities or the part which they played in the action were often more strongly present to his imagination than their personal names." [2] We shall have occasion to return to this theme in a later chapter: it is enough for the moment to suggest that if this was the attitude of the poet in composition, it might well affect the conception of the actor in the interpretation of his part.

More important than the stage-directions, cast-lists and speech-headings, is the text itself; and here the early editions can be of the greatest use to an actor who will take pains to study them. It is not a new discovery that the punctuation of the Folio can help the speaker to interpret Shakespeare's intention. McKerrow came to the conclusion that "throughout the [Elizabethan] period there seems to have been in progress a gradual change-over from a method of punctuation based simply upon the natural pauses in reading to one which took account mainly of the logical relationship of the parts of a sentence, with the natural result of much confusion between the two systems". He goes on: "In the majority of texts, at any rate in those that are printed from the First Folio, it will, I think, be found that though the punctuation may at first seem somewhat strange, and though it is undoubtedly less regular than we are accustomed to nowadays, it really presents no more difficulty to the reader than the old spelling does, while it often suggests the way in which a speech is intended to be uttered more clearly than does the more 'logical' punctuation of the modern texts." [3] But it was as recently as 1948 that Dr. Richard Flatter's book, *Shakespeare's Producing Hand,* in less than two hundred pages made plain the truth that the First Folio is a gold-mine of instruction for producers. It is not only the punctuation that over and over again indicates the intended pause: one need only dip into *Julius Caesar* to believe this, or to speak from the Folio page Hamlet's first soliloquy, and the subsequent dialogue with Horatio, Marcellus and Bernardo, or to hear Othello's dying speech.

---

[2] *Prolegomena to the Oxford Shakespeare,* 57.
[3] *op cit.,* pp. 41–2. The reader is also referred to Percy Simpson's monograph on *Shakesperian Punctuation.*

A trivial comic example occurs in *The Merry Wives of Windsor*: when Mrs. Quickly tells Falstaff that Ford "will be absence from his house, between ten and eleven", Falstaff reiterates the time "Ten, and eleven", and each mention has the comma to mark his deliberation and his anxiety to be sure. But Flatter makes it equally clear that the lineation is deliberately planned and that it contains, as plainly as a musical score, the instructions of the poet to his players. If a line is "defective", it is meant to be short: there is a pause to be filled by action, gesture, or the natural hesitation of profound feeling; or else an actor may be ignoring an interruption and continuing his own rhythm from a previous speech; or there may be simultaneous speaking of two or more speakers. Such is the trend of Flatter's skilful and convincing argument, and its corollary is that Nicholas Rowe and Pope and the other editors of Shakespeare have obscured these directions by "regularising" the verse and imposing a logical punctuation.

It should be added that while these early printed texts can be of the greatest value in interpretation, it is unwise to push the argument too far and to expect exactitude or consistency in the transmission of Shakespeare's purpose or the practice of his fellows. There is a carefree artlessness, a very human proneness to blunder in the compositors, an occasional twinge of impatience or a sly dig of exasperated humour. Leonato's brother is at first called *Bro.* in the speech-headings, but when Leonato persists in naming him, the printer yields under pressure of the repetition and marks him *Ant.* for Antonio. As Romeo and Juliet are parting for the last time, they are interrupted by the Nurse, who cries "Madam" to her newly-married charge: Juliet answers "Nurse". The compositor, his attention straying, puts in a direction—*Enter Madam and Nurse.* Hamlet asks Rosencrantz and Guildenstern to invite the King and Queen to come and see the play: "Will you two helpe to hasten them?" "We will my Lord": and the Second Quarto adds *Exeunt they two.* One wonders whether that compositor was altogether guiltless of a sense of humour who made Laertes say to Claudius "To his good Friends, thus wide Ile ope my Armes: And like the kinde Life-rend'ring Politician [*for* Pelican], Repast them with my blood". Exasperation and absence of mind and naïveté and impishness present the textual critic with untidy, unreliable material for his exact science: to the student of the theatre they add touches of reality and humanity to the imagined atmosphere.

One must not neglect, nor yet overstress, a further positive—if more intangible—advantage in using the contemporary editions. By their aid we see the whole drama through Elizabethan spectacles.

The sub-structure of Shakespeare's stage-vision is habitually Elizabethan: his Athenian yokels are grounded in Warwickshire, his
Roman senators have a palpable kinship with the nobles at Queen
Elizabeth's court. We shall have occasion to develop this theme in
the opening of Chapter V. For the moment it is enough to say that
the very look of the page and the individual freedom of the spelling
helps to project our imagination into the atmosphere of the time,
gives us the feeling that we are back in the Globe playhouse in the
most astonishingly adventurous years of our theatrical history.

3

PLOTTING WITH THE BOOK-KEEPER

SOMEONE—or some two or three—in the Chamberlain's Company must have fulfilled the function of our producer. A play does not come to life in the theatre without some guiding hand in plotting and rehearsal; nor is it sensible to accept as fact the satirical picture of muddle made delightfully familiar by Sheridan in *The Critic* and with more specific reference by Maurice Baring in his *Diminutive Dramas*. We do not know exactly who gave the instructions—whether Burbadge or (as seems unlikely) Shakespeare himself or the book-keeper—but it is plain that the instructions were recorded by the "book-keeper" in the "book" to which the actors would refer their individual parts, and that the "book" was held by the prompter or "book-holder", who no doubt controlled the whole action during performance. Greg has a note on the subject: "The book-keeper was properly the person charged with the custody of the company's stock of 'books'. Presumably it was his business to see to the writing of the prompt-book, to prepare it in accordance with the needs of production, and to provide for its safe custody. I suppose he also attended to the writing of the plot and the actors' parts. The technical name for the prompter was the 'book-holder'. . . . It does not perhaps necessarily follow that the book-keeper and the book-holder were always the same person, but since it must be difficult to distinguish their functions it is simple to assume that they were." [1] Since we are embarked upon a voyage of conjecture, we may gratefully use the person of the book-keeper for our compass. Even if he is only acting as secretary for some other controlling spirit in the playhouse, we can look over his shoulder and see what he jots down in the prompt-book. To dally still more recklessly with surmise, we may follow Dover Wilson as he talks, in his "Note on the Folio Text" of *A Midsummer Night's Dream*, of Tawyer and his trumpet in the last act: "Tawyer is the name of an actor or rather a playhouse servant, who died in 1625 and was described in the sexton's register as 'Mr. Heminges man'. Now it is perfectly obvious that the bulk of the

---

[1] W. W. Greg, *The Editorial Problem in Shakespeare*, 158–9.

Q. stage-directions, before coming into the hands of the F. compositors, had been amplified, rectified and generally overhauled by some masterful person. The entry of Tawyer with his trumpet and of Bottom with 'the ass-head' tells us who this masterful person was: he was the stage-manager of Shakespeare's company, possibly Heminge himself or his friend Condell . . ." [2] T. W. Baldwin points out that Peter Quince exercises a triple function as book-keeper, prompter and stage-keeper,[3] and Peter Quince is, after all, in farcical guise, the model of the man we are looking for. The harassed Peter Quince or the masterful Heminges? We do not know his identity. Let us call him the Book-Keeper and take leave to look over his shoulder.

(i) Scene-Rotation

With the manuscript of the new play before him, one of his first problems will be to decide which scene is to be played on which part of the multiple stage. Shakespeare is presumably at his elbow to tell him his intention and, though we are not so lucky, there are usually clues enough for us to recapture the original scene-rotation.

In the first place, we must become used to the idea of the Platform being quite self-sufficient: it is not an apron in front of a proscenium; it is the main acting arena, to which the other stages are subsidiary. To test this, one need only begin reading on page 461 (125) of the Folio in 2 *Henry VI*. After the scene of the arrest of the Duchess of Gloster,[4] who appears *aloft*, there is no occasion for, or possibility of, using the upper stages for at least ten pages—nearly an hour in acting time. We get the impression that it was habitual to expect the main action on the Platform. This play was written before the Chamber had been developed as an acting stage. But even later, the traditional pre-eminence of the Platform persists. It appears that it was not an invariable rule that the Study should be open at the end or climax of a play. For instance, the last scene of *Much Ado About Nothing* cannot make use of the Study, which still contains the monument-furniture of the penultimate scene. Cranford Adams places the last four scenes of *King Lear* entirely on the Platform.[5]

The Platform can be anywhere or nowhere: it can assume its visible appearance, of a street with a row of houses; it can represent anything suggested by the words of the speakers, or by the furniture

---

[2] *A Midsummer Night's Dream* (*New Cambridge Shakespeare*), 155. See below, p. 157.
[3] T. W. Baldwin, *Organization and Personnel of the Shakespearean Company*, 135.
[4] 2 *Henry VI*, I. iv.
[5] J. Cranford Adams, *The Original Staging of King Lear*, 332 ff.

of the Study, if open. Almost any scene which is supposed to take place in the open air—whether in the streets, in the wood, on the heath, or on the field of battle—will be acted on the Platform, with or without the addition of the Study. It is also used for an interior scene, often in conjunction with the Study which contains the solid furniture of such a scene.

The Study is sometimes used by itself for an interior setting, such as Friar Lawrence's cell. Scenes before and after show the characters entering or leaving the house in which the Study-scene takes place: an elaborate example of this is in *Troilus and Cressida*, during the first four scenes of Act IV [6]: the Folio makes clear the sequence which is obscured by the scene-headings of modern editions. Sometimes the Study represents an interior scene related to an exterior on the Platform, as when in the last scene of *Romeo and Juliet* the churchyard on the Platform leads to the monument in the Study. But more often it is combined and merged with the Platform and gives a colour to it by its furnishings, whether of indoors or outdoors. One thinks of the recurrent throne-room,[7] the orchard of *Julius Caesar*, the garden of *Twelfth Night*, the woods of *A Midsummer Night's Dream* and *As You Like It*, and the church of *Much Ado About Nothing*.

Of the upper stages, the Tarras is generally used in conjunction with the Platform, and represents battlements for parley at Bordeaux and Angiers,[8] or assault at Orleans, Rouen and Harfleur [9]: it serves Richard of Gloucester for his crowning hypocrisy *aloft, betweene two Bishops* on the leads of Baynards Castle [10]; Arthur falls to his death from these "walles" [11]; the Tarras is the gallery from which the Duchess of Gloucester watches the conjurers at their mumbo-jumbo [12]; it is probably the hill from which Pindarus, at Cassius' bidding, scans the battlefield of Philippi.[13] Occasionally it is used in isolation, without reference to the Platform: Hamlet's first sight of his father's ghost [14] must presumably be aloft, so that he may follow him to "a more removed ground" on the Platform itself; Hector must part from Andromache, one supposes, on the walls of Troy [15]; that legendary scene could hardly be set elsewhere than on the Tarras.

The Chamber, as distinct from the Tarras in front of it (which to all intents and purposes ceases to exist as soon as the Chamber

---

[6] See below, pp. 80 ff., where the sequence is studied in detail.
[7] *Henry VI*, IV. i; *Richard III*, IV. ii; *Richard II*, I. i; *King John*, IV. ii; *King Lear*, I. i.
[8] 1 *Henry VI*, IV. ii; *King John*, II. i. 201.
[9] 1 *Henry VI*, II. i; III. ii; *Henry V*, III. i.
[10] *Richard III*, III. vii. 94.   [11] *King John*, IV. iii.   [12] 2 *Henry VI*, I. iv. 16.
[13] *Julius Caesar*, V. iii. 20.   [14] *Hamlet*, I. iv.   [15] *Troilus and Cressida*, V. iii.

curtains are drawn apart), is hardly ever related to the Platform: it is usually a self-contained unit, and naturally becomes associated with domestic interiors. The ladies are at home there: in *The Comedy of Errors*, whose traffic is mostly in the streets of Ephesus, the cue for the first use of the Chamber is when we must go indoors to see Adriana and her sister; thereafter the whole play takes place on the Platform level except for the scenes when the ladies are at home. In *Romeo and Juliet* the Chamber is exclusively reserved for the heroine's apartment, and the sequence of her mock-death on the occasion of her projected marriage to Paris gains greatly in clarity if that distinction of locality is strictly preserved. Probably Prince Hal is at home in the Chamber for some of his informal scenes, as a contrast to the formality of throne-room and council-scenes which need the Platform and the Study in combination.[16] Portia talks gossip here with Nerissa,[17] so does Hero with her gentlewomen and Beatrice.[18] Hither by a natural and highly dramatic rotation Hamlet mounts the stairs to his mother's closet.[19] A neat scheme for *Twelfth Night* would set all Orsino's scenes (except the last, when he leaves home to visit Olivia) in the Chamber: they are mostly static and involve a minimum of movement.[20] In *King Lear* Cranford Adams reserves the Chamber exclusively for the sub-plot scenes, thereby revealing most vividly the design of Shakespeare's architecture: "For as long as the Edmund sub-plot runs parallel to the main plot, it is staged on the second level of the multiple stage. As the two plots merge into one the staging merges also, and the final episodes of the combined action are played on the main level." [21]

Familiar scenes of serenade and elopement suggest themselves as proper to the Window-Stages. False Proteus courts Silvia at her window in true Julia's hearing [22]; Juliet's window is the scene of more than one crisis in her story [23]; Jessica's window leans over Shylock's door, and out of it she throws her father's jewels to Lorenzo [24]; the second scene of *Troilus and Cressida* seems to begin on the Tarras, but when Pandarus urges his niece to come and watch the heroes passing by, saying: "Heere, heere, here's an excellent place, heere we may see most bravely," it looks as if he led her to

---

[16] e.g. 1 *Henry IV*, I. ii; 2 *Henry IV*, II. ii.   [17] *The Merchant of Venice*, I. ii.
[18] *Much Ado About Nothing*, III. iv.   [19] *Hamlet*, III. iv.
[20] See Appendix II, p. 319.
[21] J. Cranford Adams, *The Original Staging of King Lear*, 316.
[22] *The Two Gentlemen of Verona*, IV. ii.
[23] *Romeo and Juliet*, II. ii; III. v; Cranford Adams has a most interesting explanation of the latter scene, in which the proper use of Chamber and Window-Stage in combination heightens the tension of the drama. *The Globe Playhouse*, 273, 4.
[24] *The Merchant of Venice*, II. vi. 26.

B

one of the Window-Stages overlooking the Platform.[25] Brabantio is roused in the night to his window by Iago and Roderigo [26]; and the elaborate manœuvres of Cleopatra's monument and the hoisting of Antony seem to employ both Window-Stages and the Tarras in between them.[27]

On the third level, the Music Gallery is sometimes used by the actors when extra height is needed by some circumstance in the plot. The most obvious use would be for the ship-boy at the masthead in shipboard scenes; the dramatist may need to show the keep of a castle, or a lofty gallery overlooking both the Tarras and the Platform, or a high vantage point from which La Pucelle can signal with a torch.[28] Cranford Adams analyses the scene in *The Tempest* in which the enemies of Prospero are deluded by the magic banquet, and suggests that the only person who can control and synchronise the complicated movements and numerous personnel (both on and off stage) of that scene is—most appropriately—Prospero himself, standing aloft in front of the Musicians' Gallery.[29]

When we come to plot a play of Shakespeare on this multiple stage, it will usually be found that the story flows easily from one acting area to another, the action taking place largely on the Platform, but moving logically indoors to the Study, or upstairs to the Chamber, or making combined use of Tarras and Platform, or Window-Stage and Platform: often the opening of the Study and the showing of characteristic furniture will alter the appearance of the whole combined area of Study and Platform. Common sense will show that two succeeding scenes can seldom be played in the same area: the furniture of Study or Chamber suggests a definite locality, and to change the furniture and the locality takes time. But even the Platform will not readily give the impression in two successive scenes of a distinction between two widely different places or sets of circumstances, unless a transition is marked by the opening or closing of the curtain of the Study, or the use of Chamber or Tarras or Window-Stage. Sometimes the logic of the story's sequence will make the transition clear: something happens that we have been led to expect will happen, and we know where it will be. For instance, in 2 *Henry VI*, Act II, Scene ii takes place, as York quickly informs us, "in this close Walk". As soon as he and his fellow-peers leave the

---

[25] *Troilus and Cressida*, I. ii. 194.   [26] *Othello*, I. i. 81.

[27] Cranford Adams has an elaborate explanation of the method of staging the scene of Antony's hoisting, in *The Globe Playhouse*, 346 ff. A different and equally ingenious interpretation is that of Bernard Jenkin, published in *R.E.S.*, vol. xxi, No. 81 (January, 1945).

[28] 1 *Henry VI*, III. ii. 26: *Enter Pucell on the top, thrusting out a Torch burning.*

[29] *The Tempest*, III. iii. See J. Cranford Adams, *The Globe Playhouse*, 319 ff.

Platform, the Folio reads: *Sound Trumpets. Enter the King and State, with Guard, to banish the Duchesse.* We have been told in the last scene but one that this business was to take place in London. The King's opening words make the situation quite clear: "Stand forth Dame *Elianor Cobham, Gloster's* wife." Exactly whereabouts in London we are hardly matters: and indeed it is best not to ask, for in the same scene the Platform becomes the "Lysts" for the combat between Horner and Peter, who enter with their drunken supporters *at one Doore and at the other Doore.* The logic of the story makes the transition clear. Or it may be that a different group of characters appears whom we associate with a different place: in 1 *Henry VI*, the arrival of Talbot or Pucelle carries us at once from England to France: Rome and Egypt are thus easily differentiated in *Antony and Cleopatra.* But it will generally be found that when the story requires a drastic change of place or time, the transition marked in the dialogue is reinforced by some variation in the area of acting. It may be no more than the fact of making the action revolve round first one door and then, for a different locality, the other: thus Act IV, Scene ii of *Twelfth Night* revolves round one Door, Sir Thopas baiting Malvolio through the wicket, but the following scene opens with Sebastian stepping from the other Door, and when he says "This is the ayre, that is the glorious Sunne," we know he is out-of-doors but we do not associate his situation with the neighbourhood of Malvolio's prison. In reconstructing the scene-rotation the acid test is to try it out, and see what is plausible: if, with the aid of Shakespeare's dialogue, a transition is still not clear, then there should be some adjustment made in the plotting of the scene-rotation. But to apply the acid test, we need a rebuilt Globe. Cranford Adams puts the matter succinctly thus: "In Shakespeare's plays the dialogue, the logical sequence of events, and the corresponding movement from one stage to another enabled his audience to follow the action from beginning to end without difficulty, even when the scene shifts rapidly from place to place. In its ability to present a dramatic tale without interruption and without programme notes, yet with as many scenes and settings as the dramatist desires, the Elizabethan drama anticipated the motion picture of today."[30]

Let us study a sequence of ten pages in the Folio from *The Merchant of Venice.* On page 167 (Act II, Scene ii in modern editions) Launcelot Gobbo makes his first entry: the scene is in the street, as is plain from the arrival of old Gobbo and his wish to be directed to "Maister Jewes": a street-scene will of course be on the Platform.

---

[30] *The Original Staging of King Lear*, 318.

Shylock's house is identified by the first appearance of Jessica on page 169 (II. iii), at, let us say, the left-hand Door, Bassanio and Gratiano having departed by the right-hand Door. II. iv circulates round the right-hand Door. Shylock in II. v enters, of course, from his own (the left-hand) Door. The "penthouse" of II. vi is the over-hanging Tarras, "under which *Lorenzo* Desired us to make a stand". As Lorenzo approaches Shylock's house ("Here dwels my father Jew"), Jessica appears in the Window-Stage above the Door. Hither-to we have been all the time in the streets of Venice: there follows the first casket-scene, with Morocco, and the change of locality to Belmont is simply marked by the disclosing of the Study. The curtains drawn aside at the beginning of the scene and closed again at the end on Portia's instructions are either the alcove hangings between window and door in the rear wall of the Study, or "traverses" specially hung across the Study for the purpose.[31] Thereafter we continue with alternate street-scenes and casket-scenes down to page 176, the scene in which Shylock baits Antonio on his way to prison (III. iii).

Or, in a different vein, consider the opening sequence of *Henry V*. One must guess the position of the speaker of the Prologue, and it seems not unlikely that he would appear between the curtains of the Chamber on the Tarras. The Bishops (I. i) would converse on the Platform, for the Study would be set ready for the throne-room. I. ii would then use the Platform and Study in combination. At the end of the scene the Study would be closed again, and the Chorus would appear, this time on the Platform. II. i, a domestic scene of low life, strongly contrasted with the public splendour of the pre-vious scene, would rightly be in the Chamber; II. ii, the long scene of the exposure of the conspirators, on the Platform; II. iii, the account of Falstaff's death, once again in the Chamber, making a natural continuity with the previous Quickly scene; II. iv, involving the French King's "state", must have Study and Platform. Then the Chorus comes from the centre of the Study-curtains as soon as they are pulled: the action runs continuously into III. i, where the scaling-ladders carry the assault up to the "breach" on the Tarras; III. ii, as the comics are left behind by the attackers, takes place on the Platform. III. iii is the scene of the King's entry into Harfleur: it will need Study and Platform, with the wall and gates indicated in the Study, and the Tarras for the Governor to hold parley. Immedi-ately after the King's triumphant entry into the town, we have the delicious contrast of Princess Katherine being taught English by her

---

[31] J. Cranford Adams, *The Globe Playhouse*, 186 ff.

old Gentlewoman: this scene, of course, takes place in the Chamber, where the ladies are habitually at home.

Some plays, by the nature of their plots, are especially easy to set. One thinks of *A Midsummer Night's Dream* which, for most of its length, can be acted in front of the same woodland set. There is indeed no logical reason why there should be any change of scene from Titania's sleeping (II. ii. 26) till Bottom's waking (IV. i. 206): throughout the interval—more than seven pages in the Folio—the Study is open, and set with Titania's bank and Bottom's hawthorn-brake. *Romeo and Juliet* is so planned that the arrangements of Capulet's establishment fit the architecture of the Tiring-House and Platform. One need only follow the course of Juliet's projected marriage with Paris: it is first suggested in III. v, which begins with Romeo's descent from Juliet's window; it reaches its dismal conclusion at the end of Act IV. The interim, with its great variety of mood and atmosphere and incident, flows quite naturally from stage to stage: Juliet's apartment in the Chamber and Friar Lawrence's cell in the Study are the constants, and the rest of the movement is quite simply related to these. We shall see later in this chapter how street sequences fit easily into this setting, as the stage assumes its visible shape, with doors and doorposts and bay-windows and penthouse. We shall see also how battle-sequences, so familiar a feature in Shakespeare's plays, are skilfully organised in these conditions to seem clear in pattern and dramatically effective.

Of course, as one sets about the business of trying to reconstruct Shakespeare's scene-rotation, problems arise which are not always easy to solve on paper: but there are none, I think, which look likely to be insoluble in practice—to a company acting in a replica of the Globe. We cannot tell, till we have such conditions: and we cannot be sure that our paper theories are right until they are tested in the conditions of performance.

Reading the Folio or the Quartos, one has the impression of continuous action with no scene divisions. Those divisions of Act and Scene that appear in the Folio seem to be literary and unrelated to stage practice or the poet's conception.[32] Intervals there may have been for the convenience of the audience, or to rest the actors or give them time to change, even sometimes—though I think very rarely—to make it possible to alter a Study scene. But, whatever the practice of other dramatists, there is seldom if ever any logical reason in the architecture of a play of Shakespeare's own and only composition for a break: even the occasional Chorus figures (*Henry V, The Winter's*

---

[32] McKerrow's view is expressed in his *Prolegomena to the Oxford Shakespeare*, 49 ff.

Tale) are there to bridge a gap rather than to create one. The gain in continuity which can be achieved so easily by the scene-rotation of the Globe multiple stage, cannot be stressed too strongly. It is not merely a matter of saving time—even a mechanically rapid production in modern conditions can suffer from the loss of tension in transition from one scene to the next; for the fact of dropping a curtain over the whole stage, or switching off a light, breaks the continuous attention of the audience; they relax and have to be won all over again. It was the practice of the Elizabethan dramatist to write his story in many scenes, some very short, and with a great variety of place and personnel: the modern dramatist prefers long acts with unchanging scenes. The latter pays the price in lack of flexibility, but it should be recognised that the Elizabethans were acutely conscious of the problem of preserving continuity, and we shall see in a later chapter that the greatest of them solved the problem over and over again with a skill which is not generally realised by those who present his plays to-day.[33]

(ii) Furnishing and Properties

That the Chamberlain's Men were rich in furniture and properties, stored in the great lofts on the third level of the Tiring-House and perhaps in the capacious depths of Hell below the Platform, we can infer from Henslowe's inventories of the stock-in-trade of the Admiral's Men.[34] That they were sparing in their use of them, however, seems likely from the limited opportunity offered by the architecture of their stage. The areas available for setting solid, heavy furniture were just the Study and the Chamber.

The Chamber, as we have seen, usually represented a private apartment, whether Juliet's, Portia's, Princess Katherine's or Queen Gertrude's. Because of a characteristically modern objectivity in Shakespeare's turn of mind, to which we shall pay more attention in Chapter V, it is likely that this apartment would be furnished, without regard for the period of the play's plot, in the mixture of styles familiar to the eye of his Elizabethan audience. A modern producer will do well perhaps to use no furnishings of a period later than the Elizabethan, but need set himself no bounds before that date. It is

---

[33] In the Appendix at the end of this book will be found a suggested scene-rotation for *Twelfth Night*; J. Cranford Adams' rotation for *King Lear* is published in his paper, *The Original Staging of King Lear*. A complete rotation for *Macbeth* is included in Chapter 6 of this book.

[34] W. W. Greg, *Henslowe Papers*, 113–21. A selection from this list appears in J. Cranford Adams' *The Globe Playhouse*, 325–6.

the Elizabethan vision of Roman, Athenian or early Briton that we want to recapture: a Georgian or Victorian note can shatter the whole illusion.

The Study, besides being, like the Chamber, an interior on its own, can also give a great variety of effects in conjunction with the Platform. There were, one supposes, some stock and recurrent settings, turning up in play after play, and perhaps greeted by the audience with the sort of pleasure one feels in seeing old acquaintances crop up in a new guise and a new set of circumstances. There

Throne-room Set in the Study

is the Throne-Room set, with its great throne or "state" on a dais with an overhanging canopy, rich carpets on the steps and floor, and tapestries hung all round on the three walls. Inevitably it turns up in the English history plays, and often to keen dramatic purpose, as when Richard of Gloucester appears *in pompe*, with his ambition satisfied at last but not his hunger for blood, and turning to Buckingham says: "Thus high, by thy advice, and thy assistance, Is King Richard seated: But shall we weare these Glories for a day?" One thinks of a similar and even more dramatic moment when Macbeth, at last enthroned, finds that "To be thus is nothing . . . Our feares in *Banquo* sticke deepe."

Another standard set is that of the Wall-and-Gates, used often as the attacking force tries to force an entry into the castle. "Traverses (akin to modern 'flats') painted in imitation of castle walls are suspended at the rear of the Study (and at the sides as well?). In the middle of the rear traverse the usual curtained opening . . . is supplied with a practical door for use as the castle gate." [35] Cranford Adams points out that this would represent the outside of Gloucester's castle in *King Lear*, where Kent is put in the stocks for thrashing Oswald: this gate it is which Cornwall bids Gloucester shut against the old King after he has gone forth in high rage into the storm.

Wall-and-Gates Set in the Study

This set too will be a commonplace in the history plays, and will no doubt be used in the last act of *Macbeth*, when Malcolm is bidden by old Siward "This way my Lord, the Castles gently rendred."

For the garden-sets needed in *The Merchant of Venice*, *Twelfth Night* and *Julius Caesar*, there will be a different disposition of foliage and solid properties according to the various plots: Lorenzo's bank and Maria's box-tree dictate their own needs. The foliage—for single performances rather than for continuous runs—will probably be of natural leaves and branches, and even for three or four days evergreens will keep their freshness and their semblance of life: ilex especially will grace either wood or garden in the Study. The woodland set will again suit the needs of the particular play, whether it is

---

[35] J. Cranford Adams, *The Original Staging of King Lear*, 320,

Garden Set in the Study—*Lowlynesse is young Ambitions Ladder*

the hunting sequence in *Titus Andronicus*, the fairy-haunted wood of
A Midsummer Night's Dream (in which play the necessary bank for
Titania's lullaby and the hawthorn-brake for Bottom's tiring-house
already fill the space available in the Study), or the forest of Arden.

It is not hard to identify, from the action or from the text itself,
some of the solid properties used in the Study: "London Stone"
supports the weight of Jack Cade as he begins his short-lived reign [36];
the "Mole-hill" upon which the Duke of Yorke is made to stand,
while he receives the insults of Queen Margaret and his other
enemies, seems (by a sort of poetic justice) to be the same property
which serves as a seat for King Henry as he reflects in solitude when
chid by his friends from the battle of Towton [37]; one thinks also of
the "Monument" of *Romeo and Juliet* and *Much Ado About Nothing* [38];
the "Councell-Boord" of 1 *Henry IV*, I. iii [39]; "this Rocke" on which

[36] 2 *Henry VI*, IV, vi. 1.
[37] 3 *Henry VI*, I. iv. 67; II. v. 14.
[38] *Romeo and Juliet*, V. iii; *Much Ado about Nothing*, V. iii.
[39] Mentioned by Hotspur subsequently in describing how the King "Rated my
Unckle from the Councell-Boord". 1 *Henry IV*, IV. iii. 99. See below, p. 175.

Brutus's "poore remaines of friends" are invited to rest [40]; the "Banke of Flowers" instanced in the "dumbe shew" in Hamlet.[41]

Sometimes in the course of a scene furniture or properties are brought on from within the Tiring-House, such as the stocks for Kent in *King Lear* [42]; they are moreover often enough carried forward on to the Platform itself, as when attendants set chairs for the spectators of a play in *A Midsummer Night's Dream* and in *Hamlet* [43];

Woodland Set in the Study

or when the sick King John is "brought in", presumably like Bedford in I *Henry VI* "brought in sicke in a chayre", or like King Lear "in a chaire carried by Servants" [44]; or when Caesar's coffin becomes the focus of the celebrated forum-scene.[45] It seems to be not an uncommon practice to carry a banquet forward on to the Platform: one may suppose that there is not much room in the Study for the nine to sit at table who are present at the end of *The Taming of*

---

[40] *Julius Caesar*, V. v. 1.   [41] *Hamlet*, III. ii. 147.   [42] *King Lear*, II. ii. 146.
[43] *A Midsummer Night's Dream*, V. i. 84; *Hamlet*, III. ii. 116.
[44] *King John*, V. vii. 28; I *Henry VI*, III. i. 41; *King Lear*, IV. vii. 21.
[45] *Julius Caesar*, III. ii.

the Shrew, and that the Study is too far back for scenes of such dramatic importance, with complex movement and shifting emphasis, as the gruesome repast of *Titus Andronicus* and the ghost-ridden supper of *Macbeth*.[46] I think it is likely that so elaborate a manœuvre as the carrying on of a banquet would be done with formality to music of the Hoboyes (specifically mentioned in *Titus Andronicus*) or with some by-play on the part of the comedians acting as serving-

Turne the Table up

men. No doubt the table would be of the trestle kind that can be turned up.[47] "Turne the Table up," is the instruction of Capulet when he wants room for his guests to dance.[48] But such large-scale scene-shifting in view of the audience would, I think, be the exception rather than the rule. Nothing would destroy more effectively the tension so skilfully nursed by the poet than an undramatic pause for redistribution of furniture on the Platform. For the most part, no solid furniture would be used which could not be set in the Study or

---

[46] *Taming of the Shrew*, V. ii; *Titus Andronicus*, V. iii; *Macbeth*, III. iv.
[47] A specimen of such a table is to be seen in the house of Mary Arden, Shakespeare's mother, at Wilmcote, three miles from Stratford.
[48] *Romeo and Juliet*, I. v. 31.

the Chamber, or be carried on and off easily in the course of the play. In practice, it will seldom be found necessary to break this "rule".

Other means there are also of introducing solid furniture and properties on to the Platform: objects can be let down through a trap in the Heavens from the Huts above, and others can be raised from Hell through the big central trap in the Platform itself. Three suns appear in the air to the three sons of brave Plantagenet,[49] and Jupiter descends from Heaven sitting upon an eagle [50]; up from Hell a *Spirit riseth* at the bidding of its conjurer,[51] and no doubt much infernal luggage can be delivered from the same quarter. But the number of situations in which the use during performance of the traps in the Heavens and in Hell would be plausible is very few. Nor does it seem likely that in many Elizabethan plays—with their habitual shifting of the locality and circumstances—solid furniture would be allowed to rest on the Platform throughout the performance of a play.

Yet here it must be insisted once again that the practical test is the only sure way of knowing what is and what is not effective in the theatre. A carpet of reeds on part of the Platform must often be present throughout a performance: sometimes it will signify the usual strewing of a nobleman's house or a hall at Court; in the following scene it will be transformed by the poet into "these greenes before your Towne" [52]; for long stretches of the play it will not be noticed at all. I am reminded of an effect in the production of *Julius Caesar* at Harrow, in 1946: against one of the Stage-Posts, with its back to the audience, stood a bust (Elizabethan style) on a plinth. This did duty in the opening scene for one of the "Images" that the tribune will not allow to be "hung with Caesars Trophies": Cassius made great play with it as he confronted Brutus with the comparison "*Brutus* and *Caesar*: What should be in that *Caesar*?" [53] But later, in the Senate-house, it became Pompey's statue, and Caesar fell dead at its base. For the battlefield in the second half of the play it would obviously have been out of place: so it was carried offstage in triumph (as Caesar again) by the rioters in the Forum as they ran amok. And no one in the audience noticed the discrepancy.

I think it probable that the Platform was usually left un-encumbered by furniture: and for the rest, there was clearly no room or opportunity for elaboration—it looks as if the Chamberlain's Men were content with what was *necessary for the action* or what

---

[49] 3 *Henry VI*, II. i. 25.   [50] *Cymbeline*, V. iv. 93.   [51] 2 *Henry VI*, I. iv. 25.
[52] *King John*, II. i. 242.   [53] *Julius Caesar*, I. i. 72; I. ii. 141.

in their view was *significant in helping the words to create their desired effect*. The problem of the modern producer, therefore, is to see what this support in any given case might have been, and his success will depend upon the depth of his insight into their methods: in reconstructing their stage-sets we would do well to stick to the same limits—both in furniture and properties—as they.

As examples of what was *necessary* we have already seen that in *A Midsummer Night's Dream* we can infer from the text the furniture of the Study for the woodland sequence. When Olivia snubs Sir Andrew in favour of Viola ("Let the Garden doore be shut, and leave mee to my hearing"),[54] the probability is that III. i follows continuously upon II. v, and that the furniture of the Study includes the "Garden doore" as well as the box tree. As one reads the last scene of *Romeo and Juliet*, it is easy to make a substantial list of necessary "props": a torch for Paris, and a bunch of flowers; a torch for Romeo's boy, afterwards planted by Romeo in the vault, where its unexpected presence is twice mentioned with foreboding, a "Mattocke" and a "wrenching Iron", a Letter to be delivered early in the morning to Romeo's Lord and Father, a cup for the Appothecarie's drugs; "Lanthorne, Crow, and Spade" for Friar Lawrence; the "Masterlesse, and goarie Swords"; Juliet's "Happy Dagger". The Monument in the Study contains, of course, a tomb for Juliet's supposedly dead body to lie on, and perhaps also a suggestion of Tybalt lying in his "bloudy sheet". "Yond Young [*read* Yew] Trees," to which Paris points at the beginning of the scene, are created merely by poetical means out of one of the Stage-Posts, and likewise the bare Platform needs no tangible furniture to seem "loose, unfirme with digging up of Graves". An instructive example of how to select the necessary properties is in an earlier scene from the same play [55]: Capulet's "old accustom'd Feast" is quickly projected on the stage in a scurry of Servingmen who *come forth with their napkins*. It is plain that their immediate task is to "take away"—shifting and scraping trenchers, removing joint-stools and "the Court-cubbord", providing more light, turning up the tables and quenching the fire. The more of this detail that is reproduced with the appropriate properties in the action, the better: after all, the selection has been made by Shakespeare himself, whose eye for the significant detail is that of an artist of genius.

To illustrate the kind of furnishing which is *significant in helping the words*, without being actually necessary, let me quote examples from my own experience. In the episode of the highway robbery on Gads

---

[54] *Twelfth Night*, III. i. 105.　　　　　[55] *Romeo and Juliet*, I. v.

Now my Masters, happy man be his dole, say I

Hill, Shakespeare is at great pains to make clear the layout of his
scene: we shall have cause to examine this scene in detail in
Chapter V,[56] but for the moment it is enough to say that he creates
through the dialogue the impression that the actors are on the slope
of a hill: Falstaff has climbed up the hill, the prospective victims are
stretching their legs down it; the highwaymen take cover in "the
narrow Lane".[57] This lane would no doubt be indicated by a parting

---

[56] See below, pp. 203 ff.   [57] 1 *Henry IV*, II. ii. 65.

of the Study-curtains and a suggestion of trees on either side: a battered fingerpost with one arm pointing downwards reinforces the notion of up- and down-hill, and adds greatly to the atmosphere of highway robbery. In the Boar's Head scenes of the same play, the wall of the Study may be hung with a threadbare tapestry portraying Dives in Hell and Lazarus in Abraham's bosom. We hear from Falstaff himself of Mistress Quickly's flybitten tapestries, his chamber at Windsor (which we do not see) is "painted about with the story of the Prodigall, fresh and new",[58] and the theme of Dives is an appropriate commentary on Falstaff's mode of life and a reminder of his recurrent fits of conscience-stricken melancholy. The visible presence of this painted parable adds much point to a scene in which Falstaff is trying to cure his melancholy by familiar gibes at Bardolph's face. "Why, Sir *John*," says the indignant Bardolph, "my Face does you no harme." "No, Ile be sworne," he retorts: "I make as good use of it, as many a man doth of a Deaths-Head, or a *Memento Mori*. I never see thy Face, but I thinke upon Hell fire, and *Dives* that lived in Purple; for there he is in his Robes burning, burning." [59] Of the same kind of conjectural reconstruction of the Globe furniture is the idea of setting a ladder against a fruit tree in the Study, so that as the reflective Brutus strolls in his orchard and his hand unconsciously falls upon a rung, the action suggests to him his metaphor of "young Ambitions ladder".[60]

It would be absurd to suggest that these guesses are comparable with the deduction of necessary items from the dialogue or the action. Nevertheless they are defensible, it seems to me, provided they are made sparingly, and have a clear value in interpreting the poet's dramatic intention. In general the choice of furniture and properties should be the minimum needed to enact and illustrate the dialogue and action of Shakespeare: they will have, as Granville-Barker says, "rather the utility of furniture than the value of scenery" [61]: but the minimum may be understood in a liberal sense: simplicity is what is wanted, not parsimony; simplicity by being always relevant and significant can have a richness far more effective than unweeded luxuriance.

(iii) Use of Stage Features

The permanent features of the Globe stage were remarkably positive in character: two uncompromising front doors with

---

[58] 2 *Henry IV*, II. i. 163; *M.W.W.*, IV. v. 8.   [59] 1 *Henry IV*, III. iii. 32 ff.
[60] *Julius Caesar*, II. i. 22.
[61] Granville-Barker, *Prefaces to Shakespeare* (Second Series), 136.

Tut, I have done a thousand dreadfull things

Come my Masters, let us share

knockers, side-posts and overhanging lintels; above which, bay-windows such as you can see jutting out over the shopfronts in Gloucester or Tewkesbury or Stratford to-day; a wicket in each door; rails round the edge of the Platform; the balustrade of the Tarras between the two Window-Stages; the most prominent feature, the two great mast-like Stage-Posts (perhaps masts indeed), with their three-foot square-shaped bases; and supported by these above the third level the stage-cover, the "Heavens", painted underneath with the signs of the zodiac. All this was visible throughout a performance, and the audience were used to seeing rushes strewn on part of the platform, and trap-doors opening in other parts.

Each item of these features was used when the story demanded its use—either in its visible shape or in some imaginary likeness conjured by the words of the dramatist or the miming of the actors. Thus the Stage-Posts, Cranford Adams tells us, were used "as trees; as a means of hiding from others on the platform; as posts to which notices of various sorts are affixed, or to which rogues or victims are bound; as a seeming may-pole, or road-side cross, or the gates of a bridge".[62] It seems likely that Aaron the Moor was to be hanged

---

[62] J. Cranford Adams, *The Globe Playhouse*, 112.

You have forgot the Will I told you of

from one of the Stage-Posts, and that he speaks his great tirades from the top of a ladder, with a halter round his neck.[63] When Launce makes his first appearance in *The Two Gentlemen of Verona*, "*Crab my dog*" is no doubt "tide" to one of these Posts.[64] Helena will pursue Demetrius round such a tree in the wood near Athens.[65] On Gads Hill, Prince Hal and Poins (*two Rogues in Buckrom Sutes*) will hide behind the two Posts, with backs to the audience, while Falstaff and his confederate are sharing the swag in the centre.[66] One can imagine Mark Antony jumping up on to the base of one of them, as he cries to the mob "You have forgot the Will I told you of."[67]

The two Doors will appear in their own likeness in street-sequences such as those in *The Comedy of Errors*, *The Taming of the Shrew*, *The Merchant of Venice* and *The Merry Wives of Windsor*. But whenever the Platform-and-Study represent a great hall for court or banquet—as for instance at Macbeth's "solemn Supper" [68]—then they will naturally be taken as the interior doors of a palace. When the Platform is being used for an outdoor scene in wood or on heath or battlefield, the Doors simply do not exist. As we read the Fisher Quarto of *A Midsummer Night's Dream*, we are forcibly reminded of their presence in the stage-direction: *Enter the King of Fairies, at one doore, with his traine; and the Queene, at another, with hers*. But the audience in the playhouse have forgotten them long before "Ill met by moonlight, proud Tytania".[69]

The Door-Posts come in handy for concealing assassins, as when Iago bids Roderigo lie in wait for Cassio "behinde this Barke [*read* Bulk]".[70] The wicket is used for prolonged recriminations in *The Comedy of Errors*,[71] and for the baiting of Malvolio in prison.[72] The

[63] *Titus Andronicus*, V. i. 53 ff.   [64] *The Two Gentlemen of Verona*, II. iii.
[65] *A Midsummer Night's Dream*, II. i. 188 ff.
[66] I *Henry IV*, II. ii. 114. For the effect of this positioning, see below, pp. 136 f.
[67] *Julius Caesar*, III. ii. 243.   [68] *Macbeth*, III. iv.
[69] *A Midsummer Night's Dream*, II. i. 60.   [70] *Othello*, V. i. 1.
[71] *The Comedy of Errors*, III. i.   [72] *Twelfth Night*, IV. ii.

I know his gate, 'tis he

penthouse formed by the overhang of the Tarras is used as a *rendez-
vous* by Gratiano and Salarino as they wait for Lorenzo,[73] and by the
drunken Borachio and Conrade as shelter from the drizzling rain.[74]
The Traps are used for sprites and witches and apparitions:
the Study-trap was specially known as the "grave-trap" from
its frequent use for burying the dead: Ophelia is formally (if with
maimed rites) buried there,[75] and Oswald by Edgar with hasty

---

[73] *The Merchant of Venice*, II. vi. i.
[74] *Much Ado About Nothing*, III. iii. 109.
[75] *Hamlet*, V. i. 240 ff.

improvisation [76]; in *Titus An-dronicus* it is used as a pit to trap the living.[77] Even the platform rails, we are told, are sometimes pressed into service by the actors.

Imagine the setting of the opening scene of *The Tempest*, which is nowadays often cut or, if not cut, is unintelligibly con-fused. A ship-board scene fits admirably into the structure of the Globe. There is the ship-boy at the masthead in the Music Gallery; the Ship-Master on his bridge on the Tarras; the Bote-swaine and Mariners ranging freely on the Platform, some looking over the Platform-rails as if over the taffrail out to sea (the fact that there are two masts in parallel matters little in so dramatic a storm as the poet creates); and the distinguished company of villainous passen-gers come surging in their panic through the Study-Trap as if up the companion-way. Remem-ber that the Huts above the

Keepe your Cabines; you do assist the storme

Heavens are meanwhile busy with the thunderbolts, and that all available members of the stage-gang are ready to make the *confused noyse within* ("Mercy on us. We split, we split") [78]—and you will have some idea of the versatile and comprehensive capacity of the Globe Playhouse. "This most excellent Canopy the Ayre, look you," says Hamlet, with a gesture at the Heavens; and "You here this fellow in the selleredge," as he stamps on the boards that separate him from Hell.[79] One has indeed the feeling that the Chamberlain's Men were well equipped for most experiences between Hell and Heaven.

"It was the habit of Elizabethan dramatists," says Cranford

---

[76] *King Lear*, IV. vi. 281 ff. See J. Cranford Adams, *The Original Staging of King Lear*, 331 ff.

[77] *Titus Andronicus*, II. iii. 186 ff.

[78] *The Tempest*, I. i. 65.

[79] *Hamlet*, II. ii. 318; I. v. 151.

Adams, "to accept the equipment of their stage rather literally and to refer to that equipment in dialogue. . . . Doors, door posts, wickets, stage posts, windows, 'penthouses' . . . all were actual parts of the visible scene, and all were made a part of the sphere of dramatic action and were referred to realistically." [80] These dramatists, the better among them, were practical men of the theatre. They made use of what they had at hand. It is especially true of the best of them, Shakespeare. He often made literal use; but still more often he translated the features for his purpose: we can but be astonished at his dexterity, and the quickness with which he concentrates focus on one feature and makes us forget the others. For long stretches we are allowed to forget altogether the conventional background: then we suddenly recognise (with the pleasure of the sudden-obvious) a happy stroke of the dramatist in exploiting or translating the familiar features of the playhouse.

The playhouse is indeed fully equipped: Shakespeare, however, is never distracted from his artistic purpose by the lure of the machinery—he uses it only when the theme warrants, and we should do well to re-plot likewise.

(iv) Costume

Peter Quince and Bottom are not unconcerned about problems of wardrobe. But when we try to overhear the Book-Keeper's conversation with Burbadge on this theme, the task is not easy. The building of a twentieth-century Globe would, one hopes, breed its own literature—among which there might be a practical manual on the costume and another on the music appropriate for different plays. Meanwhile, before we begin to rehearse the players in this theatre which we are trying to rebuild in imagination, let us make some kind of conjecture as to their appearance when dressed for the play.

Shakespeare himself had an eye for costume, as for almost everything else: frequent passages turn on it: he was able to make dramatic use of its beauty, its splendour, its incongruity, its absurdity, and the tyranny of its fashions. Moreover, we know from Henslowe's inventory that the acting companies spent large sums and had a large stock in their wardrobes. But the prices are high in Henslowe's list, and a moment's reflection will suggest that with their constantly changing repertory of plays, the players are unlikely to have had accurate period costumes for them all. One's admiration

---

[80] J. Cranford Adams, *The Globe Playhouse*, 233.

of their practical sense and good housekeeping increases with further acquaintance; and in this matter we must expect them to cut their coat to suit their cloth. Shakespeare certainly does not offend by capricious impracticability, and one imagines he would be quick to see that the dramatic needs of the story were more important than historical or national or period accuracy. This consideration, I think, is partly the cause of his obvious inclination for the common denominator of Elizabethan colour.

Shakespeare's stage-vision is essentially modern. It has long been a habit among commentators to point out his anachronisms, but it is perhaps only lately that he has been credited with a deliberate purpose in his modernity. E. M. W. Tillyard remarks it as being especially prominent in the two parts of *Henry IV*: "There is nothing archaistic," he says, "about the Eastcheap tavern and its hostess, about the two carriers in the inn yard at Rochester, about the bill found in Falstaff's pocket, about the satin ordered from Master Dombleton for Falstaff's short cloak and slops, or about the life Shallow liked to think he had led at the Inns of Court: they are all pure Elizabethan" [81]; and he suggests that Shakespeare, by this Elizabethan colour, is deliberately expressing his own feelings about his fatherland. But in fact there is what might be called an Elizabethan substructure in all the plays. Miss M. St. Clare Byrne, commenting on this feature of Shakespeare's imagination, says: "The point of it all is—verisimilitude, actuality," and she speaks of Oswald, Osric and Parolles as "accurate topical portraits, which must undoubtedly have made Shakespeare's own audience more at home in ancient Britain and at Elsinore." [82]

We shall return in Chapter V to the theme of Shakespeare's objective modern vision. Its relevance to the subject of costume is simply this: we cannot do better as a beginning than to use modern dress—by which I mean Shakespeare's modern dress, an Elizabethan wardrobe. And on this basis of an Elizabethan wardrobe, disregarding archaism, we must work at the dramatic emphasis of the story.

Out of this wardrobe the non-period plays would certainly be furnished. *The Taming of the Shrew* bears much evidence of contemporary costume as well as of other details of contemporary life. We have elaborate description of Petruchio and Grumio in their grotesque wedding-garments, we hear of how the serving-men came short of their proper apparel (their new fustian, and white stockings, and their blew coats brush'd), Kate's humiliating interview with the

---

[81] E. M. W. Tillyard, *Shakespeare's History Plays*, 299.
[82] *A Companion to Shakespeare Studies* (Cambridge), 193.

Tailor and the Haberdasher gives interesting information about current fashions, and Tranio's borrowed plumes are itemised by the indignant Vincentio.[83] In *Much Ado About Nothing*, Hero's wedding-dress loosens the tongue of her gossiping gentlewoman on the subject of "the Dutchesse of *Millaines* gowne that they praise so". "O that exceedes they say," cries Hero, and Margaret retorts: "By my troth's but a night-gowne in respect of yours, cloth a gold and cuts, and lac'd with silver, set with pearles, downe sleeves, side sleeves, and skirts, round underborn with a blewish tinsel, but for a fine queint gracefull and excellent fashion, yours is worth ten on't." [84]

In these examples there are no special contrasts of style needed: nor will there be any in *Twelfth Night*, save that it is important to get the social grades right: many a performance of this shapely comedy has been marred by a misunderstanding of the composition of an Elizabethan household: by a Sir Toby who pays court to Maria in the manner of an Edwardian policeman's back-door wooing, or by a Malvolio who could not possibly have aspired (even in his own ambitious mind) to the hand of his lady. In *The Merchant of Venice*, except when we are in the enchanted air of Belmont, the important thing is to present not a period Venice with accurate Italian costume but the contrast between Jew and Christian. Granville-Barker points out that Shakespeare's Venice is "the Venice of his dramatic needs; a city of royal merchants trading to the gorgeous East, of Jews in their gaberdines . . . and of splendid gentlemen rustling in silks", and he explains how important a part in creating this atmosphere is played by the words of Solanio and Salarino. Quoting

> There where your Argosies with portly saile
> Like Signiors and rich Burgers on the flood,
> Or as it were the Pageants of the sea,
> Do over-peere the pettie Traffiquers
> That curtsie to them, do them reverence
> As they flye by them with their woven wings—

he adds: "They are argosies themselves, these magnificent young men, of high-flowing speech; pageants to overpeer the callow English ruffians, to whom they are here displayed." [85] For the modern producer it is important that their costume and that of their fellow-Christians should have a splendour and dignity to match their language, and that they should by their manner and appearance constrain such traffickers as Shylock and Tubal instinctively to curtsy to them and do them reverence.

---

[83] *The Taming of the Shrew*, III. ii. 44 ff.; IV. i. 49, 93; IV. iii. 60 ff.; V. i. 67 ff.
[84] *Much Ado About Nothing*, III. iv. 16 ff.
[85] Granville-Barker, *Prefaces to Shakespeare* (Second Series), 80 ff.

In *A Midsummer Night's Dream* the Athenian colour hardly exists at all: we may assume that the *chiton* and *himation* are as far from Shakespeare's thoughts as the Acropolis and the Pnyx. The courtiers will be Elizabethan courtiers, the craftsmen good Londoners, and there is life in the idea that the fairies should imitate their mortal counterparts, the King and Queen like Theseus and Hippolyta, and the fairies dressed as courtiers, prelates, soldiers and the like; the materials will, of course, be gathered from the woods and fields in which they live. There is a negative virtue in this choice of wardrobe— that it cuts out the irrelevant overtones of ballet-fairyland. A bold principle begins to assert itself: a producer of to-day will be wise to use no costume of a period later than Shakespeare's own day: he may range freely before that date, but subsequent fashions are to be avoided as being foreign to Shakespeare's vision.

The great tragedies are also non-period in their timeless quality. Little stress in matters of detail and local colour is laid upon Hamlet's Denmark, on Venice and Cyprus in *Othello*, on Lear's ancient Britain or on the Scotland of *Macbeth*. For instance, the porter at Inverness has none of the national eccentricities of Captain Jamy, and between Macduff and Hotspur's friend, the Douglas, there is no doubt which is the better Scotsman. Such hints of costume as there are in these tragedies are contemporary Elizabethan. Again the principle applies, that it is more important to suit the dress to the emphasis of the story than to be accurate. Thus Hamlet's "Inky Cloake" at his first appearance must be in startling contrast to the ostentatious brilliance of Claudius and his courtiers, so that when he says "I am too much i' th' Sun", a glance to left and right will make his point clear at once. But later, when he puts his "Anticke disposition" on, he must

assume the guise so graphically described by
the affrighted Ophelia:

> his doublet all unbrac'd,
> No hat upon his head, his stockings foul'd,
> Ungartred, and downe gived to his Anckle.[86]

A clear, dramatic contrast can be marked by
differentiating in costume Horatio the student,
Fortinbras the soldier, and Osric the "water-
flie". Othello should be dressed to emphasise
his difference from those of Desdemona's "owne
Clime, Complexion, and Degree"—not so as to

preserve the romantic likeness of a popular actor.
The description in the Folio of Portia's tawny
suitor may serve as a guide: the costume there
is designed to startle rather than soothe the spectator, and a similar suggestion is made by the
appearance of Aaron, paramour of the Queen
of the Goths, in a contemporary theatrical
sketch.[87] Goneril and Regan should no doubt
be "gorgeous", as Lear in the climax of his anger

---

[86] *Hamlet*, II. i. 78–80.
[87] The drawing of Henry Peacham (1595) is reproduced
in E. K. Chambers' *William Shakespeare*, vol. i, 312, and also
in *Shakespeare Survey*, I, where it is discussed at length by
J. Dover Wilson (17 ff.).

Lord Hamlet with his doublet all unbrac'd

lets us know.[88] Pains should be taken over Edgar's "the thing it selfe". Lear cries at sight of him "unaccommodated man, is no more but such a poore, bare, forked Animall as thou art": but we have a more exact view of him given by himself in advance:

> my face Ile grime with filth,
> Blanket my loines, elfe all my
>   haires in knots,
> And with presented nakednesse
>   out-face
> The Windes——

and he means to adopt the practice

> Of Bedlam beggars, who with roaring voices,
> Strike in their num'd and mortified Armes,
> Pins, Wodden-prickes, Nayles, Sprigs of Rosemarie——[89]

If this disguise is hardly a problem for the wardrobe-master, it yet helps to bring home the point that the interpretation of Shakespeare's dramatic purpose is as important in the field of costume as in any other.

In the English histories, careful attention would, no doubt, be paid to the armorial bearings of noble families, most of which had contemporary representatives moving constantly before the eye of Shakespeare's audience. The broad issues of the long series ranging from *Richard II* to *Richard III* would be all the clearer if we came to recognise the recurrent emblems, some of which provide imagery for the poet's dialogue. But apart from this consideration, the same principle applies—that we should reinforce by the costumes the dramatic emphasis. Richard of Gloucester is "at Charges for a Looking-glasse", and we should see some striking result of his employing "a score or two of Taylors, To study fashions to adorne my body".[90] Richard II, who "every day, under his House-hold Roofe, Did keepe ten thousand men", should be a splendid figure against a sober-suited Bolingbroke.[91] We have already noticed Tillyard's

---

[88] *King Lear*, II. iv. 270 ff.
[90] *Richard III*, I. ii. 257.
[89] *King Lear*, III. iv. 109; II. iii. 9 ff.
[91] *Richard II*, IV. i. 282.

suggestion that in *Henry IV* Shakespeare is giving his picture of Elizabethan England. This gives the clue for a groundwork of contemporary costume: on this we will impose the traditional blazonry: and there is a special dramatic emphasis on the plumes of Prince Hal, which can be traced as a recurrent *motif* rising to a climax on the battlefield. Stung by his father's reproaches, the Prince declares that he will

> in the closing of some glorious day,
> Be bold to tell you, that I am your Sonne,
> When I will weare a Garment all of Blood,
> And staine my favours in a bloody Maske.

The promise is redeemed on Shrewsbury field, but with a touch of magnanimous courtesy the victor takes the plumes from his own crest and lays them on the dead Percy: "Let my favours," says he, "hide thy mangled face." Half-way between the promise and its fulfilment, we have the splendid description of the young Prince and his comrades spoken in the unwilling ears of Hotspur, by Sir Richard Vernon:

> All furnisht, all in Armes,
> All plum'd like Estridges, that with the Winde
> Bayted like Eagles, having lately bath'd,
> Glittering in Golden Coates, like Images . . .

When, within sixty lines of this description, the Prince appears on his way to the battlefield, the wardrobe-master would be failing of his duty if he did not provide him and his companions with the very best plumage and harness that the Globe store-rooms could provide.[92] On the other hand, a conspicuous absence of plumes makes a fine dramatic point when Prince Hal, now King Henry, sends defiance to the Constable of France:

> There's not a piece of feather in our Hoast:
> Good argument (I hope) we will not flye.[93]

The Roman plays present the problem in its acutest form. Here too, as the text-books remind us, the few hints of detail are contemporary—Caesar's Doublet and Night-gowne, the Night-cappes of the rabblement, the Hats and Cloakes of the conspiracie, the pocket of Brutus's gowne; Cleopatra's lace that must be cut. There is, of course, no doubt that the Elizabethans knew what Romans looked like: their pictures, their decorated books make clear what anyway is obvious. Yet it seems that it was not their stage practice to

---

[92] 1 *Henry IV*, III. ii. 133 ff.; V. iv. 96; IV. i. 97 ff.; IV. ii. 54. See below, pp. 252 ff.
[93] *Henry V*, IV. iii. 112 ff.

dress their actors accurately in period. Dover Wilson infers from the Peacham drawing of *Titus Andronicus* [94] that while the lower classes were played in "modern dress", every effort was made to attain accuracy in the attire worn by patricians. I am not convinced that the evidence of the picture is plain enough to support his contention. More plausible, perhaps, is the compromise which Granville-Barker advocates when, in his preface to *Julius Caesar*, he writes: "Are not our noble Romans, flinging their togas gracefully about them, slow-moving, consciously dignified, speaking with

An illustration from Holinshed

studied oratory and all past middle age, rather too like a schoolboy's vision of a congress of headmasters? Compare them with the high-mettled, quick-tongued crew of politicians and fighters that Shakespeare imagines; and if it comes to accuracy, has he not more the right of it than we, even though his Caesar be dressed in doublet and hose? So let the designer at least provide an escape from this cold classicism, which belongs neither to the true Rome nor to the play he has to interpret. His way can be the way of all compromise. . . . The methods of the Mask and the way of Renaissance painters with classical subjects give us the hint we need. Whether from taste or lack of information, when it came to picturing Greeks and Romans

---

[94] See above, p. 57; and *Shakespeare Survey*—I, 21,

they were for fancy dress; a mixture, as a rule, of helmet, cuirass, trunk hose, stockings and sandals, like nothing that ever was worn, but very wearable and delightful to look at." [95] Tintoretto and Paolo Veronese should therefore be among our models, and also the illustrations in Holinshed over which the poet pored so often and so long.

And halfe their Faces buried in their Cloakes

In practice, the Elizabethan touches help rather than hinder: a group of conspirators whose "Hats are pluckt about their Eares, And halfe their Faces buried in their Cloakes",[96] huddled under the foliage of a property tree in the Study, while Cassius advances to Brutus beside a Post-tree in his Orchard downstage on the Platform, suggests the feeling of the Babington plot in a contemporary woodcut,

---

[95] Granville-Barker, *Prefaces to Shakespeare* (First Series), 127, 128. Much sound sense is written on this theme by Miss M. St. Clare Byrne in her chapter on "The Social Background" in *A Companion to Shakespeare Studies* (Cambridge), 190–95. Her note (on page 194) on the illustrations in Holinshed is particularly interesting. The reader's attention is also drawn to an article on "John Speed's Theatre" in *Theatre Notebook*, Vol. III, No. 2, for January–March, 1949, in which C. Walter Hodges offers "some reflections on the style of the Elizabethan playhouse".

[96] *Julius Caesar*, II. i. 73 f.

and gains greatly thereby in verisimilitude, even to twentieth-century eyes. For Shakespeare's modernity is thus emphasised: this is the true "Shakespeare in modern dress".

And therefore, if we are to reconstruct the productions of the Chamberlain's Men, we cannot do better as a preliminary than to make a detailed study of Elizabethan costume—full as it is of beauty, individual character and variety, and in many of its fashions quite unlike the standard turn-out of the theatrical costumier. Some of the miniatures of Nicholas Hillyarde and Isaac Oliver provide fashion-plates that would enrich the characterisation of many of the plays of Shakespeare: one can identify in the "King Penguin" volume of *Elizabethan Miniatures* an Orlando, a Benedick and a Hotspur: there would no doubt be, somewhere for the finding, an appropriate and individual style for most of the Shakespearian characters. And having chosen our style, then we must learn to wear it with as much ease and comfort and grace as the portraits suggest—and with more, much more of the last quality than we are used to in the sartorial fashion of to-day.

(v) *Music*

When we turn to consider what musical plans the Book-Keeper would make, we have to use a special effort of the imagination in unthinking subsequent musical practice in the theatre. Nowadays we are used to an atmospheric overture, and an automatic musical link between scenes; indeed, the technique of the films goes further still in douching the dialogue and the action with a superficially appropriate musical comment. When this kind of treatment is applied to the production of Shakespeare, it is commonly assumed that he left no clear indications of his own preference. This is a strange assumption, when we remember his often expressed fondness for music: if he had an eye for costume, it is no less true that his works show him to have had a keen ear for music, and some knowledge of the technique of an art which in his day was more generally practised than in ours.

In fact, the musical directions in the Folio are usually quite explicit,[97] and though not exhaustive, yet they seem to miss few of the significant and emphatic cues. Some, of course, can be inferred from the dialogue itself. In the second scene of *Julius Caesar* there are three separate cues for the band in the first twenty-five lines: only

---

[97] McKerrow points out that the Folio Edition of *Titus Andronicus* seems to have been printed from a Playhouse prompt-copy "in which certain incidental music had been noted". *Prolegomena for the Oxford Shakespeare*, 70, note 2.

one (*sennet*) is marked in the stage-directions, but it can be inferred from Caesar's line "I heare a Tongue shriller then all the Musicke" that the musicians strike up on the words "Set on, and leave no Ceremony out"; and reading backwards, we can deduce another music cue for the entry of the procession, interrupted suddenly by Casca's cry of "Peace ho, *Caesar* speakes." [98] A modern producer will find no difficulty in making this kind of deduction. Moreover it is easy to understand that routine, such as could be taken for granted by the players, is often omitted from the prompt-book. Thus we do not need to be told of the normal method of calling the attention and silence of the audience at the beginning of the play: it is probably a repetition of the trumpet-call which had already been advertising from the Huts to the whole of London the fact that a play is to be given this afternoon. Once the audience is settled and attentive, the play itself can begin: more often than not it begins with dialogue or solo speech, sometimes with an uproarious crowd; exceptionally, as in *Twelfth Night*, with instrumental music; not seldom with a royal flourish of trumpets; but when music is used, it is an integral part of the performance, not a descriptive "overture" in our sense of the word.

It was neither customary nor necessary to link the scenes with music: the brisk continuity, as has been said above, was made by a natural transition created by the words and miming of the speakers, the logical sequence of the story, and the corresponding rotation from one part of the multiple stage to another. On the other hand, it was evidently usual—and indeed in practice seems almost necessary —to accompany a processional entry: it is hardly possible for a large number of actors to enter by a single stage-door with grace and dignity without some musical support; no doubt this practice was borrowed from real life.

It is important to have some knowledge of the different musical terms used in the stage-directions in the early printed texts. The subject is fully expounded by E. W. Naylor, and his help should be sought in interpreting the prompt-book.[99] Meanwhile the following observations arise from a perusal of the Folio. The *Flourish*, a blast of trumpets in the manner of a bugle-call, is the usual accompaniment of the entry of a royal or sovereign personage: but the *Sennet*, played probably by the cornets (which, though made of wood, are perhaps the counterpart of the modern brass band), is a formal musical

---

piece generally used to grace a procession. The great moment when
Richard of Gloucester mounts the throne of his ambition is thus
marked in the Folio: *Sound a Sennet. Enter Richard in pompe*.[100] The
parallel crisis in Macbeth's fortune has: *Senit sounded. Enter Macbeth
as King*.[101] The last scene of *Henry V* is rounded with a *Senet*, since
there are so many royal and noble personages to make their way
into the Tiring-House.[102] As we have already seen, Caesar's procession at the Lupercal is so elaborate as to need a *Sennet*.[103] The
ceremonious splendour of King Lear's first entry is likewise accompanied.[104] Sometimes, when a prolonged movement is required by
the action, but with no visible ceremonial, the prompt-book marks a
Long Flourish. In the opening scene of *Titus Andronicus* it is necessary
for the Tribunes and Senators *aloft* to come down from the Tarras to
the Platform below: the direction is *A long Flourish till they come
downe*.[105] The musical accompaniment of the tourney in *Richard II* is
significant: *Flourish* for the King's entry; *Tucket* for Hereford's; *A
charge sounded* for the combatants' setting forward; *A long Flourish*
while Hereford and Mowbray "draw neere and list" to their
sentence.[106]

The *Tucket* usually heralds the arrival of persons of importance,
ambassadors or messengers. Thus Mountjoy's arrogant embassies
are preceded by a *tucket*: perhaps significantly, when after Agincourt
"His eyes are humbler than they us'd to be," no mention of a *tucket*
appears in the Folio.[107] In *All's Well that Ends Well*, *A Tucket afarre off*
heralds the approach of a victorious army.[108] *Tucket within* announces
the approach of Cornwall and Regan, and the same stage-direction
precedes Goneril's entry: from this last example it seems likely that
these tuckets were sometimes recognisable as the signal of an individual owner: "What Trumpet's that?" says Cornwall. "I know't,
my Sisters," answers Regan, with savage relief and relish, as she
welcomes Goneril's support against her father.[109]

The *Hoboyes* (hautboys or oboes) are the equivalent of the modern
double-reed family of wood-wind instruments. Naylor says that a
band of oboes, cors anglais, bassoons and contra-fagotto would be
similar to the sixteenth-century Hautboy band, but more refined in
tone. "The indication of 'hautboys' in the plays," he says, "always
implies a special *importance* in the stage music, generally connected

---

[100] *Richard III*, IV. ii. 1.   [101] *Macbeth*, III. i. 11.   [102] *Henry V*, V. ii. 402.
[103] *Julius Caesar*, I. ii. 24.   [104] *King Lear*, I. i. 36.   [105] *Titus Andronicus*, I. i. 233.
[106] *Richard II*, I. iii. 1–124.
[107] *Henry V*, III. vi. 124; IV. iii. 78; IV. vii. 70.
[108] *All's Well That Ends Well*, III. v. 1.
[109] *King Lear*, II, i. 80; II. iv. 185 f. So, too, Iago's excited cry on the quayside
at Cyprus: "The Moore I know his Trumpet" (*Othello*, II. i. 181).

with a banquet, masque, or procession . . ." [110] *Hoboyes* accompany
the bringing in of the Table for the feast at the end of *Titus Androni-
cus.*[111] *Hoboyes play* during the *dumbe shew* in *Hamlet.*[112] *Hoboyes, and
Torches* are specified as Duncan and his companions approach in
cheerful mood the castle of his murderer. Again there are *Ho-boyes.
Torches* to indicate the supper with which the King is welcomed.[113]
In a different mood, they play as the Witches' cauldron sinks into
Hell [114]: and they create a wonderful dramatic effect in *Antony and
Cleopatra,* when the sentries are startled on their night-vigil; the
poet's or the Book-Keeper's instruction is specifically marked:
Musicke of the Hoboyes is under the Stage.[115]

The musical accompaniment of battle-sequences is simple and
conventional, and the different types must have been easily recognisable to the audience. A drum for marching is so common that we
read in 3 *Henry VI* the instruction: *the Drumme begins to march.*[116] The
drum is also the basis of *Alarums,* a confused noise to which trumpets,
the clash of arms and no doubt the human voice contribute. The
Alarum seems to represent the fighting itself, continuing as long as the
contest of the moment lasts: for instance, in *Troilus and Cressida,*
when Hector and Ajax fight in the lists, the alarum begins on the cue
"They are in action", but when Diomed cries: "You must no
more," we are told that the *trumpets cease.*[117] An interesting hint of
the method of preparing the battle is given by the Bastard in *King
John,* when he says:

> Do but start
> An eccho with the clamor of thy drumme,
> And even at hand, a drumme is readie brac'd,
> That shall reverberate all, as lowd as thine.
> Sound but another, and another shall
> (As lowd as thine) rattle the Welkins eare,
> And mocke the deepe mouth'd Thunder.[118]

In the course of the Battle of Shrewsbury, the significant musical
points are clearly marked in the Folio—the ceremonial *trumpets,* the
alarums, (the *excursions*), the *retreat,* the trumpets of victory.[119] Add to
these the *Parley,* quickly recognised as such by Jack Cade,[120] and
answered by another trumpet within Flint Castle,[121] and we have
most of the routine signals of playhouse battles. Especially notable

---

[110] Naylor, "Music and Shakespeare", in *The Musical Antiquary,* April, 1910, 133.
[111] *Titus Andronicus,* V. iii. 25. [112] *Hamlet,* III. ii. 147.
[113] *Macbeth,* I. vi. 1; I. vii. i. [114] *Macbeth,* IV. i. 106.
[115] *Antony and Cleopatra,* IV. iii. 12. [116] 3 *Henry VI,* IV. vii. 51.
[117] *Troilus and Cressida,* IV. v. 113–6. [118] *King John,* V. ii. 167 ff.
[119] 1 *Henry IV,* V. ii., iii., iv., and v. [120] 2 *Henry VI,* IV. viii. 4 f.
[121] *Richard II,* III. iii. 61.

C

are the *Low Alarums* so carefully marked at the points of emphasis in
the defeat of Philippi.[122] All these different effects make immediate
impact, we must suppose, on the audience, and help thereby in
telling them the story.

Of the more elaborate music, as opposed to formal fanfares and
flourishes, the songs form a study by themselves and have been considered in detail by Richmond Noble.[123] He points out that with
Shakespeare's increasing skill they become more and more an
integral part of the drama. We may wonder at the diversity of effect
that Shakespeare so produced, and it is enough to mention *Who is
Sylvia?* the serenade made doubly dramatic by the presence of the
rejected Julia; *Tell me where is Fancie bred*, with its riddling applica-
tion to guide Bassanio in his choice; Lucius' song with its drowsy

This is a sleepy Tune

cadence, tactfully devised to leave Brutus alone with the atmosphere
which breeds ghosts; the musical comments of *As You Like It* (the
nearest thing among Shakespeare's plays to a musical comedy);
Come away death, an example of the music that is the food of love;
Ophelia's mad songs, reflecting the confusion of her grief-stricken
mind; Desdemona's Song of Willough, most poignant of all Shakespeare's effects in music; *Full fadom five*, giving an air of magic
unreality to the supposed bereavement of Ferdinand so that he may
be ready for his meeting with admired Miranda.

Most of these songs, and particularly those of Lucius and Feste
and Desdemona, are examples of atmospheric music in Shakespeare,
and there are other occasions where he uses instrumental music for
such effect. There is, for instance, the music which Richard II hears

---

[122] *Julius Caesar*, V. iii. 96; V. iv.
[123] Richmond Noble, *Shakespeare's Use of Song.*

in prison and whose broken time provokes him to much irritable comment and yet at last makes him grateful to the player [124]; and the music on which Orsino feeds his passion in the opening phrases of *Twelfth Night*. Music is likewise used to heighten the pathos of a sickbed (though the explicit reason is to relieve the patient or to heal him); King Henry IV asks for music in his last illness,[125] and the Doctor prescribes louder music for the waking of Lear after his frenzy.[126]

An interesting example, where the dramatist seems to have an ironical purpose in employing music, occurs in *Much Ado About Nothing*.[127] Balthasar's song *Sigh No More Ladies* is, Benedick thinks, for Claudio's benefit; in fact, Claudio is not in a melting mood, but a mischievous one, and presumably the song is meant to hale Benedick's soul out of his body—in spite of himself. *Sneakes Noyse*, which is summoned to the Boar's Head to please Mistress Tearsheet, is surely a parody of the conventional love-music, appropriate to Falstaff's maudlin romance.[128] But in all these examples it will be noticed that the music is *part of the play*; it is *heard on the stage* and is never a comment shared only by the dramatist and the audience to the exclusion of persons of the play.

There is great versatility in the type of music and also in the instrumentation; there is nothing perfunctory or hidebound about Shakespeare's demands. He is audaciously experimental here as elsewhere. He attempts, for instance, to differentiate nationality in music, but usually for dramatic, never for archæological reasons. In 1 *Henry VI*, when La Pucelle persuades Burgundy to break away from his alliance with the English, the political issue is emphasised by a distinction between an *English March* for Talbot and a *French March* for Burgundy.[129] The flourish of cornets that announces the Prince of Morocco's presence at Belmont, suggests an appropriate characterisation.[130] Lady Mortimer's Welsh air, accompanied probably by the harp,[131] and the *Danish March* which introduces Claudius and his Court as they are "comming to the Play",[132] prove that Shakespeare is ready to take whatever is available or fashionable in London at the time. There is indeed a remarkable variety of instrumentation: besides the normal instruments—trumpets, drums, cornets, hautboys, viols and recorders—we get pipers at the end of *Much Ado About Nothing*; Lucius' song for Brutus [133] is sung to an

---

[124] *Richard II*, V. v. 41–66. [125] 2 *Henry IV*, IV. v. 3. [126] *King Lear*, IV. vii. 25.
[127] *Much Ado About Nothing*, II. iii. 60. [128] 2 *Henry IV*, II. iv. 12.
[129] 1 *Henry VI*, III. iii. 31, 34. [130] *The Merchant of Venice*, II. 1; II. vii.
[131] 1 *Henry IV*, III. i. 123, 248. See *Variorum* edition, *ad loc.*
[132] *Hamlet*, III. ii. 96. [133] *Julius Caesar*, IV. iii. 256 ff.

instrument, presumably the lute, and Pandarus likewise asks for an instrument before he sings for Helen of Troy [134]; we have already noticed Glendower's harp. Besides the solo voices, which are sometimes accompanied but often free (as, for instance, with Ophelia, Lear's fool, Autolycus), we have indications of choral singing when the fairies sing Titania to sleep [135]; when a "solemn hymne" is sung in the Monument of Leonato [136]; and twice in *As You Like It*—when the direction reads *Altogether heere* for "Who doth ambition shunne"; and again when in the dénouement Hymen announces a "Wedlocke Hymne".[137] There is a burden (*Ding, dong, bell*) in *The Merchant of Venice* [138] and another (*bowgh wawgh*) in *The Tempest*,[139] and a delightful, spontaneous duet in *As You Like It*, when one of two pages asks Touchstone: "Shall we clap into it roundly, without hauking, or spitting, or saying we are hoarse, which are the onely prologues to a bad voice?" [140]

As a further symptom of enterprising experiment, the musicians are made to travel all about the playhouse. In *The Two Gentlemen of Verona* they appear on the stage to serenade Sylvia.[141] In *2 Henry IV*, by the sickbed of the dying King, they are "in the other Roome" [142]; so the supposition is that they play off stage on the ground floor of the Tiring-House. In *Troilus and Cressida*, when Pandarus visits Paris and Helen, it is apparently a chamber scene, and the prompt-book says: *Musicke sounds within*.[143] One need only mention again Glendower's music which is said to "Hang in the Ayre a thousand Leagues from thence"—it looks as if they would play in the customary gallery—and the Hoboyes in *Antony and Cleopatra* under the Platform, and we may be said to have boxed the compass.

It seems then that in re-plotting the play, we should use the directions in the Folio and Quarto texts as a basis for the formal and ceremonial music of trumpets, etc.; follow the points of emphasis marked in the prompt-book; infer other cues from the dialogue (as in *Julius Caesar*, above); and expand on similar lines, but not unless the situation calls for it; covering a processional entry is a legitimate reason for expansion. The songs should be done as Shakespeare means them (and Noble is here a safe guide), without repetition or expansion. The instrumental music should also serve exactly the dramatic purpose of Shakespeare, and no more.

It is no mere archaistic affectation to stick to the period music—

---

[134] *Troilus and Cressida*, III. i. 106, 126.
[135] *A Midsummer Night's Dream*, II. ii. 7 ff.
[136] *Much Ado About Nothing*, V. iii. 11.
[137] *As You Like It*, II. v. 38; V. iv. 144.
[138] *Merchant of Venice*, III. ii. 72.
[139] *The Tempest*, I. ii. 375.
[140] *As You Like It*, V. iii. 12.
[141] *Two Gentlemen of Verona*, IV. ii. 18.
[142] *2 Henry IV*, IV. v. 4.
[143] *Troilus and Cressida*, II. iii. *fin.*

either genuine, if there is any suitable, or an imitation if the stanza of a lyric is metrically too complicated to find a tune that will fit. The overwhelming reason is that this was the golden age of English music, and that a strain of Byrd or Gibbons or Morley or Weelkes can evoke sooner even than Shakespeare's words the astonishing poetical freshness and vigour and strength of the age. Indeed, if we use the music of these composers, we may even find it easier to listen to Shakespeare himself with a less jaded ear, and hear his freshness anew. If we stick to the period for the purely musical pieces, then it is hardly less important to preserve a simplicity in the fanfares as well: anachronisms in musical texture are quicker than anything to destroy the sense of style; and they would soon undo the effect we are trying to build up of a performance such as the Chamberlain's Men would have given.

(vi) Effects

The back-stage crew at the Globe would have had plenty to do, and one can imagine that their work was done—like that of most stage-crews—with skill and enthusiasm. They worked in the Huts above the Heavens, and in Hell below the Platform, and at any other point of the Tiring-House or the whole playhouse where their services were required for the illusion. Details of their means and devices can be found in Cranford Adams and in W. J. Lawrence, and to the works of these authors the producer who wishes to re-construct the Globe performance should refer.[144] But for our present purpose, of seeing how far it is possible to re-plot with the Book-Keeper, it must be said that, as with the music, so the other sound-effects are mostly marked in the Quarto and Folio texts or easily inferred from them.

Let us consider, for instance, the oft-repeated cue of *Thunder*. Lawrence tells us of some of the dodges by which the effect was produced—"rolling an iron bullet down an inclined wooden trough provided here and there with slight obstructions over which it crashed"; "simulation of the thunder-clap by rolling a barrel half filled with stones"; or a thunder-roll on the base-drum; and "blow-ing rosin through a candle flame (the approved method of making stage lightning)." [145] As with the trumpet-calls, so here too the points of emphasis are marked in the early texts; we must no doubt

---

[144] J. Cranford Adams, *The Globe Playhouse*; W. J. Lawrence, *Pre-Restoration Stage Studies*.
[145] *Op. cit.*, 210, 263.

expand the number of cues but still use the effect sparingly; the words must be heard. We can guess at the practice if we consider the storm in *Julius Caesar*. If we open the Folio at page 702 we find the cue *Thunder and Lightning* at the beginning of what we now call Act I, Scene iii. There is only one other cue (*Thunder still*) marked by the prompter. But one can perhaps legitimately add a roll or clap at Cicero's "This disturbed Skie is not to walke in". A lightning flash might well greet the arrival of Cassius, who boasts that he has:

> . . . bar'd my Bosome to the Thunder-stone
> And when the crosse blew Lightning seem'd to open
> The Brest of Heaven, I did present my selfe
> Even in the ayme, and very flash of it.

Other suitable moments are at Cassius' "Most like this dreadfull Night," and again when he says, just before the entry of Cinna:

> And the Complexion of the Element
> Is [*read* In] favors like the Worke we have in hand,
> Most bloodie, fierie, and most terrible.

The purpose, in all these additions, is to use the effects to point the dialogue. Then the thunderstorm drops for Brutus' orchard where it would obviously be inappropriate and disturbing both to Brutus' philosophic brooding and to the whispered colloquy of the conspirators, and indeed to the hushed intimacy of the Portia scene. But it picks up again with a sudden clap of *Thunder* just before the end of the Ligarius scene so as to remind us of the portentous night for the opening of the dialogue between Caesar and Calpurnia.[146] This is an instructive example of how the minimum of means can produce the necessary effect. The recurrent direction *Storme still* in *King Lear* reads also like a kind of reminder; as if these were the points where the noise becomes obtrusive above the dialogue. This can only be tested in practice, but we may take it for granted that a little will go a long way in creating the effect, and the kind of continuous bombardment that drowns the dialogue defeats the poet's end in an attempt at irrelevant realism.

Nevertheless there was no tendency to avoid verisimilitude on doctrinaire grounds. Quite the contrary: just as the visual effects in *Macbeth* would be real—the Apparitions, Banquo's ghost, Macbeth's severed head (but not, of course, the "Dagger of the Minde")—so with audible effects too: not only will clocks strike and bells jangle, but the owl, "the fatall Bell-man", will be heard to hoot through the

---

[146] *Julius Caesar*, I. iii; II. i. and ii. We shall notice a similar phenomenon when we come to study the night of Duncan's murder in *Macbeth*. See below, p. 291.

medium of a good mimic.[147] The cocks will crow to drive away King Hamlet's ghost. Such skilful scene-painting as the Inn Yard scene in I *Henry IV* (II. i) can be clinched by the neighing of Neighbour Mugge's poor jade Cut, and the whinnying reply of Gadshill's gelding.[148] It needs a good deal of skill with the coconuts to make the horses not only approach but also "goe about" in the Banquo murder scene: Lawrence, after mentioning as stage-directions "a noise within, as of a horse falling" and "a noise within of driving beasts",

Prompter and Effects

remarks that "few dramatists hesitated about setting the players posers of this order".[149] It needs skill, too, to get the right kind of sound for the famous knocking in *Macbeth*, different, for instance, from the knocking in Brutus' orchard; or to hit the appropriate timbre for the little bell which tells Macbeth that his "drinke is ready"; to make the noise of banqueting offstage in *Macbeth;* to let

---

[147] "We may be sure that when Puck said warningly to Oberon: Fairie King attend and mark/I do hear the morning lark, it was the lark and no other sort of bird that was imitated."—W. J. Lawrence, *op. cit.*, 205.

[148] I *Henry IV*, II. i.

[149] W. J. Lawrence, *op. cit.*, 218; see also p. 199, where Lawrence says: ". . . if the prime conveyance of atmosphere was the poet's prerogative, none the less was it the producer's duty to prolong its vibrations. He had at his beck a rich comprehension of the science of the illusion of sounds, that subtler kind of realism which, when deftly brought into play, proves such a quickener of the imagination. As procured by him, it reinforced the pen-picture sketched in by the poet and gave it colour."

the storm-sounds penetrate into the farmhouse in *King Lear* every time the door opens.[150] One may wonder what they made of the sea-fight in *Antony and Cleopatra*.[151]

In this matter of "effects", it seems unlikely that the Book-Keeper would ignore the judgment of Shakespeare himself: his selective eye and ear for significant sight and sound (which we shall study further when we discuss his stagecraft in Chapter V) would be invaluable. It is perhaps not fanciful to imagine the poet constantly saying "don't overdo it". The gang would be inhuman if they did not err in this direction. The mechanicians of the theatre are easily intoxicated with the opportunities of their craft and want to use every trick in every play. Shakespeare, with the judgment of a great artist, could say that this is significant, that is irrelevant; this helps, that hinders. The Globe Playhouse, as Lawrence and Cranford Adams have shown, was fully equipped. Riches can be an embarrassment in this department. Probably Shakespeare lost the battle in the end: one cannot escape a suspicion that one reason why he was content to withdraw to Stratford was the fact that a new generation and a new fashion gave too much glory to the machinery: the masked displays of *Cymbeline* and *The Tempest* must have gone against the grain with the poet who knew that without such aids he had "bedymn'd The Noone-tide Sun". Perhaps the mishandling of the poetic drama began even thus early, the cleavage which Collier suggested when he wrote on a kindred theme: "The introduction of scenery . . . gives the date to the commencement of the decline of dramatic poetry." [152]

(vii) *Plotting Entries*

Now we are ready for the Book-Keeper to begin putting his actors on to this stage. If the problem of scene-rotation is satisfactorily solved, the plotting of the entries usually follows as an automatic corollary. It becomes simple because of the limited possibilities of entry on the Globe ground-plan. Disregard for the moment the upper stages and the "freak" entries of trap in floor and ceiling; the main action of any play takes place on the Platform with or without the addition of the Study. The possible entries therefore are: (without the Study) the two doors R and L, and through the centre of the Study curtain; (with the Study) the two doors, the sides of the Study R and L, and—if visible (neither, for instance, would be seen in the

---

[150] *King Lear*, III. vi.   [151] *Antony and Cleopatra*, III. viii. 10.
[152] Collier, *English Dramatic Poetry*, Vol. III, 170 (Second Edition).

throne-room)—the door or the alcove (hardly both) in the rear wall of the Study.[153]

This limited number of available entries, at first sight a drawback, proves in practice a great help in clarifying the story and is quite adequate to handle even so complicated an operation as the three-day battle of Actium in *Antony and Cleopatra;* indeed, a more complicated architecture which attempts to differentiate several directions serves merely to confuse. What does the Book-Keeper in fact do in this matter? With his scene-rotation already mapped out, he chooses a door for his first entry and the rest follow almost inevitably from that initial choice. The result will read like very plain common sense, but it is worth emphasising the simplicity because it makes for remarkable clarity in presenting a swift-moving story.

With only two main entries to the Platform, the third through the curtain being accessory, he will often be confronted with a purely mathematical elimination. The fact that one character or group of characters has gone out of one door, means that the next-comer will enter by the other—to avoid the appearance of their having met outside. For instance in Cranford Adams' reconstruction of *King Lear*, banished Kent goes out through "Door A", and France and Burgundy enter at "B".[154] To indicate that they come from elsewhere, Hamlet and Horatio will use the opposite door to Ophelia's funeral procession.[155] If at the beginning of a scene both R and L doors are preoccupied with entrance, then the scene before (if it is not on an upper stage) must end with the departure into the Study, whether the curtain is drawn or not. Simultaneous entry of two persons or groups, meeting each other, will probably use the two doors; and this is sometimes so marked in the text. In *Richard III,* II. iii, where modern editions print "enter two Citizens, meeting", the Folio has: *Enter one Citizen at one Doore, and another at the other.* So in III. vii of the same play: *Enter Richard and Buckingham at severall* (i.e. different) *Doores.* We have already noted the Fisher Quarto's description of the first appearance of Oberon and Titania.[156] The simplicity of the convention is well seen in *King John,* when the rival armies outside Angiers leave the Platform for a battle, and after an indecisive engagement (occupying thirty-four lines of dialogue) return *at severall doores* to continue their dispute.[157]

But it must be remembered that, as with the music-cues, so the directions for entry in the contemporary texts will not be complete; the Book-Keeper will not need to be reminded of ordinary stage

---

[153] See ground plan on p. 18, above.
[154] J. Cranford Adams, *The Original Staging of King Lear,* 316.
[155] *Hamlet,* V. i. 60, 239.　　[156] See above, p. 50.　　[157] *King John,* II. i. 334.

practice. Thus, as Cranford Adams points out,[158] we need no *exit* or *enter* when an actor passes from the Platform through a stage door into the Study. Conversely, directions beginning *Enter* do not necessarily imply motion. *Enter Brutus in his Orchard* is the Folio's instruction when Brutus is presumably discovered in the Study (furnished with a garden set).[159] We have a similar case in *All's Well That Ends Well*: *Enter one of the Frenchmen, with five or six other souldiers in ambush.*[160]

So far, all is fairly obvious common sense. Sometimes for a number of scenes one door becomes associated with one group of characters and the other with another. Thus in the prelude to Shrewsbury Field one door will be Hotspur's tent (perhaps with his pennant hoisted on the corresponding stage-post) and the other the King's. A critical point is the transit of Worcester and Vernon back to Hotspur from their embassy: I fancy they must enter through the Study curtains, and make the tour outside the posts towards Hotspur's "tent".[161] Similarly throughout the fourth act of *Henry V* (the sequence of Agincourt), it is possible for the French to monopolise one door and the English the other, until in Scene vi the Platform (and the battlefield) belongs to King Harry. Mountjoy, in Scene vii, will still use the French door, but thereafter both doors are at the disposal of the English.

Sometimes over a long period a sense of direction prevails, as was the custom of the Roman Comedy—where the entries "from the town", "from the harbour", and so on, were fixed by convention. It is particularly true, as we shall see, of the street sequences, but one can find other examples: for instance, the audience are much helped if in *Twelfth Night* the geography of Olivia's garden is made clear to them; if, that is to say, one door may be thought to lead from the house, and the other from the street.[162] But of course the run of the story sometimes makes it impossible to persevere with this arrangement. The sense of locality suggested by the furniture of the Study or by the words of the actors will sometimes dictate the position of an entry. Cranford Adams makes clear, for instance, that when the wall-and-gates set is in the Study in *King Lear* (II. ii), neither of the stage-doors is used by any actor purporting to enter the Castle but only by those approaching it from outside. This kind of illusion is quite naturally taken for granted by an audience. By a similar

---

[158] J. Cranford Adams, *The Globe Playhouse*, 145.   [159] *Julius Caesar*, II. i.
[160] *All's Well That Ends Well*, IV. i. 1.   [161] 1 *Henry IV*, V. ii.
[162] On a small scale, the geography of the Study in the carriers' scene (1 *Henry IV*, II. i) should be quite clear—the inn towards L, the stable R—and in the sequel of the highway robbery we should be clear which direction is up hill and which down hill.

reasoning in the "Farmhouse" scene which is confined to the Study, all entries are made through the one door in the rear wall, so as to give the impression that there is only one way out of the hut to the stormy heath outside.[163]

Modern scholars speak of a "law of re-entry" which Cranford Adams defines by an illustration from *King Lear:* "Kent enters as this scene opens (III. i), yet is presumed to be at some little distance from Gloucester's Castle, the place where he last appeared. To make this remove seem possible in a scheme of dramatic time, he was withdrawn ten or more lines (there twenty-two lines) before the close of Scene ix (the preceding scene)." [164] The practice so formulated is an intelligible one. But the law is not inviolate: Brutus seems to break it twice in the last act of *Julius Caesar*. His impulsive entry on the battlefield—"Ride, ride Messala" (V. ii)—follows immediately after his departure from the Platform at the end of the previous scene. I take it that the transition in thought is made partly by the *Alarum*, a prolonged one for the start of the battle, and possibly also by the drawing of the Study curtain to reveal the battlefield set. Later, too, when after seeing Cassius' dead body, he leaves the Platform to "try Fortune in a second fight" (V. iii), he reappears at once in the thick of the battle. Here too a loud and prolonged *Alarum* marks the transition of both time and place.

But the fact is that poets and actors often recognise when it is justifiable to break the laws and principles formulated from their own practice by critics and scholars: the measure of success is the consideration of what is plausible, what creates the illusion. Much of it turns out to be common sense—common theatrical sense, such as any producer of to-day would think of as his a b c. The difference between what the Chamberlain's Men did and what is commonly done now is the difference between simplicity and complication. Three points of entry for the Platform, the main arena, are enough and to spare for Shakespeare.

We may now examine the effective simplicity of Shakespeare's stagecraft by plotting the entries in the first two acts of *Julius Caesar*. The play opens, I take it, with distant shouting to indicate the progress of Caesar's triumph: this will not swell to its full volume until the entry of Caesar's procession, but its general direction is at once made clear if the clamour is made on the left-hand side of the Tiring-House. The handful of citizens, the "idle Creatures", therefore stream on to the Platform from the R door, running towards the noise; and perhaps the liveliest of them, the "Mender of bad soules",

---

[163] J. Cranford Adams, *The Original Staging of King Lear*, 325; *King Lear*, III. vi.
[164] J. Cranford Adams, *The Original Staging of King Lear*, 323.

will jump up on to the base of the left-hand Stage-Post. Flavius and
Marullus follow them in by the R door, and when they have cowed
their enthusiasm, send them skulking back through the same
entrance. When the two tribunes part on their mission to "Disrobe
the Images", Marullus goes by the R door "towards the Capitoll"
and Flavius through the centre of the Study curtain, thus leaving the
L door free for Caesar's entry.

The citizens, who have had time to travel round the back of the
Tiring-House, reappear through L door, forming an avenue for the
procession, which makes a circular tour in front of the Stage-Posts.
After the encounter with the Soothsayer, they all proceed through
the R door, leaving Brutus and Cassius alone on the Platform. The
repeated *Flourish and Shout*, which so disturb Brutus, are of course
made on the right-hand side of the Tiring-House, and the reappearance of Caesar followed by the "chidden Traine" is through
the R door: his second departure will therefore be by the L door.
Casca, after his blunt description of Antony's offer of the crown and
Caesar's swoon, follows out L, but Brutus naturally takes the other
door when he parts from Cassius. Cassius, at the end of the scene,
goes through the centre of the Study curtain.

We can be sure of this, because Scene iii opens with the meeting
of Cicero and Casca, who need both doors: Casca, who has recently
gone out L, will conveniently return by the same entry: so Cicero
uses the R door, and leaves (at line forty) by the L door. Cassius'
simultaneous and sudden appearance is therefore by the R door. At
first calculation Cinna's direction appears not to matter, but if we
work backwards from the end of the scene, we can argue thus: the
rendez-vous is Pompey's porch, and thither Cassius may be presumed
to have been heading when he first appeared on the R; the L door
therefore leads (for the moment) to Pompey's porch, and so Cassius
and Casca will go out L at the end of the scene; but Cinna is sent on
a job by Cassius which takes him first in a contrary direction; thus
we may presume that he has entered by the L door, coming from
Pompey's porch, but that he leaves by the R door to "bestow those
Papers" at Cassius' bidding.

Actus Secundus begins: *Enter Brutus in his Orchard*. The Study is
revealed for the first time in the play, and contains a garden-setting.
The geography of the Study must be established and kept con-
sistently: at line 60 Brutus says "Go to the Gate, some body knocks",
and Lucius takes nine lines of Brutus' deliberate soliloquy to get
there and back; it is therefore plain that the "Gate" is out of sight,
not visible in the Study; we must choose a direction—let us say,
Study R—for the gate, and the other—Study L—will thus lead

towards the house. This decision made, the scene plots itself. Lucius
comes and goes by Study L until line 60, when he will take the other
way. The conspirators enter by Study R and leave by the same
course. It is worth suggesting in parenthesis that at line 110, when
Casca tells us that "the high East Stands as the Capitoll, directly
heere", he should point his sword towards the R of the Platform, a
direction which already in the opening scene of the play has become
associated with "the Capitoll". Portia's entry and departure are
Study L, from the house and back again, and when the knocking at
the gate disturbs her talk with Brutus, Lucius slips across the Study
from L to R and brings back Ligarius from Study R. At Brutus'
"Boy, stand aside," the inquisitive Lucius will reluctantly return
into the house, and at the end of the scene Brutus will be leading
Ligarius towards Study R, as the curtains are once more pulled
across the orchard-set.

We now have the bare Platform again, with its entries by the two
doors and the centre of the curtain. *Thunder & Lightning. Enter Julius
Caesar in his Night-gowne.* He will take the centre entry: the Servant
uses the L door, which we may associate with the domestic quarters
of the house; Calpurnia naturally follows her lord through the
curtain. Decius and all the rest of Caesar's visitors use the only other
available entry, the R door; and at the end of the scene, when Caesar
bids them "go in, and taste some wine", the whole party goes
through the Study curtains.

No sooner are they gone than Artemidorus crosses the Platform
from L door to R: it is plain from his words that he is in the street,
and therefore when Portia and Lucius dart out of the centre of the
Study curtains, they too may be understood to be in the street. Our
attention is drawn throughout the breathless agitation of this little
scene to the direction of the Capitoll. Lucius, bewildered by his
mistress's incoherence, says: "Madam, what should I do? Run to
the Capitoll, and nothing else?" Portia hears a "bussling Rumor like
a Fray, And the winde brings it from the Capitoll". The Soothsayer,
who wants to confront Caesar, goes to take his stand "To see him
passe on to the Capitoll." The Book-Keeper will, I fancy, direct his
players to follow the suggestion already established by Flavius and
by Casca, that the Capitoll lies to the right-hand side of the Platform. The Soothsayer will go from L to R, and at the end of the
scene, when Portia, saying "I must go in", retreats back into the
Study curtains, Lucius will run off by the R door. Then we are all
ready to expect the entry of Caesar's formal procession by the L
door as he approaches the Capitoll.

We shall have cause later in the argument to return to the scene

of Caesar's murder. For the moment, it is, I hope, established that on
the simple ground-plan of this playhouse the plotting of entries can
be decided by a process of logical reasoning; and that the clarity of
the narrative and the dramatic emphasis are sharpened in focus
rather than blurred by this very simplicity.

(viii)   Street Sequences

Street scenes are common in Shakespeare as in other Elizabethan
dramatists and their audiences would be quick to recognise the every-
day geography of Jack Cade's campaign through London—
London-Stone, the Savoy and the Inns of Court, up Fish Street,
down St. Magnus' Corner—and not slower to imagine the setting of
the mob-scenes in *Julius Caesar* and *Coriolanus*. In such sequences
where the emphasis is mostly on the mob itself, the architecture of
the playhouse has no more importance than to differentiate by use
of the Tarras the nobles from the rabble. Thus Lord Scales is seen
. . . *upon the Tower walking;* and again King Henry appears *on the
Tarras,* locality unspecified, to receive the submission of the *Multi-
tudes with Halters about their Neckes.*[165]

But it is natural that several of the plays should make literal use of
the visible shape of the Tiring-House, which has on either side of
the curtained inner stages the recognisable façade of an Elizabethan
town house—a street-door with knocker, and two doorposts supporting an overhanging bay-window.[166] Either of these doors can—with
the readiness of the Elizabethan playwrights, noted above, to accept
the features of their stage—become for the moment the focus of a
scene. For instance, in *Richard III*, when Lord Stanley sends a midnight warning to Lord Hastings, we read: *Enter a Messenger to the
Doore of Hastings:* and the envoy uses the knocker to rouse Hastings
from his bed.[167] This direction is the opening of a new scene, but the
doorway can rise up before our eyes in a flash while a scene is in
progress. An interesting example of this process is the opening scene
of *Othello* where, after a deliberately unlocalised start, we are
suddenly told "Heere is her Fathers house",[168] and Brabantio appears
Above, in the Window-Stage over the door. The effect is as if Iago
and Roderigo have been walking along the street and opportunely
find themselves outside the particular house. It is Roderigo who
notices the house, but Iago is the opportunist, Iago has led him there

---

[165] *2 Henry VI*, IV. v. 1; IV. ix.   [166] See above, pp. 20 ff.
[167] *Richard III*, III. ii. 1.   [168] *Othello*, I. i. 74.

as if by accident; or is it his creator, Shakespeare, who has found the door and window opportune for his dramatic purpose?

Sometimes the illusion of a street outside a specific house is kept up for some time. Intermittently it will "not exist", but it will not be anywhere else meanwhile. *The Comedy of Errors* is a notable case where, except when we see the ladies Adriana and Luciana at home (probably in the Chamber), the whole play takes place in the streets of Ephesus. For much of the play—but of course intermittently— one of the stage-doors is the front door of Antipholus of Ephesus (the action including a prolonged altercation through the wicket): later in the play the other door is identified as the Abbey. It is usual in such cases that when one door is identified, the other disappears, and it would be possible in the course of a long scene to seem to move from one house to another at a distance. At other times we are just in the street with no special local definition.[169]

In *The Taming of the Shrew* the two doors are likewise allotted to the house of Hortensio and the lodging of Lucentio; while sometimes we penetrate to the interior of Baptista's and Petruchio's houses by opening the Study.

We have already seen how, in *The Merchant of Venice*, where for a long sequence (punctuated by the Belmont scenes which are differentiated by the drawing of the Study curtain) the action of the play takes place in the street, one door is identified with Shylock's house, and Jessica throws her casket from the window above this door: in the same scene opportunist's use is made of the Tarras which, as Cranford Adams tells us, "resembled a feature common to many London house-fronts, namely the 'penthouse', a sloping, tiled ledge extending over shopfronts to protect the counters from the rain".[170]

In *The Merry Wives of Windsor*, if the left-hand door becomes at first associated with Page's house (in I. i and ii, and again in II. i), then by the time the story reaches Ford's house for the buck-basket

---

[169] It should be mentioned here that W. W. Greg declares (*The Editorial Problem in Shakespeare*, 140) that the directions in the Folio text of *The Comedy of Errors*, "*from the Courtizans*", "*from the Bay*", "*to the Priorie*", "*to the Abbesse*" indicated an unusual disposition of the stage such as would not be practicable in the public theatre. I think that these directions are of a type which tells the story rather than indicates the geographical features of the stage: for instance, Antipholus E., on p. 91, tells us that he means to dine with "a wench of excellent discourse" (III. i. 109); his next appearance (IV. i. 14) is therefore quite naturally marked "*from the Courtizans*". Antipholus S. bids his Dromio "hie thee presently, post to the rode" (III. ii. 154)—i.e. the road-stead. Dromio's next entry (IV. i. 86) is "*from the Bay*". A similar narrative direction in the Folio is *Enter Angelo with the Chaine* (III. ii. 171). So, too, in 2 *Henry VI*, II. iii, *Enter the King . . . to banish the Duchesse.*

[170] J. Cranford Adams, *The Globe Playhouse*, 249.

scene (III. iii) we shall readily expect the R door to be Ford's front-
door: by it Ford and his fellow searchers will approach the house,
meeting the buck-basket in the very doorway. The search for Falstaff
is conducted partly upstairs; Ford is heard speaking on the way
down the staircase which connects the first and second levels of the
Tiring-House. "I cannot finde him," he says, and Mrs. Page in the
Study whispers to Mrs. Forde "Heard you that?" The search-party
come out for a moment into the street again, when Evans says "If
there be any pody in the house . . ." and then back into the house
for the promised dinner at the end of the scene. We have here
an example of the flexibility of the multiple stage by which we
can see the actors pass from the street through the front-door into
the house and even go upstairs. It is easy to conjure up a picture
of this scene in progress at the Globe, with the Study set in
the style of Anne Hathaway's Cottage or Mary Arden's house at
Wilmcote.

To prove how this combination of street-exterior with domestic
interior clarifies the dramatist's narrative (which is of course written
for it), it will be worth following in close detail the sequence of
Cressida's fetching from Troy. Act IV of *Troilus and Cressida* opens
with a midnight encounter in the streets between Aeneas *at one doore
with a Torch, at another Paris* conducting Diomedes, the Greek who
has come to fetch Cressida, and Antenor, the Trojan who has been
liberated in exchange for her. Aeneas goes off in advance of the rest
(IV. i. 50) towards the house where Cressida is to be found: hitherto
the Platform represents no more than the street; the doors are no
more than entrances, and the sole need is that a sense of direction
should be established. Aeneas has entered L (let us say), the others
who have come for Cressida have entered R: L therefore is the
direction towards Cressida's house, and both Aeneas and the rest of
the party will go out L. As soon as the Platform is clear, Troilus and
Cressida appear—probably in the Study; since they are certainly
indoors, and Uncle Pandarus is to be called down ("He shall unbolt
the Gates," IV. ii. 3). Pandarus appears (at line 20) through the
permanent door in the Study, having just descended the Tiring-
House stairs. Aeneas crosses the Platform from L to R in time to
knock (line 35): thereby we take the right-hand stage-door to be
Cressida's front-door. Cressida says to Troilus "I would not for halfe
Troy have you seene here," and leads him back into her chamber—
that is to say, they withdraw from the Study, perhaps through the
Study door and up the staircase. Pandarus lets Aeneas in through
the right-hand door, and they move directly into the Study, with no
interruption in the dialogue. Troilus joins them there, and when he

Street Scene

hears of the Greek mission, says hurriedly "I will goe meete them: and my Lord *Aeneas*, We met by chance; you did not finde me here." They go out into the street by the right-hand door, and make a tour of the Platform, leaving it by the left-hand door. Meanwhile Cressida rejoins Pandarus in the Study and hears from him the disastrous news. Weeping and distracted, she rushes from the Study with the words, "I will not goe from *Troy*." I think it likely that at this point the curtains of the Study are closed: the visitors enter the Platform by the left-hand door: "It is great morning," says Paris, "and the houre prefixt Of her deliverie to this valiant Greeke Comes fast upon." Troilus invites them all to "walke into her house", and seems to precede the others through Cressida's door by no more than three lines of dialogue. Nevertheless, when the Study curtains re-open and disclose Pandarus counselling Cressida to "be moderate", it is nine lines before Troilus joins them, and more than one hundred before the rest of the party, after expostulations (*within*) from Aeneas and Paris at the length of the lovers' parting, are allowed to appear in the Study. When Troilus insists on accompanying Cressida and Diomedes "to the Port", they once again pass through the right-hand door on to the Platform and across to the left-hand door. But immediately after their departure, the battle-trumpet blows, the narrative ceases to be domestic and intimate, and moves once more on the public plane. This consideration, besides the technical need for clearing the Platform for the crowded entry of Scene v, makes it probable that the Study curtains close upon Aeneas' concluding couplet (IV. iv. 148). The sequence of events—including night and "great morning"—is quite clear to the audience, and it may be said in parenthesis that the reconstruction in the mind's eye of such a sequence suffers not at all from imagining a basis in costume and furniture of contemporary style.

But it is not only in sustained sequences that the stage can be thought of as a street: it is naturally the commonest of all transformations, the quickest and most obvious assumption, that the stage is what it seems; and as the examples in *Richard III* and *Othello* show, the transformation can be made in a single line or speech or a gesture of an actor: no miracles of stagecraft are needed for the poet to evoke this familiar picture. But it is always ready to the poet's hand when his story needs it. It is indeed an actually visible picture, and the poet's task is often the opposite one, of making it disappear. The fact that the house-façade is permanently before the eye makes this task too a simpler one; through the very fact of familiarity it becomes easy to look through the visible scene, to forget it and ignore it.

(ix) Battle Sequences

Shakespeare in approaching the theme of Agincourt chooses to be in a mood of anticipatory apology: but just as we learn to take his words about the new playhouse with a pinch of salt, so we must not think him too abject about his "foure or five most vile and ragged foyles". His imagined warfare finds substantial expression in the words of Othello:

> Farewell the plumed Troopes, and the bigge Warres,
> That makes Ambition, Vertue! Oh farewell;
> Farewell the neighing Steed, and the shrill Trumpe,
> The Spirit-stirring Drum, th' Eare-piercing Fife,
> The Royall Banner, and all Qualitie,
> Pride, Pompe, and Circumstance of glorious Warre:
> And O you mortall Engines, whose rude throates
> Th' immortall Joves dread Clamours, counterfet,
> Farewell: *Othello's* Occupation's gone.[171]

To this we may add the tang of saltpetre in Hotspur's sharp objective picture of the aftermath of Holmedon,[172] and Helena's terror lest her Bertram should be "the marke of smoakie Muskets" when she prays to the bullets:

> O you leaden messengers,
> That ride upon the violent speede of fire,
> Fly with false ayme, move the still-peering aire
> That sings with piercing, do not touch my Lord.[173]

Battle-scenes were popular in the Elizabethan theatre: that is obvious from the number of them, and from the fact that so many plays, including some of the deep-felt tragedies—*Julius Caesar* and *Macbeth*—end with a prolonged sequence on the battlefield. The Bastard Faulconbridge, that pattern of military glory, speaks of the shilly-shallying citizens of Angiers ". . . As in a Theater, whence they gape and point At your industrious Scenes and acts of death",[174] and we can imagine the excitement of the groundlings in the pageantry and rhetoric and athletic skill of those battles.

It may be said at once that the Globe Platform, spacious for manœuvring, centrally placed like a boxing-ring, and by the very reason of its position easy to make seem full, was ideal for presenting these battle-pieces. The indistinct muddle of the picture-stage, with everybody getting in everybody else's way and a general

---

[171] *Othello*, III. iii. 350 ff.
[173] *All's Well That Ends Well*, III. ii. 111 ff.
[172] 1 *Henry IV*. I. iii. 29 ff.
[174] *King John*, II. i. 375 f.

Stand ho, speake the word along

uncertainty among the audience as to who is who and which side is which, makes many a finale a sad anti-climax. Yet some of these Shakespearian battles are so well written that there is no reason for confusion; and in its proper setting the play often ends as it should, with a splendour of finality. Notable examples of such success are to be found in the last acts of 1 *Henry IV*, *Julius Caesar* and *Macbeth*, and to appreciate their quality it is worth spending a little time in examining elementary models of the same genre.

As we have seen, both in the preliminaries and the action itself, one stage-door will probably become associated with the forces of one side and the other with the other: but it will obviously not always be possible to keep this distinction hard and fast. Shakespeare apologises for his "foure or five" at Agincourt, and it will be readily understood that considerations of manpower and of wardrobe will confine the armies to a minimum strength: one would say the minimum to avoid the ludicrous, but the phrase is too negative; there would often be a positive splendour in the "plumed troop"— the best that the gang of hired men and the wardrobe-master could do. It is easy enough when Brutus and Cassius lead their armies on from open doors to parley in mid-stage, to use no more than three soldiers apiece—banner, drum and trumpet—and an officer or two:

Loe, where George of Clarence sweepes along

the cries of "Stand, stand, stand" echoing at various distances off-
stage will multiply a hundredfold. But when the forces have to leave
their base at the Door and march across the Platform, more will be
needed.

There is, in 3 *Henry VI*,[175] an elaborate scene in the course of
which no fewer than five "armies" appear on the Platform. Warwick
the King-Maker stands with the Mayor *upon the Walls* of Coventry
(on the Tarras), awaiting reinforcements: he is especially anxious
that the Duke of Clarence, lately become his son-in-law, should
arrive in time. His drum is expected from the direction of Southam
(let us say from the actors' left). Instead, a drum is heard from the
right, and through the right-hand door march King Edward,
Gloucester, *and Souldiers*. Edward and Gloucester are having the
better of the ensuing parley, when from the left-hand door *Enter
Oxford, with Drumme and Colours*. The newcomers are immediately
admitted into the city: that is to say, they march through the gates,
set in the Study alcove. Gloucester urges his brother to follow, with

---

[175] 3 *Henry VI*, V. i.

a characteristically impulsive cry of "The Gates are open, let us enter too." But Edward counsels caution: "Stand we in good array: for they no doubt Will issue out againe, and bid us battaile." Two more armies arrive from the left, led by Montague and Somerset, and likewise march through the gates. Then as the climax of the scene, "loe, where *George* of Clarence sweepes along, Of force enough to bid his Brother Battaile". The perjured Clarence takes the red rose from his hat and throws it at his father-in-law: then he joins forces with his brothers. The scene ends with mutual defiance between the Tarras and the Platform: "I will away," says Warwick, "towards Barnet presently, And bid thee Battaile, *Edward*, if thou dar'st." And the King retorts: "Yes, *Warwicke*, *Edward* dares, and leads the way," and he and his reinforced army march off by the left door to Barnet. If each of the armies is no more than eight men, such a scene will nevertheless tax the resources of the company to the full, and no doubt some discreet doubling, with quick change of helmets and weapons will be needed to keep the "conveyor belt" of soldiery supplied.

It will be noticed that there is nothing awkward on this Platform about the convention of the cross-stage wrangle. With Plantagenet's head fixed on the battlements of York, Lancastrians and Yorkists hurl invective at each other for nearly one hundred lines of dialogue.[176] Moreover, it is possible for superior defiance to leave the stage to their enemies in such circumstances. When the Triumvirs thus confront the conspirators at Philippi, at first there seems to be danger of an immediate clash. "Stirre not untill the Signall" commands Octavius: but after nearly forty lines of mutual recrimination he cries, "Defiance Traitors, hurle we in your teeth. If you dare fight to day, come to the Field." [177]

The procedure for assault of a town is simply exemplified in a passage of 1 *Henry VI*. At Orleans, Talbot, Bedford and Burgundy enter *with scaling Ladders*. "Ascend brave *Talbot*," says Bedford, "we will follow thee." "Not altogether," advises Talbot: "Better farre I guesse, That we do make our entrance severall wayes." "Agreed," says Bedford: "Ile to yond corner." "And I to this," says Burgundy. "Yond corner" and "this" are perhaps the two stage-doors, so that Talbot shall be given a clear run at the Tarras. The English scale the walls, and almost at once *The French leape ore the walles in their shirts*, no doubt amid the derisive cheers of the whole playhouse.[178] The classic instance is, of course, at the assault upon Harfleur which

[176] 3 *Henry VI*, II. ii. 81 ff.
[177] *Julius Caesar*, V. i. 21 ff.
[178] 1 *Henry VI*, II. i.

on the picture-stage can hardly reach perfection.[179] The movement
is initiated by the Chorus and it seems likely that the Platform begins
to fill with the attacking force while his words are creating the
picture:

> Worke, worke your Thoughts, and therein see a Siege
> Behold the Ordenance on their Carriages,
> With fatall mouthes gaping on girded Harflew.

Although the "Ordenance" would no doubt be safer unseen, there
might well be harquebusiers giving covering fire from beside the
Stage-Posts.[180] The soldiers of the attacking force, engaged with

God for Harry, England and S. George

scaling ladders, throw themselves down on the Platform exhausted
and discomfited, one perhaps binding a superficial wound with his
torn shirt, another mending a broken pike. The figure of the Chorus,
moving among them, tells us that

> . . . the nimble Gunner
> With Lynstock now the divellish Cannon touches.

With a deafening roar and a blinding flash and the stifling smell of
gunpowder the *Chambers goe off* in the Huts.

> And downe goes all before them . . .

---

[179] *Henry V*, III. Chorus and Scenes i and ii.
[180] A contemporary picture of The Assault, reproduced in G. B. Harrison's *Elija-
bethan Journal* (for 1591-4) opposite p. 36, gives a sort of diagrammatic version
of the orthodox process of attack.

that is to say, the curtains of the Chamber are parted to make a gap
—the breach in the wall—and some agitated Frenchmen appear
through it on the Tarras. At this juncture King Harry and his peers
enter the Platform and he rallies his despondent troops with the
famous cry:

> Once more unto the Breach,
> Deare friends, once more.

During his exhortation the soldiers on the Platform recover their
morale: they "Stiffen the sinewes, summon up the blood, Disguise
faire Nature with hard-favour'd Rage"; they "stand like Grey-
hounds in the slips, Straying [*read* Strayning] upon the Start"; and
when with the cry of "God for *Harry*, England and S. *George*" and a
further volley from the Chambers in the Huts, they swarm up the
ladders on to the Tarras after their leaders—then what groundling
in the Yard will be so mean and base as not to give them a rousing
cheer? Nothing—be it said in parenthesis—is more characteristically
Shakespearian than the sequel to this exhilarating scene. Bardolph
and his cronies are left at the heels of the assault, cheering with the
best of us, but all agreed that "the Knocks are too hot" to follow up
the ladders. "I would give all my fame," says their attendant Boy,
"for a Pot of Ale, and Safetie."

We may notice certain recurrent devices by which Shakespeare
gives dramatic interest to the pitched battle itself: the mere instruction to his hired men to indulge in *Excursions* is a trick that soon
wears thin and that has in itself little tragic or dramatic force.

Sometimes, to stir the interest of the audience the poet gives us a
high-sounding list of names of the principal combatants—a kind of
"match-card", sold to the spectators before the first ball of the Test
Match is bowled. The brief scene between the Archbishop of York
and Sir Michell [181] which leads on to the politics of 2 *Henry IV* has
little dramatic point in its position in the first part except as such a
"match-card" for the Battle of Shrewsbury:

> To morrow, good Sir *Michell*, is a day,
> Wherein the fortune of ten thousand men
> Must bide the touch—

and we are told of Northumberland's sickness and the absence of
Glendower and Mortimer: after which the principal figures on both
sides are announced. So, too, before Agincourt, the French King
gives us a very full list of his peers, calling upon them to "high
[*read* hie] to the field".

---

[181] 1 *Henry IV*, IV. iv.

> *Charles Delabreth,* High Constable of France,
> You Dukes of *Orleance, Burbon,* and of *Berry,*
> *Alanson, Brabant, Bar,* and *Burgonie,*
> *Jaques Chattillion, Rambures, Vaudemont,*
> *Beaumont, Grand Pree, Roussi,* and *Faulconbridge,*
> *Loys, Lestrale, Bouciquall,* and *Charaloyes,*
> High Dukes, great Princes, Barons, Lords, and Kings—[182]

The English team is, with its characteristic conciseness, no less moving:

> *Harry* the King, *Bedford* and *Exeter,*
> *Warwick* and *Talbot, Salisbury* and *Gloucester.*[183]

A corollary of the practice is to be seen in the casualty lists after the battle; the French no less imposing than before, the English by a miraculous contrast which the King duly ascribes to God,

> *Edward* the Duke of Yorke, the Earle of Suffolke,
> Sir *Richard Ketly, Davy Gam* Esquire.[184]

Often after parley and ultimatum the commanders will address their troops. Before Bosworth Field both Richmond and Richard deliver a speech, the former's described in the Folio as *His Oration to his Souldiers.*[185] The French King's speech in *Henry V,* quoted above, is such another. So too Hotspur, although he protests "I professe not talking", yet stirs his followers with the exhortation: "Let each man do his best." He ends his brief harangue by crying aloud:

> Sound all the lofty Instruments of Warre,
> And by that Musicke, let us all imbrace:
> For heaven to earth, some of us never shall
> A second time do such a curtesie.

And the moment of high chivalrous ceremony is specified in the Folio direction: *They embrace, the Trumpets sound.*[186] A similar musical stirring of the blood is created by Macduff's prelude:

> Make all our Trumpets speak, give them all breath
> Those clamorous Harbingers of Blood, & Death.[187]

Then the engagement will begin with *Alarums:* the opening *alarum* of battle might well sometimes take the form so vividly described by Faulconbridge.[188]

---

[182] *Henry V,* III. v. 40 ff.
[183] *Henry V,* IV. iii. 53 f. So in *Troilus and Cressida,* V. v. 6 ff., Agamemnon recites a somewhat perfunctory "match-card" of the battle already in progress.
[184] *Henry V,* IV. viii. 85 ff.   [185] *Richard III,* V. iii. 238 ff., 315 ff.
[186] 1 *Henry IV,* V. ii. 91 ff.   [187] *Macbeth,* V. vi. 9 f.
[188] See above, p. 65.

The normal procedure of battle itself is exemplified at St. Albans [189]; apology for the absence of horses; two single combats; one set of *Excursions; Alarum a farre off* while the non-combatants—the *King, Queene and others*—are on the Platform; one notices as characteristic the trumpet's *Retreat* to mark the end of the battle and the post-mortem description to complete it. At Wakefield [190] there is *A March afarre off*, followed eight lines later by an *Alarum:* then York goes to the battle: the child Rutland is murdered by Clifford. Then *Alarum. Enter Richard, Duke of Yorke.* York describes the course of the battle. *A*

Alarums, Excursions

short Alarum within: and he cannot escape from his pursuers. Bosworth Field [191] is the simplest example of the normal. *Drum afarre off* interrupts Richard's address to the troops. *Alarum, excursions.* Catesby describes the King's prowess. *Alarums. Enter Richard.* "A Horse, a Horse, my Kingdome for a Horse" (the absence of horses turned to dramatic advantage). *Alarum* again. The fight between the two principals. *Retreat and Flourish* for the new King.

Two battles in *King John* make it clear that Shakespeare's method is to select his emphatic incidents and build his battles round them. The fine rhetorical scene in which the Papal Legate Pandulph comes

[189] 2 *Henry VI*, V. ii. and iii.
[190] 3 *Henry VI*, I. ii., iii., and iv.   [191] *Richard III*, V. iii. and iv.

to the help of Constance in breaking up the newly made alliance between King John and King Philip ends with a great dramatic *crescendo* of inflamed tempers. "To Arms let's hie," cries King John. But the battle itself is over in ten lines, sandwiched between two sets of *Alarums, Excursions,* the second followed by the trumpet signal for *Retreat*.[192] The incidents are the decapitation of Austria and the capture of young Arthur—the first perfunctory, the second developed in the sequel. In the fifth act of the play the battle is more prolonged, but again one notices how the poet selects the salient incidents and builds round them: in this case there are three main points to be made—first, King John's sickness and retirement to Swinsted, secondly Melun's dying confession which stirs the English "Revolts" to return to their own side, and thirdly the Dolphin's reception of the news of their falling off and of the wreck of his supply on the Goodwin Sands.[193] Shakespeare sticks to these points and does not dally by the way; the insistent relevance of his dramatic narrative is a characteristic which we shall study further in Chapter V.

It is possible in some battles to trace a sort of Homeric pattern in the incidents. A hero is singled out for his ἀριστεῖα—his brief hour of triumph—and his defeat and death follow hard upon it: the weary struggle of the Wars of the Roses is thus given a perceptible rhythm in 2 and 3 *Henry VI*. Or a minor contest precedes the clash of mighty opposites: as at Shrewsbury, Blunt is killed by Douglas before Prince Hal and Hotspur meet. Sometimes the hero who is ultimately defeated is allowed to show his prowess in the earlier combat, just as Homer lets Hector kill Patroclus before he is himself killed by Achilles; so Macbeth (as we shall see in Chapter VI) must have young Siward for his victim before he is confronted by Macduff. It is perhaps true to say that the most obviously successful battle-pieces are built round personalities. Shrewsbury Field, the climax of 1 *Henry IV*, is a notable *tour-de-force*. The preliminaries, as we have seen, give some geographical clarity to the narrative: it may be that one Stage-Post bears the pennant of *Esperance*, and the other the Royal pennant. Prefaced by the "match-card", the oration to the troops, and an elaborate and moving ceremonial fanfare, the battle itself is brilliantly enriched—first by Blunt's masquerade and the insatiate Douglas' cry, "Ile murder all his Wardrobe peece by peece, Untill I meet the King"; then by the Prince's rescue of his father, and by the suspense so well sustained, as we wonder if the madcap Hal will rise to the great occasion; by Falstaff's ironical mumbling commentary; by the master-stroke of his "fight" with

---

[192] *King John*, III. i. and ii. [193] *King John*, V. iii., iv., and v.

Single Combat—*They are in action*

Douglas, simultaneous with the clash of Hal and Hotspur, so that while we are still laughing at Falstaff's swift demise, the inevitable death of Hotspur shocks us with all the sudden dismay of the unexpected; and again by the vastly funny anti-climax of Falstaff's resurrection and his last triumphant trick of "killing" Percy.

Agincourt is of a wholly different kind. We have, it is true, some of the familiar features; the parley, the "match-card", and the oration to the troops. We have also an unique masterpiece in the prolonged night-prelude: first the arrogant and irritable Frenchmen impatiently wondering "Will it never be Morning?"; then the atmospheric painting by the Chorus of the night between the two camps; then the series of conversations in the English camp, culminating in Harry's soliloquy "Upon the King" and his prayer to the God of battles; then the stirring reveilles in both camps, the Crispin speech, the final interview with Mountjoy; and all for— what? All we are shown of the battle itself is the ludicrous encounter between Pistol and Mounsieur le Fer. The heroic tone of the prelude is picked up again when the battle is over. Shakespeare seems for once to have been at a loss for a point of emphasis: his interest wanders rather than flags: he is intrigued by the inner man in King Henry, which emerges sometimes in Prince Hal, and which the poet is trying to reveal in the conversation with the three common soldiers and in the subsequent soliloquy. He is also, perhaps, interested in the army as a whole—all ranks—rather than in personalities. There is no chance of a Homeric pattern here: York's death, for instance, is presented to us (very movingly) in narrative, not in action.

By the time he wrote *Julius Caesar*, Shakespeare had begun to resolve his problem of projecting the inner man dramatically in his narrative. As we approach the climax at Philippi, the "match-card", though not actually proclaimed, is full of clear-cut characters round which the battle can be shaped. The incidents too are ready to hand in Plutarch. The geographical clue is given by Shakespeare at the very beginning of Act V:

> *Ant.* *Octavius*, leade your Battaile softly on
>   Upon the left hand of the even Field.
> *Octa.* Upon the right hand I, keepe thou the left.
> *Ant.* Why do you crosse me in this exigent.
> *Octa.* I do not crosse you: but Ì will do so.

Octavius, of course, has his way. If the producer has chosen to have them enter from the right-hand side of the Tiring-House, the upshot of this little dispute will be that Octavius' wing of the army (the right wing) will attack the left-hand side of the Tiring-House, and Antony's the right-hand side. This is in fact the plan which is simply followed in the sequel. We learn later that the disposition of forces is: Octavius *v.* Brutus, Antony *v.* Cassius. In the former of these matches Brutus wins the opening round, in the latter Cassius is quickly defeated. Let us pick up the story at the moment when Octavius and Antony hurl defiance at the conspirators. "Why now blow winde," cries Cassius, "swell Billow, And swimme Barke: The Storme is up, and all is on the hazard" (V. i. 676), and, after expressing his mood of superstitious disquiet, takes his affecting leave of Brutus:

> For ever, and for ever, farewell *Brutus*:
> If we do meete againe, wee'l smile indeede;
> If not, 'tis true, this parting was well made.

No sooner have they left the Platform (by, let us say, the L door) than the *Alarum* for battle begins. I think that at the same moment the Study is opened to reveal a battlefield-set—something simple, bleak and forlorn, with "this Rocke" visible for Brutus' "poore remaines of friends" in Scene v. The pulling of the curtain, as we have seen,[194] helps to save Brutus from violating the "law of re-entry": he returns immediately by the L door in a strongly contrasted mood of optimism, and sends instructions by Messala to Cassius' "Legions, on the other side". His words are interrupted by a *Lowd Alarum*, but if we do not hear them and take in their sense, Shakespeare's dramatisation of the whole battle will go for nothing: Brutus' misguided instructions are:

> Let them set on at once: for I perceive
> But cold demeanor in *Octavio's* wing:
> And sodaine push gives them the overthrow:
> Ride, ride *Messala*, let them all come downe.

Messala goes out by Study R towards Cassius, and Brutus returns as he came by the L door. The *Alarums* swell again, and Cassius comes in with Titinius by the R door, already in despair at Brutus' mistake: Titinius makes the point clear, and his every word must be heard throughout the theatre:

> O *Cassius, Brutus* gave the word too early,
> Who having some advantage on *Octavius*,
> Tooke it too eagerly; his Soldiers fell to spoyle,
> Whil'st we by *Antony* are all inclos'd.

Pindarus, Cassius' Parthian slave, comes to bring his master news of the burning of his tents: these may be taken to be in roughly the same direction from which Cassius made his entry. Let Pindarus therefore come in by Study R. Titinius is sent to investigate "yonder Troopes" who, in the tragic sequel, prove to be friend, not enemy: so he departs on his errand by the L door, towards Brutus. Pindarus is bidden "get higher on that hill", and Cassius' two and a half lines of melancholy brooding give him time to mount to the Tarras, whence he can "regard *Titinius*" by looking out towards the left. The *Showt* which Cassius misinterprets is also from the same quarter. *Enter Pindarus*, says the Folio, and again the Parthian is given time to come down from the Tarras. After he has killed Cassius, and left his body at the very front of the Platform, he takes to his heels, "Farre from this Country", and will therefore do well to choose the Study L, away from his previous entry. He cannot take the L door, for that is occupied by the reappearance of Titinius with Messala. The dialogue runs thus:

---

[194] See above, p. 75.

> *Messa.* It is but change, *Titinius*: for *Octavius*
> Is overthrowne by Noble *Brutus* power,
> As *Cassius* Legions are by *Antony.*
> *Titin.* These tydings will well comfort *Cassius.*
> *Messa.* Where did you leave him.
> *Titin.* All disconsolate,
> With *Pindarus* his Bondman, on this Hill.
> *Messa.* Is not that he that lyes upon the ground?
> *Titin.* He lies not like the Living. O my heart!
> *Messa.* Is not that hee?
> *Titin.* No, this was he *Messala,*
> But *Cassius* is no more.

The producer of *Julius Caesar* should read and re-read Granville-Barker's exposition of this wonderful fifth act. Of this passage he writes: "The stagecraft of this entrance, as of others like it, belongs, we must remember, to the Elizabethan theatre, with its doors at the back, and its distance for an actor to advance, attention full on him. Entrance from the wing of a conventional scenic stage will be quite another matter. . . . Stage direction is embodied in dialogue. We have the decelerated arrival telling of relief from strain, the glance around the seemingly empty place; then the sudden swift single-syllabled line and its repetition, Titinius' dart forward, Messala's graver question, the dire finality of the answer." [195]

We shall return, on a later page,[196] to the atmospheric creation of Titinius' ensuing words, as he kneels beside the fallen Cassius. Meanwhile we are concerned chiefly with the plotting of the battle. Messala goes to meet Brutus by Study L, and returns with him and his companions by the same entry, only to find that Titinius has followed Cassius in taking "a Romans part". The approach of Brutus to the pair of dead bodies in the front of the Platform is similar to the former discovery by Titinius and Messala. The *Low Alarums* of distant battle are heard on the right-hand side of the Tiring-House as Brutus kneels beside his friend: at the end of the scene (V. iii) he calls upon Lucilius and young Cato: "Let us to the Field," and they go off Study R toward the battle, while the dead bodies are borne off Study L. It will be noticed that all through the act so far the left-hand side of the Tiring-House has been associated with Brutus' base, and that he has been successful against Octavius. Cassius' base has been to the R, and has been the centre of defeat and despondency: the danger-point is now aptly towards the R. The battle surges on to the Platform for the first time, and all the

---

[195] H. Granville-Barker, *Prefaces to Shakespeare* (First Series), 116 f.
[196] See below, p. 216.

combatants therefore enter from the R door or from Study R. Brutus and young Cato are engaged in a fighting retreat: their backs are to Brutus' base, the left-hand side of the Tiring-House. Brutus drives some of the enemy off by Study R, but meanwhile young Cato (a kind of Patroclus in this battle) is killed on the Platform: Lucilius stoops over his body in a lull of the fighting, and is surprised by some of the enemy and made prisoner: his pretence of being Brutus repeats, with variation, the masquerade of Sir Walter Blunt at Shrewsbury. Antony will presumably make his entry from the R door or from Study R; his departure will certainly be towards the left—probably Study L—for he is making for Octavius' tent, and we may now assume that Brutus' base is captured. It will be seen that it has been quite easy throughout to preserve the general notion of Antony beating Cassius on the right-hand side, and Brutus having a momentary advantage over Octavius on the left. Now at this point the right-hand side of the Tiring-House is the focus of the victory of the triumvirs. Brutus and his "poore remaines of friends" struggle in from Study R, and "this Rocke" is part of the battlefield-set in the Study.

The beauty of this last scene has been eloquently expounded by Granville-Barker.[197] As for the moment we are concerned chiefly with the technicalities, it is enough to underline one or two of his— of Shakespeare's—points. The distance across the Platform gives verisimilitude to the whispered request which Brutus makes to each of his friends in turn; it enhances too the moment when, at Octavius' entry, Strato stands impassively beside the body of his dead lord: "What man is that?" says Octavius from the Study, and Strato and Brutus' body are right forward on the Platform. The dramatic *Low Alarums* and *Alarum still* rising to a *crescendo* of *Alarum. Retreat* after Brutus is safely dead—these sounds will probably come from the left-hand side of the Tiring-House, and Antony and Octavius will make their triumphant entry by Study L. On the other hand, the *Cry within, Flye, flye, flye* will come more appropriately from the right, and Clitus, Dardanius and Volumnius will make their escape (where Brutus, if he were not Brutus, might have followed them) by Study R. The final procession, with the carrying of Brutus' body, will travel (with a drum beating a march) round "this Rocke" and out through Study L towards Octavius' tent. No doubt the Study curtains will be pulled together as soon as may be, and before the last figures have disappeared from the Study.

This is indeed one of Shakespeare's most successful battle-pieces,

---

[197] *Op. cit.*, 118 ff.

and a close analysis of its mechanics is instructive for the producer who wishes to understand his methods. But of course, in this as in every other feature, Shakespeare will be bound by no rules: beside the orderly perfection of *Julius Caesar* and *Macbeth*, we must put also the deliberately skimped engagement in *King Lear*, when the *result* is all that matters; and on the other hand the magnificent expansiveness of the three-day battle of Actium in *Antony and Cleopatra*, where the military prowess of the doting general is a major theme in the drama.

(x) Some Other Settings

We have already noticed that some plays—such as *The Taming of the Shrew*, *Much Ado About Nothing* and *Twelfth Night*—have mainly domestic settings. In *The Merry Wives of Windsor*, the scenes which revolve round Ford's house (III. ii, the buck-basket scene, and IV. ii, where Falstaff makes his second escape disguised as Mother Prat) show how the architecture of the Tiring-House is naturally helpful to such plays, providing both interior and exterior, like a doll's house. Another such example is the sequence in *Troilus and Cressida* examined above.[198] In all these cases the flow of the narrative is much helped by the natural disposition of the playhouse. An interesting development of this running sequence is that of the prison episode in *Measure for Measure*. This begins at the opening of Act III and continues until the end of IV. iii (from page 70 to page 78 in the Folio), and is conducted in the prison or in the street outside it, except for the brief interlude of Mariana in the moated grange (IV. i). Apart from this scene, the whole eight pages can be played as a running sequence with the Study as the prison and the Platform as the street leading to it, one of the stage-doors being the means of communication between exterior and interior. Mariana's scene, which is domestic in character, is naturally placed in the Chamber.

The Chamber, it will be noticed, is often capable of absorbing the digressions from a continuous sequence: for instance, the poet is sometimes able to confine the sub-plot of his play to the second level of the playhouse, and thereby make the pattern of his double plot much clearer to his audience. We have already had occasion to quote J. Cranford Adams' interesting suggestion in reference to *King Lear*: "For as long as the Edmund sub-plot runs parallel to the main plot, it is staged on the second level of the multiple stage. As the two plots merge into one, the staging merges also, and the final

---

[198] See pp. 80 ff.

D

I see a voyce; now will I to the chinke

episodes of the combined action are played on the main level." [199]
How far this was a conscious æsthetic device of the poet's, and how
far a practical necessity, it is difficult to say: but it is quite likely that,
here as elsewhere, necessity was the mother of invention. It would be
interesting to apply the same idea to the plotting of *Hamlet*: but a
moment's reflection will show that the other calls upon the Tarras
and Chamber for ghost-scenes and for Gertrude's closet, preclude
the tidy pattern which Adams suggests for *King Lear*.

Apart from the sequences where the literal architecture of the
multiple stage is employed, certain conventional scenes will fall into
habitual shape. One thinks, for instance, of the throne-room scenes
which occur so frequently in the historical plays. The king's "state"
was a bulky piece of furniture, capable sometimes of seating others
beside the monarch: in *All's Well That Ends Well* the King, restored
to health by Helena, invites her with the words "Sit my preserver by
thy patient's side " [200]; when the desperate Queen Margaret visits
King Lewis of France, he bids her "Sit downe with us: it ill befits thy

---

[199] J. Cranford Adams, *The Original Staging of King Lear*, 316.
[200] *All's Well That Ends Well*, II. iii. 53.

State, And Birth, that thou should'st stand, while *Lewis* doth sit." [201] Since there is little space for manœuvring in the Study to right and left of the throne, the approach to the royal presence would presumably be made through the stage-doors. A lane would be formed by the lords and attendants for the approaching king or duke, though sometimes an alternative method was adopted, the courtiers coming on in the usual processional way, while the king was afterwards discovered seated on his throne.[202] The King himself and his intimates might use the entries to right and left in the Study.

More than once Shakespeare invites us to be spectators of a play within a play. There is the tedious brief comedy of Pyramus and Thisbe,[203] and its earlier cartoon in the show of the nine Worthies[204]: there is the "Mouse-trap" in Hamlet[205]; and Prospero's "most majesticke vision" for Ferdinand and Miranda.[206] In all these cases a likely disposition would be to set the "play" in the Study or against the background of the Tiring-House, while the chief spectators would be seated at intervals round the front edge of the Platform: they form thereby, as it were, the front row of the audience standing in the Yard, and if one or two groundlings were put to inconvenience by having to crane their necks round the seated nobility, it would be a familiar touch of reality for those who were used to struggling in a mob for a better view. The satirical comments of the Athenian court and the intense drama of Hamlet's feverish commentary would both gain greatly by the proximity to the playhouse audience. This is a theme to which we shall return in the next chapter. An opposite grouping in *The Taming of the Shrew* is the exception rather than the rule. Christopher Sly, who is not himself an actor in the play, presumably occupies the Chamber and watches in listless fashion from aloft: and indeed before the play is half-way through he seems to disappear from sight and likewise from mind.

Scenes of banqueting are interesting as an example of the carrying forward of solid furniture on to the Platform.[207] That this was a normal practice we may infer from the directions for the gruesome feast which brings *Titus Andronicus* to its violent conclusion, *Hoboyes. A Table brought in;* for the parallel comic climax of *The Taming of the Shrew, The Servingmen with Tranio bringing in a Banquet;* and for Macbeth's "solemne Supper", *Banquet prepar'd.* We may suppose that the complicated business of bringing forward the trestle-table and stools,

---

[201] 3 *Henry VI*, III. iii. 2 f.
[202] W. J. Lawrence, *Pre-Restoration Stage Studies*, 319.
[203] *A Midsummer Night's Dream*, V. i. 108 ff.
[204] *Love's Labour's Lost*, V. ii. 486 ff.   [205] *Hamlet*, III. ii. 147 ff.
[206] *The Tempest*, IV. i. 60 ff.   [207] See above, p. 42.

and the Dishes and Service, was executed by the comedy-gang and
hired men of the company, and that sometimes the musicians helped
with a tune on the hoboyes. The opposite process must presumably
have taken place at the end of the *Macbeth* Banquet scene (since it is
not at the conclusion of the play): Shakespeare gives us an instructive example with full dialogue in *Romeo and Juliet*.[208] Capulet's
"old accustom'd Feast", which is already over and has to be cleared
for the dancing, is probably set and disclosed in the Study—because
it is already over.

Scenes of conference, involving the use of a table, seem to be disclosed in the Study. King Henry IV rates Worcester from the
council-board [209]; and we must suppose therefore that the scene [210]
begins in the Study round the Table—a sort of Council Chamber
meeting, such as that at which Queen Elizabeth boxed the ears of
Essex. In the same play Glendower, Hotspur, Worcester and
Mortimer are disclosed at the conference-table, and return to it after
an altercation to study the map.[211] In the course of the long scene in
Brutus' tent, the generals and their officers sit "close about this
Taper heere" and make their plans of action.[212] These examples all
suggest that the business of the conference was not usually prolonged, but that one or more of the actors took an early opportunity
to advance on to the Platform. A contrary example is that of the
triumvirs' proscription,[213] which probably takes place in the
Chamber, so that there is no possibility of advancing. But it will be
noticed that this is a very brief scene.

The natural inference from a contemplation of these last two
typical settings—the banquets and the conferences—is that a prolonged
scene in the Study was not effective, that there is an undramatic gap
before the eyes of the spectators if the platform is not in use. Certainly
in practice the producer will find an insistent urge to bring his actors
forward from the Study. We may even occasionally detect such an
urge in Shakespeare's own dispositions: the remote position of the
"State" and the etiquette of facing the royal presence make a
problem by limiting the manœuvrability of the other characters. Is it
for this reason that in the tilting-scene of *Richard II* the King is at
pains after less than fifty lines to leave his throne and come forward
on to the Platform? [214] Antony, too, who begins his oration in the
Pulpit (which must be in the Study), is made to descend half-way
through the scene to show the mob sweet Caesar's wounds.[215] Very

[208] See above, p. 43.
[210] 1 *Henry IV*, I. iii.
[212] *Julius Caesar*, IV. iii. 163.
[214] *Richard II*, I. iii. 54.

[209] See above, p. 41.
[211] 1 *Henry IV*, III. i. 71.
[213] *Julius Caesar*, IV. i.
[215] *Julius Caesar*, III. ii. 165.

interesting, from this aspect, is the climax of the court-scene in *The Merchant of Venice*, which is conducted without any apparent reference to the presiding Duke. Is this the direct result of the scene's setting? For the Duke sits on his "state" in the Study, while the disputants and Antonio's friends are presumably all on the Platform, with Portia central between them—and so inevitably usurping the Duke's authority. With proper courtesy—after the climax—she reminds us all of the Duke's presence.[216] Cranford Adams in a rare mood of special pleading is at pains to show that the Study and the Chamber were used often and for long stretches by themselves. For instance, he seems to set the long Boar's Head scene of 1 *Henry IV* (the two-rogues-in-buckram scene) in the Study, and the parallel scene of 2 *Henry IV* (with the "drawers" and Doll Tearsheet) in the Chamber: and he tells us that "an analysis of plays written between 1599 and 1609 shows that nearly half as many scenes were acted on the rear stage as on the platform; and, furthermore, that the tendency to place scenes of dramatic importance on the rear stage, and scenes of climax on the combined stage (the platform and the rear stage), was growing every year".[217] In such a calculation the length of scenes is perhaps more important than their number, and it is well to remember that our tendency is to exaggerate the importance of the curtained inset over that of what we incurably think of as an annexe. It is timely to reiterate that the Platform was the main arena, quite self-sufficient for the main run of the action: that it is not even necessary to have the Study always open at the end of a play: that Cranford Adams himself in his scene-rotation of *King Lear* places the last four scenes on the bare Platform: and that the action of *Julius Caesar* takes place for most of its length out of doors—in the streets, in the orchard, in the forum, and on the field of battle— so that the Platform is constantly the main field of action. This is all the more remarkable if *Julius Caesar* is rightly dated as one of the first Globe plays. It shows that Shakespeare was by no means preoccupied with his inner and upper stages, and was not to be diverted from his dramatic inspiration by the mechanics of his playhouse.

Among the sequences that make prolonged use of the Platform level are the woodland scenes, usually indicated by the furnishing of the Study with suggestive properties—such as a "thick growne brake",[218] the "cheefest Thicket of the Parke",[219] and Herne's Oak

---

[216] *The Merchant of Venice*, IV. i. 176–364: throughout this passage the Duke never opens his mouth.
[217] J. Cranford Adams, *The Globe Playhouse*, 168.   [218] 3 *Henry VI*, III. i. 1.
[219] 3 *Henry VI*, IV. v. 3.

with perhaps "a pit hard by" in the Study-trap.[220] The setting is sometimes perfunctory, as for the cardboard Outlaws of *The Two Gentlemen of Verona*.[221] The dialogue helps us with no more detailed description than "this wildernesse". Sometimes it is elaborate for the needs of the play, as for instance in the prolonged forest-sequence of *Titus Andronicus*. Tamora and Aaron meet in "a Counsaile-keeping Cave" in the Study: later Bassianus' body is cast into a pit, into which two other persons jump; and a bag of gold is found "Among the Nettles at the Elder tree: Which over-shades the mouth of that same pit"—that is to say, at the foot of one of the Stage-Posts, which may be said to over-shade the central Platform-trap.[222] We have already seen how the furniture of the woodland-set of *A Midsummer Night's Dream* can be deduced. This play shows an example of an exceptionally long sequence during which the locality has definition and consistency. Two long stretches seem to be definitely placed—first, while Titania is asleep before our eyes, and secondly, from Demetrius' first slumber till Bottom's waking.[223] Indeed, once Titania's bank is disclosed, there is no reason why the whole sequence until we leave the forest should not be played before the same woodland-set. With *As You Like It* the problem is different: we are constantly shifting our ground in the Forest of Arden and the transitions are made clear by the appearance of different sets of characters. The time shifts too: there is an instance where modern editions obscure the fact that we pass rapidly from moonlight to daytime. *Actus Tertius. Scena Secunda* opens with the entry of Orlando, who hangs one of his poems on a tree and then addresses the moon, the "thrice crowned Queene of night": after ten lines he runs off on his errand of carving Rosalind's name upon the trees: the subsequent scene between Corin and Touchstone is certainly a daylight meeting. It seems probable that Orlando's ten lines are spoken in the Study, and that the curtains pulled over his departure mark a transition in place and time. No doubt similar opening or closing of the Study marks other changes of venue in the forest, but the evidence of the dialogue suggests that the whole sequence would demand no change of furniture in the Study: rather there would be a generalised indication of woodland in the permanent setting. The occasional digressions involving Duke Frederick and Oliver would of course be relegated to the Chamber.

One must recognise, therefore, what may be called comprehensive

---

[220] *The Merry Wives of Windsor*, V. iii. 14.
[221] *The Two Gentlemen of Verona*, IV. i. 63.
[222] *Titus Andronicus*, II. iii. 24, 186, 272 f.
[223] *A Midsummer Night's Dream*, II. ii. 26—III. i. 136; III. ii. 87—IV. i. 226.

settings. As with the battlefield and the street sequences, so too with woodland and heath—the storm scenes in *King Lear* are an example of the latter—it is possible to have a succession of scenes on such a general background, supposed to take place in different parts, without changing the furniture of the Study, or indeed without opening it at all. The illusion of a change in locality is sometimes, but by no means always, indicated by the opening or closing of the Study or the Chamber. But the question of locality on the Globe stage is an important one, and deserves a section to itself.

(xi) Locality and Unlocalisation

In no respect is the reading of the Quarto and Folio texts a more salutary corrective than in the matter of locality. The editorial practice since Rowe has been to divide into scenes and to give each scene a locality in a heading, such as *A street in Rome, Another part of the plain, Another part of the Forest, A Room in the Castle.* Granville-Barker has made it clear that this practice leads to much confusion and a fundamental misunderstanding of Shakespeare's stagecraft.[224] A kindred belief which also dies hard suggests that it was the regular practice in the playhouse to indicate the whereabouts of each scene by exhibiting locality-boards on the wall of the Tiring-House. This was probably the exception rather than the rule,[225] and a careful perusal of the Folio, with an eye to the practical problems of the producer, leads to the plain conclusion that nowhere in Shakespeare (neither in the simplicities of the early histories nor in the complications of the mature tragedies) are such crude indicators necessary. That he would have thought them crude appears likely, if we read between the lines of the theatrical experiments of Peter Quince and company: for instance, the expedients discussed for presenting Moon-shine and Wall.[226] In Shakespeare's own plays, the rule holds that *you know where you are when you need to know.*

Often he makes a simple and direct statement of locality. Thus each of Talbot's three actions against the French is clearly notified with an introductory sentence: "At pleasure here we lye, neere Orleance"; "These are the Citie Gates, the Gates of Roan"; "Go to

---

[224] Granville-Barker, *Prefaces to Shakespeare* (Second Series), 130 ff. ("A digression, mainly upon the meaning of the word 'scene'.")

[225] J. Cranford Adams, *The Globe Playhouse*, 166.

[226] *A Midsummer Night's Dream*, III. i. 50 ff.

the gates of Burdeaux Trumpeter".[227] Of the same kind is the
question with which Richard II opens a scene: "Barkloughly Castle
call you this at hand?" [228] Such too the question and answer in
Twelfth Night: "What Country (Friends) is this?" "This is Illyria
Ladie." [229]

But just as often Shakespeare is not at all concerned to tell us
where we are. Talbot, outside Bordeaux, is in desperate need of
reinforcements. York and Somerset in their bitter rivalry both fail to
come to his assistance: we see each in turn dallying and abusing the
other: where either of them is, we neither know nor care; the point
is that they are *not at Bordeaux*, as the plot of the play, swift-moving at
this juncture, makes amply clear. As soon as Talbot returns to the
Platform, we know we are back at Bordeaux.[230] There is shrewd
relevance here, and to cumber us with exact geographical information would obscure the main issue.

Shakespeare finds it easy to shift his locality from one place to
another, sometimes so swiftly and deftly that the change happens
without a stop or cadence in the middle of what we call a "scene".
A process like the travelling of the cinema-camera's lens can be seen
twice in *Julius Caesar.* We shall examine in detail on a later page the
scene of Caesar's murder. It is enough here to point out that it begins
in the streets, that is to say, on the bare Platform: Cassius prevents
the importunate Artemidorus from approaching Caesar, with the
words: "What, urge you your Petitions in the street? Come to the
Capitoll." Then, whilst the movement is covered by a tense inter-
change between the conspirators and Popilius Lena, the Study
curtains are drawn aside and Caesar mounts his "state": after
twenty lines the seated dictator opens the proceedings with the
words: "Are we all ready?" and the Platform-cum-Study has already
become the Senate-house.[231] Later in the play, by a precisely similar
process, Brutus and Cassius, who have confronted each other at the
heads of their armies, move into the Study, set for Brutus' tent, to
discuss their differences: *Manet Brutus and Cassius,* says the Folio: and
the great quarrel-scene, with its prolonged sequel ending in the
appearance of Caesar's ghost, ranges freely over the whole Platform,
which has changed from open ground to the interior of the tent.[232]
So too in *Romeo and Juliet* the masquers, after Mercutio's Queen
Mab speech *march about the Stage, and Servingmen come forth with their
napkins.* No doubt the remains of the banquet are discovered in

---

[227] 1 *Henry VI,* I. ii. 6; III. ii. 1; IV. ii. 1.   [228] *Richard II,* III. ii. 1.
[229] *Twelfth Night,* I. ii. 1.   [230] 1 *Henry VI,* IV. ii–v.
[231] *Julius Caesar,* III. i. 1–31.   [232] *Julius Caesar,* IV. ii and iii,

the Study and duly removed by the servants, and the Platform-
cum-Study changes in a trice from the street to the interior of
Capulet's hospitable and festive house.[233] Another example can
be seen in 2 *Henry IV*, when in the Folio text the King is made to
say:

> I pray you take me up, and beare me hence
> Into some other Chamber: softly 'pray.
> Let there be no noyse made (my gentle friends)
> Unlesse some dull and favourable hand
> Will whisper Musicke to my wearie Spirit.

Here the modern editors mark the beginning of a new scene after the
King's second line: in fact, as the Folio makes clear, the invalid is
carried to his bed in the Study, the curtains being drawn aside at
this moment to mark the change "into some other Chamber".[234] It
is important to realise that in all these cases, on the opening of the
Study curtains, even if there is a momentary confinement to that
area, afterwards the whole Platform changes its locality under the
influence of the Study furniture.

These examples have a logical basis in the movement of the
characters, but there are others where there is no such logical
explanation. In 2 *Henry VI* a scene begins with the ceremonial
arraignment of "Dame *Elianor Cobham, Gloster's* wife": exactly *where*
we are hardly matters, and indeed it is best not to ask, for without
any indication of a change of locality the Platform becomes the
"Lysts" for the combat (with staff and sandbag) between Horner
and his man Peter, who enter with their drunken supporters *at one
Doore . . . and at the other Doore.*[235] The painful and intimate "Closset
Locke and Key" scene of *Othello* clearly suggests Desdemona's
private apartments, but ends with a duologue between Iago and
Roderigo, who quite obviously has no access thither: the end of the
scene—probably on the Platform—is therefore without locality.
Conversely, the following scene begins publicly, on the Platform,
and continues in Desdemona's apartment where she is " un-pinned"
by Aemilia.[236] What the Folio calls *Scaena Secunda* of the third act of
King John [237] is an interesting example of a shifting locality. It begins
in the battle itself outside Angiers, and its last line tells us that we are
bound for Calais and home: meanwhile the locality is vague, first in
the battle, then after it, but nowhere in particular. It is John's
speech to Hubert which sets the scene, by playing tricks with

---

[233] *Romeo and Juliet*, I. iv. and v.   [234] 2 *Henry IV*, IV. iv. 131 ff.
[235] 2 *Henry VI*, II. iii.   [236] *Othello*, IV. ii. and iii.
[237] *King John*—in modern editions Act III, Scenes ii. and iii.

daylight, and complaining that it is not the right time and place for murder:

> . . . If the mid-night bell
> Did with his yron tongue, and brazen mouth
> Sound on into the drowzie race of night:
> If this same were a Church-yard where we stand,
> And thou possessed with a thousand wrongs:
> Or if that surly spirit melancholy
> Had bak'd thy bloud . . .

There are seeds here which grow to ripeness in Hamlet's "Tis now the verie witching time of night," and in Macbeth's "Now o're the one halfe World Nature seemes dead, and wicked Dreames abuse The Curtain'd sleepe." [238] We find indeed in this lifting of the imagination away from the visible scene an extreme example of what Granville-Barker calls the "unlocalised" stage.[239]

The question of the unlocalised stage needs further exploration. It is not simply that sometimes the idea of locality is, as it were, suspended in favour of the circumstantial situation of the characters, who by their dress, their properties, or their very presence tell us all we need to know about the *mise-en-scène*—as, for instance, at the first entry of Dogberry, Verges and their fellows, the familiar sight of the Watch, with a lantern, is of itself enough to tell us that it is night and the open streets, or as the appearance of Buckingham *with Halbords* suggests at once the way to execution with no further need of defining the locality—but often for several pages of the prompt-book, the continuity of the play lies in something other than the sequence of time and place. *Much Ado About Nothing*, for instance, is remarkable as being a play where the continuity is made chiefly by the intrigue and locality is incidental. If we read Act V in the Folio there is no indication of *where* we are supposed to be, except for the brief interlude in the Monument of Leonato: it is probable that Benedick's visit to Beatrice is located as a domestic scene in the Chamber: for the rest the story is strung quite logically on the thread of intrigue. As Granville-Barker puts it: "His drama is attached solely to its actors and their acting; that, perhaps, puts it in a phrase. They carry place and time with them as they move." [240]

In the great tragedies, too, sometimes our preoccupation with the story makes us forget altogether where we are supposed to be. From the beginning of Act III, Scene iii of *Othello* there is no question of

---

[238] *Hamlet*, III. ii. 413; *Macbeth*, II. i. 49.
[239] The reader is referred to *Prefaces to Shakespeare* (First Series), xix ff.—a passage in which Granville-Barker discusses "the Convention of Place".
[240] *Op. cit.*, xxiii.

locality until Act IV, Scene ii, (the "Closset Locke and Key" scene), which is presumably in the Chamber. For more than eight pages of the Folio, instead of scenery or visual suggestion of any kind, we are enthralled by the pervading themes, out of which the drama is built: the persons of the drama are all that matter and particularly their speech: there is, indeed, hardly any physical action during this period. And who is to tell us where, between Heaven and Hell, the last scene in *King Lear* is supposed to take place?

Buckingham, with Halberds, led to execution

The opportunities of this unlocalised platform were quite early on appreciated by Shakespeare, both in the speed with which its locality could be changed, and also in the fact that it could lose all sense of being anywhere. The technique, familiar from Greek drama, of creating a dramatic scene through the medium of a Messenger's Speech was often employed by him, and the effect of the unlocalised platform was to bring such scenes more vividly before the imagination of the audience. Hotspur's indignant description of the aftermath of Holmedon, and his painting of the encounter between Mortimer and Glendower are quite detached from the background of the council-chamber in which the scene opens.[241] Oberon's

---

[241] 1 *Henry IV*, I. iii. 29 ff; 93 ff,

familiar description of the origin of the "little westerne flower" becomes far more vivid if the fairy king's voice is for the moment disembodied, as it were, and not fettered to the irrelevant picture of the Athenian wood.[242] When Queen Gertrude tells the tale of Ophelia's drowning, the very speaker here is in a sense unlocalised: the sentiment is quite unlike Gertrude. Ophelia's death is itself an event in the play, and we almost see it before our eyes: it has its immediate dramatic effect upon Laertes.[243] All these descriptive and narrative speeches are the better for being detached from a suggested locality. It is as if the Platform was a white screen upon which a series of images was being projected in quick succession: Shakespeare's poetical imagination is the projector and the speed is as rapid as his thought.

The effect is still more telling when the substance of the speech is not merely objective narrative, but a tissue of changing imagery. This is a theme to which we shall return again, both in considering the acting tradition of the Chamberlain's Men, and in discussing the poet's stagecraft. But it is appropriate to mention it here, as we look over the shoulder of the Book-Keeper, while he plots the play upon the unlocalised Platform and the multiple stage of the Globe Playhouse.

---

[242] *A Midsummer Night's Dream*, II. i. 155 ff.
[243] *Hamlet*, IV. vii. 167 ff.

4

THE ACTING TRADITION OF THE CHAMBERLAIN'S MEN

NOW that we have examined the main problems of the Book-Keeper in plotting a play upon the multiple stage of the Globe, we have reached a point in our investigation where it will be profitable to make closer acquaintance with his colleagues, the player members of the Chamberlain's or King's Company. In this chapter we will begin by considering in general some of the elements in the company's technical accomplishment, and later pay attention to their individual qualities in so far as they help to elucidate the characterisation and the casting of Shakespeare's plays.

But first it is proper to correct what seems still to be a fashionable belief—that they were a set of crude mountebanks or incompetent barnstormers, living a reckless hand-to-mouth life in bohemian circumstances. Popular fiction, touching this theme, likes to paint them in lurid colours, and the sponsors of a film version of *Henry V*, addressing a world-wide audience, were at pains to guy their predecessors in the art of the theatre with the facile assumption that they knew their job less well than themselves.

The evidence is mostly to the contrary. No one who has read the comprehensive account of them given in T. W. Baldwin's *The Organization and Personnel of the Shakespearean Company*—a book which should be more widely known than it is [1]—can doubt that they are more aptly described in the dialogue *Historia Histrionica* (1699) as "grave and sober men, living in reputation".[2] Baldwin presents us with a picture of a company financially prosperous, rigidly organised

---

[1] The strictures of E. K. Chambers (as expressed, for instance, in his *William Shakespeare*, vol. ii, 82, 83) have perhaps been largely responsible for the neglect in this country of Baldwin's work. Chapter III in Chambers vol. i may be read as a corrective in points of detail, but hardly diminishes the importance of the main contention.

[2] Granville-Barker in his essay *From Henry V to Hamlet* (p. 25) refers to this passage, and adds "it is likely to be the truth: for there is confirmation of it. Heminge and Condell were two of them. Does not the introduction to the First Folio reflect as much gravity and sobriety as you like". One could cite also the example of Edward Alleyn, principal actor of the neighbouring company, and founder of Dulwich College.

and carefully guarded in law—its shareholders or "housekeepers" few and privileged, its other members striving to be thought worthy of succeeding, when opportunity arose (through death or withdrawal), to that privilege, its apprentices chosen young and often passing from the tuition stage as boy actors to full membership in adult parts.[3] In addition to the members and apprentices, the Chamberlain's Men would regularly employ more than a score of hired men as "Musitions and other necessary attendants". It is clear that the experienced actors educated their pupils carefully and that thus the repertory had its own school of acting, and a continuous tradition. It is equally certain that they were the most successful company of their time in London, no doubt largely because they had the services of Shakespeare as one of their playwrights. Shakespeare had a powerful effect upon their "box-office" receipts, but it is conversely probable that they had a notable effect upon Shakespeare's plays: they were his acting material, and he wrote for them: Baldwin hardly exaggerates when he declares that "Shakespeare's plays represent not only his own individual invention but also the collective invention of his company".[4] For this reason, if for no other, it is worth while exploring their acting tradition, and seeing how far we can reconstruct it.

It may be said straight away that the view expressed in the following pages makes the optimistic assumption that the Chamberlain's Men were worthy of the chance which Shakespeare gave them. The plays themselves are a tribute to their resourcefulness, their versatility and their all-round accomplishment. Contemporary records suggest that they were in their time "the best in this kind". That is implied too in the familiar passage of Hamlet's advice to the players. The outspoken criticism of acting methods is surely not a hint from Shakespeare to his colleagues in public—it is difficult to imagine the company rehearsing without embarrassment for such an effect—but a suggestion to the audience to notice how favourably they compared with the other London companies. The suggestion lies in the words of the Player: "I hope we have reform'd that indifferently with us, Sir." [5] This is a politely modest way of saying, "That's what the others do, but we don't, do we?"

But even if it were possible to prove that this assumption was too optimistic, it would still be worth making. There can be no harm in so doing; on the contrary, there would be positive good, if some of our modern repertories could thereby be induced to study the

---

[3] The question of the apprenticeship of the Boy Actors is a point of fundamental difference between Chambers and Baldwin: see *William Shakespeare*, vol. ii., 82 ff.
[4] *Op. cit.*, 303.   [5] *Hamlet*, III. ii. 41.

technique Shakespeare and his fellows aimed at, and reproduce or excel (but in their own kind) their performance. Shakespeare probably wrote, as most playwrights do, for an ideal performance, but he shaped his plays for his fellow-actors, asking them for the best they could do—and sometimes (as genius will) for more. If we examine their acting tradition, we may find fresh clues to that shape: if we revive it in our own acting companies, we shall at least be aiming at that same best which Shakespeare asked for, and may even find inspiration now and then to achieve that more which genius evokes.

(i) Speech

In the forefront of any discussion of the acting tradition of the Chamberlain's Men must be put their command of speech—their most important accomplishment, as it should be still for the Shakespearian actor: for the spoken word is Shakespeare's sharpest weapon. An actor of to-day must not be content if he is assured by his critics that he satisfies a general demand, somewhat vaguely expressed, that the language should be clearly and beautifully spoken. The Chamberlain's Men did very much more than such a phrase seems to imply. They were helped, no doubt, by the easy and flexible acoustic of their playhouse, which could reflect the silver-sweet whispers of Romeo and Juliet, or of Lorenzo and Jessica, as clearly as the roaring of Macbeth or Lear, the asides of Falstaff or Iago as well as the rhetoric of Mark Antony. But the evidence of the plays themselves gives some idea of a range of accomplishment throughout the company which all but a few of our modern actors have ceased to aim at—as if they did not know that such tricks and devices and skills were part of the technique which Shakespeare took for granted.

Nor is it altogether the fault of the modern actor—though it is a fault he can go a long way to remedy. Circumstances are against him, and the history of the development of our language, now in a decline—or at least in a depressed period awaiting a new injection, perhaps from across the Atlantic, to rouse it to vitality. We must never forget, in dealing with Shakespeare's plays, that in his time the language was in a state of springtime freshness. The literary man and the courtier were positively adventurous in their experiments, but even the man in the street, even the groundling in the Yard, had a lively interest in language for its own sake. "A gathering of energy and confidence," says G. D. Willcock,[6] "is one of the striking features

---

[6] *A Companion to Shakespeare Studies* (Cambridge), 128 f.

of the years 1580–96. It shows itself in every department of life, art and thought, and is expressed in *language* with even less hesitation than elsewhere . . . there was a buccaneering spirit abroad in language as well as on the high seas." We, therefore, who are less sensitive to the stimulus of language, are in danger of missing the point by flattening out Shakespeare's words, reducing them by a depressingly automatic process to something nearer to the drabness of our own speech.

In an age when language was held in honour, Burbadge and his fellows had more complicated tasks than merely to bring out the meaning and point the right emphasis of their lines. Yet it is proper to pause and consider how often, even in this respect, we are disappointed to-day. The plain meaning of a sentence, at least from the earlier plays before the poet had developed the compressed complexity of his later style, should not, one would think, be difficult to bring out. Yet quite often nowadays, as one sits in the theatre, the meaning of what an actor says wholly escapes us. The reason is often that the actor (or his producer) takes too perfunctory and casual a view of the poetical content of Shakespeare's lines, as for instance when he understands as a cliché what is really an exact and pointed sentence. King Claudius inciting Laertes against Hamlet says, "Revenge should have no bounds," and the words may easily be spoken as a familiar catch-phrase: in fact they have an exact sense, as the context makes clear:

> *Kin.*   what would you undertake,
> To show your selfe your Fathers sonne indeed,
> More then in words?
> *Laer.* To cut his throat i'th' Church.
> *Kin.* No place indeed should murder Sancturize;
> Revenge should have no bounds . . .[7]

So too Achilles, when he hears that Ajax is to have the honour of fighting Hector, says "I see my reputation is at stake": the sentence sounds prosaic until he continues, "My fame is shrowdly gored"[8]; then we realise that the metaphor comes from the neighbouring bear-pit.

There are of course differences of opinion as to what Shakespeare meant by this passage or that. Lines as familiar as

> The quality of mercy is not strain'd . . .

or—

> She should have dy'de heereafter;
> There would have beene a time for such a word . . .

admit of more than one interpretation. Here the Chamberlain's Men were at an advantage, for Shakespeare himself was there to tell

---

⁷ *Hamlet*, IV. vii. 124 ff.   ⁸ *Troilus and Cressida*, III. iii. 228 f.

them what he meant. We must rely upon the editors, and where
they disagree, ultimately on our own judgment. But it is worth
repeating here that help can be derived from the punctuation of the
Quarto and Folio texts, especially when it represents a system not of
grammatical but of declamatory pointing.[9] When we have decided
on the meaning, we must bring it out: then the critics will agree or
disagree with our interpretation, but they cannot complain that we
have shirked the issue: what is inexcusable is that the lines should
appear to have no meaning or force at all. This is too often the effect
of the perfunctory gabble which is fashionable among Shakespearian
actors of to-day. Nor is this style of speech merely a miscalculation of
speed. The Chamberlain's Men, we may be sure, could speak
"trippingly on the tongue". Hamlet, after his interview with the
Ghost, or when the play has caught the conscience of the King, or as
he tells Horatio about his adventure with the Pirates, speaks through
the lips of Burbadge at a feverish and breakneck speed. Borachio (a
minor actor) prompting the villainous Don John has a diabolical
energy suggestive of Iago at his most active.[10] The unintelligent and
unintelligible delivery of Shakespeare's lines almost always arises not
from an excess of pace but from a probably unconscious under-
rating of the dramatist's poetical skill.

Where we often fail to-day is in giving substance to the imagery,
the metaphors and similes, the language that speaks of an image
which is not present to the eye. The Chamberlain's Men must have
been skilled in such realisation, for so much of their task consisted of
precisely this. We shall see on a later page how gesture and mime
can help here, but gesture and mime without great vocal skill would
seldom bring the point home, and there are moments when they
would help hardly at all and when the whole responsibility of bringing the image to the mind's eye lies with the voice. The sick King
Henry, wakeful in the small hours of the night, appeals to the gentle
Sleep who will not visit him:

> Wilt thou, upon the high and giddie Mast,
> Seale up the Ship-boyes Eyes, and rock his Braines,
> In Cradle of the rude imperious Surge,
> And in the visitation of the Windes,
> Who take the Ruffian Billowes by the top,
> Curling their monstrous heads, and hanging them
> With deaff'ning Clamors in the slipp'ry Clouds,
> That with the hurley, Death it selfe awakes?

---

[9] See above, pp. 27 f.

[10] *Much Ado About Nothing*, II. ii. 33 ff. Another example of such rapid delivery is
the scene in the last act of *The Winter's Tale* (V. ii.) where three anonymous Gentlemen give us enough information to supply the dramatist with an extra act.

> Canst thou (O partiall Sleepe) give thy Repose
> To the wet Sea-Boy, in an houre so rude:
> And in the calmest, and most stillest Night,
> With all appliances, and meanes to boote,
> Deny it to a King? Then happy Lowe, lye downe,
> Uneasie lyes the Head, that weares a Crowne.[11]

How is this done? The eye can help here a little by seeing the ship-boy in the rigging, and by cowering before the mountainous billows: the hand and the whole body can react to the terror of the storm: an unexpected smile of contentment can register the beatific slumber of the ship-boy, and a frown the uneasy head of kingship. But the main task is with the voice, which must mime too—and rhythm will help to make the contrast between the storm at sea and "the calmest, and most stillest Night". I would hazard a guess that unless the actor himself, every time he speaks the speech, projects his mind into the imagined scenes of the storm and the King's apartment, he will not carry his audience there: if he does, he will. There are limits to such a process; the image is sometimes contained in a couple of words— as, for instance, when earlier in the same speech the restless couch of the King is compared to a "Watch-case" (a sentry-box) "or a common Larum-Bell" and there is not time to match Shakespeare's swift thought with action, hardly even with vocal change. But we must prepare to be as agile in passing from image to image, as the Chamberlain's Men probably were, or as Shakespeare certainly wanted them to be. It will be noticed that in striving to recreate the poet's imagery the actor will have to depart from realistic characteri-sation, to speak "out of character": for the tone that does justice to the deafening clamours of the storm will not be the feeble murmur of a man sick to death. Such agility of speech Shakespeare asked of Burbadge as he keyed up his audience to the idea of murdering Duncan:

> Now o're the one halfe World
> Nature seemes dead, and wicked Dreames abuse
> The Curtain'd sleepe: Witchcraft celebrates
> Pale *Heccats* Offrings: and wither'd Murther,
> Alarum'd by his Centinell, the Wolfe,
> Whose howle's his Watch, thus with his stealthy pace,
> With *Tarquins* ravishing strides, towards his designe
> Moves like a Ghost.[12]

We shall return in a later chapter to the means by which the player gave this soliloquy its utmost force.[13]

But when we have said that the Chamberlain's Men were able to

---

[11] 2 *Henry IV*, III. i. 18 ff.   [12] *Macbeth*, II. i. 49 ff.   [13] See below, p. 288.

bring out the plain meaning and the imagery, we are only at the
beginning of their accomplishments: there is far more to it than this.
Whether we complain with Matthew Arnold of Shakespeare's
"irritability of fancy and over-curiousness of expression", or remark
with Coleridge "the activity of thought in the play of words", we
must accept the fact that the poet was addicted to the habit of word-
play. It would be possible indeed to propound the view—though
this is not the place to do so—that it was one of the fundamental
elements of his style, developed from the crude and painful punning
of Speed and Launce [14] to the subtle verbal irony of Hamlet, and
including in its range not only the simple force of *"Puzel* or *Pussel,*
Dolphin or Dog-fish . . ."* or *"For Suffolks Duke, may he be suffo-
cate"* [15] and the shrinking pathos of Desdemona's "I cannot say
Whore, It do's abhorre me now I speake the word . . .",[16] but also
such semi-conscious echoes of sound as "the half-atchieved Har-
flew" [17] and "All length is torture: since the Torch is out . . ." [18]
Even as early as *Richard III* the nimble tongue of Burbadge was asked
to make no mistake about putting over "We are the Queenes *ab*jects,
and must obey," and in the same play it was a boy-actor who,
responding to the royal murderer's "Your Reasons are too shallow,
and to quicke," must make the most of the Queen's punning retort
"O no, my Reasons are too deepe and dead, Too deepe and dead
(poore Infants) in their graves." [19] In Shakespeare's maturity the
boy Edmans must give us the full horror of Lady Macbeth's "Ile
guild the Faces of the Groomes withall, For it must seeme their
Guilt." [20] If the actor fails to make these verbal points, he is like
a musician who has no phrasing and who omits the *sforzandos*
marked by the composer: the emphasis need not, of course, be
heavy, any more than the *sf.* in a *pp* passage will be heavy; it will
keep within the range of dynamics of the whole passage. The Elizabethan audience would be quick to take the point, or in the case of
the semi-conscious echoes to feel the poetical effect; for, as has been
said above, it was an age of linguistic expansion and enterprise.
"Punning and verbal acrobatics," says Willcock, "show the same
eager attention to words on the part of all classes . . ." and after
mention of Feste, Olivia's "corrupter of words", he goes on
". . . People loved, then, to follow words; they were also trained to

---

[14] Though even these two are not allowed to be complacent about it: one says to
the other, after an outrageous example, "Well, your old vice still: mistake the
word" (*The Two Gentlemen of Verona,* III. i. 285).
[15] 1 *Henry VI,* I. iv. 107; 2 *Henry VI,* I. i. 125.   [16] *Othello,* IV. ii. 161 f.
[17] *Henry V,* III. iii. 8.   [18] *Antony and Cleopatra,* IV. xii. 46.
[19] *Richard III,* I. i. 106 (the italics are mine); IV. iv. 362 ff.
[20] *Macbeth,* II. ii. 57 f.

listen strenuously." [21] After all, we to-day are in the habit of listening, if not strenuously, at least continuously and—until television
supersedes the radio—without the aid of the eye. Maybe this habit,
imposed upon us by the capricious progress of scientific invention,
will effect a renewed interest in the spoken word: certainly one of the
symptoms is already apparent, for the popularity of Tommy
Handley's half-hour depended largely upon Ted Cavanagh's word-
play: the puns seemed funny enough as they were shot at us in rapid
fire. The difference between to-day and 1600 is that the language
itself was fresh and in the making then. This difference puts a strain
upon the actor of to-day, which his predecessor had not: both to
Burbadge and to his audience the words themselves were alive and
potentially provocative of wit and beauty; our actors, to revive the
tradition, must not only recapture that interest in and love of the
language, but must find the means to communicate it to their
audience.

The frequent wit-contests of the comedies are prolonged and
elaborate examples of such verbal acrobatics. The Princess in *Love's
Labour's Lost* commends two of her ladies for "a set of Wit well
played".[22] Both typical and tiresome is this dialogue of Romeo and
Mercutio:

Rom. Good morrow to you both, what counterfeit did I give you?
Mer. The slip sir, the slip, can you not conceive?
Rom. Pardon *Mercutio*, my businesse was great, and in such a case as
    mine, a man may straine curtesie.
Mer. That's as much as to say, such a case as yours constrains a man
    to bow in the hams.
Rom. Meaning to cursie.
Mer. Thou hast most kindly hit it.
Rom. A most curteous exposition.
Mer. Nay, I am the very pinck of curtesie.
Rom. Pinke for flower.
Mer. Right.
Rom. Why then is my Pump well flowr'd.
Mer. Sure wit, follow me this jeast, now till thou hast worne out thy
    Pump, that when the single sole of it is worne, the jeast may remaine
    after the wearing, sole-singular.
Rom. O single sol'd jeast,
    Soly singular for the singlenesse.
Mer. Come betweene us good *Benuolio*, my wits faints.
Rom. Swits and spurs,
    Swits and spurs, or Ile crie a match.[23]

---

[21] *A Companion to Shakespeare Studies* (Cambridge), 130 f.
[22] *Love's Labour's Lost*, V. ii. 29.   [23] *Romeo and Juliet*, II. iv. 52 ff.

This is but half the length of the battle, which must have been fought at so brisk a pace that, when Mercutio's "wits faints", those of the audience have long been in a swoon. Trained in this kind of exercise, the actors would be well equipped to give full flavour to the greater subtleties of Beatrice and Benedick, Rosalind and Orlando, Hal and Falstaff, and, in the tragic frame, of Hamlet's fencing with Rosencrantz and Guildenstern. Indeed, in the central phase of Shakespeare's composition, which included in four years the two parts of *Henry IV*, *Much Ado About Nothing*, *As You Like It*, *Twelfth Night* and *Hamlet*, it is hard to resist the belief that the poet's witty writing was for the time matched by the witty delivery of some half dozen at least of his player colleagues.[24]

As with most Elizabethan writers, a part of Shakespeare's stock-in-trade, from his earliest days, was rhetoric: and while language was a general contemporary interest, the art of rhetoric had long been a study of the educated man. The figures of classical rhetoric—especially balance (including antithesis) and repetition—influence the shape and design of English sentences: they are pervasive in Spenser and rife in the drama of the University Wits. They were thus a part of Shakespeare's heritage.[25] T. S. Eliot goes so far as to say that "we cannot grapple with even the simplest and most conversational lines in Tudor and early Stuart drama without having diagnosed the rhetoric in the sixteenth- and seventeenth-century mind. . . . An understanding of Elizabethan rhetoric is as essential to the appreciation of Elizabethan literature as an understanding of Victorian sentiment . . . to the appreciation of Victorian literature . . ."[26] Without insisting that it is necessary for the modern actor to make an exact study of an abstruse subject, it is however proper to reflect that the delivery of rhetorical passages, in such a way as to make them interesting or exciting in themselves, was as much a part of the Chamberlain's Men's stock craft, as it was Shakespeare's to compose them. Shakespeare not infrequently, even in his mature plays, when his purely dramatic inspiration flags, falls back—as other artists will do, not only at the start of their career—upon his technique. A case in point is Juliet's cadenza on the sound "I", a *tour de force* compounded of word-play and rhetorical conceit. The Nurse, clumsily breaking the news that Romeo has killed Tybalt, gives the poor girl the impression that it is her newly-wed

---

[24] T. W. Baldwin says (*op. cit.*, 309 f): ". . . it is natural that Shakespeare's heroines should appear in cycles, not necessarily because Shakespeare was interested in that type of woman at that particular time but because he had the apprentice whose natural expression was that type of woman."
[25] I paraphrase Willcock, *A Companion to Shakespeare Studies* (Cambridge), 126.
[26] T. S. Eliot, *The Sacred Wood*, 31.

husband who is dead. Juliet, aged fourteen, expresses her grief in
these terms:

> Hath *Romeo* slaine himselfe? say thou but I,
> And that bare vowell I shall poyson more
> Then the death-darting eye of Cockatrice,
> I am not I, if there be such an I.
> Or those eyes shot [*read* shut], that makes thee answere I:
> If he be slaine say I, or if not, no.
> Briefe, sounds, determine of my weale or wo.[27]

As an expression of genuine feeling the passage fails, but the rhetoric
carries the scene forward without flagging, and it is not hard to
imagine the apprentice Juliet being "taught his scales" in rehearsal
of this passage. In the same vein the rhetorical excesses of Bassanio,
particularly the discourse on "ornament" while he ponders his
choice among the caskets, and the subsequent description of "Faire
Portias counterfeit" demand great skill from Burbadge:

> Here are sever'd lips
> Parted with suger breath, so sweet a barre
> Should sunder such sweet friends: here in her haires
> The Painter plaies the Spider, and hath woven
> A golden meeh t'intrap the hearts of men
> Faster than gnats in cobwebs: but her eies,
> How could he see to doe them? having made one.
> Me thinkes it should have power to steale both his
> And leave it selfe unfurnisht . . .[28]

It is because this virtuoso rôle of Burbadge's is so often given to an
inexperienced actor that the play seems lopsided: the neglect of the
lyrical-conceited-rhetorical element, contained largely in the speeches
of Bassanio, helps to give Shylock his overweight—after all, his part
is little longer than Bassanio's and much shorter than Portia's—and to
make the rest of the play (by an attempt at realistic interpretation) dull.

King John, the companion of *The Merchant of Venice* (1596–7) in
Chambers's list,[29] is an interesting play in this respect. We have, side
by side with the moving sincerity of the mourning Constance, King
Philip's strained conceit:

> Binde up those tresses: O what love I note
> In the faire multitude of those her haires;
> Where but by chance a silver drop hath falne,
> Even to that drop ten thousand wiery fiends [*read* friends]
> Doe glew themselves in sociable griefe,
> Like true, inseparable, faithfull loves,
> Sticking together in calamitie.

---

[27] *Romeo and Juliet*, III. ii. 45 ff.
[28] *The Merchant of Venice*, III. ii. 73 ff ; 118 ff.   [29] See Appendix I, p. 318.

We have, in the scene of the attempt to blind Arthur, a strange compound of genuine emotion, stirred by the situation but also expressed in some of the speeches and artificial conceits. The simplicity of Arthur's pleading:

> Will you put out mine eyes?
> These eyes, that never did, nor never shall
> So much as frowne on you—

and Hubert's straightforward reply:

> I have sworne to do it:
> And with hot Irons must I burne them out—

are followed by this complex fancy from the lips of the frightened boy:

> Ah, none but in this Iron Age, would do it:
> The Iron of it selfe, though heate red hot,
> Approaching neere these eyes, would drinke my teares,
> And quench this fierie indignation,
> Even in the matter of mine innocence:
> Nay, after that, consume away in rust,
> But for containing fire to harme mine eye:
> Are you more stubborne hard, then hammer'd Iron?

It is necessary to insist here that, whatever we think of the poet's device, it was—and still should be—part of the actor's job to give the rhetoric its full force. That even rhetorical conceits can be profoundly moving on the tongue of a fully-realised character is plain from the Bastard's words to Hubert as he sees the body of Arthur newly fallen from the Tarras:

> If thou didst but consent
> To this most cruell Act: do but dispaire,
> And if thou want'st a Cord, the smallest thred
> That ever Spider twisted from her wombe
> Will serve to strangle thee: A rush will be a beame
> To hang thee on. Or wouldst thou drowne thy selfe,
> Put but a little water in a spoone,
> And it shall be as all the Ocean,
> Enough to stifle such a villaine up.[30]

Compare this speech with the patterned incantations of Pembroke, Salisbury and Bigot in the same scene, and it may appear that a part of the secret of the Bastard's vitality is the rhythmical strength of his lines. Compare the Arthur-blinding scene with the scene of the blinding of Gloucester in *King Lear*—with its bullying iteration of "Wherefore to Dover?" [31]—and there is no doubt that the rhythm is

---

[30] *King John*, III. iv. 61 ff.; IV. i. 56 ff.; IV. iii. 125 ff.   [31] *King Lear*, III. vii.

half the battle. The wonders of Shakespeare's rhythmical effects have been the object of much study, and it has become clear that the punctuation and lineation of the Quarto and Folio texts often preserve for us a record of the poet's intention in this particular.[32] Certainly, if one reads *Julius Caesar* in the Folio, one has the impression that the punctuation is mostly very good for speaking. The same thing is true of the Folio version of Hamlet's first soliloquy—it is the rhythm of Hamlet's soliloquies which is half the secret of their vitality—and the subsequent dialogue with Horatio, Marcellus and Barnardo. Othello's last speech is printed thus in the Folio:

> Soft you; a word or two before you goe:
> I have done the State some service, and they know't:
> No more of that. I pray you in your Letters,
> When you shall these unluckie deeds relate,
> Speake of me, as I am. Nothing extenuate,
> Nor set downe ought in malice.
> Then must you speake,
> Of one that lov'd not wisely, but too well:
> Of one, not easily Jealious, but being wrought,
> Perplexed in the extreame: Of one, whose hand
> (Like the base Iudean) [*read* Indian] threw a Pearle away
> Richer than all his Tribe: Of one, whose subdu'd Eyes,
> Albeit un-used to the melting moode,
> Drops teares as fast as the Arabian Trees
> Their Medicinable gumme. Set you downe this:
> And say besides, that in *Aleppo* once,
> Where a malignant, and a Turbond-Turke
> Beate a Venetian, and traduc'd the State,
> I tooke by th' throat the circumcised Dogge,
> And smoate him, thus.[33]

One is tempted to say that the highly dramatic rhythm of this speech is unmistakable in the punctuation and lineation of the printed text.

It was the task, then, of the actors in Shakespeare's theatre to study the rhythm of their speeches, with something of the care that musicians bestow upon this element of their art. The poet taxed their utmost resources; he asked them to do justice to the rhythm peculiar to individual characters—the cringing, calculating, race-proud, venomous utterance of Shylock; Hotspur's stumbling impetuosity; two distinct types of Welsh lilt, Glendower's and Fluellen's; the contrast between the febrile persuasion of Cassius and the measured gravity of Brutus' hesitation, with the dry cadences of the blunt

---

[32] The reader is once again referred to Percy Simpson's *Shakesperian Punctuation*, and to Richard Flatter's *Shakespeare's Producing Hand*.
[33] *Othello*, V. ii. 337 ff.

Casca as a third voice in the trio—the list is endless, and the individuality of speech is largely compounded of characteristic rhythm. He asked them also to render rhythmically the change of mood in the course of a scene. Two boy actors must study the exquisitely judged transition from witty prose to romantic verse, in Viola's first embassy to Olivia: Viola leads the way with her comment on Olivia's face:

> Tis beauty truly blent, whose red and white,
> Natures owne sweet, and cunning hand laid on—

and Olivia follows suit, after a last attempt with the inventory of her beauty (in prose) to resist her romantic mood.[34] Brabantio, brokenhearted by Desdemona's elopement, accepts the *fait accompli* in wry couplets which parody the canting consolation of the Duke:

> But words are words, I never yet did heare:
> That the bruized heart was pierc'd through the eares—

then breaks abruptly into prose as he dismisses the theme:

> I humbly beseech you, proceed to th'Affaires of State.[35]

Kent's couplets put the brake on Lear's frenzy:

> Fare thee well King, sith thus thou wilt appeare,
> Freedome lives hence, and banishment is here.

Goneril's iambics—

> Not only Sir this, your all-lycenc'd Foole—

bring us sharply back to formality after the Fool's ungoverned prose. There is an opposite effect when, at the end of the tempestuous opening scene at King Lear's court, the wicked sisters scurry cynically into prose for the deliberate calculation of their intrigues.[36] The players had to study also and reproduce the eloquence of short lines, of calculated gaps in the rhythm, like the pauses or the silent bars of a musical score. Horatio's harrowed urgency as he confronts the illusion, the Ghost that looks so "like the King that's dead", is obscured in the lineation of the Folio: but the Second Quarto gives the actor plainer instructions:

> If thou hast any sound or use of voyce,
> Speake to me, if there be any good thing to be done
> That may to thee doe ease, and grace to mee,
> Speake to me.
> If thou art privie to thy countries fate
> Which happily foreknowing may avoyd
> O Speake:[37]

---

[34] *Twelfth Night*, I. v. 259 ff.
[36] *King Lear*, I. i. 183 f.; I. iv. 223 ff.; I. i. 286 ff.
[35] *Othello*, I. iii. 218 ff.
[37] *Hamlet*, I. i. 128 ff.

Cordelia's refusal to respond to her father's demand seems doubly obstinate in that it shatters the compulsive rhythm of the old King's speech:

> *Lear.*   What can you say, to draw
>   A third, more opilent then your Sisters? speake.
> *Cor.* Nothing, my Lord.
> *Lear.* Nothing?
> *Cor.* Nothing.
> *Lear.* Nothing will come of nothing, speake againe.[38]

Burbadge would no doubt urge forward the rhythm of his infatuate question: then Cordelia's curt answer, his indignant echo and her still more abrupt repetition are without bar-lines: only after the King has had time to recover his balance does the interrupted rhythm proceed again.

These are but the characteristic details of a practice which Shakespeare at his best sustained over long passages of dialogue. The prose-duets of Rosalind and Orlando, of Hal and Falstaff, of Beatrice and Benedick are continuously rhythmical, with a variety of pace and tread which can be felt even in reading from the printed page. To refresh the memory, the reader is referred to the mock wooing in *As You Like It*, to the rogues-in-buckram scene at the Boar's Head Tavern, and to the compound of raillery, tenderness and ferocity with which Beatrice, half confessing her love for Benedick, prompts him to revenge her cousin's dishonour.[39] Greater than these masterpieces, because in the tragic key, are the verse-duets of Othello and Iago—the two long movements, with but brief intermission, in which Iago lures Othello from secure happiness to savage despair—and of Macbeth and his Lady after his descent from the King's chamber with the words "I have done the deed" until the frenzied self-pitying cry of "Wake *Duncan* with thy knocking: I would thou could'st." [40]

It was not only the principals who were able to sustain such dialogue: the whole team were trained in this art. The long rhythm of concerted scenes is one of the glories of Shakespeare's maturest poetic drama. From the moment when Lear comes forth from his unsuccessful attempt to see Regan and Cornwall:

> Deny to speake with me?
> They are sicke, they are weary,
> They have travail'd all the night? meere fetches,—

---

[38] *King Lear*, I. i. 87 ff.
[39] *As You Like It*, IV. i. 70–231; 1 *Henry IV*, II. iv. 128 ff.; *Much Ado About Nothing*, IV. i. 257 ff.
[40] *Othello*, III. iii. 92–480; *Macbeth*, II. ii. 16–75.

to his desperate sally out into the storm—

O Foole, I shall go mad—

the rhythmical tension is not once relaxed (not even by the poignant jesting of the Fool).[41] The last scene of *Othello* [42]—with its *adagio* opening, the terrified swiftness of Desdemona's last pleading, the momentary timeless pause before Aemilia is admitted, Desdemona's smothered cry, the splendid courage of Aemilia's "itterance" ("My Husband?" "My Husband say she was false?" "My Friend, thy Husband; honest, honest *Iago*"), the revelation of the murder, Aemilia's rounding on the Moor and her husband, her pathetic singing at her death, the revival of Othello ("Behold, I have a weapon") and his agony as he looks upon his dead wife, the obdurate silence of the convicted Iago, the valediction of Othello with the startling climax of his death—the unflagging tension of this whole scene makes a great rhythmical movement, as carefully devised for variety of pace and pause, and also *crescendo* and *diminuendo*, as a symphonic first movement of Beethoven. A performance of *Othello* needs to be almost operatic in conception, and it was not Burbadge only, but half a dozen of his colleagues, who must feel and reproduce these great rhythmical movements. If the Chamberlain's Men did not always rise to the height of their author's hopes, it was not, I think—as one sometimes suspects nowadays—for want of study and practice of this particular part of their technique.

It may be said that some scenes depend almost wholly on the rhetoric to sustain them. From the distance of the Study, Phillips and Burbadge held their audience in the fine but long scene in which Prince Hal takes the crown from the King's pillow.[43] The situation— the dying father, the son seemingly filching the crown, the question of whether the madcap Hal will rise to the stature of the Ideal King —is intrinsically dramatic. But the treatment is not, and this poetical and rhetorical handling of political commonplaces was a popular feature of the historical plays. We shall see, when in a later chapter we come to deal in detail with *Macbeth*, that the long conversation between Malcolm and Macduff at the English court is another such exercise in rhetoric. Other scenes depend for their motive power upon witty conversation: such are the battle of wits between Beatrice and Benedick in the early exchanges of *Much Ado About Nothing*, and the first appearance of Prince Hal and Falstaff in the exposition of 1 *Henry IV*. To both rhetoric and wit, rhythm is usually an indispensable ally, and often if the rhythm of the dialogue is neglected, the play is marred. Listen how Leonato offers his daughter

---

[41] *King Lear*, II. iv. 89–289. [42] *Othello*, V. ii. [43] 2 *Henry IV*, IV. v. 90–223.

Hero to the Count Claudio in marriage: Beatrice, her cousin, is present, and also the gallant Prince Pedro:

> *Leona.* Count, take of me my daughter, and with her my fortunes: his grace hath made the match, & all grace say, Amen to it.
> *Beatr.* Speake Count, tis your Qu.
> *Claud.* Silence is the perfectest Herault of joy, I were but little happy if I could say, how much? Lady, as you are mine, I am yours, I give away my selfe for you, and doat upon the exchange.
> *Beat.* Speake cosin, or (if you cannot) stop his mouth with a kisse, and let not him speake neither.
> *Pedro.* Infaith Lady you have a merry heart.
> *Beatr.* Yea my Lord I thanke it, poore foole it keepes on the windy side of Care, my coosin tells him in his eare that he is in my [*read* her] heart.
> *Clau.* And so she doth coosin.
> *Beat.* Good Lord for alliance: thus goes every one to the world but I, and I am sun-burn'd, I may sit in a corner and cry, heigh ho for a husband.
> *Pedro.* Lady *Beatrice*, I will get you one.
> *Beat.* I would rather have one of your fathers getting: hath your Grace ne're a brother like you? your father got excellent husbands, if a maid could come by them.
> *Prince.* Will you have me? Lady.
> *Beat.* No, my Lord, unlesse I might have another for working-daies, your Grace is too costly to weare everie day: but I beseech your Grace pardon mee, I was borne to speake all mirth, and no matter.
> *Prince.* Your silence most offends me, and to be merry, best becomes you, for out of question, you were born in a merry howre.
> *Beatr.* No sure my Lord, my Mother cried, but then there was a starre daunst, and under that was I borne: cosins God give you joy.[44]

Between the lines of this dialogue, the rapturous hesitation of Claudio, the eloquent silence of Hero (who never speaks), the impetuous wit of Beatrice, with its undertone of affectionate envy of the lovers, its impulsive apology to the Prince, its sweet change of mood as she speaks of her birth—"No sure my Lord, my Mother cried, but then there was a starre daunst, and under that was I borne"—these are effects which can only come to spontaneous life by careful rehearsal.

Pure music of speech is the essence of such "set pieces" as the opening of the last scene in *The Merchant of Venice*:

> . . . in such a night
> *Troylus* me thinkes mounted the Trojan walls . . .

or the lyrical distraction of Silvius in *As You Like It*:

> If thou remembrest not the slightest folly,
> That ever love did make thee run into,
> Thou hast not lov'd——

---

[44] *Much Ado About Nothing*, II. i. 315 ff.

or the measured quartet from the same play:

> *Phe.* Good shepheard, tell this youth what 'tis to love
> *Sil.* It is to be all made of sighes and teares,
>   And so am I for *Phebe*.
> *Phe.* And I for *Ganimed*.
> *Orl.* And I for *Rosalind*.
> *Ros.* And I for no woman.[45]

Here the dialogue is as musical as a song. There are whole plays, such as *Love's Labour's Lost* and *The Merchant of Venice*, which depend very largely on a relish for the music of words in the audience, and which demand therefore an unusual skill in performing the music of words; and this together with the other vocal skills of the Chamberlain's Men makes the most important element of their technique: their art, we must never cease to remind ourselves—at least when they were interpreting Shakespeare—was the art of the poetic drama.

(*ii*) *Miming*

The present revival on the stage of athletic activity, especially in the single combats, is a welcome change from the perfunctory "one, two, and the third in your bosom" of ten years ago. It is certainly in the tradition of the Chamberlain's Men, whose audiences relished a display of martial vigour and skill, and were accustomed to such sights as Burbadge's twenty-six-year-old Orlando wrestling and carrying Shakespeare on his back, and Falstaff also twice a performance shouldering Hotspur in full armour, and Puck breaking records for speed, and the angry Roman mob lynching Cinna, and witches vanishing by trap-doors, and (as the crowning marvel) Ariel flying from the Heavens on a wire. The mere size of the stage would invite an all-out chase as the lovers quarrel in the Athenian wood, and in a pitched battle or in the storming of the Tarras we may be sure that the armies did not hold their punches.

But it is plain that the miming of the Chamberlain's Men must have gone much further than athletic skill and a willingness to take an active part in a scene of riot, revelry or battle. To create some of the effects which Shakespeare asked of them, they needed the art of Ruth Draper or Jean-Louis Barrault—the pure art of make-believe, of making us believe that we see things which are not there. And this art must have been studied and practised not by the principals alone, but by every member of the company: it must have been part of the

---

[45] *The Merchant of Venice*, V. i. 3 f.; *As You Like It*, II. iv. 34; V. ii. 90 ff.

You are now within a foote of
th'extreme Verge

tradition, and the result such teamwork of expressive mime as our generation have seen perhaps only in the performances of the *Compagnie des Quinze*. It was a common practice with the Chamberlain's Men to act a night scene on the day-lit stage. It might be the "black brow of night" in which Hubert seeks out the Bastard to give him "newes fitting to the night, Blacke, fearefull, comfortlesse, and horrible" [46]; or it might be the "soft stilnes" of the night in which Lorenzo and Jessica listen to the "musicke of the house" [47]; or the "perillous" night in which Cassius and Casca meet, "when the crosse blew Lightning seem'd to open The Brest of Heaven".[48] Each would require a different physical reaction from the players on the bare Platform. If Burbadge had the difficult task of creating in mid-air his "Dagger of the Minde", another actor, Lowin, must make us see the flight of the swallow as it swoops across the playhouse yard to its "pendant Bed, and procreant Cradle" in the imaginary buttresses of the Tiring-House façade.[49] So too Cassius (Phillips) must make us feel with the doomed army of the conspirators that

> Ravens, Crowes, and Kites
> Fly ore our heads, and downward looke on us
> As we were sickely prey; their shadowes seeme
> A Canopy most fatall, under which
> Our Army lies, ready to give up the Ghost.[50]

At least eight of the company could make the flat stage seem like the steep slope of Gads Hill—the slope which causes Falstaff so much trouble when his horse is removed by Poins, and down which the luckless travellers walk to ease their legs.[51] One thinks of the skilled

---

[46] *King John*, V. vi. 17 ff.
[47] *The Merchant of Venice*, V. i. *init.*
[48] *Julius Caesar*, I. iii. 47 ff.
[49] *Macbeth*, II. i. 33 ff.; I. vi. 3 ff.
[50] *Julius Caesar*, V. i. 85 ff.
[51] 1 *Henry IV*, II. ii. See below, pp. 203 f.

miming which preserves for so long the illusion of storm in *King Lear;* of the miracle at Dover Cliff when Edgar persuades his blind father to hurl himself down a precipice which is not there [52]; of Macbeth and Banquo on their first appearance thrusting their way head-down through foul weather, and dimly glimpsing the weird sisters through the fog and filthy air.[53] These effects with little scenic aid demand the expressive movement of dancers, and one fancies that Shakespeare's colleagues must have been very cunning in the art of mime.

A familiar feature of Shakespeare's drama is the re-enacting of an episode in pantomime by an actor. We may have seen this episode ourselves already, in which case the re-enaction is a commentary on what we have seen. Immediately after the rehearsal of the mechanicals in the wood, with Bottom's translation and Titania's awakening, Puck gives a circumstantial report to Oberon of how "My Mistris with a monster is in love". Each incident of the episode we have just witnessed is mimed for us with an extra twist of satire by the mischievous contriver.[54] Benvolio's account to Prince Escalus of the fray in which Mercutio and Tybalt were slain, sharpens our appreciation of the horrible dilemma which confronted Romeo. No doubt the player would recreate for our benefit Romeo's "calme looke, knees humbly bow'd", and "the unruly spleene Of *Tybalts* deafe to peace", and give us Mercutio

> Who all as hot, turnes deadly point to point,
> And with a Martiall scorne, with one hand beates
> Cold death aside, and with the other sends
> It back to *Tybalt*, whose dexterity
> Retorts it: . . .

We should see Romeo as he "beats downe their fatall points", and the "envious thrust" of Tybalt under Romeo's intervening arm: then the climax of the return of Romeo to revenge Mercutio's death.[55] A similar recital but given with a malign rather than friendly intent, is Iago's recapitulation of the brawl in which Cassio has lost his reputation. The villain interprets what we have just seen in such a way as to ensure Cassio's disgrace, but so subtly is the story presented that Othello says:

> I know *Iago*
> Thy honestie, and love doth mince this matter,
> Making it light to *Cassio.*

---

[52] *King Lear*, III. i., ii. and iv.; IV. vi. See below, pp. 204 f.
[53] *Macbeth*, I. iii. 38 ff.   [54] *A Midsummer Night's Dream*, III. ii. 6 ff.
[55] *Romeo and Juliet*, III. i. 158 ff.

This trick of commenting on and interpreting the action of the play
in speech is a point to which we shall return on a later page.[56] For
the present purpose, it is enough to observe that Iago's account is
highly circumstantial and is recreated for Othello's benefit and ours
in lively mime.[57]

More often, however, the episode re-enacted in speech and mime
is one which we have *not* seen but which is important in the run of
the plot. Salarino's account of the parting of Anthonio and Bassanio
is such a narrative: the player would show us the action of the kind,
melancholy merchant, as he speaks the cadence:

> And even there his eye being big with teares,
> Turning his face, he put his hand behinde him,
> And with affection wondrous sencible
> He wrung *Bassanios* hand, and so they parted.

Earlier in the same scene, which consists entirely of narration, we
have Solanio's account of Shylock's tragi-comic distress at Jessica's
elopement:

> My daughter, O my ducats, O my daughter,
> Fled with a Christian, O my Christian ducats!

Shylock himself in this condition we are to see in a later scene, but
the clever miming parody of Solanio kindles our anticipation.[58]
Hotspur's caricature of Bolingbroke—

> Why what a caudie [*read* candie] deale of curtesie,
> This fawning Grey-hound then did proffer me.
> Looke when his infant Fortune came to age,
> And gentle *Harry Percy*, and kinde Cousin:
> O, the Divell take such Couzeners . . .

re-enacts a conversation in *Richard II*, but we may not have seen, or
may not remember, the earlier play.[59] The episode and the attitude
make themselves vivid enough in Hotspur's contemptuous burlesque.
A capital example of such miming is Harry Percy's brilliant presentation of the aftermath of Holmedon field, how he was "so
pestered with a Popingay" that he answered neglectingly the King's
demand for the surrender of his prisoners.[60] Other instances occur to
mind at random—an anonymous Lord's account of Jaques and the
"poore sequestred Stag" [61]; Cassius' two pictures of Caesar's "feeble

---

[56] See below, pp. 215 f., 228 f.   [57] *Othello*, II. iii. 222 ff.
[58] *The Merchant of Venice*, II. viii. 35 ff.; 12 ff.
[59] 1 *Henry IV*, I. iii. 251 ff.; *Richard II*, II. iii. 45 ff.
[60] 1 *Henry IV*, I. iii. 29 ff.   [61] *As You Like It*, II. i. 29 ff.

temper", swimming in the Tiber, and fever-stricken in Spain [62]; Casca's sarcastic tale of Caesar's "swound" in the market-place [63]; Malvolio's daydream of himself after three months of marriage with Olivia—"sitting in my state. . . . Calling my Officers about me, in my branch'd Velvet gowne . . ." ("looke how imagination blowes him," says Fabian, and we can see Phillips, who was also Cassius, revelling in the opportunity for mime) [64]; the boy Ophelia's description of Hamlet's distracted visit:

> He tooke me by the wrist, and held me hard;
> Then goes he to the length of all his arme;
> And with his other hand thus o're his brow,
> He fals to such perusall of my face,
> As he would draw it. Long staid he so,
> At last, a little shaking of mine Arme:
> And thrice his head thus waving up and downe;
> He rais'd a sigh, so pittious and profound,
> That it did seeme to shatter all his bulke,
> And end his being. That done, he lets me goe,
> And with his head over his shoulders turn'd,
> He seem'd to finde his way without his eyes,
> For out adores he went without their helpe;
> And to the last, bended their light on me. [65]

In all these cases—and there are many more—the player's ability to mime his story is an essential part of the poet's conception. It will be noticed that the demand is made upon the supporting actors as much as upon the principals.

We may add an occasional *tour de force* such as the charades in the Boar's Head Tavern, where Falstaff first stands for the King taking his son to task, and then, the parts exchanged, Hal plays his father, and Falstaff tickles us for a young Prince [66]; or the grim, tragic equivalent when Lear arraigns Goneril in the person of a joint-stool before a bench of justices consisting of the disguised Kent, the Fool and Tom o' Bedlam [67]; or Jaques' cadenza of the seven ages of man (imagine a Barrault giving us the whole gallery in succession) [68]; or Armin holding conversation between Feste and Sir Thopas outside Malvolio's prison [69]; or Ophelia's mad scenes [70]; or Lady Macbeth's sleepwalking, when (as we shall see on a later page) the boy-actor with his miming must re-evoke the horrors of the play in memory. [71]

---

[62] *Julius Caesar*, I. ii. 100 ff.
[64] *Twelfth Night*, II. v. 50 ff.
[66] 1 *Henry IV*, II. iv. 418 ff.
[68] *As You Like It*, II. vii. 139 ff.
[70] *Hamlet*, IV. v.

[63] *Julius Caesar*, I. ii. 234 ff.
[65] *Hamlet*, II. i. 87 ff. See above, p. 57.
[67] *King Lear*, III. vi. 38 ff.
[69] *Twelfth Night*, IV. ii. 21 ff.
[71] *Macbeth*, V. i. See below, pp. 305 f.

E

If it is true that the Chamberlain's Men practised their tongues to give life to the imagery, so also must they have called in gesture and movement for the same end. Few actors or producers on the modern stage seem to realise the need or the possibility of such mimetic interpretation of the imagery. Sometimes, indeed, no gesture suggests itself, and there is a danger of overdoing the method: nevertheless, it would be helpful if Friar Lawrence made a comment with his hands to bring his comparison to life, as he said:

> These violent delights have violent endes,
> And in their triumph: die like fire and powder;
> Which as they kisse consume. [72]

Puck can enrich his narrative of the panic when Bottom appeared among his fellows with the Ass-head, by acting his simile:

> when they him spie,
> As Wilde-geese, that the creeping Fowler eye,
> Or russed-pated choughes, many in fort
> (Rising and cawing at the guns report)
> Sever themselves, and madly sweepe the skye:
> So at his sight, away his fellowes flye . . . [73]

When Worcester suggests to his daredevil nephew a plot which shall be

> As full of perill and adventurous Spirit,
> As to o're walke a Current, roaring loud
> On the unstedfast footing of a Speare—

he must create for us the roaring torrent and the spear-bridge by voice and gesture; and Hotspur in making his impetuous response:

> If he fall in, good night, or sinke or swimme—

must show with his whole body the toppling balance and the desperate plunge. [74] One could multiply examples, each to be studied on its merits, many perhaps controversial and only to be approved in practice, if the actor can bring them off. But I hazard the suggestion that, just as the actor must sometimes use his voice "out of character", so too it is often more important for him to be using his powers of mime to interpret the imagery than to be making a realistic gesture or movement appropriate to his assumed character.

That Shakespeare knew the difference between good and bad miming appears from more than one passage in the plays; most vividly, perhaps, in Buckingham's boast:

---

[72] *Romeo and Juliet*, II. vi. 9 ff. The folio's colon seems to obscure the sense.
[73] *A Midsummer Night's Dream*, III. ii. 20 ff.
[74] 1 *Henry IV*, I. iii. 191 ff.

> Tut, I can counterfeit the deepe Tragedian,
> Speake, and looke backe, and prie on every side,
> Tremble and start at wagging of a Straw:
> Intending deepe suspition, gastly Lookes
> Are at my service, like enforced Smiles.[75]

The other side of the picture appears in the exhibition given by the First Player in his Pyrrhus-Hecuba speech, and more especially in Hamlet's comment—

> Is it not monstrous that this Player heere,
> But in a Fixion, in a dreame of Passion,
> Could force his soule so to his whole conceit,
> That from her working, all his visage warm'd [read wanned],
> Teares in his eyes, distraction in's Aspect,
> A broken voyce, and his whole Function suiting
> With Formes, to his Conceit? [76]

The man acts with his whole body: this is surely what the poet would have his players do.

If we return once more to consider the "Messenger's Speeches" mentioned above,[77] we find that many of these can be illuminated by the miming of the players, but that some are mostly vocal in their means of expression: as Shakespeare develops his art towards the maturity of the great tragic period, the speech becomes more important and more powerful, and carries more of the dramatic responsibility. As one thinks of the death of Ophelia, of the unvarnished tale of Othello's whole course of love, of the anonymous Gentleman's account of Cordelia's grief at hearing of her father's sufferings, of the bleeding Captaine's speech in *Macbeth*, of Enobarbus' famous description of Cleopatra in her barge, of Ariel's account of the shipwreck he has caused [78]—one recognises a kind of speech-miming, a drama whose medium is almost wholly the voice, demanding the utmost skill on the part of the actors and—be it noted—finding a much more vivid reality of expression on the unlocalised Platform of the Globe than on a picture-stage competing through the eye for the imaginative attention of the audience.

(iii) Positioning

Both the technique of the actors and the impression received by the audience were radically different in the Globe Playhouse from

---

[75] *Richard III*, III. v. 5 ff.   [76] *Hamlet*, II. ii. 585 ff.   [77] pp. 107 f.
[78] *Hamlet*, IV. vii. 167 ff.; *Othello*, I. iii. 128 ff.; *King Lear*, IV. iii. 13 ff.; *Macbeth*, I. ii. 7 ff.; *Antony and Cleopatra*, II. iii. 198 ff.; *The Tempest*, I. ii. 195 ff.

what we are used to on the picture stage. The effect of the shape, dimensions and central forward position of the Platform is easily felt in practice, but harder to convey on paper. Nevertheless, until the Globe is rebuilt and in continual use, we must strive to win converts with a paper exposition of its merits.

We can begin by stating the difference geometrically with a comparison of diagrams:

Fig. (a)   *Fig. (b)*

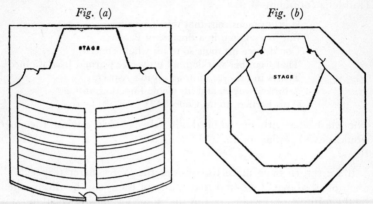

Diagrams contrasting the Globe Platform and the Picture-Stage

It is plain at once

   (i) that the angle of vision reduces the impression of depth to a minimum in *Fig. (a)*, giving an image flat like a picture: but magnifies the impression of depth in *Fig. (b)*, so as to produce a feeling of three dimensions, like sculpture. The result is that the Globe stage not only *is* a little deeper than most modern stages, but also *seems* (which is more important) very much deeper;

  (ii) that whereas the bane of the picture-stage is "masking", there is very little of that danger in *Fig. (b)*; indeed, a figure on the forward edge of the Globe Platform will in practice hardly ever obscure a figure up-stage;

 (iii) the outer limits of vision allowed by the sight-lines because of the proscenium in *Fig. (a)* make a tapering effect of the opposite kind from that in *Fig. (b)*: the result is that the stage and even the play are, as it were, turned inside out, with an enfeebling effect upon much of the grouping, as will appear in what follows.

The most immediate and obvious effect of the ground-plan of the Globe is the real sense of distance, not only across the Platform, but also between the forward (down-stage) and backward (up-stage) positions, making one group seem close to us in the audience, another remote. This, be it noticed, is the effect not only of the size but also of the central position of the platform. The impression of near and far, of perspective, makes lively sense of many scenes which are in danger of awkwardness on our picture-stage. Thus outside Flint Castle, Northumberland acts as ambassador going backwards and forwards between Bolingbroke, standing presumably outside one of the forward Stage-Posts, and Richard on the Tarras. When Richard descends with bitter humility to the "base Court", Bolingbroke bids his company "Stand all apart", and himself converses privately with the King: the two must be central and forward, the rest up-stage, close to the Tiring-House.[79] At the first interview between the Jew and the Merchant in *The Merchant of Venice*, Shylock makes a deliberate pretence of not seeing Antonio: the savage aside—"How like a fawning publican he lookes"—must be spoken right at the front of the Platform, while Bassanio goes up-stage to prompt his friend. Bassanio, returning, comes forward towards Shylock, who only after five or six lines "recognises" and greets Antonio: "Rest you faire good signior, Your worship was the last man in our mouthes."[80] So too Caesar's prolonged comment on "that spare *Cassius*" gains greatly in effectiveness by the opportunity of three-cornered grouping afforded by the Globe Platform: the dictator, irritable after his fit in the market-place, calls Antony to his side in front of one of the Stage-Posts; the "chidden Traine" of his companions linger close to the stage-door through which he has just entered; Cassius and Brutus, who have held their long conversation during Caesar's absence, are all the width and depth of the stage away from the rest, so that the words "Yond *Cassius* has a leane and hungry looke" put no strain upon the imagination of the audience.[81] Likewise the moment of panic outside the Capitol when Popilius Lena whispers to the conspirators "I wish your enterprize to day may thrive" is easy to plot on this Platform with the maximum of dramatic effect: we shall examine this scene in close detail at the end of this chapter.[82] We have already dealt with the moments in the battle of Philippi where the depth of the Platform adds pathos to the discovery of the dead bodies of Cassius and Titinius, and to the solitary figure of Strato standing like a sentinel beside the fallen Brutus.[83] In the graveyard scene Hamlet and Horatio enter *a farre*

---

[79] *Richard II*, III. iii. 72–end.   [80] *The Merchant of Venice*, I. iii. 41 ff.
[81] *Julius Caesar*, I. ii. 189 ff.
[82] *Julius Caesar*, III. i. 13 ff. See below, pp. 175 ff.
[83] See above, pp. 95 f.

off. If the grave is in the centre of the Study (the grave-trap), then the Prince and his friend will hold their subsequent conversation in front of one of the Stage-Posts—that is to say, quite close to their audience, as is appropriate to their reflective comment. When they stand aside as the funeral approaches, they presumably hide by the doorposts on the opposite side to the procession's entry.[84] Cassio

Yond Cassius has a leane and hungry looke

asking Desdemona to intercede for him, takes a hurried leave on the approach of Othello: Iago pounces on his opportunity:

> *Iago.* Hah? I like not that.
> *Othel.* What dost thou say?
> *Iago.* Nothing my Lord; or if—I know not what.
> *Othel.* Was not that *Cassio* parted from my wife?
> *Iago.* *Cassio* my Lord? No sure, I cannot thinke it
>   That he would steale away so guilty-like,
>   Seeing your comming.
> *Othel.* I do beleeve 'twas he.
> *Des.* How now my Lord?
>   I have bin talking with a Suitor heere,
>   A man that languishes in your displeasure.
> *Othel.* Who is't you meane?
> *Des.* Why your Lieutenant *Cassio*: [85]

Othello and Iago have come swiftly through one door towards the nearest Stage-Post: Iago's embarrassed whispers are as close to the

---

[84] *Hamlet*, V. i. 61 ff.   [85] *Othello*, III. iii. 35 ff.

audience's ear as to Othello's; Desdemona and Aemilia are meanwhile beside the other door through which Cassio has made his
over-hasty departure.

Sometimes the sense of remoteness afforded by the Chamber or
the Study helps the interpretation of a scene. Cranford Adams sets
the blinding of Gloucester in the Chamber.[86] Certainly the horror
would be more tolerable at that distance; for perhaps even the
proverbial callousness of the Elizabethans might have been jolted if
Cornwall had perpetrated his savagery in their midst; the objective
detail of the spoken dialogue and the brutal rhythm of the verse
make no bones about the barbaric business, but there is a saving
grace of detachment for the audience if the physical action is set
remotely up aloft. I imagine that the chair to which Gloucester's
tormentors "Binde fast his corky armes" would have its back set
against the middle of the Tarras rail, so that the old man's face would
be invisible to us, but the onslaught facing the audience would be
made through him upon us as well. A different, but no less justly
calculated, effect is contrived in the scene of the murder of Clarence
in *Richard III*.[87] Here there is a long and deliberately comic exchange
between the two murderers—played presumably by two of the
company's comic gang, who otherwise have little employment in
this play—while their unwitting victim lies asleep. The incongruity
of this vaudeville-turn, intervening between Clarence's eloquent and
tragic nightmare and his unavailing pleading and murder, is an
almost insoluble problem for the modern producer. The difficulty
hardly exists if Clarence sleeps remotely in the Study, while the
comedians play their ghoulish comedy at the front of the Platform.
The sudden change of mood when Clarence wakes and advances on
to the Platform seems then a natural transition and the tragedy is
even heightened by the contrast.

The Stage-Posts have an important influence on the positioning of
the actors: for they seem to give a kind of perspective to the Platform
itself. Outside them there is a semicircular perimeter, leading by a
roundabout tour from one doorway to the other; inside them an
inner central area, seeming more distant than the perimeter though
less remote than the Tiring-House, its various stages and its immediate vicinity. The convenience of this deep perspective is seen in many
different circumstances. Romeo, on his way to the Capulets' ball,
declares his intention of carrying a torch and not dancing. He sticks
to this plan, for this is how he is employed when he first catches sight
of Juliet.

---

[86] *King Lear*, III. vii. 28 ff. See J. Cranford Adams, *The Original Staging of King
Lear*, 326.   [87] *Richard III*, I. iv. 84 ff.

Rom. What ladie is that which doth inrich the hand
    Of yonder Knight?
Ser. I know not sir.
Rom. O she doth teach the Torches to burne bright . . .

The dance, in which Juliet is taking her part, is in progress in the
central area: Romeo, torch in hand, questions the servant on the
perimeter. Tybalt's indignant argument with Capulet is also outside
the Stage-Posts. But when Romeo addresses himself to Juliet, he
probably joins her in the dance within, and the formal gallantry of
their first conversation is spoken to the measure of the music.[88] A
scene in *Much Ado About Nothing* presents an interesting variant on
this theme: there the dance takes place off-stage, but we are shown
the Maskers walking about with their partners *before* the music
strikes up. In the game of mistaken identity, the ladies have the
advantage. There are four pairs, and presumably the formal parade
round the perimeter brings each pair in turn to the front central
point of the Platform for their *tête-à-tête*. The pace of their walking
must match the dialogue: Beatrice and Benedick, who come last and
speak the most, linger in their progress: when the music begins,
Claudio is left behind, at a distance from Don John and Borachio.[89]
A similar manœuvre, but without the conversational interest, is
indicated by the Folio direction when the Montagues approach the
festive house of Capulet: *They march about the Stage.*[90] A circular tour
of the perimeter is the technical basis of the scene in *Troilus and
Cressida* where the Greek heroes "put on A forme of strangenesse" as
they pass along in front of the tent of Achilles. Achilles and Patroclus
stand in the entrance of the tent—that is to say, in a gap of the Study
curtains. The Greeks, making the circuit of the perimeter, "passe by
strangely", either ignoring them or with disdainful air, and so go out
by one of the stage-doors. Ulysses, coming last in the queue, delays
his progress by reading a book, while Achilles speaks his twenty
lines.[91]

One remarkable result of the central position of the Platform in
relation to the auditorium can best be illustrated from scenes of
waylaying and ambush. At Gads Hill Prince Hal and Poins, disguised in their buckram suits, lie in wait to rob the robbers: Falstaff
and his gang, after driving their victims out of sight, return to the
Platform to share the booty. Now in Shakespeare's playhouse the
Prince and Poins will hide outside the two Stage-Posts, that is to say,

---

[88] *Romeo and Juliet*, I. v. 45 ff.
[89] *Much Ado About Nothing*, II. i. 90 ff. An earlier example of the same pattern of
four pairs can be seen in *Love's Labour's Lost*, V. ii. 212 ff.
[90] *Romeo and Juliet*, I. iv. 115.   [91] *Troilus and Cressida*, III. iii. 38 ff.

in the front of the Platform close to the groundlings: the dramatic effect of their hiding is thus doubled, for we too in the audience seem to be lying in wait to pounce on Falstaff.[92] So, too, the murderers of Banquo will lurk in the shadow of the Stage-Posts, and we with them will twitch a dagger behind our backs as "neere approches The subject of our Watch".[93]

The deep and wide perspective of the playhouse helps the actors when there is a shifting of dramatic emphasis from one group to another. For instance, in *The Two Gentlemen of Verona*, Proteus for his own ends is helping the foolish Thurio to serenade Silvia in one of the window-stages: his faithful Julia, seeking him in the disguise of a page, has found him in the very moment of his infidelity: there follows a moving dialogue, charged with pathetic irony, between Julia and the innkeeper who has befriended her. The emphasis shifts from the pair of them to the serenade and back again; and it seems plain that the whispered conversation is held close to the audience at the front of the Platform while the musicians and Thurio and the faithless Proteus are under Silvia's window. After some time, Julia says hurriedly: "Peace, stand aside, the company parts," and while she and the Host retreat to the opposite door, Proteus and Thurio advance down-stage to capture the attention of the audience.[94] A characteristic grouping can be seen in the prelude to Philippi in *Julius Caesar* when, after the cross-stage wrangle between the opposing parties, "The Storme is up, and all is on the hazard." Brutus takes Lucilius aside and we do not hear their conversation; Cassius calls Messala to him and tells him of his superstitious foreboding. The emphatic conversation is right forward on the Platform, the incidental one behind: it would be impossible to look beyond a nearer group to a more distant one, and still seem to hear them in intimate discussion.[95] A very interesting example is the critical moment when Troilus, conducted by Ulysses, is a witness of Cressida's dalliance with Diomed. All four are on the Platform: Troilus and Ulysses stand "where the Torch may not discover us", and the indignant outbursts of the betrayed lover are suppressed to whispers by his Greek escort: Cressida and Diomed, unconscious of their audience, are not at pains to hush their speech. It is plain that their amorous duet is up-stage, while the hidden eavesdroppers are right forward and close to the groundlings: from this position it is easy for them to fulfil their author's purpose—for though talking in whispers, they speak as freely and as fully as the other two. On the

---

[92] 1 *Henry IV*, II. ii. 102 ff.
[94] *Two Gentlemen of Verona*, IV. ii. 28 ff.
[93] *Macbeth*, III. iii.
[95] *Julius Caesar*, V. i.

picture-stage the length of the "aside" dialogue is an embarrassment: on Shakespeare's stage it is simply effective.[96]

That "asides" were not always spoken from the forward position
is clear from two scenes of eavesdropping in *Much Ado About Nothing*
—and it is to be expected of the brilliant opportunism of Shakespeare
(and, indeed, of his profession) that there will be no rigid rules of
stage-practice that cannot be broken to suit a particular set of
circumstances. The match-makers' plot induces both Benedick and
Beatrice to overhear a conversation deliberately staged for their
enlightenment. Benedick, spying the approach of the Prince with
Leonato and Claudio, betakes him to "the Arbor", which is presumably set in the Study. After a song calculated to put the sceptic
(in spite of his protestations to the contrary) in melting mood, the
conspirators approach their prey: "Stalke on, stalke on," whispers
Claudio, "the foule sits." There follows a long circumstantial tale of
Beatrice's concealed love for Benedick, punctuated by occasional
whispered comments on Benedick's reception of the news, and a rare
interjection from Benedick himself. I fancy that the conspirators hug
one doorway, while their quarry is at the opposite end of the Study
"in the Arbor". Then, when their work is done, Leonato says to the
Prince, "My Lord, will you walke? dinner is ready." The two
ensuing speeches, delivered so that Benedick cannot hear their
further plotting, must be spoken as the three conspirators tour the
perimeter of the Platform to depart by the opposite door. The ladies'
half of the conspiracy is conducted on exactly similar lines: Hero says

> looke where *Beatrice* like a Lapwing runs
> Close by the ground, to heare our conference—

and Ursula tells us that their prey

> even now,
> Is couched in the wood-bine coverture . . .

Once more, then, the victim is in the Study, and the plotting ladies
approach her sideways ("Then go we neare her that her eare loose
nothing"), hugging one of the doorways—perhaps for variety the
opposite one from that in the last scene. The departure of Hero and
Ursula is probably also done by a tour of the perimeter—though
faster this time, as behoves the boy-ladies, with but four skipping
lines of dialogue.[97] In the box-tree scene of *Twelfth Night*, the
situation is reversed: the victim speaks aloud, the conspirators aside.
The interruptions of Sir Toby and his crew come from the Study,

---

[96] *Troilus and Cressida*, V. ii.
[97] *Much Ado About Nothing*, II. iii. 39 ff.; III. i. 24 ff.

where the box-tree is set. But the writing of the scene seems designed for this disposition, for the emphasis is all upon Malvolio in front of the Platform. Moreover the considerable distance between him and the Study makes it possible for the surrounding audience to feel as if they were between the two groups, as if they too (like the conspirators) were poking fun at the infatuated steward's back.[98]

The sense of intimate contact between actors on this Platform and audience in the Yard must be felt to be fully realised. The steady daylight helps, for with the audience not only near but plainly visible, there is no artificial frontier at the footlights. From this close contact springs the popularity of the conventional "aside". Shakespeare used this device continually in his early plays and never grew tired of it. There is, for instance, in 1 *Henry VI*, a long scene in which Suffolk woos Margaret of Anjou by proxy for the King: the fact that he himself desires her touches the scene with irony, and there is a vein of deliberate comedy in the pattern of the "asides". First she speaks *to him* and he *aside;* then both *aside* together; then he *to her* and she *aside;* the culmination is her mocking "I cry you mercy, 'tis but *Quid* for *Quo*." [99] Of even longer duration is the four-part conversation when King Edward woos Lady Gray. The match is an unpopular one with the King's relations, and Gloucester and Clarence give a witty but bitterly outspoken commentary on the progress of their brother's suit.[100] The mourning scene at Towton with its ritual of lament needs triangular perspective to persuade an audience. The pious King sits on his Mole-Hill in the Study. The Son that has killed his Father and the Father that has killed his Son enter at opposite doors, and presumably come to rest in front of the corresponding Stage-Posts. All speak independently of each other, though their words form a pattern.[101] Falstaff, of course, is a past master in the use of speech "aside". He is continually ogling his audience and making us privy to his deceptions—the rogue's most powerful means of engaging our sympathy. Imagine him at a critical point of his narrative of the highway-robbery—the terrible odds of four against sixteen. "Pray Heaven," says Poins, "you have not murthered some of them," and something in his sniggering manner betrays the truth to Falstaff. Nimbly the old villain sees his way to turn the tables: "Nay, that's past praying for," he says; "I have pepper'd two of them: Two I am sure I have payed, two Rogues in Buckrom Sutes." Picture the scene: the Prince and Poins

---

[98] *Twelfth Night*, II. v. 18 ff.

[99] 1 *Henry VI*, V. iii. 72 ff. Shakespeare learnt later to do this more deftly: less naïve but in the same vein is Falstaff's successful attempt to score off the Lord Chief Justice "tap for tap, and so part faire" (2 *Henry IV*, II. i. 210.)

[100] 3 *Henry VI*, III. ii.   [101] 3 *Henry VI*, II. v. 55 ff.

up-stage enjoying their joke together, Falstaff right forward on the perimeter, enjoying *his* with the groundlings: the close contact with the audience, the intimate wink, at first sharing his secret only with his immediate neighbours in the Yard, conveys by infection to the whole playhouse the truth that "I have pepper'd two of them" means "I have seen through your stratagem." And the ensuing tale with its monstrous arithmetical progression is seen by the audience for what it is—Falstaff's ripost to the Prince's trick.[102] Granville-Barker has explained how the conditions of the Elizabethan playhouse give added point to Iago's cynical comment on the civilities that pass between Desdemona and Cassio on the quayside

I have pepper'd two of them

at Cyprus: "He takes her by the palme: I, well said, whisper. With as little a web as this, will I ensnare as great a Fly as *Cassio*. I smile upon her, do . . ." Here we have the sculptured and the pictorial together, the round and the flat: the pair Iago is describing make a flat picture against the curtain of the Study; the villainous interpreter stands in the round, in our midst, and his devilish insinuations make us accessory to his wickedness.[103]

A logical development of the "aside" is the soliloquy and this device too is admirably suited to the conditions of the Elizabethan

---

[102] 1 *Henry IV*, II. iv. 213 ff. Dover Wilson has given the hint of how we should read between the lines of this famous scene. See *The Fortunes of Falstaff*, 53.

[103] *Othello*, II. i. 168. See Granville-Barker, *Prefaces to Shakespeare* (Fourth Series), 19. He describes the visual effect of this moment as being "of a fully rounded statue placed before a bas-relief",

playhouse.[104] Shakespeare's restlessly experimental mind invented constantly new variations of method and motive for solo speech, and it is impossible to lay down a hard-and-fast rule for the position and manner of its delivery. The informative tell-the-audience-the-story type—such as those of York in 2 *Henry VI*, of Richard of Gloucester

He takes her by the palme: I, well said, whisper

in 3 *Henry VI* and *Richard III*, of Proteus in *Two Gentlemen of Verona*, and (in the mature tragic period) of Iago [105]—addresses the audience almost as if lecturing, and is appropriately delivered from the centre

---

[104] Granville-Barker has a section on "The Soliloquy" in the Introduction to the First Series of his *Prefaces to Shakespeare*, xxx ff.

[105] 2 *Henry VI*, I. i. 215 ff.; III. i. 331 ff. 3 *Henry VI*, III. ii. 124 ff.; *Richard III*, I. i. 1 ff.; I. i. 144 ff.; I. ii. 229 ff.; I. iii. 324 ff. *Two Gentlemen of Verona*, II. iv. 193 ff.; II. vi. 1 ff.; IV. ii. 1 ff. *Othello*, I. iii. 389 ff.; II. i. 298 ff.; II. iii. 345 ff.

of the Platform. The same is true of the rhetorical *tours de force* of the
Bastard in *King John:* when he discourses on "observation" or
"commoditie", he takes the stage and harangues the meeting.[106] But
Richard II's "still breeding Thoughts" at Pomfret must have been
incarcerated in Study or Chamber.[107] Prince Hal's preliminary
statement of motive ("I know you all, and will a-while uphold The
unyoak'd humor of your idlenesse") was probably delivered from
the Chamber, while his more intimate address to his father's crown
("O pollish'd Perturbation! Golden Care!") is from the neighbourhood of the Study, where stands the bed of the dying King.[108] The
grave but detached philosophic reflection of Brutus would perhaps
pace the rushes of his Orchard strewn in the Study.[109] But after his
first interview with Isabella, Angelo's dynamic outburst, betraying
his uncontrolled passion, races off as the climax of the preceding
scene. " 'Save your Honour," says the virtuous maid in formal
valediction: "From thee," cries the Deputy, as soon as she has gone:
"even from thy vertue." The ensuing soliloquy must range over the
whole Platform. When we next see Angelo, he is revealed at prayer
in the Study, and speaks his dilemma from there.[110] King Claudius
must do likewise in similar vain attempt to pray: but Hamlet's subsequent breathless hesitation in the same scene ("Now might I do it
pat . . .") would then move round the perimeter, away from Claudius
but close to us. How well this scene brings out the greater expressiveness of the Elizabethan multiple stage! Putting up his sword again,
the Prince continues his way round the front of the Platform and
goes out by the opposite door: he is bound for his Mother's Closet,
and after the King's despairing couplet—

> My words flye up, my thoughts remain below,
> Words without thoughts, never to Heaven go——

the play flows on in its uninterrupted course on the upper level.[111]
The solitary heart-searching of Hamlet's "Oh that this too too solid
Flesh, would melt" and "To be, or not to be, that is the Question"
and the hair-raising calculations of Macbeth ("This supernaturall
solliciting . . ." and "If it were done, when 'tis done . . .") strike pity
or terror into each one of us as Burbadge stands at the hub of the
octagon.[112]

The clowns are a law apart. The shape of the theatre and the fact
that the auditorium as well as the Platform was in steady daylight

---

[106] *King John*, I. i. 182 ff.; II. i. 561 ff.   [107] *Richard II*, V. v. 1 ff.
[108] 1 *Henry IV*, I. ii. 217 ff.; 2 *Henry IV*, IV. v. 20 ff.
[109] *Julius Caesar*, II. i. 8 ff.
[110] *Measure for Measure*, II. ii. 161 ff.; II. iv. 1 ff.   [111] *Hamlet*, III. iii. 36 ff.
[112] *Hamlet*, I. ii. 129 ff.; III. i. 56 ff. *Macbeth*, I. iii. 130 ff.; I. vii. 1 ff.

are partly responsible for their technique of frontal assault, their
frequent direct appeals to the audience. Even a summary review of
the practice of soliloquy shows that the serious characters often so
address the playhouse, with varying degrees of explicitness: one
thinks of Faulconbridge, Iago, Edmund, each (be it noted) with a
touch of humour in his make-up. But it is of course a much com-
moner trick with the comic figures. No picture rises more vividly to
the mind's eye than Launce (in the person of Kemp) with his dog
Crab, surrounded by the laughter of the groundlings: "I thinke
Crab my dog, be the sowrest natured dogge that lives: My Mother
weeping: my Father wayling: my Sister crying: our Maid howling:

Yet did not this cruell-hearted Curre
shedde one teare

our Catte wringing her hands, and all our house in a great per-
plexitie, yet did not this cruell-hearted Curre shedde one teare." [113]
Another such turn in the music-hall style is that of Launcelot Gobbo,
drawn this way and that between his conscience and the fiend at his
other elbow.[114] Kemp's successors of to-day would envy him his
forward position in the centre of the playhouse, as they show by their
tendency to walk into the footlights. It is the vaudeville comedians
of to-day and yesterday who come nearest in their genre to the
manner of the Elizabethan theatre: Saturday night at the old
Palladium—twenty years ago—had the feeling, at least of the comic
side of the business.

   Falstaff, as we have seen, by taking the audience into his con-

---

[113] *Two Gentlemen of Verona,* II. iii. 5 ff.   [114] *The Merchant of Venice,* II. ii. 1 ff.

fidence, makes us feel in collusion with his villainies. If the dramatist
can do that, he has gone a long way to make his play live. We must
expect him, and his actors with him, to do their utmost to lure us
into the game too. But Falstaff has more than one trick up his
sleeve: and if he cannot always carry the audience with him as
confederates, he will sometimes associate them with those whom he
wishes to make his dupes. When, standing in the central area within
the Stage-Posts, he is in the full career of his ridiculous lies about the
robbery on Gads Hill, Prince Hal and Poins (now on the perimeter)
turn, as they think, the tables on the braggart: the Prince gives his
version of the business, his plain tale to put Falstaff down, and cries
"What trick? what device? what starting hole canst thou now find
out, to hide thee from this open and apparent shame?" Falstaff, as
always, has the last trick: blandly, amid the expectant silence, he
says "I knew ye as well as he that made ye." Then if the player is
doing his job, not only Hal and Poins but the audience too will burst
into incredulous and uproarious laughter, and as he cries "Why
heare ye my Masters . . ." Falstaff will have to silence the whole
playhouse, shouting at the Prince and Poins, but through them at
you and me in Yard and galleries. When he has reduced us all to
silence, he need not raise his voice to say "was it for me to kill the
Heire apparant?" For the nonce, the whole audience is within the
hospitable four walls of mine Hostess' tavern.[115]

This taking up of the audience into the play lies at the root of the
matter: as they stood or sat in the same steady light which shone on
the actors, and were themselves easily visible by them, they were a
constant and obvious and no doubt vocally explicit reminder to
dramatist and players alike of the danger of failure. When there is a
ring of critical spectators within a few feet of the stage, whose expres-
sions are not concealed by the merciful darkening of the auditorium,
then the actors and the playwright must take their courage in both
hands, they must do or die; and in practice it is astonishing what
people will succeed in doing rather than die. Certainly the Chamberlain's Men would be at great pains to make and keep a contact of
sympathy with their audience, and to break down in imagination
the barrier of the stage-rails between Platform and Yard. We can see
them at it constantly, taking the groundlings into alliance. It may
be that they are made the audience of a play within the play, when
the nobility on the stage sitting at intervals round the Platform-rails
seem but the front row of a larger company.[116] It may be that they

---

[115] 1 Henry IV, II. iv. 283 ff.
[116] See above, p. 99. The references there given are to A Midsummer Night's
Dream, Love's Labour's Lost, Hamlet and The Tempest.

become the spectators of a duel, either on the battlefield or in single combat. The fencing-match which makes the climax of *Hamlet* has at the Globe all the tense excitement of a prizefight in the ring, and indeed at the duel between Hector and Ajax in *Troilus and Cressida* it looks as if some of the Greek chiefs watched from the Tarras, thereby completing the ring.[117] On other occasions the groundlings may seem to be the rest of the crowd, of whom typical members appear on the Platform itself. This seems to be Shakespeare's intention in his handling of the mob-scenes of *Julius Caesar*. The Folio text refers to the crowd as *certaine Commoners* on their first appearance, and their leader is introduced to us as a lively personality. Later they are called *the Plebeians*. In the Forum scene four individual speakers are instanced, and the folio seems to differentiate them with some care as 1, 2, 3 and 4. We may be tempted to change a number here and there, but there is certainly a robust independence and initiative discernible in the speeches assigned to Number 4. The stage-crowd would, I fancy, amount to no more than twelve all told, and can be thus few and individualised because by being thrust out among the

He poysons him i'th'Garden for's estate

---

[117] *Hamlet*, V. ii. 294 ff.; *Troilus and Cressida*, IV. v. 113 ff.

groundlings of the Yard they can seem to be but the fringe or front
row of the groundlings themselves. A good Antony, helped by
"infectious" crowd-actors (recruited from the comedy-gang of the
Chamberlain's Men) would sway the whole Yard with his oratory.
Yet another device for drawing the Yard into the action of the play
is that of making them seem, as it were, the rest of a symbolical stage
army. The occasion commonly arises when the generals address their
troops before battle.[118] Especially stirring is the moment in *Henry V*

*God send you sir, a speedie Infirmity, for the better
increasing your folly*

of the assault on Harfleur, when on the cry of "God for *Harry*,
England, and S. *George*," the whole Yard seem to hurl themselves
into the breach. An interesting case is that of the French King's
appeal in the same play when he mentions by name a far greater
number of his peers than can be mustered among the Chamberlain's
Men. The audience in the playhouse become for the time being the
assembled chivalry of France.[119] The proclamation of Othello's
Herald delivered presumably from the Tarras shows how, even

---

[118] A number of such occasions are listed on p. 89, above.
[119] *Henry V*, III. i. 34; III. v. 38 ff.

when the Platform is empty, the streets of Cyprus will—under the influence of an established convention—still seem full.[120]

In short, the architecture of the playhouse, and especially the shape, dimensions and central forward position of the Platform, are the basis of much of Shakespeare's stagecraft: they affect the positioning and grouping of his scenes, which were after all written for performance in this theatre. In these conditions we can bring his plays to vivid life again: for thus the action will be in the round, not flat; grouping will be easy and natural, not strained by the need to avoid "masking"; we in the audience shall be once again participants on the edge of a central group, not detached spectators of a distant, moving picture. In this playhouse we can co-operate almost physically in the play: we can see over an actor's shoulder, if he is down-stage, and so feel with him: we can make immediate response to his suggestion, and thereby help him to cast his spell. We can have a sense of being "in it". "It was like being out in the wood yourself," said a spectator of *A Midsummer Night's Dream* in such conditions. I have seen the Roman mob on such a Platform hobnobbing with their acquaintance in the audience. Not the least important result of such a revolution in stage-practice is this—that to make such a powerful and immediate impression on the audience, the technique of the actor must be more robust, more direct, more do-or-die than the methods we are used to now.

(iv) Characterisation

If we want to recapture the characterisation of the Chamberlain's Men, we shall have little help in contemporary references to performance, which are scanty and unhelpful.[121] Although we are not as fortunate as the poet's colleagues who could put their questions direct, yet even for us the most fertile field of evidence is Shakespeare himself; for the characterisation is very often fully prescribed somewhere in the words of one speaker or another. Shakespeare seldom leaves us in doubt about any of the major figures: yet he does not rely on the long descriptive character-notes of the modern dramatist, nor does he use bracketed adverbs to indicate the tone of a speech. If we can find out how he achieves this, we have gone some way to understanding the technique of poetic drama. We shall see, in the next chapter, how it is a feature of Shakespeare's poetic drama that the characters, like the scenery and the atmosphere (and sometimes the very action itself), are all contained in the spoken dialogue.

---

[120] *Othello*, II. ii.
[121] Even the familiar tribute of Leonard Digges does little more than tell us which figures were the most popular.

It is surprising, therefore, how often producer or actor seems to prefer his own interpretation. How seldom do we see a Polonius who succeeds in making his manifest absurdities compatible with the sound wisdom of his advice to Laertes, the shrewdness which underlies his absent-minded verbosity as he briefs Reynaldo, and the philosophical humility of his comment on his blundering judgment of Hamlet's "tenders" to Ophelia:

> It seemes it is as proper to our Age,
> To cast beyond our selves in our Opinions,
> As it is common for the yonger sort
> To lacke discretion . . .

so that we can feel that there is some substance in the Queen's posthumous tribute to the "good old man".[122] Horatio is not always of a stature to deserve Hamlet's moving panegyric:

> Since my deere Soule was Mistris of my choyse,
> And could of men distinguish, her election
> Hath seal'd thee for her selfe. For thou hast bene
> As one in suffering all, that suffers nothing.
> A man that Fortunes buffets, and Rewards
> Hath 'tane with equall Thankes. And blest are those,
> Whose Blood and Judgement are so well co-mingled,
> That they are not a Pipe for Fortunes finger,
> To sound what stop she please. Give me that man,
> That is not Passions Slave, and I will weare him
> In my hearts Core: I, in my Heart of heart,
> As I do thee.[123]

But how much the play suffers if Hamlet has not this comforting support to lean on in his time of need. We do not often see a Caesar who can reconcile the opposite colours in which Shakespeare deliberately paints him—on the one hand, the irritable epileptic who, fresh from his posturing hypocrisy in the market-place, mutters pettishly in Antony's ear "Let me have men about me, that are fat . . .", vacillating between the superstitious fears of his wife and his own self-esteem, and falling an easy victim to the subtle flattery of Decius; on the other, the man whose word might have stood against the world, who could pronounce himself before the Senate

> constant as the Northerne Starre,
> Of whose true fixt, and resting quality,
> There is no fellow in the Firmament.[124]

---

[122] *Hamlet*, I. iii. 58 ff.; II. i. 1–74; II. i. 114 ff.; IV. i. 12.
[123] *Hamlet*, III. ii. 68 ff.
[124] *Julius Caesar*, I. ii. 191 ff.; II. ii; III. i. 60 ff.

Heminges could do it, if it is true that he played both Polonius and the Earl of Kent. And when shall we see again the right Shakespearian Gloucester in *King Lear*, who can combine the impression of the opening sentences of the play with that of Edmund's dupe, who can be the casual and cheerful lecher, prone to superstition and suspicion, and gullible; and at the same time heroically loyal to the King, and eventually pitiable to us all? [125]

In the history plays there is even less reason than elsewhere for the misconception of Shakespeare's purpose in characterisation; for different plays of the cycle often offer hints of his conception, and if we read backwards and forwards we shall find that one play throws light upon the interpretation of another. True, it is a commonplace of criticism that King Henry V is not the same character as Prince Hal—an opinion which does not command unreserved acceptance. But even Prince Hal, as we see him in the theatre to-day, is seldom consistent with himself. The fault is usually one of casting: the star actor will not take this rôle, preferring Hotspur or Falstaff; so Hal is given to a young rising actor who unconsciously plays the part as if he were a foil to the star of Falstaff, not (as he should) as the heir-apparent, the central figure of the story. Here is a side of Shakespeare's conception which seldom appears in the performance of Hal's madcap escapades:

> hee is gracious, if hee be observ'd:
> Hee hath a Teare for Pitie, and a Hand
> Open (as Day) for melting Charitie:
> Yet notwithstanding, being incens'd, hee's Flint,
> As humorous as Winter, and as sudden,
> As Flawes congealed in the Spring of day.

Here too is a precise and explicit account of his way of life:

> The Prince but studies his Companions,
> Like a strange Tongue: wherein, to gaine the Language,
> 'Tis needfull, that the most immodest word
> Be look'd upon, and learn'd: which once attayn'd,
> Your Highnesse knowes, comes to no farther use,
> But to be knowne, and hated. So, like grosse termes,
> The Prince will, in the perfectnesse of time,
> Cast off his followers: and their memorie
> Shall as a Patterne, or a Measure, live,
> By which his Grace must mete the lives of others,
> Turning past-evills to advantages.[126]

---

[125] It is the more surprising that Gloucester is habitually misplayed when Granville-Barker has made an admirably Shakespearian study of the character in his *Prefaces to Shakespeare*, First Series, 202 ff.

[126] 2 *Henry IV*, IV. iv. 30 ff.; 68 ff.

If an actor were to begin the building of his interpretation upon these two passages, he could be sure that the foundation was Shakespeare's own, and finding opportunity to reveal these aspects of the character, would greatly enrich the high spirits of the earlier scenes by the contrast of serious mood and purpose. Hotspur projects his personality as soon as he opens his mouth, but there is plenty of other material to study for the full interpretation of the character. Lady Percy gives us his immediate mood when he is restless and uneasy in plotting rebellion: the description is reminiscent of Portia's account of Brutus in like circumstances, but the reaction of the two conspirators is characteristically different.[127] Harry Percy's general habit of speech and movement is drawn for us in his widow's posthumous panegyric:

> He was (indeed) the Glasse
> Wherein the Noble-Youth did dresse themselves.
> He had no Legges, that practic'd not his Gate:
> And speaking thicke (which Nature made his blemish)
> Became the Accents of the Valiant.
> For those that could speake low, and tardily,
> Would turne their owne Perfection, to Abuse,
> To seeme like him.[128]

Prince Hal's caricature throws another light on him: "he that killes me some sixe or seaven dozen of Scots at a Breakfast, washes his hands, and saies to his wife; Fie upon this quiet life, I want worke"; and the burlesque throws into strong relief the Prince's generous praise of his rival in the parleys before Shrewsbury Field. Worcester's bitter comment adds something to the picture:

> My Nephewes trespasse may be well forgot,
> It hath the excuse of youth, and heate of blood,
> And an adopted name of Privilege,
> A haire-brain'd *Hotspurre*, govern'd by a Spleene:

Hotspur's demeanour in his single combat with Hal is described vividly in the sequel, and might surprise some of the actors who represent him:

> But these mine eyes, saw him in bloody state,
> Rend'ring faint quittance (wearied, and out-breath'd)
> To *Henrie Monmouth*, whose swift wrath beate downe
> The never-daunted *Percie* to the earth,
> From whence (with life) he never more sprung up.

---

[127] 1 *Henry IV*, II. iii. 42 ff.; *Julius Caesar*, II. i. 237 ff.
[128] 2 *Henry IV*, II. iii. 21 ff.

The growth of the character in Shakespeare's mind can be studied in his brief but not insignificant appearance in *Richard II*.[129] Nor is it perhaps irrelevant to remember that his familiar speech on honour is burlesqued in *The Knight of the Burning Pestle* when Ralph, being asked to speak a "huffing part", delivers Hotspur's lines.[130] From this rich variety of material it is possible to make a synthesis which approximates to Shakespeare's own intention: there is no need for producer or actor to work up a personal interpretation of the part.

The hunt for Shakespeare's intention is not always so easy as in the case of Hotspur. Sometimes we must clear away the errors of subsequent theatrical tradition. A not infrequent source of misunderstanding is a neglect of Shakespeare's habit of modern objective vision. The point is readily illustrated by the usual manhandling of the sub-plot in *Twelfth Night*. The social position of Malvolio as a dignified gentleman who is Steward of a great household, makes his aspiration to the hand of his mistress a quite credible ambition: "There is example for't," says he, and Miss M. St. Clair Byrne, in an admirable passage on this theme, quotes more than one precedent from contemporary history. Such a figure as this (a victim worth the gulling) together with a Maria who is a well-educated gentlewoman, a Sir Toby for all his cakes and ale still unequivocally my lady's kinsman, a Sir Andrew in spite of his absurdity a man of substance and position, worth the humouring (for he is "a great quarreller") so long as Sir Toby can hope for any profit from him—here is material for pure comedy very different from the farcical riot that is now the traditional rendering. The clues to Shakespeare's meaning are, as usual, embedded in the dialogue, but the producer must here seek some expert elucidation of the Elizabethan social background.[131] Falstaff himself suffers if producer and actor have not a firm conception of his social status, if the actor is hail-fellow-well-met with all men and does not insist on his gang of parasites keeping their place and distance: as his creator draws him, he never forgets his position; indeed his aloofness is an offence below-stairs at the Boar's Head, where he is known as "proud Jack" among the Drawers.[132] Even in

---

[129] I *Henry IV*, II. iv. 117 ff.; V. i. 85 ff.; V. ii. 16 ff.; 2 *Henry IV*, I. i. 107 ff.; *Richard II*, II. iii. 21 ff.; III. iii. 20 ff.

[130] Beaumont and Fletcher, *The Knight of the Burning Pestle*, Induction. E. M. W. Tillyard, commenting on this fact, says that "Hotspur, however captivating his vitality, verges on the ridiculous from the very beginning, through his childish inability to control his passions" (*Shakespeare's History Plays*, 283).

[131] The reader is referred to Miss M. St. Clare Byrne's chapter in *A Companion to Shakespeare Studies* (Cambridge), 187 ff. (and especially 209 ff.); and also to Charles Lamb's observations on *Twelfth Night* in his essay "On Some of the Old Actors" (*Essays of Elia*).

[132] I *Henry IV*, II. iv. 12.

the ecstasies of courtship he makes it clear to Mistress Ford that he knows himself to be a cut above her.[133]

Sometimes a light is thrown upon the characterisation by a comparison of similar parts in different plays. The likeness may be in habitual circumstances. The Countess' Steward in *All's Well That Ends Well* is a highly privileged and trusted servant: he first discloses Helena's passion to his mistress, and later is asked to write a confidential letter for the Countess to her son.[134] A virtuous Oswald we might call him (Oswald also writes his Lady's letters),[135] a discreet Malvolio; his name is Rinaldo, to remind us of Polonius' confidential envoy [136]; the comparisons are not without value in helping an actor of any of these four parts to conceive his performance. It may be the immediate situation that is similar: thus Roderigo, Iago's financial backer and his dupe, gulled into thinking himself a likely suitor for the hand of Desdemona, is the tragic equivalent of Sir Andrew, who stands in a like relation to Sir Toby and Olivia. Or the resemblance may be in temperament: there is common ground between Iago and Edmund, though their station differs, and bastardy is not the only affinity between Edmund and Faulconbridge, though their characters are fundamentally unlike. But this line of approach needs discretion: it is easy to overstress the similarity in observing a superficial resemblance.

We are trying all the time to get closer to Shakespeare's intention, and one obvious way of achieving that is to examine his sources and see how paragraphs, and even single phrases, give a hint of what was in the poet's mind. Sometimes the poet adopts the version of his predecessor, sometimes he alters it: either process is interesting to the student who wants to follow the working of Shakespeare's mind. Plutarch is the most fertile field here, because Plutarch himself had so keen a dramatic sense, as Shakespeare acknowledges in the extent of his borrowing. There is a wonderful feeling at times of looking over the poet's shoulder as he "Opens his Plutarch, puts him in the place Of Roman, Grecian". While he was writing *Macbeth*, we may suppose that his evening reading was the life of Marcus Antonius: one night he was occupied with the passage where a soothsayer visits Antony and warns him to depart from Rome and the neighbourhood of Octavius: "For thy Demon, said he, (that is to say, the good angell and spirit that keepeth thee) is affraied of his: and being coragious and high when he is alone, beccommeth fearefull

---

[133] *The Merry Wives of Windsor*, III. iii. 52 ff.
[134] *All's Well That Ends Well*, I. iii. 112 ff.; III. iv. 29 ff.
[135] *King Lear*, I. iv. 359.   [136] *Hamlet*, II. 1.

and timerous when he commeth neere unto the other." [137] Next day
he made Macbeth say of Banquo that

> under him,
> My *Genius* is rebuk'd, as it is said
> Mark *Anthonies* was by *Caesar*.[138]

And in his next play, the episode in Plutarch is elaborated into a
scene which changes the course of the drama.[139] The producer of
Julius Caesar, if he would give us Shakespeare's intention, must study
Plutarch's lives of Brutus and Caesar in North's version.[140] There he
will find much of the characterisation and many of the episodes
already in being, and can observe the added touches of the poet's
genius. Holinshed and Hall, and the other known sources, though to
a lesser degree, are nevertheless indispensable aids to the understanding of Shakespeare's intended characterisation.

At second remove from Shakespeare's shoulder, but nearer to the
practice of his colleagues, is the evidence of the Quarto and Folio
texts, which give us an idea of the intention not only of the poet but
also of the Book-Keeper, or sometimes indeed a reporter's recollec-
tion of the performance.[141] We may have a hint of the calculated
emphasis in the plot from the Quarto title-page. For instance, the
1602 text of *The Merry Wives of Windsor* begins with an elaborate
programme note: "A Most pleasaunt and excellent conceited
Comedie, of Syr *John Falstaffe*, and the merrie Wives of *Windsor*.
Entermixed with sundrie variable and pleasing humors, of Syr *Hugh*
the Welch Knight, Justice *Shallow*, and his wise Cousin M. *Slender*.
With the swaggering vaine of Auncient *Pistoll*, and Corporall *Nym*."
The 1608 (Pied Bull) *King Lear* speaks of "M. William Shak-speare:
His True Chronicle Historie of the life and death of King LEAR
and his three Daughters. *With the unfortunate life of* Edgar, *sonne* and
heire to the Earle of Gloster, and his sullen and assumed humor of
Tom of Bedlam." More useful, perhaps, are the occasional cast-lists
in the Folio. At the end of *Measure for Measure* "The names of all the
Actors" include *Lucio, a fantastique; Elbow, a simple Constable; Froth, a
foolish Gentleman; Clowne* (which means Pompey); and *Barnardine, a
dissolute prisoner.* A similar list at the end of *Othello* describes Cassio as
an Honourable Lieutenant, Iago as *a Villaine,* and Rodorigo as *a gull'd*

---

[137] Plutarch's *Life of Antonius* (North's Translation, 1579).

[138] *Macbeth*, III. i. 55 ff.

[139] *Antony and Cleopatra*, II. iii. 10 ff.

[140] A full, if not exhaustive, selection of the relevant passages can be conveniently
studied in Verity's edition of the play in the Pitt Press series.

[141] See Chapter II, "The Prompt Book", pp. 25 ff., above.

Gentleman (further link with Sir Andrew, who is called "a gull" by Sir Toby in parting).[142] It will be noticed that there is a marked tendency in these lists to label the characters by their type, or rather according to the part which they play in the plot: it is not insignificant that Brabantio is described not in his quality as a reverend senator, but as *Father to Desdemona*.

Scattered here and there among the stage-directions are epithets or phrases that help us to interpret the poet's characterisation. We learn from the Folio that Princess Katherine's attendant Alice is *an old Gentlewoman*, our only direct indication of her age. *Enter young Osricke* has just the right tone of patronage in speaking of "this water-flie", and reflects perhaps also the condescension of the member to the apprentice-player.[143] An occasional direction, indicating action or appearance, helps to suggest to the player his demeanour at a certain moment: *Enter one blowing*, as a messenger brings the news of the Duke of York's death; *Enter the Queene with her haire about her ears, Rivers & Dorset after her; Enter Richard, and Buckingham, in rotten Armour, marvellous ill-favoured; Enter the King and his poore Souldiers; Enter Ofelia playing on a lute, and her hair down, singing* (this last example from the First Quarto).[144]

Perhaps the most interesting of all the suggestions to be derived from the texts is the habit (noted above, in discussion of the prompt-book)[145] of varying the speech-headings—of writing type-names instead of personal names, or rather names showing the quality or the function of the character in the play. Thus in *Love's Labour's Lost* we have *Braggart* alternating with *Armado*, *Pedant* with *Holofernes*, *Curate* with *Nathaniel*. In *Romeo and Juliet*, *Capulet* is described as *Father*, *Lady Capulet* as *Mother*. In the vastly entertaining quarrel-scene of *Henry V* in which the four corners of the Kingdom are participants, Fluellen's speech-heading is changed to *Welch* as soon as the international issue is raised, and Macmorice and Captaine Jamy are described as *Irish* and *Scot* throughout.[146] It is most instructive to follow the nomenclature of the Countess in *All's Well That Ends Well*, who first appears as *Mother* with the line "In delivering my sonne from me, I burie a second husband"; next with her Steward and the Clowne she is properly designated *Countesse*; and then in the middle of the same scene, when Helen appears, the speech-heading alters to *Old Cou.* with the words "Even so it was

---

[142] *Twelfth Night*, V. i. 216.   [143] *Henry V*, III. iv. 1; *Hamlet*, V. ii. 81.

[144] 3 *Henry VI*, II. i. 43. *Richard III*, II. ii. 34; III. v. 1. *Henry V*, III. vi. 94. *Hamlet*, IV. v. 21. The reader is strongly recommended to glance at the appendix of stage directions in W. W. Greg's *The Editorial Problem in Shakespeare*, 158 ff.

[145] See pp. 26 f.   [146] *Henry V*, III. ii. 76 ff.

with me when I was young". In each case her relation to the immediate situation—to the other characters—dictates the appropriate style.[147] We seem to be very close to the original manuscript of Shakespeare here and, as we have seen above, McKerrow infers that this is the way the poet's mind worked: in the heat of composition the qualities of the characters or the part which they played in the action were often more strongly present to his imagination than their personal names.[148] If this is true, then the same general attitude to the characterisation should be present in the mind of a producer, and through him communicate itself to the actors.

A highly interesting field for speculation—if not research—is to be found among the individual personalities of the Chamberlain's Men. We must remember that Shakespeare was writing his plays not only for a particular playhouse but also for a particular company of players, and that, as Baldwin says, "the play was regularly fitted to the company, not the company to the play".[149] It follows that, if the cast-lists themselves had survived, as they have occasionally for the plays of Ben Jonson and others, their importance as evidence of characterisation could hardly be exaggerated; and that we may learn much even from conjecture, when it is based on so close a study as Baldwin's. From the point of view of the present enquiry, it is obviously interesting to find that Augustine Phillips, who played Cassius, turned his lean and hungry look in the same year to good effect as Malvolio; that the same actor (Pope) played Shylock, Falstaff and Fluellen; that Burbadge played Bassanio and Prince Hal—both parts distorted by under-casting nowadays. A glance at Lowin's portrait suggests that his Gloucester in *King Lear* would have shown a more full-blooded semblance of the "Goatish disposition" indicated in the opening dialogue of the play, than we are used to in the dry, doddering impersonations of to-day; and he, it seems, also played the "blowt king" Claudius. The succession of Robert Armin to the place of Will Kemp, who left the company in 1599, made a fundamental change—as has often been pointed out—in Shakespeare's conception of the principal comedian's rôle.

---

[147] *All's Well That Ends Well*, I. i. 1; I. iii. 1; 136.
[148] See above, p. 27.
[149] T. W. Baldwin, *Organization and Personnel of the Shakespearean Company*, 197. In another passage (305, 307), Baldwin uses the analogy of a tailor, calling Shakespeare a good tailor-playwright, as opposed to Ben Jonson, who was not adaptable. The distinction chimes with what we know of their contrasted temperaments.

(v) The Repertory

This, then, is an appropriate place to turn aside for a moment and become more closely acquainted with some individual members of the company.[150]

Richard Burbadge, who with his brother, Cuthbert, held a half of the total number of shares in the playhouse, joined the company about 1590, when it came to his father's theatre. Once he had proved himself as Talbot and *Richard III*,[151] he remained the leading man as long as he was with the company. Baldwin assigns to him Berowne, Romeo, Demetrius (*A Midsummer Night's Dream*), Bassanio, Prince Hal, Claudio (*Much Ado About Nothing*), Henry V, Brutus, Orlando, Orsino, *Hamlet*, Ford, Bertram, Angelo, *Othello*, *Lear*, Macbeth, Antony (*Antony and Cleopatra*), Timon, Pericles. We have already noticed that he played Bassanio and Prince Hal, and no doubt the weight of his personality preserved the balance where nowadays these plays usually suffer distortion; the same may be said, perhaps, of his playing Claudio in *Much Ado About Nothing*, and Orsino. Berowne and Romeo are akin to this style, which shows him a master of subtle speech-music, wit and decorative conceit. The parts grow in stature with him: Brutus "with himself at warre" marks a turning point, compensating for the comparative failure in the mature Hal of *Henry V*, and indeed developing some of the depth of introspection attempted in the prelude to Agincourt. Thereafter, in the sequence of great tragedies Shakespeare sets him a task, in study and performance, second only to his own in composition. There is no reason to think that he failed him. The mere mention of Hamlet, Othello, Lear, Macbeth and Antony speaks volumes for Burbadge's versatility—which seems to have stopped short only of pure comedy, of which quality, says Baldwin, "he had almost none, his comic effects being procured by a half satiric contrast of high ideals turned

---

[150] For fuller information about the players, the reader is referred to T. W. Baldwin's *The Organization and Personnel of the Shakespearean Company*. A number of Baldwin's conjectural cast-lists are reproduced below in the Appendix III, pp. 320 ff. Baldwin uses an unorthodox chronology, and in listing the parts assigned to the various players, I have adjusted the order to the chronology of E. K. Chambers, which is reproduced below in the Appendix I, p. 318. Baldwin goes too far in drawing inferences about the appearance and personality of the actors from references to the characters they played, and even reaches the extremity of supposing that Shakespeare habitually fitted the age of his character to the age of his actor. For a more orthodox and less adventurous account of the players, the reader is referred to E. K. Chambers' *William Shakespeare*, vol. i, Chapter III, and vol. ii, Appendix A, Section VIII, "Shakespeare and his Fellows"; and also to the same author's *Elizabethan Stage*, vol. ii, 192, 295.

[151] Characters printed in italics indicate certain ascriptions, for which there is recognised evidence.

Richard Burbadge
(*from the picture in the Gallery of Dulwich College*)

loose to be laughed at in a practical world, somewhat after the manner of Cervantes".[152] If in looking at his portrait, our first instinct is to exclaim "Was this the face . . .?" it is worth recording the opinion that the best actors are those who can assume a great variety of characters, not those who are content to exploit or have exploited for them their own graceful or attractive personality: if the art of acting consists of the deliberate assumption of other characters, it is quite probable that the face in repose when not making that effort will bear no trace of the distinction of its many impersonations.

If this guess hits the mark, that Burbadge was able to assume so many different rôles, because his own personality was neutral, then he was probably an exception in the company. Though all his colleagues show some measure of versatility, there is a remarkable gallery of distinctive and forceful personalities among them. John Heminges, a house-keeper from the building of the Globe till 1631, the business manager of the company (to everybody's satisfaction) for more than a quarter of a century, who survived all the original members of 1595 to join with Cundall in honouring Shakespeare's memory in the Folio of 1623, lives even through the phrases of the preface to that volume: Dover Wilson has an interesting suggestion that he might have been the masterful person who overhauled the Quarto stage-directions of *A Midsummer Night's Dream*, and so perhaps the stage-manager of the company, since it was certainly "Mr. Heminges man", Tawyer, who was detailed in the Folio text of the play to blow his trumpet before the entry of Quince's dumb-show.[153] A glance at the parts ascribed to him reinforces the impression of a man to be respected among his fellows, seeming elderly, able easily to assume gravity or hot temper or prosiness or sardonic wit. He is down for (among other parts) Boyet, Capulet, Egeus, Glendower, the Lord Chief Justice, Leonato, Exeter (*Henry V*), Caesar, Duke Senior, Fabian (unexpectedly), Polonius, the Host (*The Merry Wives of Windsor*), Lafeu, Brabantio, Kent (*King Lear*), Ross. It is easy to see a resemblance in treatment between Capulet, Egeus, Glendower (the same phrase occurs on the lips of Capulet and Glendower, "a peevish selfe-will'd Harlotry"),[154] Leonato, Polonius and Brabantio —all concerned with refractory daughters. Baldwin points out, not inappositely, that Heminges had himself more than a dozen children.[155] Exeter and Ross are alike in their gravity, especially in reciting bad news; and Kent has something in common with these

[152] Baldwin, *op. cit.*, 203.
[153] *A Midsummer Night's Dream* (New Cambridge Edition), 155. See above, pp. 30 f.
[154] *Romeo and Juliet*, IV. ii. 14; 1 *Henry IV*, III. i. 197.
[155] Baldwin, *op. cit.*, 249.

two. Already one catches a glimpse of Baldwin's theory, upon which
he bases his conjectural cast-lists, that it is possible to establish the
"lines" or types of part appropriate to each of the principal actors
and boys. And already it is apparent that a study of the similar parts
of the same "line" can help in forming our idea of Shakespeare's
intended characterisation. To Heminges is ascribed "the line of the
old dignitary, upon occasion merry or peppery, Shakespeare's
'humorous man' ".[156]

Very interesting is the "line" represented by Thomas Pope and
passing, when he left the company, to John Lowin. Pope was
evidently himself something of a character in private life, with an
oddly-assorted household which, as Baldwin says,[157] was perhaps the
target of Ben Jonson's slanderous insinuations, but which might also
suggest affinity with the establishment of the generous-hearted Dr.
Sam. His parts include Petruchio, Speed, Armado, Quince, the
Bastard Faulconbridge, Shylock, Falstaff,[158] Benedick, Fluellen,
Casca, Jaques and Sir Toby.

The mixture is at first bewildering, but a closer inspection shows
him a master of a kind of robust, bluff comedy part. Petruchio and
Benedick have much in common; so have Sir John and Sir Toby.
He was able to be heroic as the Bastard, and even for a brief
moment tragic as Mercutio; and there is more than one echo of
Mercutio's speech in the Bastard's. To this mixture Armado and
Jaques add a touch of the fantastic. Baldwin detects a "scolding
streak" in the Bastard, Casca and Jaques "who has been considered
everything from a plain clown to the deepest philosopher. Since he
was Pope, he was exactly that". Shylock is described as "hero-
villain-clown. The Elizabethan Shylock is a characteristic part for
Pope . . . but it must be admitted that Pope would not be much at
home with the heroic figure Shylock has become". Baldwin adds his
verdict that "possibly the best composite representative of this line
is the clownish Welsh soldier Fluellen".[159] If it is true that the actors
did much to inspire Shakespeare's characterisation, then we owe a
debt of gratitude to Thomas Pope, as his rich and varied list shows.

Succeeding Pope, John Lowin takes up this same "line", but gives
it a slight twist, no doubt due to some difference of temperament or
personality: there is certainly an individuality of character in his

---

[156] Baldwin, op. cit., 235.   [157] Baldwin, op. cit., 234.
[158] The part of Falstaff is often assigned to Kemp. The two renderings would be
fundamentally different. The producer, before he finds his Falstaff, must in fact
decide whether he is looking for a Pope or a Kemp. I have little doubt that the
part was written for the actor of Pope's "line" rather than for the "creator" of
Bottom, Launcelot Gobbo and Dogberry.
[159] Baldwin, op. cit., 246.

ÆTAT. 64
A° 1640.

John Lowin
(*from the picture in the Ashmolean*)

portrait. Baldwin gives him Claudius in *Hamlet*, Falstaff in *The Merry Wives of Windsor*, Parolles, Lucio (*Measure for Measure*), Iago, Gloucester (*King Lear*), Banquo, Enobarbus. The robust bluffness takes a more sombre turn, with the change of mood of Shakespeare's composition; even the Falstaff of *The Merry Wives of Windsor* is indicative of a different personality. Perhaps the substitution of Lowin for Pope (as also of Armin for Kemp) was a contributory factor in Shakespeare's change of tone. But it is essentially the same "line" as Pope's, and it is interesting to find Iago and Enobarbus in the succession. Baldwin hits it off when he says that "the fundamental characteristic of Lowin is a certain bluff gruffness, which may be of the 'honest' soldier type, or that of the rather domineering villain".[160]

William Sly, whose portrait also shows a pronounced personality, is suited with Tybalt, Lewis (*King John*), Lorenzo, Hotspur, The Dauphin (*Henry V*), Octavius (*Julius Caesar*), Silvius (*As You Like It*), Sebastian (*Twelfth Night*), Laertes, Fenton, Claudio (*Measure for Measure*), Roderigo, Edmund, Macduff—a "line" that in most details speaks for itself, stressing youth, romantic or soldierly, calculating or impulsive, in early days the stage Frenchman, and growing in stature to the scope of Edmund and Macduff. Baldwin has an interesting suggestion that the mercurial, nervous temperament of Shakespeare's Hotspur, which is not to be found in the source, was perhaps suggested by Sly's own personal bearing.[161] In some cases, he is the rival to Burbadge's hero, and on several occasions literally crosses swords with him. Roderigo comes rather oddly in the list, and suggests that, though he is in a sense the tragic equivalent of Sir Andrew, the part and the play itself loses some force if the actor makes him wholly ridiculous.

Henry Cundall, who deserves like honour with Heminges as his collaborator in editing the 1623 Folio, though not himself one of the first seven house-keepers who built the Globe, was with Sly a member of the older generation of actors.[162] His parts show a bewildering variety and include Friar Lawrence, Antonio (*The Merchant of Venice*), Mark Antony (*Julius Caesar*), Horatio, Cassio, the Duke in *Measure for Measure* (his longest), Edgar, Malcolm, and Octavius Caesar. Mark Antony was perhaps his first big chance, and it is noteworthy that the obvious difference between this Antony and the later hero of *Antony and Cleopatra* corresponds with a difference in calibre between Cundall and Burbadge.

---

[160] Baldwin, *op. cit.*, 186, note.   [161] Baldwin, *op. cit.*, 253.
[162] Baldwin, *op. cit.*, 83, and note.

Particularly instructive is the succession of Armin to Kemp. William Kemp is credited by Baldwin with Costard, Peter (*Romeo and Juliet*), Bottom, Launcelot Gobbo, Shallow (with Cowley as Silence), *Dogberry* (with Cowley as Verges). Kemp was a famous figure of the time, whose triumphal progresses of morris-dancing to Norwich and again over the Alps to Rome suggests the fan-mail and star-gazers of modern times. His style of clowning was obviously set and formal, and his parts would no doubt have been played with much stock "business" and gagging, to the discomfiture, no doubt, of his authors. Baldwin quotes a scene from *The Pilgrimage to Parnassus* which caricatures Kemp's method when left on the stage to his own devices. Dromo draws in a clown with a rope and tells him "Clownes have bene thrust into playes by head and shoulders ever since Kempe could make a scurvey face; and therefore reason thou shouldst be drawne in with a cart-rope." "But what must I doe nowe?" says the Clown. "Why, if thou canst but draw thy mouth awrye, laye thy legg over thy staffe, sawe a peece of cheese assunder with thy dagger, lape up drinke on the earth, I warrant thee theile laught mightilie. Well, I'le turne thee loose to them; ether saie somwhat for thy selfe, or hang and be *non plus*." Left alone, the Clown faces his audience: "This is fine, y-faith! nowe, when they have noebodie to leave on the stage, they bring mee up, and, which is worse, tell mee not what I shoulde saye! Gentles, I dare saie youe looke for a fitt of mirthe . . ." and so he proceeds to do his stock turn.[163]

Robert Armin, who succeeded him in 1600, was a very different person; himself a playwright, and author of pamphlets on the subject of Fooling. We may think of him as something of a doctrinaire therefore, and it is reasonable to suppose that Shakespeare had discussions with him on the subject, and that his joining the company had an even more direct effect upon Shakespeare's composition than the collaboration of the rest of his colleagues. Armin's parts are listed thus: Touchstone, Feste, First Grave-digger, Evans, Pompey (*Measure for Measure*), Fool (*King Lear*), Porter (*Macbeth*), Clown (*Antony and Cleopatra*). The Touchstone-William scene (*As You Like It*, V. i) is interesting as being the first Armin-Cowley association: comparison with Shallow-Silence and Dogberry-Verges illuminates the difference between Kemp and Armin. Kemp and Cowley are a pair; with Armin and Cowley there is an intellectual distinction between the wit and the simpleton. The next Armin-Cowley association is Feste and Aguecheek. Duke Senior's comment on Touchstone

---

[163] Baldwin, *op. cit.*, 242.

William Sly
(*from the picture in the Gallery of Dulwich College*)

hits off Armin's style as opposed to Kemp's: "He uses his folly like a stalking-horse, and under the presentation of that he shoots his wit." [164] The idea of wiseman-fool is the novelty. Viola's comment on Feste—

> This fellow is wise enough to play the foole,
> And to do that well, craves a kinde of wit:
> He must observe their mood on whom he jests,
> The quality of persons, and the time:
> And like the Haggard, checke at every Feather
> That comes before his eye. This is a practice,
> As full of labour as a Wise-mans Art:
> For folly that he wisely shews, is fit;
> But wisemens folly falne, quite taint their wit . . .

reads like an extract from Armin's treatise.[165] Both Touchstone and Feste suggest that Shakespeare was much taken up at this time with conversations with Armin; and Jaques' long dissertation after his first meeting with Touchstone probably reflects these conversations; as also perhaps the passage about clowns in Hamlet's advice to the players.[166] The combined triumph of poet and player came five years later in Lear's Fool, of whose shrewd commentary on the follies of his misguided master we have a foretaste in Feste's "proofe" that Olivia is a fool to mourn for her brother's death. Like Viola, Kent says of him too, "This is not altogether foole my Lord." [167]

One of Baldwin's most convincing character-sketches is that of Richard Cowley, who played second fiddle to both Pope and Kemp, and afterwards to Armin. He is known to have been *Verges* to Kemp's Dogberry, and other parts assigned to him are Robert Faulconbridge, Old Gobbo, Silence, William in *As You Like It*, Aguecheek and Slender. Baldwin tells us: "Cowley seems to have been decidedly thin, and to have capitalized this characteristic for comic effect. Thus half-faced Robert has legs that are

> two such riding-rods,
> My arms, such eel-skins stuffed, my face so thin,
> That in mine ear I durst not stick a rose
> Lest men should say, "look where three farthings goes".

Aguecheek is 'a thin-faced knave', named accordingly. Slender is also labelled with this characteristic, having but 'a little whey face'.

---

[164] *As You Like It*, V. iv. 112 ff.   [165] *Twelfth Night*, III. i. 68 ff.
[166] *As You Like It*, II. vii. 13 ff.; *Hamlet*, III. ii. 43 ff.
[167] *Twelfth Night*, I. v. 62 ff.; *King Lear*, I. iv. 166.

F

Also Aguecheek's hair 'hangs like flax on a distaff', and Slender has 'a little yellow beard—a cane-coloured beard'. As Slender walks, 'does he not held up his head, as it were, and strut in his gait?' In these youthful caricatures, Cowley was represented as approximately his own age, William in *As You Like It*, for instance, being twenty-five. But this slenderness was also used for aged comic caricatures. Here are Silence, Gobbo, and Verges, this last character being one that we know from contemporary evidence was Cowley's. As this comic old man, Cowley was usually paired with Kemp; but as the comic young man he was usually connected with Pope." [168]

These are some of the leading personalities among the members of the Chamberlain's-King's company of players, whose number never rose to more than a round dozen at a single time. Among so few the choice for distribution of parts is not as difficult to make as might be expected, and Baldwin's "lines" become plausible. With a score or so of hired men, and at most, five or six boy apprentices, the full strength of the company engaged in a normal performance would be between thirty-five and forty. Of the hired men not much need here be said, except to point out that they were a very necessary part of the company, and that their functions were much varied; we have a list of twenty-one names—hardly more than names—dating from 1624, and the list is described as "Musitions and other necessary attendantes". We must think of them as playing and singing when needed, as being handymen behind the Tiring-House wall to move furniture and properties, as being at the beck and call of the Book-Keeper, often as appearing on the Platform in minor parts (parts over which Shakespeare often takes pains to give them dramatic life), or as attendants on a royal or noble personage, as armies in the field, as mobs in the streets, and used of course to frequent doubling of parts. *Julius Caesar* is a particularly interesting play from the point of view of casting—where there is a kind of cleavage half-way, the mob turning into the soldiers of the rival armies, and the rear-rank conspirators into their officers. The fairies for *A Midsummer Night's Dream* and *The Merry Wives of Windsor* would need to be specially recruited for the occasion—perhaps from one of the Choir Schools, perhaps as Chambers suggests from the musical establishment of the second Lord Hunsdon. [169] And no doubt sometimes a musician of special accomplishment would be enlisted for a particular occasion. But in general there would be a collection of about twenty hired men available, working on a wage basis, with little chance of belonging

---

[168] Baldwin, *op. cit.*, 254. *King John*, I. i. 140 ff. *Twelfth Night*, V. i. 215; I. iii. 110. *The Merry Wives of Windsor*, I. iv. 22 ff.

[169] E. K. Chambers, *William Shakespeare*, vol. ii, 86.

to the class of masters, but content to renew their contracts every two or three years with so successful a company as the Chamberlain's Men. "At least in theory," says Baldwin, "they accepted Menenius' orthodox parable of the belly, and were not ill content."[170] Their descendants in the modern theatre are more specialised in their functions: many of the Globe hired men were no doubt Johannes Factotum, and if there is any truth in the tradition mentioned by Malone that Shakespeare's "first office in the theatre was that of *Call-boy*, or prompter's attendant", then that is perhaps why—as his stagecraft shows—he had such a firm grip on the practical technique of his art.

(vi) *The Boy Actors*

But the apprentices, the boy-actors, need separate treatment; for they raise a fundamental issue in examining the art of Shakespeare's theatre. The conditions of their employment are obscure. It is tantalising to read in Baldwin that the master of an apprentice "took the boy at ten and broke him in on minor parts supplied by the dramatist. As the boy grew older, his parts become more difficult till a few years before his graduation at the age of twenty-one he was playing the leading part in his line . . ." and that "this system of training necessitated the closest co-operation on the part of the dramatist also. It was his business in co-operation with the master (of the apprentices) to supply proper parts for each youngster to begin with and develop in. He had also to be careful not to create any female part for which there was not a properly trained actor."[171] It is tantalising because Chambers will not allow us to believe in this picture. Baldwin's speculations are, he says, "vitiated by a misconception as to the nature of theatrical apprenticeship" and he will only allow us to "take the engagements to have been for terms of two or three years, rather than of seven years or longer, and not under formal indentures of apprenticeship, but, as in the case of men, ordinary contracts of service with individual sharers, backed by bonds".[172] Whatever the facts, we can readily assume that the boy-actors were carefully trained by the full members of the company, one being groomed as successor to another whose voice was "crack'd within the ring", and that if they proved apt pupils, their contracts were likely to last long enough for them to be admitted in time to full membership of the company. Many of them had long enough to wait, and some were never admitted. It is, moreover,

[170] Baldwin, *op. cit.*, 147.   [171] Baldwin, *op. cit.*, 227.
[172] E. K. Chambers, *William Shakespeare*, vol. i, 82; vol. ii, 85.

likely that some of the boys were still capable of playing female parts
at the age of twenty: and we may presume that some of the maturer
rôles were designed for players who had grown beyond the stage of
boyhood.

To dally once more with surmise—for it is easier to see in concrete
examples if a theory is plausible or not—Baldwin's conjecture gives
us Eccleston as Moth, Nerissa, Juliet's Nurse, Mrs. Quickly (*Henry IV*),
Beatrice, and after a long gap "Lord E." in *All's Well That Ends
Well;* and Goffe as Juliet, Portia, Princess (*Love's Labour's Lost*) and
Lady Mortimer, and "Lord G." in *All's Well That Ends Well;*
Rosalind and Viola are the climax of Ned Shakespeare's list of boy
parts, which also include Francis the Drawer and Doll Tearsheet.
Edmans is the "creator" of Regan, Lady Macbeth and Cleopatra.
Crosse, who plays Mrs. Quickly in *Henry V* and *Merry Wives of
Windsor*, Audrey in *As You Like It*, Maria in *Twelfth Night*, Mistress
Overdone, Queen Gertrude, and Emilia, is perhaps not in-
appropriately described in *Measure for Measure* as "A Bawd of eleven
yeares continuance".[173] With the shifting personnel of adolescence,
one would not expect here the same assurance of conjecture as with
the adult members, nor the same clear demarcation of "lines".
Nevertheless, one can play with the idea of a contrast between
Eccleston's vein of impudent merriment and Goffe's of tender
dignity; Ned Shakespeare's flair for a type of candid wit; Edmans'
for tragic intensity.

In general it must be said that Shakespeare's expectation of the
boys, as indicated by the parts he wrote for them, suggests a very
high range of accomplishment. The tragic queens of the early histories
are compounded largely of rhetoric. Juliet is a landmark, for while
her tragic development draws upon the rhetorical intensity of the
tragic characters in the histories, the background of her daily
circumstances is akin to that of the comedies. For the comic vein,
Rosalind gives us some of the tricks of the trade when she makes up
for Orlando's benefit her story of how she cured a lover of his
malady:

> Hee was to imagine me his Love, his Mistris: and I set him everie day
> to woe me. At which time would I, being but a moonish youth, greeve,
> be effeminate, changeable, longing, and liking, proud, fantastical, apish,
> shallow, inconstant, ful of teares, full of smiles; for everie passion some-
> thing, and for no passion truly any thing, as boyes and women are for the
> most part, cattle of this colour: would now like him, now loath him: then
> entertaine him, then forswear him: now weepe for him, then spit at him;
> that I drave my Sutor from his mad humor of love, to a living humor of

---

[173] *Measure for Measure*, III. ii. 212.

madness, w^c was to forsweare the ful stream of ye world, and to live in a nooke meerly Monastick: and thus I cur'd him, and this way wil I take upon mee to wash your Liver as cleane as a sound sheepes heart, that there shal not be one spot of Love in't.[174]

And there are most explicit instructions given to the boy who is to play the part of wife to Christopher Sly in the induction to *The Taming of the Shrew*.[175] One can see the comedy parts growing; from the simple sincerity of Julia in *Two Gentlemen of Verona* and the "tongues of mocking wenches" in *Love's Labour's Lost*, through the robustly boyish skirmishing of Hermia and Helena, to Portia of Belmont (the first time a boy's part was the longest in the play). When she and Nerissa speak their quick-fire rhythmical prose, they show promise already of Rosalind and Beatrice. Portia's opening scene, with its satirical mimicry, is very well suited for a boy to play, and the unaffected candour of a boy's voice can still redeem even the hackneyed "mercy" speech from the sententiousness that has overgrown it in the intervening years since it was written. For the great comedy parts, Beatrice, Rosalind, Viola, the boy must have been quick-witted and remarkably sensitive in expressing changes of mood with his voice and in his miming. It is unthinkable that the brilliant wit of Beatrice can have been done less than justice by Shakespeare's original actor, or that the known popularity of the duets between her and Benedick [176]—

> let but *Beatrice*
> And *Benedicke* be seene, loe in a trice
> The Cockpit Galleries, Boxes, all are full—

can have arisen from the gauche antics of a boy-girl such as we saw pilloried in a recent Shakespearian film. It is perhaps less astonishing to us in this generation who have been shown over and over again on the films, from France, from Germany, from Italy, from our own studios, the powers of children in acting rôles of great intensity to wring our hearts, and their versatility in making us laugh and weep with the sincerity of their playing. Anyone who has seen *Poil de Carotte*, *Mädchen in Uniform*, *Shoe Shine* or *The Fallen Idol*, will be ready to believe that the acting of the Globe boys was not the least moving part of the performance, and will understand why it was that the boys' companies were sometimes a menace to their adult rivals.

It has often been pointed out that the trick of male disguise is a

---

[174] *As You Like It*, III. ii. 433 ff.
[175] *The Taming of the Shrew*, Induction. I. 105 ff.
[176] Leonard Digges, Commendatory Verses to Shakespeare's *Poems* (1640), reproduced in E. K. Chambers' *William Shakespeare*, vol. ii, 232 ff.

device to suit the convention, but we should notice too the ingenuity with which Shakespeare exploits the device for his comic purposes. Portia tells Nerissa

> Ile prove the prettier fellow of the two,
> And weare my dagger with the braver grace,
> And speake betweene the change of man and boy,
> With a reede voyce, and turne two minsing steps
> Into a manly stride.[177]

Viola, becoming suddenly aware of Olivia's passion, cries "Fortune forbid my out-side have not charm'd her," and there is a special piquancy in the boy-player's embarrassed realisation "I am the man".[178] In the dénouement of *The Merry Wives of Windsor*, while Anne Page is away with her Fenton, Slender is fobbed off with "a great lubberly boy" and Dr. Caius finds that he has married a "Garsoon".[179] Shakespeare is never afraid of reminding us that there is a positive pleasure in the very fact of make-believe. One of his boldest strokes of opportunism is Cleopatra's indignant outcry, as she contemplates the prospect of being taken by Octavius in triumph to Rome—

> The quicke Comedians
> Extemporally will stage us, and present
> Our Alexandrian Revels: *Anthony*
> Shall be brought drunken forth, and I shall see
> Some squeaking *Cleopatra* Boy my greatnesse
> I'th' posture of a Whore.[180]

That he can remind us of the convention with so much confidence is an indication of his own trust in the plausibility of the boys' acting: there would be no point in the irony (rather a danger of its being turned on the players themselves) if we were not for the moment under the spell.

The last of these examples is from a tragedy, and from a tragic passage in a tragedy that has many comic episodes. We may think, when we come to consider *Macbeth* in detail, that the deliberate "unsexing" of the fiendish queen is a kind of tragic equivalent of the male disguise of comedy. She and Goneril and Regan are easily within the range of a boy's expression—primitive cruelty, is it true to say? coming more easily than the more civilised emotions. The remarkable thing—but remarkable only until we remember that Shakespeare was a practical man of the theatre and knew his

---

[177] *The Merchant of Venice*, III. iv. 64 ff.   [178] *Twelfth Night*, II. ii. 26,
[179] *The Merry Wives of Windsor*, V. v. 202, 228.
[180] *Antony and Cleopatra*, V. ii. 215 ff.

material—is that the love scenes too are so written that they can be
easily played by boys. Granville-Barker has an admirable passage on
this theme [181]: ". . . it is Shakespeare's constant care," he says, "to
demand nothing of a boy-actress that might turn to unseemliness or
ridicule," and he goes on to show how discreetly the part of Juliet is
written with such intent, and contrasts Shakespeare's handling of
Cleopatra "with a Cleopatra planned to the advantage of the actress
of to-day". I would add as an example the wonderfully cunning way
in which Shakespeare portrays the love of Hotspur and Lady Percy
—his absent-minded brusqueness, her teasing, eager anxiety, "In-
deede Ile breake thy little finger *Harry*, if thou wilt not tel me true";
his bluster, "Away, away, you trifler: Love, I love thee not, I care
not for thee *Kate :* this is no world To play with Mammets, and to tilt
with lips"; and then, when she insists, "Do ye not love me? . . . Nay
tell me if thou speak'st in jest, or no," his tender parry, "Come, wilt
thou see me ride? And when I am a-horsebacke, I will sweare I love
thee infinitely." Subtler still is the comedy of the contrasted pairs in
Glendower's hall—Hotspur and his Lady bickering as before, and
the sentimental parting of the others stripped of embarrassment
because to speak one word to his wife Mortimer must depend on his
father-in-law as interpreter. How easy is this scene for the boy-singer-
player to act! [182] The midnight encounter between Brutus and
Portia is more straightforward and just as easy.[183] But it will be
noticed that in no case does the poet leave us in doubt of the real
warmth of affection between husband and wife. Granville-Barker
continues: "Shakespeare, artist that he was, turned this limitation to
account, made loss into a gain. Feminine charm—of which the
modern stage makes such capital—was a medium denied him. So his
men and women encounter upon a plane where their relation is
made rarer and intenser by poetry, or enfranchised in a humour
which surpasses more primitive love-making. And thus, perhaps, he
was helped to discover that the true stuff of tragedy and of the
liveliest comedy lies beyond sensual bounds. His studies of women
seem often to be begun from some spiritual paces beyond the point at
which a modern dramatist leaves off. Curious that not a little of the
praise lavished upon the beauty and truth of them—mainly by
women—may be due to their having been written to be played by
boys!" This paragraph, eloquent and true as it is of nine-tenths of
Shakespeare's creation in this kind, ignores the few occasions when
his story necessitates his stressing the ugliness of sensual passion. But

---

[181] Granville-Barker, *Prefaces to Shakespeare*, First Series, Introduction, xxviii f.
[182] 1 *Henry IV*, II. iii. 41 ff.; III. i. 191 ff.
[183] *Julius Caesar*, II. i. 234 ff.

even there he makes no embarrassment for his boy-actors. The
lechery of Claudius puts no strain upon the player of Gertrude: we
witness no amorous *tête-à-tête;* if we may borrow from Iago, "it were
a tedious difficulty, I thinke, To bring them to that Prospect"; once
only do we see them alone, and then in a state of panic immediately
after the death of Polonius. On the other hand, Shakespeare is ruthless and unsparing in his verbal picture, whether in metaphor—

> Nay, but to live
> In the ranke sweat of an enseamed bed,
> Stew'd in Corruption; honying and making love
> Over the nasty Stye . . .

or in objective statement—

> Let the blunt [*read* bloat] King tempt you againe to bed,
> Pinch Wanton on your cheeke, call you his Mouse,
> And let him for a paire of reechie kisses,
> Or padling in your necke with his damn'd Fingers
> Make you to rovell all this matter out.[184]

When Cressida bandies pleasantries with the Greek chiefs on her
return from Troy, Nestor describes her as "A woman of quick
sence", but Ulysses is uncompromising in his judgment:

> Fie, fie, upon her:
> Ther's a language in her eye, her cheeke, her lip;
> Nay, her foote speakes, her wanton spirites looke out
> At every joynt, and motive of her body:
> Oh these encounterers so glib of tongue,
> That give a coasting welcome ere it comes;
> And wide unclaspe the tables of their thoughts,
> To every tickling reader: set them downe,
> For sluttish spoyles of opportunitie;
> And daughters of the game.[185]

These last two examples give us a hint of the secret of Shakespeare's method: he creates his feminine characters, as indeed the
whole of his drama, by means of the words: here especially they are
the creation of the poetic drama. We can use again the analogy of
the white screen, suggested above in discussing unlocalisation.[186] The
neutral personalities of the boy players are a white screen upon
which the poet projects the images of Rosalind, Viola, Beatrice,

---

[184] *Hamlet*, III. iv. 91 ff., 182 ff.
[185] *Troilus and Cressida*, IV. iv. 54 ff. Dover Wilson expresses the opinion that
even Doll Tearsheet was well within the scope of the boy-actor (*The Fortunes of
Falstaff*, 108).
[186] See above, p. 108.

Lady Macbeth and Cleopatra. The actress will, perhaps, unconsciously and instinctively, paint something of her own upon the screen which cannot do other than blur the clear image of the poet. Desmond McCarthy says something of the kind when in criticising a performance with boy-actors he remarks that it is "interesting to see what Shakespeare took for granted: boys impersonating women. The effect of that convention was by diminishing personal interest to direct the attention of the spectator towards the character impersonated rather than upon the impersonator. This also was in harmony with that technique which required the actor never to allow the spectator to forget completely that he was 'acting', but on the contrary, to draw additional pleasure from his skill. And it may be of some significance that the decline of poetical drama to which that technique was so admirably suited, begins when women begin to take women's parts".[187] I have seen a Desdemona, unnaturally propped on a couch under a powerful spotlight, affronting the gallery with her coiffure that had "woven A golden mesh t'intrap the hearts of men Faster then gnats in cobwebs". This is the unquestioned privilege of the leading lady. The boy Wilson at the first performance would be given no such consideration: hardly visible in the depths of the Study, he would yet exist for us in the clearest and most poignant of pictures as no spotlight and make-up artist, as no camera even, could possibly show us:

> that whiter skin of hers, then Snow,
> And smooth as Monumentall Alablaster . . .

It is the voice of Burbadge that paints Desdemona for us—

> Thou cunning'st Patterne of excelling Nature, . . .
> When I have pluck'd thy Rose,
> I cannot give it vitall growth againe,
> It needs must wither. Ile smell it on the Tree.
> Oh Balmy breath, that dost almost perswade
> Justice to breake her Sword.[188]

The poetry gives us not only the impression of Desdemona's innocent sleep, but also "the pity of it". The actress, too often, offers us into the bargain a hair-do, a frock, a figure, and her personal charm. And it is in the nature of man to be distracted by such irrelevance

---

[187] The quotation is from an article in *The New Statesman* for July 12th, 1947. The decline began as early as the Restoration, and is already fully developed in Dryden's 1667 version of *The Tempest*. See Harold Child's description in *A Companion to Shakespeare Studies* (Cambridge), 331, 332. It is interesting to compare McCarthy's last sentence with the remark of Collier quoted on p. 72 above.

[188] *Othello*, V. ii. 4 f.; 11 ff.

from the point—which is not that she is beautiful or charming, but
that she is like a rose (as innocent and as easily destructible) and that
Othello who knows how easily the rose will wither, takes her inno-
cence for seeming which is really truth; and there's the pity of it.

Ultimately, of course, this condemnation of the poor leading lady
is applicable to our male actors too—though in a lesser degree, for
the instinct to obtrude themselves is less strong with them. But the
fact remains that they too, most of them, will not let Shakespeare
have his way; they too will not recognise that the essence of the
poetic drama is in the words and that their job is to speak and mime
the drama which is complete in the words—their meaning, their
emphasis, their style, their phrasing, their rhythm, their mood, their
characterisation—and to interpose nothing of their own irrelevant
invention.

(vii) *Characterisation* (recapitulated)

We may now return from this digression among the individual
personalities of the Chamberlain's Men, to consider and summarise
their practice in characterisation. We have taken note of the old-
men parts of Heminges, the Pope-Lowin "line" of robust bluffness
hardly changing in the succession, the *jeune premier* of Sly, the Kemp
"line" transformed in Armin, a hint of repetitive parts among the
boy actors. The common denominator in each case is the "line" of
the actor—made up of his voice, his person, his habitual mannerisms,
his chosen style of mimicry; the variations are Shakespeare's. Let it
not be thought that each actor could play but one type of part: the
lists assert the contrary; and it is not only Burbadge who shows considerable versatility; the "lines" are more elastic than this. But we
are surely right to follow Baldwin in studying the individuals of the
company, and if we were rebuilding a Shakespearian repertory, we
should provide a representative capable of performing each of the
main "lines". The capabilities and limitations of his principal actors
were as much part of Shakespeare's data as the conditions of his
playhouse.

We can go further than this. Professor E. E. Stoll opens his *Art and
Artifice in Shakespeare* with a forthright declaration: "The core of
tragedy (and of comedy too, for that matter) is situation; and a
situation is a character in contrast, and perhaps also in conflict, with
other characters or with circumstances. We have ordinarily been
taught that with the author character comes first and foremost, not
only in importance but in point of time, and (cause of no little confusion) that the action is only its issue. But there is no drama until

the character is conceived in a complication; and in the dramatist's mind it is so conceived at the outset." [189] For the moment, we are more concerned with the actors than with the poet, and, concurring with Stoll, we may notice that his view chimes with our interpretation of the typical speech-headings and the descriptive cast-lists of the Folio.[190] If the prompt-copy speaks of Capulet and Lady Capulet as *Father* and *Mother*, it stands to reason that not only the author but also the players were accustomed to think of these (and other) characters "in a complication"; that if Heminges were asked what part he played in *Romeo and Juliet*, he would answer instinctively "I'm the girl's father". Indeed, it would hardly be necessary to ask him: he was so used to playing the part of "the girl's father". Nothing is more revealing in this connection than the case of the Countess in *All's Well That Ends Well*, already cited.[191] The boy-actor of this rôle is all the time playing his part in the story. We must in fact think of the Chamberlain's Men as playing not with such psychological subtlety as to provoke us to speculate on the life of their characters before and after the action of the play and when they are off the stage, but simply as figures, active or passive, agent or sufferer, in a drama, made up of certain defined episodes or situations, beyond which the characters do not exist.

We shall have cause to see in the next chapter that Shakespeare's stagecraft works on such lines as these, and that he regularly thinks of his main characters with an insistent relevance only in their relation to his story. The truth is that the immediate moment is always Shakespeare's first concern, and he is careless of implications and overtones. Indeed, sometimes, if he wants his actors to create an effect of mood or atmosphere by poetical means, he will ask them to speak altogether "out of character". The night-alarm at the opening of *Othello* is created by the player of Iago's part: "Heere is her Fathers house," says Roderigo, "Ile call aloud." "Doe," cries Iago, "with like timerous accent, and dire yell, As when (by Night and Negligence) the Fire is spied in populous Citties." The same player paints Othello for us in the pangs of jealousy:

> Not Poppy, nor Mandragora,
> Nor all the drowsie Syrrups of the world
> Shall ever medicine thee to that sweete sleepe
> Which thou owd'st yesterday.

The murderer of Banquo waxes lyrical to create the atmosphere of dangerous dusk:

---

[189] E. E. Stoll, *Art and Artifice in Shakespeare*, 1. [190] See above, pp. 26 f.
[191] See above, pp. 154 f.

> The West yet glimmers with some streakes of Day.
> Now spurres the lated Traveller apace,
> To gayne the timely Inne . . .

Gertrude's vivid recital of Ophelia's drowning, the bleeding sergeant more concerned to show us the prowess of Macbeth carving out his passage through the battle than to display his own fainting condition,[192] these are all cases where characterisation is subordinated to another effect in Shakespeare's dramatic purpose.

We shall also see in the next chapter that Shakespeare's method of characterisation changed, with his changing motive, during the progress from *Henry V* to *Hamlet*, and in the following years which may be described in Professor Toynbee's phrase as the poet's years of "Withdrawal-and-Return". Always restlessly experimental, he tired of the objectively-drawn figure, made vivid by an unerring choice of significant detail, and taught himself to portray the heart of man. The desire to do so was already present perhaps in the creation of the merchant Antonio's unplumbed melancholy. We can see the contrast clearly in a comparison of Lady Percy's account of her dead Hotspur with King Henry's description of his son [193]: Harry Percy is one of the most vivid examples of Shakespeare's objective portraiture; Harry Plantagenet, although after his coronation his development causes general disappointment among the critics, nevertheless contains, in certain passages of all three plays in which he figures, the seeds of Brutus, Hamlet and Macbeth.[194] Yet even these inwardly-conceived characters are contained wholly in the spoken words of the poet's text, and we gain nothing—we lose rather—by turning aside from them to speculation on a life for the character independent of those words.

Whether he was dealing with the earlier objective or the later "inward" character, Burbadge, I think, did not digress into psychological speculations such as are supposed to have given distinction to many a new interpretation of Hamlet (for instance) since his day. His manner of acting realised that the character was already there, complete in the words the poet gives him; that he, like the poet, must stick to the matter in hand and give the fullest force to the immediate moment. Consider the closet-scene: it is no part of the player's business to bother his head about the previous relationship of Hamlet to his mother, whether he was fonder of his father in his life-

---

[192] *Othello*, I. i. 74 ff.; III. iii. 331 ff. *Macbeth*, III. iii. 5 ff.; I. ii. 7 ff. *Hamlet*, IV. vii. 167 ff.

[193] See above, pp. 149 f.

[194] E. M. W. Tillyard expresses such an opinion in his *Shakespeare's History Plays*, 313 f.

time, whether he was neglected by his mother in childhood, whether he had an "Œdipus-complex" or some other inhibition. If he wants to know with what feelings and with what aspect he must burst into his mother's presence, he has his clear instructions in a previous soliloquy:

> 'Tis now the verie witching time of night,
> When Churchyards yawne, and Hell it selfe breaths out
> Contagion to this world. Now could I drink hot blood,
> And do such bitter businesse as the day
> Would quake to looke on. Soft now, to my Mother:
> Oh Heart, loose not thy Nature; let not ever
> The Soule of *Nero*, enter this firme bosome:
> Let me be cruell, not unnaturall,
> I will speake Daggers to her, but use none . . .[195]

This is the mood Shakespeare asks for, and, if we are not properly frightened at the beginning of the closet-scene, it may be partly the Queen's fault, but it will also be Hamlet's for not making the most of the preparatory atmosphere of these lines. Burbadge, we may be sure, confronted the boy Crosse with incisive wit, with violent action, with a flood of rhetoric, launching the passionate rhythm, and then at the climax of his passion bringing in brilliant miming to reinforce the impression of the supernatural presence: the Ghost scene is explicitly created in the words of all three speakers; Burbadge, Crosse, and Shakespeare himself (as the Ghost) have but to follow the instructions contained in the dialogue, to harrow us with fear and wonder. The Ghost describes the Queen:

> But looke, Amazement on thy Mother sits;
> O step betweene her, and her fighting Soule,
> Conceit in weakest bodies, strongest workes.

The Queen describes Hamlet:

> Alas, how is't with you?
> That you bend your eye on vacancie,
> And with their corporall ayre do hold discourse.
> Forth at your eyes, your spirits wildely peepe,
> And as the sleeping Soldiours in th' Alarme,
> Your bedded haire, like life in excrements,
> Start up, and stand an end.

And Hamlet describes the Ghost in moving terms:

> look you how pale he glares,

---

[195] *Hamlet*, III. ii. 413 ff.

and

> Do not looke upon me,
> Least with this pitteous action you convert
> My sterne effects:

and again

> looke how it steals away:
> My Father in his habite, as he lived,
> Looke where he goes even now out at the Portall.[196]

It is almost as if Shakespeare was bent on leaving nothing to chance. All this detailed description is needed where, with modern stage-lighting and make-up, or with the "close-up" of the cinema, it would not be. The poetry takes the place of the lighting and the close focus. The limitation of mechanical means in the Elizabethan theatre is not wholly a disadvantage: for this very limitation breeds the poetic drama: the necessity of description gives the poet the opportunity to comment as well as to describe, to illuminate with metaphor and imagery, to suggest our mood. For instance, the words "Forth at your eyes, your spirits wildely peepe" produce an impression that no amount of grimacing could convey with certainty. The fullness of Shakespeare's description and comment is what makes many of his admirers content to read him in the armchair. It also makes the producer's and actor's task quite unmistakably clear, if only they will aim at Shakespeare's interpretation, and not seek to impose their own.

We shall return in the next chapter to this habit of "close-up" description, which is seemingly implicit in the technique of the poetic drama. Meanwhile let it be observed that it arises directly from the conditions of the playhouse. Daylight, coming mostly from overhead, though making quite clear what was happening and which character was which (in contrast to the not infrequent confusion among our elaborate lighting effects), would not illuminate the details of facial expression, as our use of strong make-up and powerful lights does. No doubt make-up was not unknown in the Elizabethan playhouse: one thinks of Othello's complexion, Bardolph's nose, Piramus' beard. But its purpose would be broad disguise rather than the revelation of facial expression or subtle visual illusion. So these, like much of the atmospheric effect, had to be supplied by the poet's words.

In summary, it is possible to draw a parallel between the essential simplicity of the stage, its furniture and properties, on the one hand, with the subtleties of Shakespeare's atmospheric transformations of

---

[196] *Hamlet*, III. iv. 111 ff.

it, and on the other, the broad lines of the actor's impersonation, with the subtleties of Shakespeare's elaboration of it. The actor had his "line", allowing of considerable variation within itself (and Shakespeare was quick to take advantage of this latitude); he also knew, every time he went on the stage, the business he was to transact, the part he was to play in carrying forward the plot of the story: to this he stuck with a clear-cut relevance, which was characteristic also of his author. I believe this is true even of so highly complex a characterisation as Hamlet, and that if your actor remembers the business, the agenda, of each scene (quite literally *what it is about*)—then, provided he has the skill and grace of voice and gesture that Burbadge had, he will give a capital performance of Shakespeare's sweet prince.

(viii) *The Method in Practice*

To recapitulate this chapter on the acting tradition of the Chamberlain's Men, we may now attempt a detailed illustration of the method in practice. What did the Chamberlain's Men do? This is the question we must ask ourselves every time we set about plotting a play in the manner of a performance at the Globe.

Each play, each scene, will present its own problems, and we must use every trick of the detective's art to solve them. Hints are often there for the observant. Corin in *As You Like It* lets us know in a later scene that his charming conversation with Silvius on the theme of love was conducted while sitting "on the Turph": there are clues here for deciding on the scene rotation—for the turf is likely to be in the Study—and the positioning of the earlier scene.[197] When Sir Walter Blunt visits Hotspur as envoy from the King before Shrewsbury field, one of the complaints that Harry Percy utters is that the King

Rated my Unckle from the Councell-Boord.

He is clearly referring to the occasion when earlier in the play Worcester is snubbed by the King:

You have good leave to leave us. When we need
Your use and Counsell, we shall send for you.

Thus we know that the earlier scene opens with a council of state, with the King and his nobles sitting round the table set in the Study.[198] It is possible to multiply such clues, which the producer with the single-minded purpose of discovering Shakespeare's intention

---

[197] *As You Like It*, III. iv. 50; II. iv. 22 ff.
[198] 1 *Henry IV*, IV. iii. 99; I. iii. 20 f. See above, p. 41 (and note 39).

will not find hard to detect; though we shall not always be so
lucky as when we catch Jaques with his food half-way to his mouth.
"Forbeare, and eate no more," cries Orlando, to startle the company; "Why I have eate none yet," retorts Jaques, with the
sang-froid of the cynic; and no doubt Pope proceeded to stuff his
mouth in spite of the stranger's desperate prohibition.[199] We must
look out especially for subsequent descriptions of a past scene, such
as Benvolio's account of the death of Mercutio and Tybalt, Puck's
version of the clowns' rehearsal and the "translation" of Bottom, or
Iago's picture of the brawl in which Cassio lost his reputation.[200] The
Constable of France, refuting the Dauphin's opinion of England's
new King as a "vaine giddie shallow humorous Youth", says:

> Question your Grace the late Embassadors,
> With what great State he heard their Embassie,
> How well supply'd with Noble Councellors . . .

A due consideration of this comment on the earlier scene might have
spared us the farcical tomfoolery which was presented on the screen
as the Chamberlain's Men's version of King Henry among his
peers.[201] Sometimes the clue precedes the scene in which it may be
applied; as when Hamlet warns us that he means "To put an
Anticke disposition on," or in his preparations for the play that he
will rivet his eyes to his uncle's face; or as, when Lady Macbeth
looks forward to the discovery of Duncan's murder, saying, "we shall
make our Griefes and Clamor rore, Upon his Death", she gives us a
hint of Macbeth's manner when he protests too loudly his horror at
the deed.[202]

So much in general terms about the method of detection. Now let
us take a specific example, and set about reconstructing what the
Chamberlain's Men did with the scene of Caesar's murder. In this
case we are not short of documentary evidence. We have two
separate accounts by Antony after the event: he speaks in the Forum
of the blow of Brutus' dagger:

> This was the most unkindest cut of all.
> For when the Noble *Caesar* saw him stab,
> Ingratitude, more strong then Traitors armes,
> Quite vanquish'd him: then burst his Mighty heart,
> And in his Mantle, muffling up his face,
> Even at the Base of *Pompeyes* Statue
> (Which all the while ran blood) great *Caesar* fell . . .

[199] *As You Like It*, II. vii. 88.
[200] These three examples are mentioned above, p. 127.
[201] *King Henry V*, II. iv. 28 ff.; I. ii.
[202] *Hamlet*, I. v. 172; III. ii. 90. *Macbeth*, I. vii. 78 f.; II. iii. 98 ff.

and he taunts the conspirators before Philippi because they uttered
no warning threat before they attacked their victim:

> Villains: you did not so, when your vile daggers
> Hackt one another in the sides of *Caesar*:
> You shew'd your teethes like Apes,
> And fawn'd like Hounds,
> And bow'd like Bondmen, kissing *Caesars* feete;
> Whil'st damned *Caska*, like a Curre, behinde
> Strooke *Caesar* on the necke.[203]

We have moreover some most graphic descriptions in Plutarch,
which suggest much of the stage-business which Shakespeare would
presumably have passed on to the Book-Keeper and to his fellow
actors. We can read, as Shakespeare read, of how "Popilius Laena,
after he had saluted Brutus and Cassius more friendlie then he was
wont to doe: he rounded softlie in their eares, and told them, I pray
the goddes you may goe through with that you have taken in hande,
but withall, dispatche I reade you, for your enterprise is bewrayed.
When he had sayd, he presentlie departed from them, and left them
both affrayed that their conspiracie woulde out".[204] We hear of "the
great prease and multitude of people that followed him" and how
Caesar "received all the supplications that were offered him, and
that he gave them straight to his men that were about him".[205]
Plutarch continues: "When Caesar came out of his litter: Popilius
Laena, that had talked before with Brutus and Cassius, and had
prayed the goddes they might bring this enterprise to passe: went
unto Caesar, and kept him a long time with a talke. Caesar gave
good eare unto him. Wherefore the conspirators (if so they shoulde
be called) not hearing what he sayd to Caesar, but conjecturing by
that he had tolde them a little before, that his talke was none other
but the verie discoverie of their conspiracie: they were affrayed
everie man of them, and one looking in an others face, it was easie
to see that they all were of a minde, that it was no tarying for them
till they were apprehended, but rather that they should kill them
selves with their owne hands. And when Cassius and certeine other
clapped their handes on their swordes under their gownes to draw
them: Brutus marking the countenaunce and gesture of Laena, and
considering that he did use him selfe rather like an humble and
earnest suter, then like an accuser: he sayd nothing to his companion
(bicause there were many amongst them that were not of the

---

[203] *Julius Caesar*, III. ii. 188 ff.; V. i. 39 ff.
[204] Plutarch's *Life of Brutus* (North's Translation, 1579).
[205] Plutarch's *Life of Caesar*.

conspiracie) but with a pleasaunt countenaunce encouraged Cassius. And immediatlie after, Laena went from Caesar, and kissed his hande: which shewed plainlie that it was for some matter concerning him selfe, that he had held him so long in talke. Nowe all the Senators being entred first into this place or chapter house where the counsell should be kept: all the other conspirators straight stoode about Caesars chaire, as if they had some thing to have sayd unto him. And some say, that Cassius casting his eyes upon Pompeys image, made his prayer unto it, as if it had bene alive. Trebonius on thother side, drewe Antonius atoside, as he came into the house where the Senate sate, and helde him with a long talke without. When Caesar was come into the house, all the Senate rose to honor him at his comming in. So when he was set, the conspirators flocked about him, and amongst them they presented one Tullius Cimber, who made humble sute for the calling home againe of his brother that was banished. They all made as though they were intercessors for him, and tooke him by the handes, and kissed his head and brest. Caesar at the first, simplie refused their kindnesse and intreaties: but afterwardes, perceiving they still pressed on him, he violently thrust them from him. Then Cimber with both his hands plucked Caesars gowne over his shoulders, and Caska that stoode behinde him, drew his dagger first, and strake Caesar upon the shoulder, but gave him no great wound. Caesar feeling him selfe hurt, tooke him straight by the hande he held his dagger in, and cried out in Latin: O traitor, Casca, what doest thou? Casca on thother side cried in Graeke, and called his brother to helpe him. So divers running on a heape together to flie uppon Caesar, he looking about him to have fledde, sawe Brutus with a sworde drawen in his hande readie to strike at him: then he let Cascaes hande goe, and casting his gowne over his face, suffered everie man to strike at him that woulde. Then the conspirators thronging one upon an other bicause everie man was desirous to have a cut at him, so many swords and daggers lighting upon one bodie, one of them hurte an other, and among them Brutus caught a blowe on his hande, bicause he would make one in murdering of him, and all the rest also were every man of them bloudied." [206] A second account, in the *Life of Caesar*, is no less graphic in detail: "So Caesar comming into the house, all the Senate stoode up on their feete to doe him honor. Then parte of Brutus companie and confederates stoode rounde about Caesars chayer, and parte of them also came towardes him, as though they made sute with Metellus Cimber, to call home his brother againe from banish-

[206] Plutarch's *Life of Brutus*.

ment: and thus prosecuting still their sute, they followed Caesar, till
he was set in his chayer. Who, denying their petitions, and being
offended with them one after an other, bicause the more they were
denied, the more they pressed upon him, and were the earnester
with him: Metellus at length, taking his gowne with both his
handes, pulled it over his necke, which was the signe geven the confederates to sette apon him. Then Casca behinde him strake him in
the necke with his sword, howbeit the wounde was not great nor
mortall, bicause it seemed, the feare of such a develishe attempt did
amaze him, and take his strength from him, that he killed him not at
the first blowe. But Caesar turning straight unto him, caught hold of
his sword, and held it hard: and they both cried out, Caesar in
Latin: O vile traitor Casca, what doest thou? and Casca in Greeke
to his brother, Brother, helpe me. At the beginning of this sturre,
they that were present, not knowing of the conspiracie were so
amazed with the horrible sight they sawe: that they had no power to
flie, neither to helpe him, not so much, as once to make any outcrie.
They on thother side that had conspired his death, compassed him
in on everie side with their swordes drawen in their handes, that
Caesar turned him no where, but he was striken at by some, and still
had naked swords in his face, and was hacked and mangeled amonge
them, as a wilde beaste taken of hunters. For it was agreed among
them, that every man should geve him a wound, bicause all their
partes should be in this murther: and then Brutus him selfe gave him
one wounde about his privities. Men reporte also, that Caesar did
still defende him selfe against the rest, running everie waye with his
bodie: but when he sawe Brutus with his sworde drawen in his
hande, then he pulled his gowne over his heade, and made no more
resistaunce, and was driven either casually, or purposedly, by the
counsell of the conspirators, against the base whereupon Pompeys
image stoode, which ranne all of a goare bloude, till he was slaine.
Thus it seemed, that the image tooke just revenge of Pompeys
enemie, being throwen downe on the ground at his feete, and yelding
up his ghost there, for the number of wounds he had upon him. For
it is reported, that he had three and twenty wounds apon his body:
and divers of the conspirators did hurt them selves, striking one body
with so many blowes." [207]

It is plain that the scene starts on the Platform and that the Study
curtains are parted as Caesar approaches the Capitol [208]: they reveal
a "state"—probably in this case a dais with chairs for Caesar himself
and a senator on either side. Casca's first blow must fall on Caesar

from behind, as he sits on the dais. Yet Caesar's dead body must be down-stage during what follows, first because it is the focus of attention at Antony's entry and when he makes his passionate address to it after the conspirators have gone; further, because the mechanical need for the entry of Octavius' servant at the end of the scene is that the body must be carried off ("Lend me your hand") and this would not be necessary if the body still lay in the Study. The logical place for the body to lie is beside one of the fore-stage Pillars—that is, at the base of Pompey's statue. How did it get there? The answer is provided by Plutarch, whose stage-business is just what is wanted.

If we cast the play according to Baldwin's list, there is new life and interest in the characterisation. Here is Burbadge exploring new ground as the reflective Brutus; here is Phillips playing Cassius with the cutting edge which he will turn to comic purpose in the same year as Malvolio; Heminges bringing to Caesar his natural gravity so near the borderline of the absurd; Pope giving life to the blunt fellow Casca, who was "quick Mettle, when he went to Schoole"; Cundall grasping his first big chance as Antony. Within the limits of this scene, there is ample scope for creative speech, and the stature of Caesar and consequently the greatness of his fall will depend largely upon the verbal skill of Heminges: there is opportunity for miming in the movements of the conspirators, their furtive manœuvring from the perimeter towards the Study, with Phillips perhaps "casting his eyes upon Pompeys image" and making his prayer to it, "as if it had bene alive", and their assumed servility, taking Caesar by the hands, and kissing his head and breast; vigorous miming too in the violent and prolonged struggle of the murder itself with its three distinct phases. Moreover, the three-dimensional positioning of the Globe stage is fully illustrated in the approach to the senate-house from the street, and the expressively dramatic episode of Popilius Lena's false alarm.

Let us then annotate the prompt-book, plotting the scene as the Book-Keeper might have done.

The Prompt Book
Annotated

Immediately after *Portia's* distracted retreat between the closed curtains of the Study, the crowd (A-H) surge in from R door, bringing with them the *Soothsayer* and *Artemidorus*: their excited murmurs and a long flourish of trumpets accompany a brisk processional entry from L door. *Caesar* is confronted with the *Soothsayer* between the two pillars, *Decius*, who came to fetch him to the senate-house, is still at his elbow, ready to intervene by drawing attention to the suit of *Trebonius*, just behind him.

10   *What, is the fellow mad?* The curtains of the Study drawn quickly to disclose the furniture of the senate-house—a dais with three chairs, the central one for *Caesar*; broad steps in front, and other steps at both ends of the dais.

11–12   *Cassius's* question and the description in Plutarch suggest what happened here. *Caesar's* progress to the Capitol is checked in midstage by a throng of petitioners kneeling in his way: this in dumb-show forms a background to the whispered dialogue of the panic-stricken conspirators at the front of the platform. The passage from the street to the Capitol is (as Granville-Barker makes clear, *Prefaces to Shakespeare*, First Series, 122) an excellent example of the simple effectiveness of Shakespeare's stagecraft. When *Caesar* reaches his "state", the crowd disperse to right and left, leaving a clear approach for the conspirators to their object.

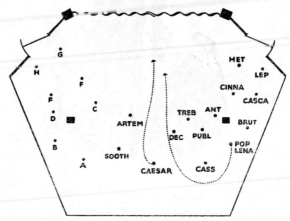

Positioning: *The Ides of March are come*

13–30   The details of both background and foreground are made clear in the dialogue—the movements of *Popilius*, the moment when *Caesar* and he are in conversation (conspicuous by being raised on the dais), the departure of *Antony* and *Trebonius*; the approach of the suitors to *Caesar*, first *Metellus*, then *Decius*; *Casca*, at *Cinna's* prompting, creeps stealthily behind the dais. *Cinna* the last to approach *Caesar* (line 74), can lend a touch of terror to the foreground by holding his dagger ready behind his back.

Flourish

Enter *Caesar, Brutus, Cassius, Caska, Decius, Metellus, Trebonius, Cynna, Antony,
Lepidus, Artimedorus, Publius,* and the *Soothsayer.*

Caes. The Ides of March are come.
Sooth. I *Caesar,* but not gone.
Art. Haile *Caesar*: Read this Scedule.
Deci. Trebonius doth desire you to ore-read
    (At your best leysure) this his humble suite.   5
Art. O *Caesar,* reade mine first: for mine's a suite
 That touches *Caesar* neerer. Read it great *Caesar.*
Caes. What touches us our selfe, shall be last serv'd.
Art. Delay not *Caesar,* read it instantly.

I wish your enterprize to day may thrive

Caes. What, is the fellow mad?   10
Pub. Sirra, give place.
Cassi. What, urge you your Petitions in the street?
 Come to the Capitoll.
Popil. I wish your enterprize to day may thrive.
Cassi. What enterprize *Popillius?*
Popil. Fare you well.
Bru. What said *Popillius Lena?*   15
Cassi. He wisht to day our enterprize might thrive:
 I feare our purpose is discovered.
Bru. Looke how he makes to *Caesar*: marke him.
Cassi. Caska be sodaine, for we feare prevention.
 Brutus what shall be done? If this be knowne,   20
 Cassius or *Caesar* never shall turne backe,
 For I will slay my selfe.

31   *Are we all ready?* The crowd, chidden by *Publius* in front of *Caesar* and
     Popilius behind him, have parted to left and right, and remain
     quiescent until the moment of the murder: a discreet actor in the
     part of *Artemidorus* can help to increase the tension by his ill-
     concealed anxiety: but the crowd are an inconspicuous frame to the
     picture of *Caesar's* greatness, raised by Shakespeare to its fullest
     stature in preparation for the catastrophic fall.

    Caesar's last two speeches have the rhythm and diction of greatness: there
is no mistaking Shakespeare's intention to build up the stature of the
dictator, so that we may afterwards recognise the dramatic force of Antony's

> *Are all thy Conquests, Glories, Triumphes, Spoiles,*
> *Shrunke to this little Measure?*

and in the Forum speech, his

> *O what a fall was there, my countrymen?*

But I am constant as the Northern Starre

47–48   Producers here must choose between the reading of the Folio and
        that other version which Ben Jonson scorned, but which may well
        seem to other critics not only characteristic of Shakespeare, but
        also preferable.

> *Know, Caesar doth not wrong, but with good cause,*
> *Nor without cause will he be satisfied—*

has the authentic ring of rhetoric, pushed to the verge of absurdity.
It is indeed very like Shakespeare to recognise that grandeur and
absurdity are not incompatible, and Shakespeare's Caesar certainly
has elements of both.

49 ff.   The conspirators, supporting the petition of *Metellus*, close in on
         Caesar, so that *Casca* and *Metellus* can begin the assault from behind.
         Cassius, Decius and *Cinna* meet him as he struggles down the steps,
         and *Brutus* confronts him in mid-stage.

Bru. Cassius be constant:
  Popillius Lena speakes not of our purposes,
  For looke he smiles, and *Caesar* doth not change.
Cassi. Trebonius knowes his time: for look you *Brutus*   25
  He drawes *Mark Antony* out of the way.
Deci. Where is *Metellus Cimber*, let him go,
  And presently preferre his suite to *Caesar*
Bru. He is addrest: presse neere, and second him.
Cin. Caska, you are the first that reares your hand.   30
Caes. Are we all ready? What is now amisse,
  That *Caesar* and his Senate must redresse?
Metel. Most high, most mighty, and most puisant *Caesar*
  Metellus Cymber throwes before thy Seate
  An humble heart.
Caes. I must prevent thee *Cymber:*   35
  These couchings and these lowly courtesies
  Might fire the blood of ordinary men,
  And turne pre-Ordinance, and first Decree
  Into the lane [*read* law] of Children. Be not fond,
  To thinke that *Caesar* beares such Rebell blood   40
  That will be thaw'd from the true quality
  With that which melteth Fooles, I meane sweet words,
  Low-crooked-curtsies, and base Spaniell fawning:
  Thy Brother by decree is banished:
  If thou doest bend, and pray, and fawne for him,   45
  I spurne thee like a Curre out of my way:
  Know *Caesar* doth not wrong, nor without cause
  Will he be satisfied.
Metel. Is there no voyce more worthy then my owne,
  To sound more sweetly in great *Caesars* eare,   50
  For the repealing of my banish'd Brother?
Bru. I kisse thy hand, but not in flattery *Caesar:*
  Desiring thee, that *Publius Cymber* may
  Have an immediate freedome of repeale.
Caes. What *Brutus?*   55
Cassi. Pardon *Caesar: Caesar* pardon:
  As lowe as to they foote doth *Cassius* fall,
  To begge infranchisement for *Publius Cymber.*
Caes. I could be well mov'd, if I were as you,
  If I could pray to moove, Prayers would moove me:
  But I am constant as the Northerne Starre,   60
  Of whose true fixt, and resting quality,
  There is no fellow in the Firmament.
  The Skies are painted with unnumbred sparkes,
  They are all Fire, and every one doth shine:
  But, there's but one in all doth hold his place.   65
  So, in the World; 'Tis furnish'd well with Men,
  And Men are Flesh and Blood, and apprehensive;
  Yet in the number, I do know but One
  That unassayleable holds on his Ranke,

76   *Speak, hands, for me.* It seems likely that the Chamberlain's Men would build their action upon the vivid accounts of Plutarch as distilled through the imagination of the poet. Salient features are the initial stab of *Casca* from behind on the neck, while *Metellus* throws *Caesar's* cloak over his head; then a prolonged and violent struggle in which *Caesar* defends himself with vigour and the conspirators wound each other in panic; then a dramatic moment when *Caesar* comes face to face with *Brutus*; then *Brutus'* deliberate blow; *Caesar's* cry, and the muffling of his head; then with no further resistance, the conspirators hustle their victim to the base of Pompey's statue and dispatch him.

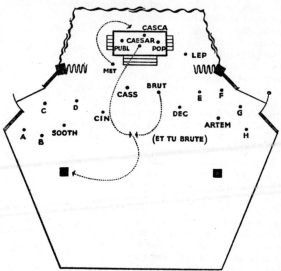

Positioning: *Speake hands for me*

On Shakespeare's stage, the action could be rendered thus: *Casca* and *Metellus* both spring their surprise attack from behind the chair of the seated *Caesar;* the prolonged struggle takes place on the dais and on the broad steps in front of it; *Brutus* confronts *Caesar* in the very middle of the Platform; after his blow, and *Caesar's* cry, the conspirators close in again and drive *Caesar* to the base of the R pillar, where the bust (hitherto *Caesar's* image) is now easily taken for Pompey's statue (see above, p. 44).

78   A moment of dead silence before *Cinna's* cry, a half hysterical outburst which loosens the pent emotions of the theatre, and launches a panic among the mob: one half of them (E, F, G, H, with *Artemidorus*) surge forward round the perimeter, communicating their terror to the groundlings.

83   In spite of *Brutus'* reassuring words, the mob (both sections) run out by R door. Their clamour is heard off-stage R until the exit of *Publius* (line 95).

95   *Trebonius* returns inset R, where he went with *Antony* earlier in the scene.

Unshak'd of Motion: and that I am he,   70
Let me a little shew it, even in this:
That I was constant *Cymber* should be banish'd,
And constant do remaine to keepe him so.
Cinna. O *Caesar.*
Caes. Hence: Wilt thou lift up Olympus?
Decius. Great *Caesar.*
Caes. Doth not *Brutus* bootlesse kneele?   75
Cask. Speake hands for me.
                              They stab Caesar.
Caes. Et Tu Brutè?—— Then fall *Caesar   Dyes*
Cin. Liberty, Freedome; Tyranny is dead,
    Run hence, proclaime, cry it about the Streets.
Cassi. Some to the common Pulpits, and cry out   80
    Liberty, Freedome, and Enfranchisement.
Bru. People and Senators, be not affrighted:
    Fly not, stand still: Ambitions debt is paid.
Cask. Go to the Pulpit *Brutus.*
Dec. And *Cassius* too.
Bru. Where's *Publius?*
Cin. Heere, quite confounded with this mutiny.
Met. Stand fast together, least some Friend of *Caesars*
    Should chance——
Bru. Talke not of standing. *Publius* good cheere,
    There is no harme intended to your person,   90
    Nor to no Roman else: so tell them *Publius.*
Cassi. And leave us *Publius*, least that the people
    Rushing on us, should do your Age some mischiefe.
Bru. Do so, and let no man abide this deede,
    But we the Doers.   95

                        Enter Trebonius.

Cassi. Where is *Antony?*
Treb. Fled to his House amaz'd:
    Men, Wives, and Children, stare, cry out, and run,
    As it were Doomesday.
Bru. Fates, we will know your pleasures:
    That we shall dye we know, 'tis but the time
    And drawing dayes out, that men stand upon.   100

5

THE POET'S STAGECRAFT

HITHERTO we have considered the playhouse, the prompt-book, the Book-Keeper's problems, and the accomplishments of the players: it is now time to turn to the poet himself, and re-study his stagecraft against a background of the conditions for which it was devised. If it can be proved that by such a process Shakespeare's intention is clarified, and new light shed upon his conception of the art of poetic drama, then this inquiry will be not merely of academic or archæological interest but a necessary pre-liminary to the interpretation and production of his plays in the future. The inquiry cannot, within the compass of this volume, be exhaustive: little more can be attempted than to indicate that there is a wide field open for new research. It is indeed doubtful whether the study can be carried much further without more practical experience of the conditions—which means, if not the rebuilding of the playhouse, at least a drastic alteration of existing conditions, and the training of a repertory in the tradition of the Chamberlain's Men. For there is no art in which theory needs practical testing more than the art of the theatre.

Nor is it intended here to attempt a detailed analysis of Shake-speare's poetry—that has been done often elsewhere and with much penetration [1]—but rather to consider how poetry is made dramatic by Shakespeare, how it is the keystone of his stagecraft, and how it is devised for the conditions of the Elizabethan playhouse. As we have already seen, a comparison of the prompt-book with the sources helps us often to guess at Shakespeare's intention [2]: we can get much nearer still—such is the contention of the present chapter—if we make a habit of imagining each play, and each scene in each play, in the setting of the Globe and through the eyes of the Chamberlain's Men.

The Globe, we must remember, and its predecessor across the

---

[1] The reader is referred to George Rylands' chapter, "Shakespeare the Poet", in *A Companion to Shakespeare Studies* (Cambridge), 89 ff., and to the select bibliography on pp. 353 ff. of the same book. Certainly an actor who has studied the mechanics of the poetry can give a better account of Shakespeare than one who has not.

[2] See above, p. 152.

river, were the scene of Shakespeare's daily life for most of his working years, and the Chamberlain's Men were his daily companions
and collaborators. Baldwin has given us a mass of evidence about
this company of players: even if his handling of the evidence is
sometimes open to criticism, yet its very bulk is impressive and its
substance most interesting, and the reconstruction of Shakespeare's
daily life in association with his colleagues, contained in his last
chapter called "Facing the Facts with Shakespeare", deserves closer
study and a wider public.[3] It certainly provides a far more plausible
background—to think of him striking fire from Burbadge, discussing
back-stage problems with Heminges, theorising on fooling with
Armin—than the romantic picture of hobnobbing with Southampton
and Essex on the fringes of the Queen's pleasure, which is not confined to the pages of popular fiction, but finds favour sometimes even
with the scholars and critics.

(i) Objectivity of Vision

"I could be bounded in a nutshell," says Hamlet, "and count my
selfe a King of infinite space———"[4] There is an exuberance in the
words which suggests Shakespeare's own imaginative freedom. His
nutshell is the Globe Playhouse, and we would do well to recognise
that neither Shakespeare nor the most part of his contemporary
playwrights were reluctant to accept the fact of the nutshell. We
have seen in Chapter III how readily the plays are set back in this
theatre, how easy it is to reconstruct the original scene-rotation and
the plotting of entries. We have been told by Cranford Adams that it
was the habit of the Elizabethan dramatists to make no bones about
the permanent features of the visible scene: he points out, moreover,
that the playwright Middleton, in his *Black Book*, makes Lucifer
remark:

---

[3] After explaining that an author's work was subject to direction and suggestion
from the players' company, Baldwin continues: "But where the dramatist and
company worked in harmony together, as did Shakespeare and his company,
dictation would be replaced by suggestion and consultation. Thus Shakespeare's
plays represent not only his own individual invention but also the collective
invention of his company. . . . Doubtless even Shakespeare's plays were the better
for the suggestions of these the most expert actors of their age, whose lives had been
spent in their profession, although the suggestions may at times have occasioned the
dramatist a wry face. In view of the social standing of these men and the training
through which they entered their profession, it is now high time that we ceased to
brand them as only a source of contamination and pollution to the dramatist,
labelling their contributions as only 'the ill-conditioned interpolations and
alterations of actors and theatrical managers'. Since their position rendered them
and not the dramatist the dictators of the drama, that drama is their sufficient
vindication" (T. W. Baldwin, *op. cit.*, 303 f.).

[4] *Hamlet*, II. ii. 264 f.

> And now that I have vaulted up so high
> Above the stage rails of this earthen globe
> I must turn actor—

and that Chapman, in his *Caesar and Pompey*, has the lines:

> We are now like
> The two poles propping heaven, on which heaven moves,
> And they are fixed and quiet.[5]

In both these examples the terms of the metaphor—the rails, the globe, the poles, the heaven—are the concrete and visible features of the playhouse.[6] Shakespeare himself is full of the same kind of imagery. Some examples are familiar, such as Duke Senior's

> Thou seest, we are not all alone unhappie:
> This wide and universall Theater
> Presents more wofull Pageants than the Sceane
> Wherein we play in . . .

and Jaques' reply:

> All the world's a stage,
> And all the men and women, meerely Players . . .[7]

or Antonio's

> I hold the world but as the world *Gratiano*,
> A stage, where every man must play a part,
> And mine a sad one . . .[8]

or Macbeth's

> Life's but a walking Shadow, a poore Player,
> That struts and frets his houre upon the Stage,
> And then is heard no more . . .[9]

or King Lear's

> When we are borne, we cry that we are come
> To this great stage of Fooles.[10]

But the image sometimes appears unexpectedly and may be overlooked if the actor does not point it with the appropriate glance or gesture. Ross, commenting on the unnatural darkness that follows on the night of Duncan's murder, says:

---

[5] See above, pp. 52 f.; and J. Cranford Adams, *The Globe Playhouse*, 100, 108.
[6] Perhaps we have here instances of what E. M. W. Tillyard calls, in a different context, the "Elizabethan hovering between equivalence and metaphor" (*The Elizabethan World Picture*, 92).
[7] *As You Like It*, II. vii. 137 ff.   [8] *The Merchant of Venice*, I. i. 77 ff.
[9] *Macbeth*, V. v. 24 ff.   [10] *King Lear*, IV. vi. 187 f.

> Thou seest the Heavens, as troubled with mans Act,
> Threatens his bloody Stage.[11]

A familiar speech in *Hamlet* mentions "this goodly frame the Earth ... this most excellent Canopy the Ayre ... this Majesticall Roofe, fretted with golden fire . . ." [12] and it seems likely that Burbadge would have made plain the reference to the frame of the playhouse, the canopy of "the Heavens", and the thatched roof lit up by the afternoon sun.[13] When we see how often Shakespeare uses this particular range of metaphor—and frequently indeed at moments of extreme dramatic tension or of spiritual exaltation or profundity—we may discount such apologies as those of the Chorus in *Henry V* as being the mock-modesty of the skilful orator, and suppose rather that he was very well pleased with the means at his disposal: it was in the first year of the new Globe that the poet was pretending to apologise for "this unworthy Scaffold", "this Cock-Pit", "this Woodden O".[14]

We may also infer that the visible features of the playhouse were constantly in his mind as he wrote. A very interesting example where we can catch him thinking *unconsciously* in the theatre rather than in the imagined scene occurs in the sequel to Hamlet's encounter with the Ghost: the unearthly voice *cries under the Stage*, and Hamlet says to his astonished companions "you here this fellowe in the Sellerige": the phrase is hardly appropriate to the supposed scene high on the battlements of Elsinore, but the Ghost (in the person of Shakespeare himself) is wandering hither and thither in the capacious cellarage of Hell beneath the Platform of the Globe.[15] It is indeed Shakespeare's constant habit to see his theme in the setting of his playhouse: he does not write *in vacuo* (as might perhaps be said of Marlowe, for instance, in *Tamburlaine*)—he is always the practical man of the theatre. There is reason to believe that, though he may sometimes deliberately ignore and sometimes transcend the visible scene, what he writes can always be acted on that multiple stage; that in fact the conventional elements of the scene underlie even the most ambitious flights of the poet's fancy.

His practical sense of the stage and his objective turn of mind are further shown by the fact that he does not forget his actors. Indeed, as we have seen, it is Baldwin's view that "the play was regularly fitted to the company, not the company to the play"; and we may quote once again his analogy of the tailor—when he calls Shake-

---

[11] *Macbeth*, II. iv. 5 f.   [12] *Hamlet*, II. ii. 317 ff.

[13] Among many further examples of playhouse imagery may be mentioned *Romeo and Juliet*, I. iv. 7 f.; *King John*, II. i. 375 f.; *Troilus and Cressida*, I. iii. 153 ff.; *Othello*, I. ii. 83 f.

[14] *Henry V*, Prologue, 10 ff.   [15] *Hamlet*, I. v. 151.

speare a better tailor-playwright than Ben Jonson.[16] We need not
accept his belief that Shakespeare wrote the parts to suit the exact
age of his players, but it is hard to ignore the probability of his theory
of "lines", by which it is to be understood that he had his principal
players in mind in planning the chief characters of his plays.

There are, by the way, some amusing topicalities which emerge
from a study of Baldwin's lists. Pope's Fluellen speaks of how Harry
Monmouth ". . . turn'd away the fat Knight with the great belly
doublet: he was full of jests, and gypes, and knaveries, and mockes,
I have forgot his name",[17] and the tone of superior contempt has an
added touch of piquancy if it is true that Pope was also the creator of
Falstaff. Polonius tells Hamlet, "I did enact *Julius Caesar*, I was
kill'd i'th' Capitol: *Brutus* kill'd me." Hamlet, in teasing voice,
replies, "It was a bruite part of him, to kill so Capitall a Calfe
there." The indifferent jest gains something from the fact that
Heminges did in fact play Caesar the year before, and Burbadge was
Brutus.[18] Goffe, as Mistress Overdone, is described as "A Bawd of
eleven yeares continuance", and the audience who had seen the boy
play many such parts would take the point of the joke at his expense.[19]
This kind of topicality is much more probable than the conjectured
caricaturing of court-figures or discussion of high political intrigues,
which were likely to be dangerous in the poet's lifetime. Actors in
revue and on the music-hall stage are still prone to make jokes about
each other, and the audience still likes such allusions as well as any.
One may suspect, without possibility of certainty, that some of the
minor rôles in the plays are individual portraits of the less prominent
players. There is the living skeleton who played Pinch in *The Comedy
of Errors* and the Apothecary in *Romeo and Juliet*, and who was
probably also the Beadle whom Mistress Quickly calls "Thou
Anatomy, thou", as he hales her and Doll off to "base Durance".
His name may have been Sinklo.[20] There is Sir Nathaniel the Curate,
who represents Alexander in the Show of the Nine Worthies, and of
whom Costard says "a foolish milde man, an honest man, looke you,
& soon dasht. He is a marvellous good neighbour insooth, and a verie
good Bowler; but for *Alisander*, alas you see, how 'tis a little ore-
parted".[21] There is Barnardine who is introduced into *Measure for
Measure* solely for the purpose of providing a substitute head for
Claudio's to be presented to Angelo; who has been drinking all the

---

[16] See above, p. 155, and note 149.   [17] *Henry V*, IV. vii. 51 ff.
[18] *Hamlet*, III. ii. 109 ff.
[19] *Measure for Measure*, III. ii. 212; and see above, p. 164.
[20] See W. W. Greg, *The Editorial Problem in Shakespeare*, 116, and note 3.
[21] *Love's Labour's Lost*, V. ii. 582 ff.

night and so will not consent to die; and who survives to be pardoned by the Duke in the last scene.[22] There is Edmund's gruff officer who, when given his sealed orders to kill Lear and Cordelia in prison, says:

> I cannot draw a cart, nor eate dride oats,
> If it bee mans worke ile do't.[23]

It is of course mere guesswork which suggests that some mannerism or cast of personality in his fellow players prompted Shakespeare to give such individual life and vitality to many minor rôles.

One notices a practical common sense in the handling of limited manpower, when in *Julius Caesar* the minor conspirators and senators and plebeians of the first half vanish to provide officers and soldiers for the plains of Philippi. The treatment of the mob which develops there from the merry truants of the opening scene to the frenzied hooligans who murder Cinna, is a *tour de force* of dramatic art; but it is worth remembering that here are the familiar comedy gang of the company leading half a dozen hired men; their parts are written accordingly with the traditional gambits, even in so sinister a scene as the lynching of the innocent poet.[24] At every turn the producer of to-day, if he follows in the steps of Shakespeare and the Chamberlain's Men, will find a shrewd realisation of the practical needs. The revolt of Laertes against Claudius, quelled as soon as mentioned, is simply achieved by the sound of a riotous mob outside the King's apartment. "Where is this King?" cries Laertes, bursting into the presence; then he turns back in the doorway and shouts "sirs stand you all without". "No lets come in," they cry. "I pray you give me leave," says Laertes, and they answer "We will, we will": their acquiescence saves the wardrobe-master a deal of trouble and expense.[25]

But Shakespeare's objective vision goes deeper than this: he conceives not only in terms of his theatre, but also in terms of the age he lived in. We must not be misled by the familiar eulogy, "not of his age, but for all time". It is his habit to see his story through modern —that is to say, Elizabethan—spectacles.[26] W. J. Lawrence suggests that this was an habitual feature of the public theatre [27]: certainly it is most clearly marked in Shakespeare. It is not merely a matter of topical jokes, such as the grave-digger's quip, when he speaks of Hamlet's being sent into England because he was mad—" 'Twill not be seene in him there, there the men are as mad as hee" [28]; or Iago's

---

[22] *Measure for Measure*, IV. ii. 132 ff.; IV. iii. 42 ff.; V. i. 479 ff.
[23] *King Lear*, V. iii. 39 f.   [24] *Julius Caesar*, III. iii.
[25] *Hamlet*, IV. v. 112 ff.   [26] See above, p. 54.
[27] W. J. Lawrence, *Pre-Restoration Stage Studies*, 29.   [28] *Hamlet*, V. i. 168 f.

G

comment on drinking in England, "where indeed they are most
potent in Potting" [29]; nor of topical caricatures such as Osric,
Parolles and Oswald [30]; nor of topical themes such as that in *Hamlet*
of the boys' companies—the "little Yases"—who have "so be-ratled
the common Stages" that the Tragedians of the City must go on
tour.[31] These instances are introduced into, or superimposed on, the
main texture of the play. But often the theme itself is worked out in
modern terms. For all its Roman feeling derived from Plutarch,
there is no archæology in Shakespeare's conception of *Julius Caesar*.
The background colour is largely modern, as may be shown in a list
of items—the pocket, the gown, the doublet, the aprons, the taper,
the closet, the striking clock. The boy Lucius' description of the
conspirators,

> their Hats are pluckt about their Eares,
> And halfe their Faces buried in their Cloakes . . .

suggests resemblance to a woodcut of the Babington plot in Carle-
ton's *Thankfull Remembrance*.[32] The opening scene of the play is a good
example of Shakespeare's mixture of the elements: Plutarch's Rome
appears in many details of the speeches of Flavius and Marullus
(Tributaries, Chariot Wheeles, *Pompey*, Tyber, the Capitoll, the dis-
robing of the Images); but side by side with these is contemporary
London (Battlements, Towres, and Windowes, Chimney tops, and
the familiar hawking image applied to Caesar's growing Feathers);
and the scene owes its initial momentum to the stock contribution of
the playhouse comics.[33] It is this habit of mind that mixes *Alcides*
with "Ale-house painted signes" in the same speech of Aaron in
Titus Andronicus [34]; that follows the opening recriminations of Oberon
and Titania—in which such names as Corin, Phillida, Peregenia,
Ariadne and Atiopa are called in question—with a homely description of the Warwickshire countryside—

> The Oxe hath therefore stretch'd his yoake in vaine,
> The Ploughman lost his sweat, and the greene Corne
> Hath rotted, ere his youth attain'd a beard:
> The fold stands empty in the drowned field,
> And Crowes are fatted with the murrion flocke,
> The nine mens Morris is fild up with mud,
> And the queint Mazes in the wanton greene,
> For lacke of tread are undistinguishable . . .[35]

---

[29] *Othello*, II. iii. 78 ff.   [30] See above, p. 54.
[31] *Hamlet*, II. ii. 362 ff.
[32] *Julius Caesar*, II. i. 73 f. The woodcut is reproduced in *Shakespeare's England*,
vol. i, p. 9.   [33] *Julius Caesar*, I. i.
[34] *Titus Andronicus*, IV. ii. 96–9.   [35] *A Midsummer Night's Dream*, II. i. 60 ff.

that dubs Hector and Ajax "Knights", and thinks no profanity to
call Helen of Troy "Nell" [36]; that makes the inmates of Vienna jail
sound like a sort of travesty of Bunyan—with Mr. *Caper*, Master
Three-Pile, yong *Dizie*, yong Mr. *Deepe-vow*, Mr. *Copperspurre*, Mr.
Starve-Lackey, yong *Drop-heire* that kild lustie *Pudding*, Mr. *Forthlight*,
Mr. *Shootie*, and wilde *Halfe-Canne*.[37]

Shakespeare's objectivity of language, especially of simile and
metaphor, hardly needs an example except for identification.
Berowne compares the wife that he seeks to

> a Germane Cloake [*read* clock],
> Still a repairing: ever out of frame,
> And never going a right, being a Watch:
> But being watcht, that it may still goe right.[38]

Silvius, imploring Phebe to let him down lightly if she must refuse
his suit, says:

> the common executioner
> Whose heart th'accustom'd sight of death makes hard
> Falls not the axe upon the humbled neck,
> But first begs pardon: will you sterner be
> Then he that dies and lives by bloody drops?

Jaques says of Touchstone that his brain is "as drie as the remainder
bisket After a voyage".[39] It is in the same play that Quiller-Couch
detected on the lips of Adam (the poet's own part) "an exquisite
instance of Shakespeare's habitual stroke!—with which the general
idea, 'unregarded age', is no sooner presented than (as it were) he
stabs the concrete into it, drawing blood: 'unregarded age *in corners
thrown*' ".[40] Perhaps if we could analyse and understand this habit of
Shakespeare's mind, the objective modernity of his vision, we could
come nearer to-day to solving the problem of how to bring poetry—
even dramatic poetry—into touch with contemporary life. When,
for instance, will a twentieth-century poet follow this example to
bring vivid life to a Roman theme, or an Elizabethan theme, or an
eighteenth- or nineteenth-century theme?

It is well to repeat here that the prompt-book (Quarto or Folio)
will help greatly to recapture this modern flavour of Shakespeare's
mind, and that the use of Elizabethan costume, or at least a substructure of Elizabethan costume, and contemporary furnishing and

[36] *Troilus and Cressida*, IV. v. 67; III. i. 152.
[37] *Measure for Measure*, IV. iii. 1–21.
[38] *Love's Labour's Lost*, III. i. 200 ff.
[39] *As You Like It*, III. v. 3 ff.; II. vii. 39.
[40] Sir Arthur Quiller-Couch, *Shakespeare's Workmanship*, 98; *As You Like It*,
II. iii. 42.

propertics, will help likewise. So, for the same reason, will the use of
the Elizabethan Platform with the conventional background of the
Tiring-House façade.

(ii) Opportunity snatched from Necessity

It should, moreover, be clear that so far from regretting his nutshell, Shakespeare seems actually to revel in it; that the inclination
of his mind, his natural bent, leans towards the acknowledgment and
exploitation of his limited resources; that he finds a positive joy in
make-believe, in turning necessity or handicap into opportunity.
Faced with a difficulty, he makes it into a chance: with him the most
effective defence is always counter-attack. Travellers are to be shown
being waylaid by highwaymen: their horses cannot appear on the
Platform—Shakespeare finds the solution, by making them stretch
their legs in a walk down the hill.[41] An explanation must be found of
why the players in *Hamlet* are on tour: he pounces on the chance to
have a fling at the children's companies, and the topical theme gives
verisimilitude to the whole episode of the players' visit. After the
first Player has shown his paces, Hamlet in soliloquy cries:

> Is it not monstrous that this Player heere,
> But in a Fixion, in a dreame of Passion,
> Could force his soule so to his whole conceit,

and the point of the speech depends on the illusion that Hamlet is
not Burbadge! [42] It is Shakespeare's (and Burbadge's) delight to
"get away" with such impudent conjuring. After the night-brawl in
which Cassio loses his reputation, Iago and his creator want to go
straight on with their plot without interruption: "Dull not Device,
by coldnesse, and delay." So night must be turned into day: a line
and a half are enough for the purpose, but how brilliantly the need
is turned to dramatic profit! Iago's words are

> bi' the masse tis morning;
> Pleasure, and Action, make the houres seeme short.[43]

Here again, Shakespeare goes straight for the heart of the problem—
that the clock has been moving almost too fast to be plausible.
That's what I thought, too, says Iago in effect, but then I've been
enjoying myself: haven't *you?* The great storm in *King Lear* has to be
established in the dialogue: it starts in a scene between Kent and an
unnamed Gentleman. "Who's there besides foule weather?" says
Kent, and the answer comes: "One minded like the weather, most

---

[41] 1 *Henry IV*, II. ii. 86 ff.   [42] *Hamlet*, II. ii. 585 ff.
[43] *Othello*, II. iii. 387 ff.

unquietly." [44] The need to create the storm confronts the poet, but the poet counter-attacks by making emotional capital out of the storm. So too at Macbeth's first entry upon the Platform, the exultation of the victorious general is brilliantly combined with the sinister jingle of the Witches' former incantation:

> So foule and faire a day I have not seene . . .[45]

and this is Shakespeare's response to the technical necessity of conveying the impression of wild and ominous weather. When the conspirators visit Brutus' orchard at night, the narrative demands that Cassius should have a brief private word with Brutus: therefore the ball must be kept rolling by the others. The dispute about the daybreak and the points of the compass not only serves to produce the appropriate effect, but also turns our anxious minds once more towards the Capitoll, combining the idea with the dawn of the Ides of March and putting it into the mouth of Casca who is to be the first to rear his hand against Caesar. "Heere, as I point my Sword, the Sunne arises," he says, ". . . and the high East Stands as the Capitoll, directly heere." [46]

This particular habit of Shakespeare's invention is well exampled in a short scene in *Twelfth Night* between Sebastian and Antonio.[47] The need is to show us Antonio *giving his purse* to Sebastian, and to remind us again of Antonio's *danger* in Illyria. Shakespeare takes the opportunity to make a lively objective scene, of which the elements are Sebastian's thanks instead of payment ("ever oft good turnes, Are shuffel'd off with such uncurrant pay"); his desire to go sight-seeing, which Antonio dare not; the *rendez-vous* ("In the South Suburbes at the Elephant"); "I will bespeake our dyet"; "Why I your purse?" "Haply your eye shall light upon some toy . . ." The scene is only fifty lines long, but instead of giving us a perfunctorily informative dialogue, the poet fills the conversation with objective detail so as to create the realistic atmosphere of the town round the idyllic atmosphere of Orsino's court: when the time comes, Sebastian is thus all the more bewildered at his experiences with Olivia and her entourage.

The Chorus in *Henry V* is typical of such resourcefulness. Created to supply the need of epic grandeur, full of apology for the lack of material resources, he is in his own person the great glory of the play, skilfully evoking the illusion of crossing the Channel, fronting Harfleur, camping at midnight before Agincourt. The very magnitude of the handicap gives the poet his great opportunity: his Muse

---

[44] *King Lear*, III. i. 1 f.
[46] *Julius Caesar*, II. i. 101 ff.
[45] *Macbeth*, I. iii. 38.
[47] *Twelfth Night*, III. iii.

does indeed ascend the brightest Heaven of Invention. It is perhaps
significant that in his later and greater works, when his imaginative
range is still more ambitious than in *Henry V*, he no longer apologises
for his resources. Think, for instance, of *Antony and Cleopatra* in this
respect: the problem is not unlike—"in little roome confining mightie
men". But in the later play there is no apology, and no need for it;
the technique is assured. He can there handle the three-day battle of
Actium with perfect clarity upon the Globe stage.[48] It is arguable
that in the plays of the last period—the so-called romances—Shakespeare, more and more out of touch with the Globe, was no longer at
pains to fit his inspiration to the practical needs of the playhouse.
But assuredly in the great tragic period, in *Othello*, *King Lear*,
Macbeth, and *Antony and Cleopatra*, while in the very act of showing
himself a king of infinite space, he is still at pains to remember that
he is bounded in a nutshell: more than that, he still takes a positive
pleasure in triumphing over his limitations, in finding that "our
meere defects Prove our Commodities", in turning handicap into
opportunity, in showing just how much can be done with the
wooden O, in proving that his material means are ideal for his
purpose, that the Globe playhouse is a perfect medium for presenting
the poetic drama.

(iii) Creation in Words—of Atmosphere

Certainly he is a king of infinite space; and we, if we take him
aright, can be made sharers of his kingdom. There is probably a
touch of autobiography in the deliberate ambiguity of Prospero's
farewell to his art:

> I have bedymn'd
> The Noone-tide Sun, call'd forth the mutenous windes,
> And twixt the greene Sea, and the azur'd vault
> Set roaring warre: To the dread ratling Thunder
> Have I given fire, and rifted *Joves* stowt Oke
> With his owne Bolt: The strong bass'd promontorie
> Have I made shake, and by the spurs pluckt up
> The Pyne, and Cedar. Graves at my command
> Have wak'd their sleepers, op'd, and let 'em forth
> By my so potent Art.[49]

What is this so potent Art? It is a question which producer and
actors must know how to answer if we are to have the full experience
of being spellbound by this great magician. It would not be amiss

---

[48] Granville-Barker's Preface to the play makes this point quite plain, and it is a
pity that we have not yet seen his advice put into practice (*Prefaces to Shakespeare*,
Second Series, 143 ff.).   [49] *The Tempest*, V. i. 41 ff.

that the audience too should have some idea of how the spell is
worked: the hypnotist invites the co-operation of his patient, and
Shakespeare (as the Chorus in *Henry V* shows) played constantly for
the active imaginative collaboration of his hearers.

The answer can be quite simply given: the potent art lies in the
spoken word. The fact is so simple and so obvious as to seem a
truism; yet it is so often ignored or only half understood that it needs
repeating and expounding. The poetry was of course supported—
and I think very skilfully supported—by effects of sight, sound and
even smell: by the clever miming of the actors, the well-chosen and
significant furniture and properties, by lightning, smoke, fog and
mist from the traps, by the waving of a branch to register the wind
on the heath; by the sound of knocking on gate or door carefully
rehearsed for its special occasion, by bells and clocks, by a horse's
whinney or hoofbeats, by the voice of the owl, by thunder or the
rushing of the wind; by the whiff of saltpetre for battle, by foliage
and rushes which breathe of the open air, by straw reeking of the
inn-yard. But for all that, it is the words that create the atmosphere,
the character and the action of the poet's play. After all, almost all
that we have left of Shakespeare is the spoken word: the stage-
directions are of the shortest, and seldom descriptive of elaborate
action or atmospheric subtlety; the scene-headings are hardly ever
geographical or descriptive; there are no descriptions of character,
no bracketed adverbs to indicate the tone of a speech or the mood of
a speaker. Yet in spite of this, even in reading, we have the most
vivid impressions of atmosphere, of character, and of action, so that
often people talk about the plays as if they were discussing real
persons, real occasions, real actions.

Let us consider first how Shakespeare sets about creating the
atmosphere which he desires. In its simplest form, this process consists of investing properties or furniture or the stage-features and the
stage itself with colour. Thus the graveyard for the climax of *Romeo
and Juliet* is fully furnished with the necessary and significant
properties by the poet's own cunningly selective eye; as we have
seen above, they are mentioned and sometimes vividly characterised
in the dialogue.[50] Thus Oberon describes for us, just before we see it
disclosed in the Study, the

> banke where the wilde time blowes
> Where Oxslips and the nodding Violet growes,
> Quite over-cannoped with luscious woodbine,
> With sweet muske roses, and with Eglantine;

[50] See above, p. 45.

> There sleepes *Tytania*, sometime of the night,
> Lul'd in these flowers, with dances and delight:
> And there the snake throwes her enammel'd skinne,
> Weed wide enough to rap a Fairy in.[51]

The stock property moss-bank is translated by his words into a couch fit for the Fairy Queen. Old Adam, who has heard of Oliver's treachery, standing outside one of the stage-doors, warns Orlando "Come not within these doores": at the end of the same scene he makes of this door a moving symbol of the house in which he has served so long and from which he must now for ever part:

> From seaventie [*read* seventeen] yeeres, till now
>   almost fourescore
> Here lived I, but now live here no more
> At seaventeene yeeres, many their fortunes seeke
> But at fourescore, it is too late a weeke . . .[52]

It would have been interesting to hear the poet himself working his own magic in the part of Adam. Bolingbroke, standing on the perimeter, points at the Tarras, saying:

> Goe to the rude Ribs of that ancient Castle,
> Through Brazen Trumpet send the breath of Parle
> Into his ruin'd Eares . . .[53]

King John likewise, arriving before Angiers simultaneously with the French, warns a Citizen on the Tarras that

> but for our approch, those sleeping stones,
> That as a waste doth girdle you about
> By the compulsion of their Ordinance,
> By this time from their fixed beds of lime
> Had bin dishabited.[54]

The greater subtlety of the painting when Duncan approaches the castle of Inverness is a sign of the poet's development in this art.[55] King Philip of France adds to the scene-painting at Angiers by translating the rushes on the Platform into "these greenes before your Towne".[56] During the battle which hastens the dénouement of *King Lear*, blind Gloucester is bidden by Edgar to "take the shadow of this Tree" [57]: so simply are the Stage-Posts converted for a momentary purpose. The orchard of the Capulets, where Romeo speaks his love to Juliet at her window, is created by poetical means. Constantly, yet without strain, the impressions of night and darkness

---

[51] *A Midsummer Night's Dream*, II. i. 249 ff.   [52] *As You Like It*, II. iii. 71 ff.
[53] *Richard II*, III. iii. 32 ff.   [54] *King John*, II. i. 216 ff.
[55] *Macbeth*, I. vi. 1 ff.   [56] *King John*, II. i. 242.
[57] *King Lear*, V. ii. 1.

and the moon, and danger and the walled orchard, are present in the dialogue: the actors, using this poetical effect and trained miming, will easily create the illusion. One notices here Shakespeare's growing skill in working the "atmospherics" into the dialogue so that they have dramatic force. Such a stroke is Romeo's impulsive oath:

> Lady, by yonder blessed Moone I vow,
> That tips with silver all These Fruite tree tops.[58]

Remarkable in this respect is the moment of Richard II's return from Ireland. For swift continuity Shakespeare wants to make clear at once the geography and the circumstances: so the King asks, "Barkloughly Castle call you this at hand?" and Aumerle replies "Yea, my Lord: how brooks your Grace the ayre, After your late tossing on the breaking Seas?" So much for necessity: but then follows the stroke of the master, as he plucks opportunity from the need. Richard replies:

> Needs must I like it well: I weepe for joy
> To stand upon my Kingdome once againe.
> Deere Earth, I doe salute thee with my hand,
> Though Rebels wound thee with their Horses hoofes:
> As a long parted Mother with her Child,
> Playes fondly with her teares, and smiles in meeting;
> So weeping, smiling, greet I thee my Earth,
> And doe thee favor with my Royall hands.

We note how he goes on to create the earth from the bare scaffoldage of the Platform—with the Spiders, the heavie-gaited Toades, the stinging Nettles, the Flower, the Adder, these Stones—so that in the end we are persuaded that "This Earth shall have a feeling".[59] We shall have cause to return to this passage later, to study an early example of the poet's preoccupation with a theme: for the theme of the "earth" runs through this phase of the play. For the moment we can but admire the skill with which the atmospheric painting is turned to dramatic effect.

It is not only the visible stage itself and its features that the poet can invest with life. Its neighbourhood too is subject to his magic. Across the Yard we see with sudden startling clarity the legendary walls of Troy, as Ulysses prophesies to Hector that

> yonder wals that pertly front your Towne,
> Yond Towers, whose wanton tops do busse the clouds,
> Must kisse their owne feet . . .

---

[58] *Romeo and Juliet*, II. ii. 107 f.   [59] *Richard II*, III. ii. 1–24.

and Hector, with moving restraint, replies

> I must not beleeve you:
> There they stand yet: and modestly I thinke,
> The fall of every Phrygian stone will cost
> A drop of Grecian blood: the end crownes all,
> And that old common Arbitrator, Time,
> Will one day end it.[60]

The illusion can in fact be extended to cover the circumstances of a scene, as, when Brutus and Cassius encounter on the Platform, the presence of great armies is swiftly indicated in the text:

> *Bru.* Hearke, he is arriv'd:
>   March gently on to meete him.
> *Cassi.* Stand ho.
> *Bru.* Stand ho, speake the word along.
>   Stand.
>   Stand.
>   Stand.[61]

The echoing order to "Stand" grows gradually more distant as it passes down the line, the furthest being perhaps spoken by someone outside the playhouse. So too when the storm is raging off the coast of Cyprus, and there is a cry *Within:* "A Saile, a Saile, a Saile." The comment of a Gentleman on the Platform

> The Towne is empty: on the brow o'th'Sea
> Stand rankes of People, and they cry, a Saile . . .[62]

has an expansive effect, making the Platform seem but one headland on a long sea-coast. A single line sometimes does the trick, as when Antony asks for the news from Sicyon, and a superior flunkey shouts through the door: "The man from *Scicion,* Is there such an one?" [63] The contemptuous casual tone of the flunkey creates for us a vista of crowded ante-chambers and long-suffering queues outside the stage-door. We have, in fact, a glimpse of "The insolence of Office, and the Spurnes That patient merit of the unworthy takes". The opening scene of *The Tempest* shows how the whole multiple stage of Platform and Tiring-House can be made to seem like a ship tossing on a stormy sea—with the Master on his bridge on the Tarras, and perhaps the Ship-Boy on the high and giddy mast in the Musicians' gallery, the Boatswain bidding the gentry keep below as they struggle up through the trap-door from the ship's hold in Hell, the Stage-Posts serving for masts, the Stage-Rails as the taffrail, and

---

[60] *Troilus and Cressida*, IV. v. 218 ff.   [61] *Julius Caesar*, IV. ii. 30 ff.
[62] *Othello*, II. i. 53 f.   [63] *Antony and Cleopatra*, I. ii. 123.

A tempestuous noise of Thunder and Lightning heard from the Huts above the Heavens.[64]

The episode of the highway robbery in 1 *Henry IV* [65] shows Shakespeare's method *in extenso*. The prelude of the two carriers in the inn-yard, sometimes omitted in the productions of to-day, is an essential part of Shakespeare's stagecraft. Throughout the first act of the play we have been at court. The change of circumstances is indicated partly perhaps by the opening of the Study, in which are set some indications of the inn-yard—a bale of straw, a pannier, a rake, bridle and harness, a bucket, a trough—but mostly by the dialogue of the two carriers. Crammed with local colour, it is a masterpiece of compression: one of them carries a lantern: it is still dark but the star over the new chimney tells him that it is "foure by the day": his "poore Jade" is galled by the saddle: the "Pease and Beanes are as danke here as a Dog": the whole place is topsy-turvy since Robin the Ostler died: we hear complaints of the fleas and the sanitary arrangements: the load is of bacon and ginger, "to be delivered as farre as Charing-Crosse": the ostler has not given the turkeys in the pannier anything to eat overnight. All this and more is given us in a matter of thirty-five lines, and then to the setting of the circumstances is added the sinister note as the two carriers show their suspicion of the inquisitive spy and "setter" Gadshill. "What time do you mean to come to London?" he asks, and one of the carriers answers: "Time enough to goe to bed with a Candle, I warrant thee. Come neighbour *Mugges*, wee'll call up the Gentle-men, they will along with company, for they have great charge." When they have gone, the Chamberlain of the inn, Gadshill's accomplice, confirms the information that he gave him yester-night: there is a Franklin with three hundred marks in gold, and a "kinde of Auditor, one that hath abundance of charge too"; they are already up and calling for breakfast. The two rogues shake hands on their villainy and take their several ways, the Chamberlain back into the inn, Gadshill towards the stable. The Study curtains close, and we proceed with no interruptions to the projected scene of operations. Now the flat Platform becomes the slope of Gads Hill: the ten players, who take part in the scene, are carefully instructed in their miming to preserve the illusion of up and down hill. Falstaff's horse has been "removed" by Poins and the "fat-kidney'd Rascall", to whom "eight yards of uneven ground, is threescore and ten miles afoot", comes puffing up the hill from the left door. The Prince tells him that Poins has walked up to the top of the hill, and himself

---

[64] *The Tempest*, I. i.   [65] 1 *Henry IV*, II. i and ii.

follows him out towards the right. The entry of Gadshill is a moment of melodramatic comedy. I fancy that as Falstaff grumbles at the Prince "Go hang thy selfe in thine owne heire-apparant-Garters", he has his back to the Study curtains, which slowly part to a gap of a few feet, and reveal the figure of a masked highwayman, pistol in hand, perhaps under a weatherbeaten signpost, one arm of which points left-handed down the hill. "Stand," roars the masked figure: "So I do against my will," cries Falstaff, and then amid laughter we recognise Gadshill. We hear that "ther's money of the Kings comming downe the hill", so that we expect the Travellers from the right door. "You foure shall front them in the narrow Lane," says the Prince, indicating the gap in the Study curtains; "*Ned* and I, will walke lower," and the pair of them retreat downhill through the left door. Falstaff and his gang bestow themselves in the Study, while the Franklin, the Auditor and the two carriers appear through the right door. "Come Neighbor," says the Franklin, "the boy shall leade our Horses downe the hill: Wee'l walke a-foot a while, and ease our Legges." We need not pursue the scene to its uproarious climax to realise that the dialogue is most skilfully contrived to create on the Platform of the Globe the circumstances and atmosphere of the London–Rochester highway. In a more leisurely vein, it is just such atmospheric painting of objective detail that gives verisimilitude to the country establishment of Mr. Justice Shallow in Gloucestershire.[66]

The classic example of the creation of circumstances not visible to the eye of the beholder is the episode of Dover cliff in *King Lear*.[67] Cranford Adams would set Gloucester's leap in the Study and provide him with a property bank to jump from—"a 'verge' evident to the audience as well as to Gloucester's limited senses."[68] I am not convinced that this concession is necessary or desirable, but would suspend judgment until it is possible to try it in practice—the only safe test in matters of dramatic illusion. Here, for once, we have the conjurer with his coat off, showing us how he does his tricks: for Edgar is casting upon his blind father such a spell as the poet is constantly attempting to cast upon his audience. Gloucester, like us, protests scepticism; and, like us, is ultimately persuaded against his judgment.

> *Glou.* When shall I come to th' top of that same hill?
> *Edg.* You do climbe up it now. Look how we labour.
> *Glou.* Me thinkes the ground is eeven.
> *Edg.* Horrible steepe.
> Hearke, do you heare the Sea?

---

[66] *2 Henry IV*, III. ii; V. i; V. iii.   [67] *King Lear*, IV. vi. 1–81.
[68] J. Cranford Adams, *The Original Staging of King Lear*, pp. 300 f.

> *Glou.* No truly.
> *Edg.* Why then your other Senses grow imperfect
>   By your eyes anguish.

The bedlam beggar leads the blind man to the supposed edge of the cliff: even the rhythm of his words suggests vertigo and the holding of the breath:

> Come on Sir,
> Heere's the place: stand still: how fearefull
> And dizie 'tis, to cast ones eyes so low—

The crows flying half-way down seem hardly as big as beetles: there is a man there gathering samphire, a dangerous business: he looks no larger than his head: the fishermen on the beach are like mice: "and yond tall Anchoring Barke, Diminish'd to her Cocke." To the visual illusion is added the aural; for though you can see the surf on the pebbles, you cannot hear it so high up. Edgar pretends that he dare not look any longer, for fear of giddiness. With a blessing for his lost son Edgar on his lips, the blind man hurls himself over the imaginary cliff. But the poet's tricks are not finished yet. Changing his voice and his manner, Edgar pretends to find the old man huddled at the bottom of the precipice. The opposite illusion, of looking up from below, is again created by poetical means:

> *Edg.* Had'st thou beene ought
>   But Gozemore, Feathers, Ayre,
>   (So many fathome downe precipitating)
>   Thou'dst shiver'd like an Egge: but thou do'st breath:
>   Hast heavy substance, bleed'st not, speak'st, art sound,
>   Ten Masts at each, make not the altitude
>   Which thou hast perpendicularly fell,
>   Thy Life's a Myracle. Speake yet againe.
> *Glou.* But have I falne, or no?
> *Edg.* From the dread Sommet of this Chalkie Bourne.
>   Looke up a height, the shrill-gorg'd Larke so farre,
>   Cannot be seene, or heard:—

Our physical eyes are of course as wide open as Edgar's: but if the mind's eye cannot see and feel with Gloucester, cannot surrender to the poet's magic, then the despairing plunge over the precipice will seem but a ridiculous tumble on a flat Platform, and Edgar's redemption of his father a childish absurdity.

A special need in the steady daylight of the afternoon performances at the Globe, with the hardly changing appearance of the Platform and the Tiring-House, was the creation of atmosphere in a more literal sense of the word—the suggestion of different times of day and night, and of varying weather. There are many night scenes in Shakespeare's plays. An episode in the course of the siege of Orleans opens with a Sentinel grumbling

> Thus are poore Servitors
> (When others sleepe upon their quiet beds)
> Constrain'd to watch in darknesse, raine, and cold.[69]

The interest of this early example lies in the fact that already we see the poet finding a dramatic justification for his atmospheric painting. The eve of Bosworth Field is admirably sketched: Richmond begins it with the words:

> The weary Sunne, hath made a Golden set,
> And by the bright Tract of his fiery Carre,
> Gives token of a goodly day to morrow.

He invites his companions to a conference, bidding them come

> Into my Tent, the Dew is rawe and cold.

The ensuing scene at Richard's headquarters is full of graphic detail: we learn that it is supper time, nine o'clock: but the King will not sup to-night: Norfolk is bidden to choose trusty sentinels, and to "Stir with the Larke to morrow": a message is sent to Stanley to

> bid him bring his power
> Before Sun-rising, least his Sonne *George* fall
> Into the blinde Cave of eternall night.

The "melancholly Lord Northumberland" with the Earl of Surrey

> Much about Cockshut time, from Troope to Troope
> Went through the Army, chearing up the Souldiers.

Richard's final orders to his aide-de-camp are:

> Bid my Guard watch. Leave me.
> *Ratcliffe*, about the mid of night come to my Tent
> And helpe to arme me.

Almost at once, from the other side of the Platform, we hear the voice of Derby saying to Richmond:

> The silent houres steale on,
> And flakie darknesse breakes within the East.[70]

The poet has bestowed such careful attention upon the painting of this night in the two camps because he is building up to the elaborate

---

[69] 1 *Henry VI*, II. i. 5 ff.   [70] *Richard III*, V. iii. 19 ff.

ghost-scene, when Richard's victims curse him and bless his antagonist. It is interesting to compare this early night-piece with a later and more mature essay in the same vein, the portrayal of the night before Agincourt. Here the main burden falls upon the Chorus, who creates the atmosphere in narrative form. I think it likely, though, that his narrative was accompanied by the gathering of the characters who were to play the following scene in the English camp. The Frenchmen have filled the Platform with their nervous, boastful bickering, protesting "Will it never be Morning?" and "What a long Night is this", and "Will it never be day? I will trot to morrow a mile, and my way shall be paved with English Faces". Now they retreat into the far corner by the right-hand door to polish their armour and play at dice, waiting for the dawn. The Chorus appears on the Tarras and bids us

> entertaine conjecture of a time,
> When creeping Murmure and the poring Darke
> Fills the wide Vessell of the Universe.

Then he proceeds with swift strokes to paint the scene:

> From Camp to Camp, through the foule Womb of Night
> The Humme of eyther Army stilly sounds;
> That the fixt Centinels almost receive
> The secret Whispers of each others Watch.

The English sentinels come from the left door, and prowl along the closed curtain of the Study: a moment later three common soldiers appear—the same three who will afterwards discuss the ethics of war with their disguised King—and erect their tripod and cauldron on the perimeter outside the left Stage-Post:

> Fire answers fire, and through their paly flames
> Each Battaile sees the others umber'd face.

There is a small trap-door in their corner of the Platform, from which, perhaps, the flames can be supplied to light up their bent, pensive faces. The neighing of horses, the strange sound of the armourers' hammers, the crowing of cocks, the clocks' tolling, all add their touch of realism. Other soldiers, no more than three or four, lie here and there upon the Platform taking their restless ease outside their tents in this fateful night. Old Sir Thomas Erpingham alone seems unmoved as, like an old campaigner, he makes a pillow of his cloak and prepares for his habitual sleep in the central space within the Stage-Posts. With a glance at the Frenchmen the Chorus points the contrast in the other camp:

> The poore condemned English,
> Like Sacrifices, by their watchfull Fires
> Sit patiently, and inly ruminate
> The Mornings danger: and their gesture sad,
> Investing lanke-leane Cheekes, and Warre-worne Coats,
> Presenteth them unto the gazing Moone
> So many horride Ghosts.

Into this picture steps the familiar figure of the King:

> O now, who will behold
> The Royall Captaine of this ruin'd Band
> Walking from Watch to Watch, from Tent to Tent;
> Let him cry, Prayse and Glory on his head . . .

He goes from group to group, bidding good morrow, and would put courage even into the shivering Pistol, who stands to warm himself by the fire his fellow-soldiers have made:

> That every Wretch, pining and pale before,
> Beholding him, plucks comfort from his Lookes.
> . . . that meane and gentle all.
> Behold, as may unworthinesse define,
> A little touch of *Harry* in the Night . . .

It seems now quite dark: every eye in the playhouse is peering through the shadows in fear of the Frenchmen, overwhelming in their numbers: the poet's apology for the resources of his stage seems needless: his audience are in camp, at midnight before the day of battle, and feel genuine comfort when they hear the hushed voice of their commander:

> *Gloster*, 'tis true that we are in great danger,
> The greater therefore should our Courage be.[71]

There in the steady light, on the unlocalised Platform of the Globe, the simple miracle is performed. Shakespeare's positive delight in make-believe infects his hearers with a like pleasure: his medium is the spoken word, poetry: all through the play he has thrown down his explicit challenge to them to use their imagination: undistracted by pictorial realism, their imagination responds to his bidding—and lo! it is midnight between the rival camps.

The robbery on Gads Hill is a good example of an incidental but important effect of the Globe's daylight convention. There is a great advantage in such a scene in being able to see who's who: in a recent performance of the play, with the stage plunged in gloom, it was as

---

[71] *Henry V*, III. vii. IV. Chorus and i.

much as the audience could do to discern the bulky silhouette of Falstaff, and most of the fun was therefore missed. I have sometimes seen
a "thriller" on the cinema-screen marred by such a miscalculation
of the degree of darkness, the audience left helplessly and irritably
bewildered by a succession of shots of muffled figures, with glinting
pistols and flickering torches pouncing on unrecognisable victims.
Compare with them the horrifying clarity of the attempted murder
of Cassio,[72] where we see every actor in the drama and yet feel we
are in the dark: the dialogue illuminates every significant detail.
Roderigo lurks "behind this Barke [*read* Bulke]", and bids Iago "Be
neere at hand, I may miscarry in't". Cassio is recognised by his gait,
but Roderigo's thrust is made ineffectual by the stoutness of his
victim's coat. Roderigo is mortally wounded, but Cassio only
"maym'd for ever". Othello, aloft on the Tarras, cannot see, but
hears enough to spur him on to follow the example of "brave *Iago*,
honest, and just". Cassio calls for a surgeon. Lodovico and Gratiano,
groping in the dark, are reluctant to approach the groaning pair:

> These may be counterfeits: Let's think't unsafe
> To come into the cry, without more helpe.

Iago returns to the scene, as if newly roused from sleep, "in his shirt,
with Light, and Weapons". He goes to Cassio's help, but hearing
Roderigo's cry from the other side of the Platform, takes the chance
to stop his mouth for ever, crying in hypocritical indignation:

> Kill men i'th'darke?
> Where be these bloddy Theeves?
> How silent is this Towne? Hoa, murther, murther.

then turns to Lodovico and Gratiano and asks them

> What may you be? Are you of good, or evill?

Cassio declares that his leg is "cut in two", and Iago cries

> Light Gentlemen, Ile binde it with my shirt.

Still bending over his task, he asks the wounded man (in a voice
tense with anxiety for his own safety):

> *Cassio*, may you suspect
> Who they should be, that have thus mangled you?

Reassured by Cassio's "No", he finishes his first-aid:

> Lend me a Garter. So:—— Oh for a Chaire
> To beare him easily hence.

[72] *Othello*, V. i.

The devilish, brilliant opportunism of Iago is only matched by Shakespeare's own unflagging invention, but how little of this masterly stagecraft survives in the confused twilight of the picture-stage!

The moonlit wood is created by lyrical repetition in the early passages of *A Midsummer Night's Dream*, such as these lines of Lysander as he reveals to Helena his tryst with Hermia:

> To morrow night, when *Phoebe* doth beholde
> Her silver visage, in the watry glasse,
> Decking with liquid pearle, the bladed grasse . . .[73]

and the moonlit garden at Belmont is even more explicitly lyrical:

> The moone shines bright. In such a night as this,
> When the sweet winde did gently kisse the trees,
> And they did make no noyse . . .

and again—

> How sweet the moone-light sleepes upon this banke,
> Here will we sit, and let the sounds of musicke
> Creepe in our eares [*read* eares:] soft stilnes, and the night
> Become the tutches of sweet harmonie . . .

and the impression of still moonlit night is reinforced by other phrases, including Portia's playful description of the rapt pair of lovers—

> the Moone sleepes with Endimion,
> And would not be awak'd.[74]

It is typical of the concise compression of Shakespeare's later style that Othello, in a tense moment of night encounter, reinforces the torchlight with a single line:

> Keepe up your bright Swords, for the dew will rust them.[75]

There is once again a dramatic motivation in Enobarbus' dying appeal to the moon as

> Soveraigne Mistris of true Melancholly.[76]

The converse process of producing daylight after darkness is of course no less necessary on the daylit stage. The eve of Bosworth and of Agincourt are both followed by vivid portrayal of the morning of

---

[73] *A Midsummer Night's Dream*, I. i. 209 ff.
[74] *The Merchant of Venice*, V. i. 1 ff.; 54 ff.; 109 f.
[75] *Othello*, I. ii. 59.   [76] *Antony and Cleopatra*, IV. ix. 12.

battle. King Richard counts the clock, consults the calendar, and observes that the sun "disdaines to shine":

> The sky doth frowne, and lowre upon our Army.
> I would these dewy teares were from the ground.[77]

At Agincourt one of the French peers, in high spirits, cries:

> The Sunne doth gild our Armour up, my Lords.[78]

The effect can be studied in detail in *A Midsummer Night's Dream*, where the plot demands, after the long sequence in the moonlit, fairy-haunted wood, that the lovers should be discovered by the Duke in the early morning. Shakespeare, as usual, meets the difficulty by turning it into an opportunity: Hippolyta the Amazon suggests to his imagination the notion of a hunting-party—she and Theseus talk the jargon of the hunt, and how beautifully it is calculated to dispel the atmosphere of moonlight and fairies. Gone is the moonlit bower of Titania: instead we have "the vaward of the day", the "Westerne valley" where the forester is to uncouple, the neighbouring mountain-top, the drooping ears of the Duke's hounds that "sweepe away the morning dew"; and when Theseus sees the lovers asleep, he says

> No doubt, they rose up early, to observe
> The right of May . . .[79]

Hot noon is vividly realised in the scene of Mercutio's untimely death. Benvolio strikes the note at once in his opening lines:

> I pray thee good *Mercutio* lets retire,
> The day is hot, the *Capulets* abroad:
> And if we meet, we shal not scape a brawle,
> For now these hot dayes, is the mad blood stirring.

The impression is casually reinforced by Mercutio's "thou hast quarrel'd with a man for coffing in the street, because he hath wakened thy Dog that hath laine asleepe in the Sun", and there is a touch of the sun-baked street too in Benvolio's anxious intervention, as the mad blood begins to stir—

> We talke here in the publike haunt of men:
> Either withdraw unto some private place,
> Or reason coldly of your greevances:
> Or else depart, here all eies gaze on us.[80]

---

[77] *Richard III*, V. iii. 277 ff.   [78] *Henry V*, IV. ii. 1.
[79] *A Midsummer Night's Dream*, IV. i. 109 ff. See my *Moonlight at the Globe*, 90 f. An earlier attempt at the same effect, for a similar purpose (to establish the idea of early morning), can be seen in the Induction to *The Taming of the Shrew*, lines 16 ff.
[80] *Romeo and Juliet*, III. i. 1 ff.; 26 ff.; 55 ff.

It is noticeable here that Shakespeare not only projects the required atmosphere upon the stage, but also makes us feel the effect of it on the tempers of his characters.

We have a vivid storm in *Julius Caesar* created by Pope and Phillips: Casca is mainly descriptive, but Cassius makes dramatic capital out of the elements:

> Now could I (*Caska*) name to thee a man,
> Most like this dreadfull Night,
> That Thunders, Lightens, opens Graves, and roares,
> As doth the Lyon in the Capitoll:

and again:

> the Complexion of the Element
> Is [*read* In] Favors, like the Worke we have in hand,
> Most bloodie, fierie, and most terrible.

It is interesting to see how Shakespeare moulds the storm to his own purposes, creating an artificial lull in Brutus' orchard as a background to the musing of the philosopher "with himselfe at warre", and reviving the cue of *Thunder* just before the end of the orchard scene as a preparation for the outcry of the sleepless Caesar: "Nor Heaven, nor Earth, Have beene at peace to night." [81] But this "disturbed Skie" is insignificant beside the "Cataracts, and Hyrricano's" of *King Lear*, where the storm is as integral a part of the texture of the drama as the darkness is in *Macbeth*. The means by which this tempest is contrived deserve a close inspection. We have a presentiment of it long before it begins in the brief interlude of Edgar's escape from the hue and cry: he tells us in soliloquy his intention to disguise himself as a Bedlam beggar,

> And with presented nakednesse out-face
> The Windes, and persecutions of the skie . . .

and to visit

>   low Farmes,
> Poore pelting Villages, Sheeps-Coates, and Milles . . . [82]

The very phrases are echoed in the storm-scenes. The first evidence of the storm itself is a stage-direction, *Storme and Tempest*, just before the King's frenzied departure from Gloucester's house. The Platform represents the courtyard outside the house, and the great gates are set in the Study. "Let us withdraw," says Cornwall, " 'twill be a Storme." Gloucester, who has "Followed the old man forth", returns in helpless agitation:

---

[81] *Julius Caesar*, I. iii. 72 ff.; 128 ff.; II. ii. 1.
[82] *King Lear*, II. iii. 11 f.; 17 f.

> Alacke the night comes on, and the high windes
> Do sorely ruffle, for many Miles about
> There's scarce a Bush.

But Regan is heartless in her determination, and Cornwall no less ruthless as he advises Gloucester—

> Shut up your doores my Lord, 'tis a wil'd night,
> My *Regan* counsels well: come out o'th'storme.[83]

The company withdraw into the house: the great gates clash to behind them, the Study curtains are pulled, and without interruption, as the Huts get busy with the mechanics of thunder and wind, Kent and a Gentleman appear, heads down against the weather, at opposite stage-doors.

> *Kent.* Who's there besides foule weather?
> *Gen.* One minded like the weather, most unquietly.

The Quarto of 1608 gives us full measure of the atmospheric painting which is an essential part of the poet's scheme [84]: it is this anonymous gentleman, a minor player, who is entrusted with the preliminary description (which gives much added pathos to the subsequent entry of the King) of how he

> Contending with the fretfull element,
> Bids the wind blow the earth into the sea,
> Or swell the curled waters bove the maine
> That things might change or cease, teares his white haire,
> Which the impetuous blasts with eyles rage
> Catch in their furie, and make nothing of,
> Strives in his little world of man to outscorne,
> The too and fro conflicting wind and raine.[85]

It would carry us too far afield to examine the details of Lear's own creation of the storm in words—that masterly fusion of imagery and rhythm which produces such explosions as

> Strike flat the thicke Rotundity o'th'world . . .

and

> Rumble thy belly full: spit Fire, spowt Raine:
> Nor Raine, Winde, Thunder, Fire are my Daughters.

---

[83] *King Lear,* II. iv. 290, 303 ff., 311 f.
[84] Already by 1623 his colleagues had initiated the process by which since their day such atmospheric poetry has been sliced wholesale from the active text.
[85] *King Lear,* III. i. 1 f., 4 ff.

But two things should be noticed in this context: first, that it was Burbadge's task not only to seem

> A poore, infirme, weake, and dispis'd old man . . .

but also to create with all the force that his voice and his gesture could command the "high-engender'd Battailes" of the elements.[86] This is a clear example of how Shakespeare will sometimes expect his player to go beyond the mere representation of the character he plays to the creation of the atmospheric effect of the scene in which he plays it. The second point has been often observed before; that this storm is itself an integral part of the tragedy, close-woven into the poet's pattern, as is clear in the King's outcry—

> Thou think'st 'tis much that this contentious storme
> Invades us to the skin: so 'tis to thee,
> But where the greater malady is fixt,
> The lesser is scarce felt . . .
>   the tempest in my mind,
> Doth from my sences take all feeling else,
> Save what beates there, Fillial ingratitude . . .[87]

We must also notice that the poet is at pains to prompt our reactions to the storm: it is not only the comments of the Gentleman and Kent, nor the pathetic chattering of the Fool —"heere's a night pitties neither Wisemen nor Fooles" and " 'tis a naughtie night to swimme in"—but Gloucester's words as the five wanderers reach shelter, "Heere is better then the open ayre, take it thankfully," make us too in the audience grateful for the relief, and correspondingly distressed (as Gloucester returns to say that they must go out again) at Kent's "This rest might yet have balmed thy broken sinewes." [88] The storm has its moments of aftermath, when Gloucester, at the mercy of his tormentors, protests

> The Sea, with such a storme as his bare head,
> In Hell-blacke-night indur'd, would have buoy'd up
> And quench'd the Stelled fires:
> Yet poore old heart, he holpe the Heavens to raine.
> If Wolves had at thy Gate howl'd that sterne time,
> Thou should'st have said, good Porter turne the Key:[89]

and when Cordelia, gazing on her father's face as he sleeps in his chair, cries

---

[86] *King Lear*, III. ii. 7, 14 f., 20, 23.
[87] *King Lear*, III. iv. 6 ff.
[88] *King Lear*, III. ii. 13; III. iv. 113; III. vi. 1 ff., 107.
[89] *King Lear*, III. vii. 59 ff.

> Was this a face
> To be oppos'd against the jarring windes?
> Mine Enemies dogge, though he had bit me,
> Should have stood that night against my fire . . .[90]

In both these last examples, it will be seen that Shakespeare is adding to his creation of the storm a strong prompting of our feelings about it and about the cruelty of those who drove the old King out into it.

From the formal ritual scene of the visitation of ghosts at the end of *Richard III*, Shakespeare advanced to the masterpieces of *Julius Caesar* and *Hamlet*. "The deepe of night is crept upon our talke," says Brutus, and calls for his gown before he bids good night to Cassius. Lucius, bringing the gown, speaks drowsily. The guards are invited to sleep on cushions in the tent. The absent-minded Brutus finds the book he had looked for in the pocket of his gown. The boy is asked to hold up his heavy eyes awhile, and play a tune: he sings, and falls asleep in the middle of his song. Brutus opens his book, finds his place, and begins to read: "How ill this Taper burnes." As always, the poet selects the details that will most easily and most vividly make his dramatic effect.[91] But the ghost in *Hamlet* is the more astonishing *tour de force*: for there is so little time to prepare the ground: within forty lines of the play's beginning the ghost is before our eyes. The strokes are swiftly made: the opening challenge unexpectedly coming from the relieving sentry not yet at his post; the punctual arrival—no, it is already "strook twelve"; the "releefe" (the word is deliberately ambiguous) of Francisco, who is "sicke at heart"; "Not a Mouse stirring"; "bid them make hast"; the arrival of the neighbour watch; "What, ha's this thing appear'd againe to night"; "this dreaded sight, twice seene of us"; "this Apparition"; the *crescendo* dwindles again before Horatio's scepticism; they sit down awhile to hear Barnardo's tale:

> Last night of all,
> When yond same Starre that's Westward from the Pole
> Had made his course t'illume that part of Heaven
> Where now it burnes, *Marcellus* and my selfe,
> The Bell then beating one . . .

and lo! the player Shakespeare has already taken his cue and "In the same figure, like the King that's dead", stalks martially across the Tarras.[92]

It grows clearer, as we contemplate more examples, that it became Shakespeare's practice not only to give us the atmosphere

---

[90] *King Lear,* IV. vii. 31 ff.   [91] *Julius Caesar,* IV. iii. 225 ff.
[92] *Hamlet,* I. i. 1 ff.

and to motivate it, but also quite often to guide and influence—
subtly sometimes and almost imperceptibly—our reactions to it; and
that the chance of so guiding us is one of the great strengths of the
method of the poetic drama. We have seen examples from *King Lear*,
and the Ghost in *Hamlet*, when he opens his mouth, not only hints at
the secrets of his prison-house but guides our feelings too:

> I could a Tale unfold, whose lightest word
> Would harrow up thy soule, freeze thy young blood,
> Make thy two eyes like Starres, start from their Spheres,
> Thy knotty and combined locks to part,
> And each particular haire to stand an end,
> Like Quilles upon the fretfull Porpentine:
> But this eternall blason must not be
> To eares of flesh and bloud . . .[93]

A most striking instance of this practice can be studied in *Julius
Caesar*. Titinius kneels beside the dead body of his friend Cassius on
the battlefield of Philippi; or rather a minor actor kneels beside
Augustine Phillips on the bare Platform of the Globe and, lifting his
eyes, gazes intently at horizon-level across the Yard. Then he cries
aloud:

> O setting Sunne:
> As in thy red Rayes thou dost sinke to night;
> So in his red blood Cassius day is set.
> The Sunne of Rome is set. Our day is gone,
> Clowds, Dewes, and Dangers come . . .[94]

Now your lighting expert with his cyclorama can manage a sunset,
and your make-up artist some red blood for Cassius. But what more
can they do than has been done for them already by the poet? And
the poet leaves them behind when he goes on to weave the two
strands together—the red rays and the red blood—in a texture that
colours the whole of that wonderful last act. Through our ears, our
imagination is pierced with the intense suffering in the minds of the
idealists, the dismal realisation that their labour has all been in vain,
and their belief that Rome has gone down with them: it is (to them)
the end of Rome. The sun of Rome is set. Our day is gone. Clouds,
dews and dangers come. The play ends in the twilight shed by those
lines—an atmosphere that no lighting-effect could produce, that any
attempt at lighting-effect would merely hinder—and we feel that we
are watching the twilight of a great cause.

We shall see when, in the next chapter, we come to consider

---

[93] *Hamlet*, I. v. 15 ff.   [94] *Julius Caesar*, V. iii. 60 ff.

Macbeth in detail, how in creating the twilight for Banquo's murder, the poet plays most powerfully upon our feelings and makes us long to be under cover, to gain the timely inn.[95]

(iv) Creation in Words—of Character

Familiar, even from the earliest plays, is the poet's habit of drawing his characters in the direct description of their fellows. The good Duke Humphrey of Gloucester thus indicts the enemies who confront him in the royal presence:

> *Beaufords* red sparkling eyes blab his hearts mallice,
> And *Suffolks* cloudie Brow his stormie hate;
> Sharpe *Buckingham* unburthens with his tongue,
> The envious Load that lyes upon his heart:
> And dogged *Yorke*, that reaches at the Moone,
> Whose over-weening Arme I have pluckt back,
> By false accuse doth levell at my Life.[96]

When York falls into the hands of the Lancastrians, Queen Margaret's mocking is bitterest of all:

> Where are your Messe of Sonnes, to back you now?
> The wanton *Edward*, and the lustie *George*?
> And where's that valiant Crook-back Prodigie,
> *Dickie*, your Boy, that with his grumbling voyce
> Was wont to cheare his Dad in Mutinies?
> Or with the rest, where is your Darling, *Rutland*?[97]

Richard Crookback's mother adds much to our understanding of him when she describes (as it were) his "four ages of man":

> Tetchy and wayward was thy Infancie.
> Thy School-daies frightfull, desp'rate, wilde, and furious,
> Thy prime of Manhood, daring, bold, and venturous:
> Thy Age confirm'd, proud, subtle, slye, and bloody,
> More milde, but yet more harmfull; Kinde in hatred . . .[98]

The actor who would play the part of Boyet in *Love's Labour's Lost* has ample material in Berowne's twenty lines of satire:

> This fellow pickes up wit as Pigeons pease,
> And utters it againe, when *Jove* doth please.
> He is Wits Pedler, and retailes his Wares,
> At Wakes, and Wassels, Meetings, Markets, Faires,
> And we that sell by grosse, the Lord doth know,
> Have not the grace to grace it with such show . . .[99]

---

[95] See below, p. 298.
[97] 3 *Henry VI*, I. iv. 73 ff.
[99] *Love's Labour's Lost*, V. ii. 316 ff.
[96] 2 *Henry VI*, III. i. 154 ff.
[98] *Richard III*, IV. iv. 169 ff.

(Who would not—absent-mindedly and without book—think he was listening to Dryden or Pope?)

The narrative portrait sketches of Jaques and Touchstone in *As You Like It* are familiar; so likewise Maria's caricatures of Sir Andrew and Malvolio in *Twelfth Night*.[100] A play especially rich in the method is *Julius Caesar*: there is, for instance, Caesar's elaborate picture of

> that spare *Cassius*. He reades much,
> He is a great Observer, and he lookes
> Quite through the Deeds of men. He loves no Playes,
> As thou dost *Antony*: he heares no Musicke;
> Seldome he smiles, and smiles in such a sort
> As if he mock'd himselfe, and scorn'd his spirit
> That could be mov'd to smile at any thing.
> Such men as he, be never at hearts ease,
> Whiles they behold a greater then themselves,
> And therefore are they very dangerous.

There is Cicero whose silver-haired gravity does not outweigh Brutus' adverse judgment:

> let us not breake with him,
> For he wlll never follow any thing
> That other men begin.

There is Casca, of whom Brutus says

> What a blunt fellow is this growne to be?
> He was quick Mettle, when he went to Schoole.

and of whom Cassius answers

> So is he now, in execution
> Of any bold, or Noble Enterprize,
> How-ever he puts on this tardie forme:
> This Rudenesse is a Sawce to his good Wit,
> Which gives men stomacke to disgest his words
> With better Appetite.

There is Antony who loves plays, who is given "To sports, to wilde-nesse, and much company", who "Revels long a-nights", who seems to Brutus "but a Limbe of *Caesar*", who is indeed a dark horse until the death of Caesar, in spite of the hint of Cassius:

> we shall finde of him
> A shrew'd Contriver. And you know, his meanes
> If he improve them, may well stretch so farre
> As to annoy us all . . .

---

[100] *As You Like It*, II. i. 25 ff.; II. vii. 12 ff. *Twelfth Night*, I. iii. 16 ff.; II. iii. 161 ff.

There is Brutus, "with himselfe at warre", whom Cassius thinks he can sum up:

> Well *Brutus*, thou art Noble, yet I see,
> Thy Honorable Mettle may be wrought
> From that it is dispos'd: therefore it is meet,
> That Noble mindes keepe ever with their likes . . .

who gains so much in vivid reality by the intimate domestic glimpse of him which Portia gives us:

> yesternight at Supper
> You sodainly arose, and walk'd about,
> Musing, and sighing, with your armes a-crosse:
> And when I ask'd you what the matter was,
> You star'd upon me, with ungentle lookes.
> I urg'd you further, then you scratch'd your head,
> And too impatiently stampt with your foote:
> Yet I insisted, . . .[101]

the whole episode, as she describes it, is eloquent of the man's inward struggle. She succeeds in conveying, in this masterly scene, with hardly a word from Brutus except the one eloquent profession of love, a complete picture of their relationship, their daily life, his recent behaviour and her own character. It is of great value in creating Brutus' portrait, and pays a big dividend later in the play at a climax of the long scene in Brutus' tent. All these characters in this play are reinforced in the description of their fellows—sometimes, be it noticed, in a contradictory sense. It is indeed a feature of the play which cannot be accidental that Shakespeare presents his characters in two diametrically opposite manifestations: the blunt Casca reappears in a state of feverish excitement in the thunderstorm; the grave dignity of Cato's daughter returns to the stage as the hysterical Portia who sends Lucius to the Senate-house on a fool's errand; Cassius, who "lookes Quite through the Deeds of men", is panic-stricken by the ambiguous greeting of Popilius Laena, and on other occasions too reveals "that rash humour which my Mother gave me"; Caesar, the vain, suspicious epileptic, shows himself at the last "as constant as the Northerne Starre"; the "gamesom" Antony becomes the prophetic voice of "*Caesars* Spirit ranging for Revenge". It is as though Shakespeare's intention was, by taking his pictures from two different angles, to give a stereoscopic roundness to his figures.

From some of these examples it will be noted that, as with the

---

[101] *Julius Caesar*, I. ii. 200 ff.; II. i. 150 ff.; I. ii. 300 f.; II. i. 157 ff.; I. ii. 313 ff.; II. i. 238 ff.

creation of atmosphere, so also in character-drawing the method of
the poetic drama not only gives us the character but also sometimes
hints at how we should react to it. Ulysses' portrait of Diomed—

> 'Tis he, I ken the manner of his gate,
> He rises on the toe: that spirit of his
> In aspiration lifts him from the earth . . .

goes beyond objective description to interpret what we see; and still
more clearly does he prompt us to understand Cressida for what
she is—

> Ther's a language in her eye, her cheeke, her lip;
> Nay, her foote speakes, her wanton spirites looke out
> At every joynt, and motive of her body . . .[102]

One may go further and observe that Shakespeare is at pains to
prevent us being misled by the public demeanour of a character
whose dramatic interest is not on the surface. That is the purpose of
Prince Hal's informative soliloquy at the end of his first scene [103]; of
Brutus' hint to Cassius not to be deceived:

> Vexed I am
> Of late, with passions of some difference,
> Conceptions onely proper to my selfe,
> Which give some foyle (perhaps) to my Behaviours:
> But let not therefore my good Friends be greev'd
> (Among which number *Cassius* be you one)
> Nor construe any further my neglect,
> Then that poore *Brutus* with himselfe at warre,
> Forgets the shewes of Love to other men.[104]

Hamlet gives us a similar lead when he tells us right at the beginning
of his part

> I have that Within, which passeth show . . .[105]

and Iago, before proceeding to deceive all his acquaintance, gives us
in the audience explicit warning that

> when my outward Action doth demonstrate
> The native act, and figure of my heart
> In Complement externe, 'tis not long after
> But I will weare my heart upon my sleeve
> For Dawes to peck at; I am not what I am.[106]

In such cases, no doubt, the actor took care to remind the audience
occasionally in his performance of the poet's anticipatory hint.

---

[102] *Troilus and Cressida*, IV. v. 14 ff.; 55 ff.   [103] I *Henry IV*, I. ii. 217 ff.
[104] *Julius Caesar*, I. ii. 39 ff.   [105] *Hamlet*, I. ii. 85.
[106] *Othello*, I. i. 61 ff.

It is not only the general character of his figures and their habitual traits and mannerisms that Shakespeare gives us (and his colleagues) in his poetry, but also an indication of their appearance and behaviour at particular moments. It seems, indeed, an important point of technique arising from the conditions of performance: the detailed description takes the place of the facial expression visible with the make-up and strong lights of the modern theatre. Shakespeare at least (if not his fellow-dramatists) has a habit of leaving nothing to chance: his poetry supplies the place of the cinema's "close-up", and as with the atmospheric description, he can do far more than merely supply a photographic impression. When Richard of Gloucester springs the news that his brother Clarence is dead, the actors look their horrified surprise, and we are not allowed to miss the fact:

> *Buc.* Looke I so pale Lord *Dorset*, as the rest?
> *Dor.* I my good Lord, and no man in the presence,
> But his red colour hath forsooke his cheekes.[107]

When "High-reaching *Buckingham* growes circumspect", the new-crowned King Richard's dangerous mood is underlined for us:

> The King is angry, see he gnawes his Lippe.[108]

The aspect of Caesar's companions after the *contretemps* of his fit in the market-place is defined in close detail by Brutus:

> The angry spot doth glow on *Caesars* brow,
> And all the rest, looke like a chidden Traine;
> *Calphurnia's* Cheeke is pale, and *Cicero*
> Lookes with such Ferret, and such fiery eyes
> As we have seene him in the Capitoll
> Being crost in Conference, by some Senators.[109]

We have had occasion to notice the serial portraiture of the visitation of the Ghost to Gertrude's closet.[110] There is a vivid momentary glimpse of Iago's hypocrisy when Othello bids him give an account of the brawl he has engineered:

> Honest *Iago*, that lookes dead with greeving,
> Speake: who began this? [111]

The appearance of Desdemona as she lies asleep in bed has been quoted above.[112] The complementary picture as she lies dead wrings the heart of all that hear it:

---

[107] *Richard III*, II. i. 84 ff.   [108] *Richard III*, IV. ii. 27.
[109] *Julius Caesar*, I. ii. 182 ff.   [110] See above, pp. 173 f.
[111] *Othello*, II. iii. 179 f.   [112] See above, p. 169.

> Now: how dost thou looke now? Oh ill-Starr'd wench,
> Pale as thy Smocke: when we shall meete at compt,
> This looke of thine will hurle my Soule from Heaven,
> And Fiends will snatch at it. Cold, cold my Girle?
> Even like thy Chastity.

Beside these two "close-ups" of Desdemona, we may set two more of
Othello himself. As he bends over her in bed, her terrified voice says:

> you're fatall then
> When your eyes rowle so.

and asks him

> Alas, why gnaw you so your nether-lip?
> Some bloody passion shakes your very Frame.

These descriptive phrases are an essential part of the stagecraft of
this playhouse: Othello's face at this moment could hardly be visible
to his audience. It is he himself who gives us the last glimpse of his
agonised countenance when he bids the ambassadors, when they
return to Venice, speak

> Of one, whose subdu'd Eyes,
> Albeit un-used to the melting moode,
> Drops teares as fast as the Arabian Trees
> Their Medicinable gumme.[113]

Moreover, just as with the general character, so also with the
particular moments, it seems that Shakespeare thought it necessary
to warn us against being misled. The young King Henry VI in an
early and characteristically unsuccessful attempt to keep the peace
between Somerset and York, causes deep offence to the latter by
wearing the red rose. After his departure, Richard of York begins to
express his feelings, but breaks off with enigmatic restraint. His
silence is interpreted for us by Exeter, whose chorus-like soliloquy
closes the scene:

> Well didst thou *Richard* to suppresse thy voice:
> For had the passions of thy heart burst out,
> I feare we should have seene decipher'd there
> More rancorous spight, more furious raging broyles,
> Then yet can be imagin'd or suppos'd.[114]

At a mature stage of the poet's development, we see the same
process at work in Horatio's anticipatory description of Ophelia's
madness:

---

[113] *Othello*, V. ii. 271 ff.; 37 f.; 43 f.; 347 ff.
[114] 1 *Henry VI*, IV. i. 182 ff.

> She speakes much of her Father; saies she heares
> There's trickes i'th'world, and hems, and beats her heart,
> Spurnes enviously at Strawes, speakes things in doubt,
> That carry but halfe sense: Her speech is nothing,
> Yet the unshaped use of it doth move
> The hearers to Collection; they ayme at it,
> And botch the words up fit to their owne thoughts,
> Which as her winkes, and nods, and gestures yeeld them,
> Indeed would make one thinke there would be thought,
> Though nothing sure, yet much unhappily.[115]

We have here a hint to the boy-actor as to how to play the mad-scenes, but also a hint to the audience how to take them—how to read between the lines. Othello, already convinced of Desdemona's guilt and determined to kill her, is obliged to conceal his intention when he meets her. "How is't with you, my Lord?" she asks, and he replies "Well, my good Lady"; then he mutters to himself, "Oh hardnes to dissemble!" [116] We must be told that he is keeping up the pretence. For the same kind of reason, Cordelia must confess to us her true feelings and express her love for her father before she seems cruelly casual in her obstinate refusal to respond to his demands. After Goneril's hypocritical protestation, she whispers aside:

> What shall *Cordelia* speake? Love, and be silent—

And when Regan has followed suit—

> Then poore *Cordelia*,
> And yet not so, since I am sure my love's
> More ponderous then my tongue.[117]

We might almost wish she would not spoil in advance the dramatic effect of her "Nothing my Lord": but to Shakespeare's judgment the conditions seem to demand that she shall not mislead the audience by her apparent heartlessness. Likewise Kent must not appear in his disguise without telling us who he is and what he is up to:

> If but as well I other accents borrow,
> That can my speech defuse, my good intent
> May carry through it selfe to that full issue
> For which I raiz'd my likenesse. Now banisht *Kent*,
> If thou canst serve where thou dost stand condemn'd,
> So may it come, thy Master whom thou lov'st,
> Shall find thee full of labours.[118]

---

[115] *Hamlet*, IV. v. 4 ff. The Folio ascribes the speech to *Horatio*, the 1604–5 Quarto to *A Gentleman*.   [116] *Othello*, III. iv. 34 f.
[117] *King Lear*, I. i. 64, 78 ff.   [118] *King Lear*, I. iv. 1 ff.

Edgar, too, tells us in advance of his intended disguise: his vivid and circumstantial description of "poore *Turlygod*, poore *Tom*" adds greatly to the impression made by his sudden appearance from the hovel in the storm; we then invest his figure with the poetical painting previously given, and we have moreover the additional pleasure which comes from a surprise that might have been foreseen.[119] Again the nameless Gentleman who meets Kent in the storm, prepares us for the appearance of the King and the Fool, and his anticipatory description of "the Foole, who labours to out-jest His heart-strooke injuries" [120] is as important to our understanding of the sequel as is Horatio's pre-view of Ophelia. At the climax of Lear's madness, Edgar is our interpreter, bidding us understand the old King's words as

> matter, and impertinency mixt,
> Reason in Madnesse.[121]

A specially interesting case of this phenomenon is the often misunderstood episode of the announcement of Portia's death in *Julius Caesar*.[122] The stirring quarrel and reconciliation of Brutus and Cassius is followed by the seemingly ridiculous interruption of the jigging poet who tries to give his canting advice to the generals. Plutarch is the source of this episode, but Shakespeare has turned it to splendid dramatic advantage. For while Cassius laughs at the intruder, Brutus explodes in quite unreasonable rage. The contrast with his former restraint is so astonishing that Cassius says, "I did not thinke you could have bin so angry." Brutus explains the reason: Portia is dead. His words are measured: it is the impulsive Cassius who breaks out with "O insupportable, and touching losse!" Now Shakespeare is anxious to make us see the greatness of Brutus' long-suffering: but stoical restraint is a difficult thing to project in the poetic drama—for the poetic drama relies for its effects upon the spoken word, and the stoic is by nature short of speech. The cinema camera can register the silent suffering of stoicism by the twitching of an eybrow and the compressing of a lip. But how does the poetic dramatist achieve his purpose? Shakespeare does it here by the elaborate process of repeating the announcement, so that we in the audience can watch Brutus under the stress of his emotion, and feel with him as he says:

> Why farewell *Portia*: We must die *Messala*:
> With meditating that she must dye once,
> I have the patience to endure it now.

---

[119] *King Lear*, II. iii; III. iv. 44.   [120] *King Lear*, III. i. 16 f.
[121] *King Lear*, IV. vi. 179 f.   [122] *Julius Caesar*, IV. iii. 128-94.

Messala's comment is in itself an explanation of Shakespeare's intention:

> Even so great men, great losses shold indure . . .

and Cassius' following words help also to interpret for us—

> I have as much of this in Art as you,
> But yet my Nature could not beare it so . . .

by which he means, I think, "I can act a part as well as you, but I couldn't bear the grief in the first place." Reading the play in detachment in our armchair, we have time to calculate that there is some disingenuousness in Brutus' deception of Messala. But, in the theatre, we are carried away by the immediate emotional effect, and ready to accept the poet's interpretative comments. A less elaborate and perhaps more satisfactory treatment of the theme of stoical restraint occurs in *Macbeth:* we shall see in due course how the descriptive "close-up" method is applied to Macduff, when he hears the news of the murder of his family.[123]

Before leaving the subject of Shakespeare's creation of character, it is proper to draw attention to a style of characterisation which is fundamentally different from the objective portraiture of most of the early and middle-period plays. Capulet, Hotspur, Cassius, Fluellen, may stand as a typical cross-section of the objective trend: we might meet them any day, and we should recognise their mannerisms, their tastes, their words, their tone of voice. Even the principal figures, Prince Hal, Benedick, Orlando, have an individual personality which brings them within our ken; and certainly the women, Rosalind, Viola, Portia of Belmont, Beatrice. The kind of character—one may not call it a type—culminates in Hamlet, whom we all feel that we know as an intimate friend. If we think now of Othello, Macbeth and Antony, of Lady Macbeth, of Goneril and Regan—these figures seem to be Olympian in stature, unapproachable, remote; without the common touch, and yet surprisingly no less potent to cast a spell upon us. Even Lear, full of changes as his age is, even Cleopatra, with her infinite variety, seem conceived on a scale quite different from the earlier kind, which nevertheless persists among the minor figures side by side with the new kind. It is unnecessary at this point to do more than mention this essential difference and suggest that it arises from a fundamental change in Shakespeare's dramatic purpose and method, dating from the years that immediately follow *Hamlet*. A full analysis of this change is outside the scope of this book. But the suggestion

---

[123] See below, p. 304.

H

will be followed up later in this chapter when we consider the development of the technique of pervasive themes, and study briefly the crucial years of experiment, the period of the poet's "Withdrawal-and-Return". We shall notice then that the new method of characterisation is no less than the old a *poetic* creation, that it is indeed still more closely bound up with the art of the poet who was constantly alert to discover new means of expressing the mystery of things in terms of his poetic drama.

(v) Creation in Words—of the Action itself

We have more than once had cause to notice the method of presenting episodes of the plot (whether prior to the action or during it) by means of narrative description, in the manner of the Messenger Speech of Greek tragedy.[124] It is enough here to remind the reader of one or two striking examples, to illustrate the fact that in Shakespeare's playhouse it was part of the habitual technique to create in words—that is to say, by poetical means—not only atmosphere and character but also the action itself. Tyrrell's conscience-stricken tale of the murder of the young princes in the Tower is one such "Messenger Speech".[125] Hotspur's account of the aftermath of Holmedon Field, when he was "so pestered with a Popingay", is such another. Another is Morton's report of the defeat and death of Hotspur.[126] King Hamlet's ghost in his detailed description of his own poisoning provides an essential element in Shakespeare's presentation of his story; its dramatic importance can be measured when later on we watch the Players' travesty of the same scene under the eyes of the usurping murderer.[127] Queen Gertrude's picture of Ophelia's death, Salarino's of the parting of Antonio from Bassanio, Othello's unvarnished tale of his wooing, the bleeding captain's speech in the opening of *Macbeth*, Ariel's account of the shipwreck he has caused [128]—these speeches all take the place of visible action. In the medium of the cinema, for instance, they would be represented visually—perhaps by a "flashback". On Shakespeare's stage there is one reason or another why they cannot be so represented: it may be the practical difficulty of exhibiting drowning or shipwreck; it may be simply that the plot is long enough without further action, as for instance it would be inconvenient to begin *Othello* so far back as the time of Desdemona's wooing; or, as in the case of *The Winter's Tale*,

---

[124] See above, pp. 107 f., 131.   [125] *Richard III*, IV. iii.
[126] 1 *Henry IV*, I. iii. 29 ff.; 2 *Henry IV*, I. i. 105 ff.
[127] *Hamlet*, I. v. 59 ff.; III. ii. 270 ff.
[128] *Hamlet*, IV. vii. 167 ff.; *The Merchant of Venice*, II. viii. 36 ff.; *Othello*, I. iii. 128 ff.; *Macbeth*, I. ii. 7 ff.; *The Tempest*, I. ii. 196 ff.

the story has already carried the poet over four and a half acts, and there is not time to show in action both the reunion of Leontes and Polixenes and Paulina's resuscitation of Hermione; so three anonymous but eloquent Gentlemen are entrusted with the task of bringing before our eyes the meeting of the two Kings—"a Sight," says one of them, "which was to bee seene, cannot bee spoken of," and proceeds to speak of it so graphically that we do indeed see the occasion: "There was casting up of Eyes, holding up of Hands, with Countenance of such distraction, that they were to be knowne by Garment, not by Favor. Our King being ready to leape out of himselfe, for joy of his found Daughter; as if that joy were now become a Losse, cryes, Oh, thy Mother, thy Mother: then askes *Bohemia* forgivenesse, then embraces his Sonne-in-Law: then againe worryes he his Daughter, with clipping her. Now he thanks the old Shepheard (which stands by, like a Weather-bitten Conduit, of many Kings Reignes). I never heard of such another Encounter; which lames Report to follow it, and undo's description to doe it." [129] In the handling of such "Messenger Speeches", unless producer and actor realise—and unless the audience are made to realise—that the narrative is an essential part of the action of the play, and not just fine speech (beautiful poetry, brilliant prose, but static and rather long and therefore perhaps to be abridged or cut), then the play is marred. It has already been pointed out that the unlocalised stage by its very neutrality of aspect helps to bring them to life, and it has been suggested that the miming of the Chamberlain's Men would also contribute to this end. Meanwhile we must recognise that the poet himself has done his part of the job with deliberate intent and with his habitual skill.

Moreover, it is not only scenes that take place off-stage that are so treated: but, as with the "close-up" method defined above, in reference to characterisation, so too the visible action is illuminated by the dialogue so that we can feel its force more fully than, in the conditions of the Globe, we can by the aid of the eye alone. The scene of the blinding of Gloucester in *King Lear* [130] is a case in point, played as it probably was at a distance in the Chamber. There is a ruthless insistence in the *verbal* presentation of Gloucester's torment, contained in such phrases as "Binde fast his corky armes . . . Hard, hard . . . To this Chaire binde him . . . 'tis most ignobly done To plucke me by the Beard. . . . These haires which thou dost ravish from my chin . . . (*Gloucester speaking of Lear*) I would not see thy cruell Nailes Plucke out his poore old eyes (*but the words reflect upon his*

---

[129] *The Winter's Tale,* V. ii. 46 ff.   [130] *King Lear,* III. vii.

own predicament) . . . Fellowes hold ye Chaire, Upon these eyes of
thine, Ile set my foote. . . . One side will mocke another: Th'other
too . . . Out vilde gelly: Where is thy luster now? . . . All darke and
comfortlesse?" This grim catalogue will make it clear that Shakespeare is determined to create the action in his words: the objective
vision contained in these phrases, and reinforced by the bullying
rhythm of the inquisitors' insistent "Wherefore to Dover?" make the
scene one of the most terrible in all the annals of the stage: and it
will be noticed that the terror is multiplied by the fact—already
familiar to us in his treatment of atmosphere and character—that
the poet not only states what we see but also prompts our feelings
towards the action.

We have already studied the objective creation of atmosphere in
the scene of the attempt on Cassio's life. Another of Iago's con-
trivances is no less remarkable—the drunken brawl in which Cassio
loses his reputation. That in a scene of such swift and complicated
action it is quite clear (without stage-directions) what is happening
is a measure of Shakespeare's uncanny skill in the poetic drama. But
it is not only the bare narrative which is worth study but also the
overtones by which Iago gives his calculated sinister twist to the
bare facts: of Cassio's drunkenness he says—

> I fear the trust *Othello* puts him in,
> On some odde time of his infirmitie
> Will shake this Island.

He whispers to Roderigo—

> go out and cry a Mutinie . . .

and cries aloud to any that will hear—

> Heere's a goodly Watch indeed.
> Who's that which rings the Bell: Diablo, hoa:
> The Towne will rise.

The measure of his success is the eloquent anger of Othello:

> For Christian shame, put by this barbarous Brawle:

and

> Silence that dreadfull Bell, it frights the Isle,
> From her propriety.

and his surprised reproach to Montano—

> What's the matter
> That you unlace your reputation thus,
> And spend your rich opinion, for the name
> Of a night-brawler?

and his concise indictment of the whole affair:

> What in a Towne of warre,
> Yet wilde, the peoples hearts brim-full of feare,
> To manage private, and domesticke Quarrell?
> In night, and on the Court and Guard of safetie?
> 'Tis monstrous . . .[131]

Here we have a capital example of Shakespeare's double process, Iago creating the action and Othello interpreting it for us— prompting us what to think. This power of *interpreting* the action is another strength of the poetic drama; in the less eloquent realism bred of the conditions of the picture-stage, such interpretation is left to the capricious and often inert imagination of the spectators.

(vi) Transcending the Visible Scene

The poetic drama does not stop there in its power to cast a spell upon the audience. Shakespeare learnt that his playhouse and his poetical medium could create the illusion of things invisible to mortal sight, and could transcend even the suggestion of a visible scene. The appearance of the Ghost in *Hamlet* is very vivid to us: we see him before our eyes, and he is given an objective portraiture, which is very moving, in the words of those who watch him on the Platform: but more moving still is what we *cannot* see—the rising from the tomb. When young Hamlet asks his dead father to tell

> Why thy Canoniz'd bones Hearsed in death,
> Have burst their cerments, why the Sepulcher
> Wherein we saw thee quietly enurn'd,
> Hath op'd his ponderous and Marble jawes,
> To cast thee up againe?

and when the dead King hints at the secrets of his prison-house, the "eternall blason" which "must not be To eares of flesh and bloud", then indeed we begin to find our disposition shaken

> With thoughts beyond the reaches of our soules.[132]

It cannot be too strongly stressed that the unlocalised Platform of the Globe gives a sharp reality to such transcendental thoughts which will be blurred and blunted by any conflicting attempt to define the battlements of Elsinore.

The theme of mortality and the state of man after death is, of course, recurrent and pervasive in the play. Hamlet—like his

---

[131] *Othello*, II. iii. 132 ff.; 158, 161 ff.; 174, 177 f., 195 ff., 215 ff.
[132] *Hamlet*, I. iv. 47 ff.; I. v. 13 ff.

creator, perhaps, and many of his contemporaries—is much concerned with "the dread of something after death". The too-familiar
soliloquy "To be, or not to be . . ." carries us, quite unexpectedly
(for the immediately preceding scenes are concerned with the
manœuvres in the duel of wits between the King and Hamlet),
away from the intrigues of the Danish court to a contemplation of
this world and the next. The transcendent vision, it may be noticed,
is based on an objective ground: the "Whips and Scornes of time"—

> The Oppressors wrong, the poore mans Contumely,
> The pangs of dispriz'd Love, the Lawes delay,
> The insolence of Office, and the Spurnes
> That patient merit of the unworthy takes,

are modern Elizabethan, and indeed still topical to-day: but the
next moment we are peering into

> The undiscovered Countrey, from whose Borne
> No traveller returnes . . .[133]

Three years after writing *Hamlet*, Shakespeare was able to carry his
audience still more surely away from the Platform, in Claudio's
terrified vision of impending execution:

> I, but to die, and go we know not where,
> To lie in cold obstruction, and to rot,
> This sensible, warme motion, to become
> A kneaded clod; And the delighted spirit
> To bath in fierie floods, or to recide
> In thrilling Region of thicke-ribbed Ice,
> To be imprison'd in the viewless windes
> And blowne with restless violence round about
> The pendant world: or to be worse then worst
> Of those, that lawlesse and incertaine thought,
> Imagine howling, 'tis too horrible.[134]

Othello transports us in a moment from the bedside of the murdered
Desdemona beyond all visible circumstance as he cries:

> when we shall meete at compt,
> This looke of thine will hurle my Soule from Heaven,
> And Fiends will snatch at it. Cold, cold, my Girle?
> Even like thy Chastity. O cursed, cursed Slave!
> Whip me ye Divels,
> From the possession of this Heavenly sight:
> Blow me about in windes, roast me in Sulphure,
> Wash me in steepe downe gulfes of Liquid fire.[135]

---

[133] *Hamlet*, III. i. 56 ff.   [134] *Measure for Measure*, III. i. 116 ff.
[135] *Othello*, V. ii. 272 ff.

But it is not only in connection with death and the world to come that Shakespeare lifts us beyond the horizon of the eye. The vast conception of the storm in *King Lear* is interesting as an example of the poet's transcendent mood. There is a characteristic contrast between Lear's picture of the storm and Kent's, which makes the point clear. Kent speaks for the most part literally:

> Since I was man,
> Such sheets of Fire, such bursts of horrid Thunder,
> Such groanes of roaring Winde, and Raine, I never
> Remember to have heard.[136]

Lear sees

> Sulph'rous and Thought-executing Fires,
> Vaunt-curriors of Oake-cleaving Thunder-bolts . . .

he bids the thunder

> Strike flat the thicke Rotundity o'th'world . . .

He addresses the tempest, and cries

> I taxe not you, you Elements with unkindnesse . . .

and speaks of their "high-engender'd Battailes".[137] His imagery lifts the drama off the plane of the visible, to the range of poetical sublimity. Kent is creating the atmosphere by Shakespeare's habitual method; he is making us see a scene that is not there. But Lear goes one further: he sublimates the scene that Kent merely creates. Kent says, "Pretend this is a thunder-storm"; Lear makes the thunder-storm part of a great poetical vision which transcends visual pretence and can exist only in the imagination. We have all seen sheets of lightning and heard bursts of thunder, but we have never known the thunder to "Strike flat the thicke Rotundity o'th'world". Moreover, to explain this transcendent vision in a paraphrase is an impossible task; the only words that will do it are Shakespeare's own. There is a like contrast, as we shall see on a later page, between the words of Macbeth immediately after the murder of Duncan and those of his wife.[138]

Once again it is pertinent to realise that this transcendental mood belongs properly to the poetic drama, that it can hardly be achieved by other means: and again we may note the paradox that often in the furthest reaches of Shakespeare's imaginative inspiration, we find ourselves (expressly or by implication) closest to the objective detail

---

[136] *King Lear*, III. ii. 45 ff.   [137] *King Lear*, III. ii. 4 ff.; 16 ff.
[138] See below, pp. 289 f.

of Elizabethan modernity or to the conventional setting of the Globe
Playhouse. The whips and scorns of the poet's own time stand side by
side with the undiscovered country. When Hamlet speaks his prose-
poem of disillusionment with the beauty of the world and the
excellence of man, he uses the images of frame, canopy and roof,
which his audience would see before them in the playhouse. When
Macbeth contemplates the hopelessness of life, his thought turns to
the

> poore Player,
> That struts and frets his houre upon the Stage,
> And then is heard no more.

Granville-Barker expresses this truth when he writes of Shakespeare's
"peculiar gift of bringing into contribution the commonplace traffic
of life. However wide the spoken word may range, there must be the
actor, anchored to the stage. However high, then, with Shakespeare,
the thought or emotion may soar, we shall always find the transcendental set in the familiar".[139]

(vii) The Architecture of the Play

This reconsideration of the detail of Shakespeare's poetic creation
may now lead us to revise our opinion of his long-range composition.
Amid a universal chorus of praise for his tactical triumphs, it is
possible to detect a fairly general opinion that his strategy is weaker:
that is certainly the inference one must draw from the somewhat
lighthearted way in which his plays are still carved about to suit the
taste of his producers. It is well to clear our heads upon this point;
and by way of beginning, to recognise that there is some strong
evidence on the other side, tending towards the belief that Shakespeare is seldom diffuse and desultory, and that the thread of
dramatic tension is broken less often than is usually supposed. There
is, for instance, a school of thought represented by J. Semple Smart,
Peter Alexander and E. M. W. Tillyard which recognises Shakespeare's authorship of all three parts of *Henry VI* as well as *Richard III*
by virtue of the masterly architectural sense with which the complicated theme of this series of plays is handled. "Shakespeare
planned his first historical tetralogy greatly," writes Tillyard,[140]
"reminding one of Hardy in the *Dynasts*. When we consider how
deficient his fellow-dramatists were in the architectonic power, we
can only conclude that this was one of the things with which he was

---

[139] Granville-Barker, *Prefaces to Shakespeare*, First Series, xxxv.
[140] E. M. W. Tillyard, *Shakespeare's History Plays*, 160 f. See also his Preface, vii.

conspicuously endowed by nature. Far from being the untidy genius, Shakespeare was in one respect a born classicist."

I need not enter further upon this controversial ground than to express agreement with the main contention [141]: meanwhile let us examine this "architectonic power" in an example which we have already studied in considering the battle sequences.[142] The Dauphin is invading England and has the support of some of King John's nobles. A cross-stage wrangle ends with mutual defiance between the Dauphin and Faulconbridge:

> *Dol.* Strike up our drummes, to finde this danger out.
> *Bast.* And thou shalt finde it (Dolphin) do not doubt.

The conventional *Alarums* mark the onset, but the battle never surges on to the Platform itself. Instead, Shakespeare keeps us, on the fringes of the fighting, always in touch with the important issues. John asks Hubert how the day goes, and Hubert answers, "Badly I feare." The King complains of a fever. A messenger brings good tidings of the wreck of the Dauphin's supply ship, but the King is too ill to welcome the news: he bids them carry him to his litter to Swinsted Abbey. The revolted English lords appear and inform us that

> That misbegotten divell *Falconbridge*,
> In spight of spight, alone upholds the day.

The French Count Melun staggers on to the Platform, "Wounded to death", and warns them of the Dauphin's intention, if he wins the day, to quit treachery with treachery and cut off their heads. His eloquent speech includes a passage of scene-painting which in its power to evoke overtones of emotion is a forerunner of the "setting Sunne" of the plains of Philippi:

> if *Lewis* do win the day,
> He is forsworne, if ere those eyes of yours
> Behold another day breake in the East:
> But even this night, whose blacke contagious breath
> Already smoakes about the burning Crest
> Of the old, feeble, and day-wearied Sunne,
> Even this ill night, your breathing shall expire,
> Paying the fine of rated Treachery,
> Even with a treacherous fine of all your lives . . .

---

[141] And to draw attention to Charles Knight's admirable essay on the same subject in the Imperial Shakespeare, vol. iii, 41 ff., where a like opinion is supported with a great weight of internal evidence.

[142] *King John*, V. ii. *fin.*, iii., iv., and v. See above, pp. 90 f,

After Melun has explained that his love for Hubert and

> this respect besides
> (For that my Grandsire was an Englishman)
> Awakes my Conscience to confess all this . . .

Salisbury voices for his fellow "Revolts" their joy in the chance of returning to their allegiance. Then he offers his arm to Melun, painting in "close-up" the agony of the dying man:

> My arme shall give thee helpe to beare thee hence,
> For I do see the cruell pangs of death
> Right in thine eye.

No sooner have they left the Platform than we are shown the Dauphin in high spirits, still ignorant of what we have heard and seen. The end of the day's engagement is briefly and fully summed up in less than twenty-five lines: again the atmospheric painting is turned to dramatic purpose:

> *Dol.* The Sun of heaven (me thought) was loth to set;
>   But staid, and made the Westerne Welkin blush,
>   When English measure backward their owne ground
>   In faint Retire: Oh bravely came we off,
>   When with a volley of our needlesse shot,
>   After such bloody toile, we bid good night,
>   And woon'd our tott'ring colours clearly up,
>   Last in the field, and almost Lords of it.
>
> *Enter a Messenger*
>
> *Mes.* Where is my Prince, the Dolphin?
> *Dol.* Heere, what newes?
> *Mes.* The Count *Meloone* is slaine: The English Lords
>   By his perswasion, are againe falne off,
>   And your supply, which you have wish'd so long,
>   Are cast away, and sunke on *Goodwin* sands.
> *Dol.* Ah fowle, shrew'd newes. Beshrew thy very hart:
>   I did not thinke to be so sad to night
>   As this hath made me.

There is a sure selection of emphasis in this sequence, an insistent relevance, which we must recognise as characteristic of Shakespeare even from his earliest years. He sees here that there is no dramatic interest in the battle itself: it is the incidental circumstances that are important in his story—King John's sickness and withdrawal to Swinsted, Melun's dying confession and the chance for England's princes to come home again, the Dauphin's reception of the news of their falling-off and of the wreck of his supply ships. To these points he sticks with an insistent relevance: and meanwhile by shrewd atmospheric painting preserves the illusion of battle in the neighbourhood.

If we put the plays back into the playhouse for which they were devised, much that now seems irrelevant to their structure will fall automatically into place. In the course of our argument, it has become clear that many passages which seem on the picture-stage unnecessary ornaments (and which therefore might be cited as evidence of desultoriness) are in fact essential elements in the technique of Shakespeare's poetic drama. Such, for instance, is Oberon's description of Titania's bank "where the wilde time blowes", necessary to convert a familiar property-bank into a couch fit for a fairy queen. Such too—as we have seen—are the hunting speeches of Theseus and Hippolyta, which are needed to change the scene from the moonlit wood to the dew of morning. Such are the passages of character-drawing and "close-up" description of mood and facial expression: and the anticipatory descriptions of Kent and Edgar and the Fool in *King Lear*: and the many speeches which create the action in "Messenger Speech" form. Such too is the opening dialogue of *The Merchant of Venice*, in which Solanio and Salarino, "cursed by actors as the two worst bores in the whole Shakespearean canon", paint for us the background of Venetian magnificence against which the figures of Antonio and Bassanio stand in sharp relief.[143] We must recognise that Shakespeare sometimes considers it fair game to reveal a character in typical speech, at first appearance or not much later, even if the speech does not forward the plot of the play: *Romeo and Juliet*—an early play, with less technical subtlety than ebullient inspiration—shows examples of this phenomenon in the introduction of the Nurse, Mercutio, and Friar Lawrence.[144] All these passages are necessary to the structure of the play, and it seems reasonable, therefore, to suppose that, in their native element, the plays would be remarkable for an insistent relevance rather than for a diffuse and episodic carelessness of structure.

In *Romeo and Juliet*, *Julius Caesar* and *Twelfth Night* there is a masterly directness of narrative exposition which hardly needs illustration: and if, even from quite early days, Shakespeare had this architectural gift in the handling of his material, it seems reckless to assume that he was often unable or unwilling to use it. The producer will do well to be humble here, to ask himself what Shakespeare is driving at, before he begins to patch what he supposes to be a

---

[143] See above, p. 55; and Granville-Barker's *Prefaces to Shakespeare*, Second Series, 80 ff.

[144] *Romeo and Juliet*, I. iii. 16 ff.; I. iv. 55 ff.; II. iii. 1 ff.

careless job, for more exacting modern tastes. There are, of course,
some baffling scenes. We know that clowning "hath a priviledge",
especially in the days of Kemp, though we may guess (from the
familiar censure in *Hamlet*) that Shakespeare was reluctant to accord
it. Such a scene as Launcelot Gobbo's wit-snapping at Belmont [145]
seems to have no better justification than that Kemp has had too few
opportunities to play the fool (it is as irrelevant as the turn of the
juggler or the acrobat in pantomime); unless, indeed, it is needed
for the benefit of the stagehands to set the court-scene in the Study.
On a higher level of art, Shakespeare may perhaps be accused of
being led sometimes into irrelevancy by Armin's theorising on folly:
and even Touchstone has an intolerable passage on the old cuckold
joke.[146] Many topical quips make the comedy out of date, as for
instance the caricatures of that excellent butt Ben Jonson, which
probably underly the figures of Ajax, Nym and Jaques.[147]

Serious passages, too, sometimes lose their force owing to the
natural change in popular interest with the passing of the years: it
is perhaps surprising how little has proved ephemeral. The opening
act of *Henry V* is a problem. The first two scenes, up to the arrival of
the French ambassadors, seem to hang fire, and to throw away all
the advantage which the Prologue has sought and gained. In such
cases, common sense will not fall to abusing Shakespeare: he has
already proved in other history plays that he knows his job. We
must understand that his audience were really interested in history
and historical theory, and we can admire the objective detachment
of his presentation of the clerics' unscrupulous policy, the swift and
vivid recapitulation of the King's reformed character, the King's
grave and dignified charge to the Archbishop, the Archbishop's
evocation of the Black Prince's prowess, and the lecture on the
honey-bees—a *tour de force* on a favourite theme. For the rest, a producer of to-day must cut in such a way as to keep the general sense
without the long detail: at all costs he must not seek a comic
diversion by such an expedient as caricaturing the Archbishop's
exposition of the Salic Law.[148]

We are at liberty to cut unless the historical material is vital to the
structure of the play. It is hardly surprising that more often than not
it *is* vital. Tillyard has made it clear how compact and close-woven
is the tapestry of themes in the first tetralogy—*Henry VI* and *Richard III*
—and finds dramatic justification for such "history lessons" as
York's recital of his claim to England's crown.

---

[145] *The Merchant of Venice*, III. v. 1–70.   [146] *As You Like It*, III. iii. 50 ff.
[147] E. K. Chambers, *William Shakespeare*, vol. i, 72.
[148] *Henry V*, I. i and ii. 1–220.

> *Edward* the third, my Lords, had seven Sonnes:
> The first, *Edward* the Black-Prince, Prince of Wales;
> The second, *William* of Hatfield . . .

so it goes on relentlessly for fifty lines until Salisbury and Warwick, weighed down with the logic of genealogy, fall to their knees, anxious to be the first

> That shall salute our rightfull Soveraigne
> With honor of his Birth-right to the Crowne.

"This scene," writes Tillyard, "is one of those stiff, factual expositions, full of resounding names, that must have been listened to breathlessly by an audience for whom the questions of titles and successions were a living issue, and the Wars of the Roses a terrible spectacle of what could so easily happen again. The bare exposition, granted a solemn versification, was enough; the bare facts had their own momentum; realism would be inappropriate, almost impious." [149] There is a danger always present in considering the history plays: if we cut, or minimise the emphasis of, the historical substance, we distort the structure of the whole play. The first part of *Henry IV* makes nonsense, if Prince Hal is not in the centre of the picture. Shakespeare made no mistake in the planning of this first part, even if in *Part Two* he did allow Falstaff (after he had won fame in *Part One*) to loom too large. It is easy to forget that even Falstaff had to make his reputation. In the first scene in which he appears he is not at the top of his form [150]: many an actor of the part must have been glad to have got that scene behind him, so that he can proceed to the easy victories of Gads Hill and the Boar's Head. The reason for the modest start is surely this, that Shakespeare is at pains in the first scene to introduce his leading character, Prince Hal (his leading player, too; for the part was Burbadge's); and Falstaff as the Prince's "mis-leader of Youth" is only incidental to that presentation. The business of 1 *Henry IV* is the history of the madcap Prince winning his spurs at Shrewsbury and saving his father from a most dangerous rebellion: Falstaff enters the play as a means of exhibiting the Prince's riotous youth, and for all his independent vitality, he does not (in *Part One*) exceed his brief; he has no scene which is unrelated to the Prince's affairs; it is only in *Part Two* that he goes off to pursue his own fortunes. Prince Hal (in *Part One*) is the centre of interest, and for this reason if for no other, your Burbadge must play him.

Even outside the strictly historical plays, the point holds good. One must beware of *injudicious* cutting in *Hamlet*, which for practical

---

[149] E. M. W. Tillyard, *Shakespeare's History Plays*, 180. 2 *Henry VI*, II. ii. 10 ff.
[150] 1 *Henry IV*, I. ii.

reasons must, of course, often be cut. At all costs we must not eliminate the public background and make the play—as it so often wrongly appears—a private psychological study. We must give due weight to the historical exposition, which Shakespeare cunningly inserts after the dramatic impact of the ghost's first appearance, and (just when there is a danger of the audience's attention wandering)— "loe, where it comes againe".[151] There is a wealth of implication in a chance word of Laertes to his sister about Hamlet:

> Hee may not, as unvallued persons doe,
> Carve for himselfe; for, on his choyce depends
> The sanctity and health of the whole State.[152]

It is when we start cutting that we most realise Shakespeare's insistent relevance: there is so little that we can spare. Anyone who has seen *Hamlet* in its entirety will realise how much clearer the design of the complete play is than the abbreviated versions we normally see. If the play is not *badly* cut, Fortinbras' final entry will have a proper inevitability about it. Almost the last articulate preoccupation of the dying Prince is with the public weal, and the public view of his career.

Always we must consider what Shakespeare's main design is. It is usually supposed that Angelo's is the principal part in *Measure for Measure*: this is against the evidence of the statistics, for while Angelo has but 320 lines to speak, the Duke has 884.[153] After Angelo's declaration to Isabella, there is nothing for him to do except await his humiliation. Perhaps the truth is that we have strayed away from Shakespeare's professed purpose. Early in the play the Duke gives to Friar Thomas an involved but definite explanation of his intention in disguising himself: it is in the main a public motive, concerning the obsolete decrees of his city where

> libertie, plucks Justice by the nose;
> The Baby beates the Nurse, and quite athwart
> Goes all decorum . . .

and only secondarily is he interested in the private problem of his "precise" Deputy who

> scarce confesses
> That his blood flowes: or that his appetite
> Is more to bread then stone: hence shall we see
> If power change purpose: what our Seemers be.[154]

---

[151] *Hamlet*, I. i. 70 ff.   [152] *Hamlet*, I. iii. 19 ff.
[153] Baldwin gives Angelo to Burbadge and the Duke to Cundall. But is it possible that Burbadge played the Duke, and gave him the necessary stature and authority to preserve the balance of Shakespeare's design?
[154] *Measure for Measure*, I. iii. 29 ff.; 51 ff.

In fact, the state of Vienna is at least equally important with the
state of Angelo. It is largely Shakespeare's doing that we get the
balance wrong. He gives us a powerful exposition, always insistently
relevant and mainly concerned with Angelo, and then after two and
a half acts of compelling tragedy he seems to lose interest and grip in
the mechanical contrivance of his dénouement: the dejected Mariana
of the moated-Grange is introduced in prose which looks oddly in
the Folio text after five pages of continuous verse and which seems
to symbolise the relaxed tension of the writing.[155]

It is well to mention here in parenthesis that *Measure for Measure*
belongs to the period of Shakespeare's writing which follows upon
Hamlet, a period which we shall study more closely in a later section
of this chapter.[156] An attempt will there be made to explain the
manifest fact that between 1601 and 1604 the poet's creative energy
was in some measure in abeyance, that *Troilus and Cressida* (1601–2),
All's Well That Ends Well (1602–3), and *Measure for Measure* (1604–5),
all show signs of tiredness and exhausted inspiration. But in all these
plays there are traces of the restless experimentation which is
characteristic of Shakespeare's mind, and *Measure for Measure*, the
last play of the interval, closely followed by the triumphant *Othello*,
must be treated as a vigorous, if not wholly successful, attempt to
present the conflict between licence and discipline in its public as
well as its private context.

Apart from the rare times of exhaustion and uneasiness, when (as
normally) Shakespeare is on top of his form, the producer of a
particular play must certainly make it a matter of first importance to
settle what his author is driving at. The poet himself would presumably have been asked for an explanation at rehearsal at the
Globe. With so volatile and restlessly experimental an imagination,
it is no good assuming that one knows. One of the most remarkable
things about the canon is the fact that Shakespeare so seldom repeats
himself. *As You Like It* is a case in point. There is obviously nothing
amiss with his inspiration at this time: the companion-play *Twelfth
Night* makes this plain, and *Julius Caesar* in the same year. The
digressive, episodic manner of *As You Like It* is not due to inability,
not therefore unintentional. At first sight there is little of the
insistent relevance of the companion-plays. The Duke Senior and
Jaques *do* nothing: whole scenes and prolonged dialogues are built
of nothing but talk and song.[157] But here Shakespeare is dramatising
(in a vein of satire) a frame of mind, a whole way of life, pastoral

---

[155] *Measure for Measure*, III. i. 182 ff.
[156] See below, pp. 267 ff.
[157] See *As You Like It*, II. v.; II. vii. 1–87; 136–66.

escapism; the plot is left to Rosalind, Orlando and the shepherds.
He was also preoccupied, I think, during the composition of this
play, with conversations with Armin on the art of fooling. Touchstone is an object-lesson from Armin's text-book. The play is full of
cadenzas, which are quite in place in this pastoral satire. The "seven
ages" of man is a cadenza, needed to fill a gap while Orlando goes to
fetch Adam: another is Rosalind's on Time travelling in divers
paces: Jaques again discourses *ad lib.* on melancholy; Touchstone
on quarrelling by the book (the Retort courteous, the Quip-modest,
the reply Churlish, and so forth)—this last again to fill a gap in the
action.[158] The songs, moreover, are, unlike those of most of the other
comedies, a loosely-knit *comment* on the action, rather than an
integral part of it: they make the play Shakespeare's nearest approach
to the operetta or the musical comedy of modern times. It is a play
for the civilised palate, for the "highbrow", like *Love's Labour's Lost*,
and of both these collector's pieces it may be said that "Time ambles
withal". The substance of *As You Like It* is hard to define: no doubt
it is of more than one kind—satire of court life and also of the
pastoral escape from court life; variations on the theme of love; a
study of different kinds of folly (in the last two particulars it is a pair
with *Twelfth Night*, and not unlike *Love's Labour's Lost*). Talk with
Armin seems a likely background to this period of Shakespeare's
composition. But if it is hard to state in precise terms the subject of
the play, yet its dramatic interest never flags: the poet meanders,
perhaps, but he meanders with conviction and determination, and
there is never any good reason to doubt what effect he is aiming at
at a given moment. He sticks to the point, and continuously fixes
the attention of his audience.

This power of fixing and holding the attention of his audience is
one of the most potent elements in his art. He proceeds from one
point of emphasis in his story to the next with that immediate continuity which can only be achieved in the conditions of his playhouse.
The insistent relevance of his writing and the speed of his transitions
from one point to another compels us to experience the drama with
his actors and prevents us from thinking over our experience while it
is in progress. Some of the not infrequent charges of inconsistency
and confusion arise from a neglect of this simple truth: such, for
instance, is the notorious absurdity in *Othello* of the fact, obvious but
only to the armchair calculator, that there is no possible opportunity for the suspected adultery of Cassio and Desdemona; such
too the inexplicable mystery of the first contemplation of regicide by

---

[158] *As You Like It,* II. vii. 139 ff.; III. ii. 328 ff.; IV. i. 11 ff.; V. iv. 71 ff.

Macbeth and his Lady, when "Nor time, nor place Did then adhere". We can see the spellbinding process in a sequence of *Hamlet*. When the Prince asks Horatio what is his affair in Elsinore, Horatio reluctantly answers

> My Lord, I came to see your Father's funerall.

From Hamlet's previous soliloquy we know that this must have been nearly two months ago. The incongruity seems an absurd one, if we have time to reckon the distance from Wittenberg: but in fact Hamlet drives all calculation from our minds with his bitter retort:

> I pray thee doe not mock me (fellow Student)
> I thinke it was to see my Mothers Wedding.

It is not enough here to give the negative explanation and say that this is an example of "dramatic time", and that the audience in the playhouse have no chance to think out the absurdity. We must ask also, what is the positive reason for Horatio's statement? I think the answer is that Shakespeare is intent on dramatising the "wicked speed" of the wedding all through this sequence of the play—in Claudius' opening apologia, in Hamlet's soliloquy, and still in the beginning of the dialogue with Horatio. The continuity is in the theme, which is kept before our notice with insistent relevance. The juxtaposition of Horatio's line and Hamlet's retort is clinched by the sequel, with its epigrammatic irony:

> *Hor.* Indeed my Lord, it followed hard upon.
> *Ham.* Thrift, thrift, *Horatio*: the Funerall Bakt-meats
>   Did coldly furnish forth the Marriage Tables . . .[159]

The strength of Shakespeare's architecture lies largely in his insistent relevance and his unflagging continuity. It will be worth while to study more closely the mechanics of this continuity.

(viii) Continuity

It has already been seen, in considering the problems of scene-rotation, that the swift continuity possible in this playhouse was a great asset to the poet. Shakespearian producers have learnt, within the memory of this generation, to value a speedy passage from scene to scene, but we still do not achieve that absolute immediacy of transition which is characteristic of Shakespeare's own theatre. Even

---

[159] *Hamlet*, I. ii. 176 ff.

the sudden black-out, the lowering of a fore-curtain to allow of a
"corridor-scene", even the insertion of a musical "join", breaks the
continuity and dissipates the concentration of the audience. Any
such expedient on the picture-stage throws the audience, as it
were, back upon itself: the spell is interrupted as it is when the
cinema-projector breaks down. In the Globe the audience are always
crowded round the great central Platform: the main field of action is
never withdrawn from their sight. There is an atmospheric difference,
which only experience can prove. We can see the normal practice of
the playhouse in a vivid simile from *Richard II*:

> As in a Theater, the eyes of men
> After a well grac'd Actor leaves the Stage,
> Are idlely bent on him that enters next,
> Thinking his prattle to be tedious . . .[160]

and we can also see in these lines the poet's problem stated in its
simplest terms: how is he to keep the interest of his audience, and
sustain the continuity of his dramatic tension? It is difficult to
formulate the methods of genius, but some general principles of procedure can be detected in Shakespeare's tackling of this problem.

Though, as we have seen in *As You Like It*, we must be wary in
making such an assumption, the logical sequence of events, the continuity of plot, is usually the main thread upon which the play is
strung. This continuity of plot has nothing to do with realism of
time: Shakespeare, as Granville-Barker points out, "knew that,
once away from watches and clocks, we appreciate the relation of
events rather by the intensity of the experiences which unite or
divide them in our minds than by any arithmetical process".[161] For
instance, the dispersal of Capulet's dancing-party so soon after its
inception reads abruptly on the printed page, but is quite plausible
in the theatre: in the interim, the first meeting of Romeo and Juliet
"stops the clock". Shakespeare cunningly leads us on from one point
of interest to another: we are told what to expect and we welcome
it when it comes.[162]

His simplest method of progress is by the direct method. When
King Henry VI hears of the magic practices of the Duchess of
Gloucester, he says:

> To morrow toward London, back againe,
> To looke into this Business thorowly. . . .

---

[160] *Richard II*, V. ii. 23 ff.
[161] Granville-Barker, *From Henry V to Hamlet*, 17.
[162] *Romeo and Juliet*, I. v. 20–131.

There follows the scene in which York expounds his claim to Salisbury and Warwick, and no sooner do they leave the Platform than (the Folio tells us):

Sound Trumpets. Enter the King and State,
with Guard, to banish the Duchesse.

King. Stand forth Dame *Elianor Cobham,*
Glosters Wife.

We know where we are at once.[163] This admirable directness of procedure is a conspicuous feature of *Richard III.* Turning page after page of the Folio, one is left with the impression that the main sequence of the play is acted out on the naked Platform, and the continuity of subject is very close and direct between one scene and the next. This direct method makes the very freest use of the un-localised Platform, as we have already seen in Chapter III. The maskers approaching Capulet's feast *march about the Stage, and Servingmen come forth with their napkins:* at once the Platform is transformed from the street into the hall of Capulet's house. In *Julius Caesar*, by a like method, we proceed from the streets into the Capitol, and from the open air into Brutus' tent.[164] Hamlet follows the beckoning of his father's ghost out by one end of the Tarras, and reappears six lines later—with a shift of focus as rapid as that of the cinema-camera—by one of the stage-doors on to the Platform: we know that the Platform is the "more removed ground" of Marcellus' fears.[165] Sometimes the scene is changed for us by the logic of the *dramatis personae.* We studied above the sequence in 1 *Henry VI* where Talbot at Bordeaux waits in vain for reinforcements from York and Somerset.[166] In *As You Like It*, it seems probable that the Study contained but one symbolical setting of woodland furniture, and that the presumption of different locality was left for the audience to infer from the appearance of different groups of characters: the Chamber would of course be reserved for the interruptions of the woodland sequence at Duke Frederick's court. Venice and Belmont are likewise simply differentiated by the presence of Antonio and Shylock on the one hand and of Portia on the other: Cleopatra means Egypt, Octavius Rome, and our imagination is not too severely strained by Pompey's galley, and by Ventidius' outlandish and gruesome triumphal procession in Parthia. The eyes of the audience, "idly bent on him that enters next", see Kemp and Cowley *with the watch*, carrying "bills" and a lantern, and are in no

---

[163] 2 *Henry VI*, II. i. 199 f.; II. iii. 1 f. See above, pp. 34 f.
[164] See above, p. 104. [165] *Hamlet*, I. iv. 86 ff.; I. v. i.
[166] See above, p. 104.

doubt of their business as the night-patrol of the Messina con-
stabulary: if they see the Sheriff and halberds, and a dignified
prisoner, they can guess the road to execution. The street-sequences
of *The Merry Wives of Windsor* and *Troilus and Cressida*, and the
prison-sequences of *Measure for Measure* employ such a direct
method, and are based, as we have seen, on the existing architecture
of the Tiring-House. So too in the battle-sequences the plotting of
entries follows a method of logical directness which is always
sustained in the dialogue. We have seen too how in a large part of
Much Ado About Nothing the method dispenses with locality altogether:
the thread of connection is not geographical at all, but consists of the
logical course of the intrigue.[167]

There are—one may notice in passing—some shrewd strokes of
juxtaposition which, if the continuity, as usually in the modern
theatre, is broken, fail of their intended effect. There is a genuine
thrill in *King John* where the pusillanimous would-be murderer finds
out suddenly from Hubert that his victim is not dead:

> Doth *Arthur* live? O hast thee to the Peeres,
> Throw this report on their incensed rage,
> And make them tame to their obedience.

He hopes that he may yet make all well with his revolted nobles:

> Oh, answer not; but to my Closet bring
> The angry Lords, with all expedient hast,
> I conjure thee but slowly: run more fast.

He is sitting on his throne in the Study, with Hubert at his elbow.
The curtain draws upon him, and immediately—

> *Enter Arthur on the walles.*

Dressed as a ship-boy, the poor Prince appears on the Tarras, and
hurls himself to death below.[168] There is a stroke of irony, surely not
unconscious, in the sequence of King Henry IV's restless soliloquy

> How many thousand of my poorest Subjects
> Are at this houre asleepe?

close upon Falstaff's "Now comes in the sweetest Morsell of the
night . . ."[169] There is no setting better than Shakespeare's playhouse to bring out the mischievous anti-climax which appears thus
in the Folio:

---

[167] See above, p. 106.   [168] *King John*, IV. ii. 260 ff.; IV. iii. 1 ff.
[169] 2 *Henry IV*, II. iv. 401; III. i. 4 ff.

> The Game's afoot:
> Follow your Spirit; and upon this Charge,
> Cry, God for *Harry*, England, and S. *George*.
> *Alarum, and Chambers goe off.*
> *Enter Nim, Bardolph, Pistoll, and Boy.*
> *Bard.* On, on, on, on, on, to the breach, to the breach.
> *Nim.* 'Pray thee Corporall stay, the Knocks are too hot . . .[170]

Likewise Edgar's soliloquy in which he compassionates King Lear with the exclamation "He childed as I fathered" is given a bitter twist of tragic irony by the immediate sequel up aloft in the Chamber of the blinding of his deluded father.[171] We shall see in the next chapter how the episode of Banquo's murder gains in dramatic effect as Macbeth's words from the Tarras

> Good things of Day begin to droope, and drowse,
> Whiles Nights black Agents to their Prey's doe rowse . . .

are followed immediately by the stealthy entry of the murderers on the Platform below.[172]

Sometimes one notices a kind of pendulum-swing of alternation in the course of a prolonged sequence. Thus in *Twelfth Night* for most of the third and fourth acts the interest is provoked first by the gulling of Malvolio and then by Sir Andrew's challenge to Viola: when one theme is temporarily played out, the other is called in to sustain the tension. In *All's Well That Ends Well* the exposure of Parolles alternates with the stratagem against Bertram. The most skilful use of this seesaw movement ends in the combination of the two, as when the alternation of Venice and Belmont culminates in Portia's appearance in the Venetian court. A capital example of this procedure is the elaborate dénouement of 2 *Henry IV*.[173] The dying King's last words are still echoing in the theatre, when we are transported to Gloucestershire, where Falstaff for his own ends is paying Shallow a return visit: the inimitable Davy sets the scene for us and also helps to make clear that Falstaff passes for an influential person—"Doth the man of Warre, stay all night sir?" he asks his master. "Yes *Davy*," replies Shallow: "I will use him well. A Friend i'th'Court, is better then a penny in purse." Pausing to soliloquise before he goes in to accept the offered hospitality, Falstaff says: "I will devise matter enough out of this *Shallow*, to keepe Prince *Harry*

---

[170] *Henry V*, III. i. 32 ff.; III. ii. 1 ff.
[171] *King Lear*, III. vi. 111 ff.; III. vii.
[172] *Macbeth*, III. ii.. 52 f.; III. iii. See below, p. 298.
[173] 2 *Henry IV*, V. i.–v.

in continuall Laughter . . . O you shall see him laugh, till his Face be like a wet Cloake, ill laid up." Without interruption the Earl of Warwick and the Lord Chief Justice transport us by their very presence back to London. The King is dead, and the Lord Chief Justice wishes he were too; for he has had occasion to incur the enmity of his successor. Warwick agrees

> Indeed I thinke the yong King loves you not . . .

and Prince Hal's younger brothers are no more encouraging about his prospects; Clarence goes so far as to say

> Wel, you must now speake Sir *John Falstaffe* faire,
> Which swimmes against your streame of Quality.

When Prince Hal appears, of whom Falstaff has just said "you shall see him laugh, till his Face be like a wet Cloake", he finds himself surrounded by sad and suspicious glances. Shakespeare cannot resist making him play "cat and mouse" with the Lord Chief Justice, but after a noble apologia the Justice is confirmed in his office and invited to be "as a Father" to the young King. We return at once back to Gloucestershire for the delicious mellow comedy of wine and dessert in Shallow's orchard, which is interrupted by Pistol's news that the old King is as dead "As naile in doore". Falstaff calls for his horse:

> Master *Robert Shallow*, choose what Office thou wilt
> In the Land, 'tis thine. *Pistol*, I will double charge thee with Dignities.
> *Bard.* O joyfull day:
> I would not take a Knighthood for my Fortune.
> *Pist.* What? I do bring good newes.
> *Fal.* Carrie Master *Silence* to bed: Master *Shallow*, my Lord *Shallow*, be what thou wilt, I am Fortunes Steward. Get on thy Boots, wee'l ride all night. Oh sweet Pistoll: Away *Bardolfe*: Come Pistoll, utter more to mee: and withall devise something to do thy selfe good. Boote, boote, Master *Shallow*, I know the young King is sick for mee. Let us take any mans Horsses: The Lawes of England are at my command'ment. Happie are they, which have beene my Friendes: and woe unto my Lord Chiefe Justice.

With horrible suddenness we see Quickly and Dol Tearesheet being dragged to prison by the Beadles. Then the Grooms strew the Platform with rushes: then Falstaff and Shallow appear in the crowd, all travel-stained: "O if I had had time to have made new Liveries," Falstaff says to Shallow, "I would have bestowed the thousand pound I borrowed of you."

> *The Trumpets sound. Enter King Henrie the Fift . . .*
> *Fal.* 'Save thee my sweet Boy.
> *King.* My Lord Chiefe Justice, speake to that vaine man.
> *Ch. Just.* Have you your wits?
>   Know you what 'tis you speake?
> *Falst.* My King, my Jove; I speake to thee, my heart.
> *King.* I know thee not, old man: Fall to thy Prayers . . .

As the procession passes on, Falstaff turns to his dupe:

> Master *Shallow*, I owe you a thousand pound.

The Lord Chief Justice, returning, gives the *coup de grâce*. The building of this alternating climax is a masterpiece of stagecraft: for its full effect the immediate continuity of the Globe stage is needed.

Shakespeare often sustains the interest by a method which may be described as keeping a rod in pickle. "Go you before to *Gloster* with these letters," says King Lear to the disguised Kent; "acquaint my Daughter no further with any thing you know, then comes from her demand out of the Letter, if your Dilligence be not speedy, I shall be there afore you." "I will not sleepe my Lord," replies Kent, "till I have delivered your Letter." Our curiosity is roused about the coming visit to Regan: we are ready to understand at his next appearance where Kent is and why—and we expect Lear to follow him closely at the heels.[174] Gloucester, asking the disguised Edgar's guidance to Dover, tells us

> There is a Cliffe, whose high and bending head
> Lookes fearfully in the confined Deepe:
> Bring me but to the very brimme of it,
> And Ile repayre the misery thou do'st beare
> With something rich about me: from that place,
> I shall no leading neede.

Thus we are ready to recognise the Platform as the brink of Edgar's imaginary cliff, when we next see him leading his blind father on to the Platform: and meanwhile we dwell with interest on the prospect of such a scene.[175] We are cleverly kept in suspense for two and a half pages of the Folio from Hamlet's first statement of his intention

> To put an Anticke disposition on

to his next appearance: meanwhile Ophelia's story of Hamlet's distracted visit and the King's hints of Hamlet's "transformation"

---

[174] *King Lear*, I. v. 1–5; II. ii. 1 ff.
[175] *King Lear*, IV. i. 74 ff.; IV. vi. 1 ff.

keep our interest alive.[176] A very clear example of this rod-in-pickle method can be found in a speech of Polonius to the King immediately after the "nunnery-scene":

> My Lord, do as you please,
> But if you hold it fit after the Play,
> Let his Queene Mother all alone intreat him
> To shew his Greefes: let her be round with him,
> And Ile be plac'd so, please you in the eare
> Of all their Conference. If she finde him not,
> To England send him: Or confine him where
> Your wisedome best shall thinke.

At this moment Shakespeare has our curiosity aroused about three possible developments in his plot—the play to "catch the Conscience of the King", Hamlet's interview with his mother (we have never seen them alone together, and the issue cannot be other than dramatic), and the possibility of his being shipped to England.[177]

Other still subtler devices for knitting together the continuity, and holding continuously the concentrated interest of his audience, were in Shakespeare's armoury. We have already seen, in considering the skilled speech of the Chamberlain's Men,[178] the powerful effect of rhythm in preserving the tension over long periods. The rhythmic tension is often deliberately relaxed at the end of a scene, not seldom with the conventional cadence of a couplet. But it is interesting to notice that sometimes the musical movement is intended to continue. Mercutio and Benvolio hunting for Romeo after Capulet's dance are foiled in their search; Mercutio mocks at him for his supposed love for Rosaline, but grows tired of his own joke, and Benvolio agrees that there is nothing for it but to go to bed:

> for 'tis in vaine
> To seeke him here that meanes not to be found.

When they have gone, Romeo, in hiding in Capulet's orchard, murmurs

> He jeasts at Scarres that never felt a wound.

Romeo's words show that he has heard the previous dialogue of his friends, and his rhyme confirms the swift continuity of his speech after Benvolio's. The change of "scene" from street to orchard is taken in the stride of a rhymed couplet.[179] We have yet to see the

---

[176] *Hamlet*, I. v. 172; II. i. 77 ff.; II. ii. 5.   [177] *Hamlet*, III. i. 189 ff.
[178] See above, pp. 119 ff.
[179] *Romeo and Juliet*, II. i. 41 f.; II. ii. 1. The lineation of the folio, which I have altered, obscures the point.

opening scenes of Lear's storm in their native element, the Platform
of the Globe: but when we do, it is to be hoped that we shall be
allowed to feel the rhythmic continuity of such transitions as that
from Cornwall's

> Shut up your doores my Lord, 'tis a wil'd night,
> My *Regan* counsels well: come out o'th'storme

to Kent's

> Who's there besides foule weather?

and that when, with Kent and the Gentleman parting at opposite
Stage-Doors, Lear and his Fool emerge from the Study curtains,
"Contending with the fretfull Elements".[180] The great rhythmic
movements in verse of the mature tragedies are among Shakespeare's
unquestioned masterpieces. No less magical in their own vein are the
rhythmical movements in prose of the comedies—with Rosalind and
Orlando, Beatrice and Benedick, Hal and Falstaff. That much more
art goes into the making of them than their spontaneity suggests, is
shown by the fact that in the hurriedly composed *Merry Wives of
Windsor* the rhythmical flow is conspicuously absent. There are
many capital phrases, but for the most part they are in isolation;
Falstaff's account of his experiences in the buck-basket is exceptional
in this play, but for rhythm it hardly compares with Mistress
Quickly accusing Falstaff of breach of promise, or recounting the
tragi-comic tale of his death.[181]

(ix) Pervasive Theme

This device of rhythmical continuity, it will be noticed, is an
exclusively poetical one, a property of the poetic drama. So likewise
is the next object of our study, Shakespeare's deliberate use of the
method of pervasive themes. Even in the first historical cycle—the
three parts of *Henry VI* and *Richard III*—the use of repeated themes is
a conscious item of the author's means to give architectural unity to
his subject. Tillyard makes this clear in his *Shakespeare's History
Plays*, naming among others the theme of "order and degree" and
showing how it is worked out in the repetition of symbols. "Warwick's dying soliloquy at Barnet," he says, for instance, "is full of the
traditional commonplaces associated with degree. Speaking of himself, he says—

---

[180] *King Lear*, II. iv. 311 f.; III. i. 1 ff.; III. i. 55; III. ii. 1 ff.
[181] *The Merry Wives of Windsor*, III. v. 98 ff.; 2 *Henry IV*, II. i. 95 ff.; *Henry V*,
II. iii. 9 ff.

> Thus yields the cedar to the axe's edge,
> Whose arms gave shelter to the princely eagle,
> Under whose shade the ramping lion slept,
> Whose top branch overpeer'd Jove's spreading Tree
> And kept low shrubs from winter's powerful wind.

Warwick is thinking of his own power in making and unmaking kings. He is not the oak, the king of trees, but a cedar overtopping the oak; and he refers to a whole sequence of primates in the chain of being: God or Jove in heaven, the King on earth, the lion among beasts, the eagle among birds, and the oak among plants." [182] These themes, and the imagery which sustains them, are derived from the poet's models and are the commonplaces of contemporary political and historical theory: they are the bricks ready to hand, and it is the dramatist's chief task to build them into his architectural structure. Comparison with the later historical cycle—*Richard II, Henry IV* and *Henry V*—is instructive here. Inevitably, with the Tudor interpretation of history, there are patterns of orthodoxy in the treatment of this period too. The theme of regicide is prominent on the lips of the uneasy Bolingbroke, particularly the notion of crusade for penance, which dominates his dying thoughts; when he hears that the room where he was first taken ill is called Jerusalem, he says:

> Laud be to heaven:
> Even there my life must end.
> It hath beene prophesi'de to me many yeares,
> I should not dye, but in *Jerusalem*:
> Which (vainly) I suppos'd the Holy-Land.
> But beare me to that Chamber, there Ile lye:
> In that *Jerusalem*, shall *Harry* dye.

The notion of retribution for Richard's murder recurs unexpectedly in King Henry V's prayer on the eve of Agincourt:

> Not to day, O Lord,
> O not to day, thinke not upon the fault
> My father made, in compassing the Crowne.[183]

These themes, like those in the earlier cycle, stand ready to hand and are an intrinsic part of the dramatist's material. But, side by side with these, we can detect also themes of his own creation, whose repeated emphasis is the poet's deliberate choice in order to give dramatic life to his play. I would instance the very interesting case in *Richard II* of the theme of the earth. We have seen above [184] how on

---

[182] E. M. W. Tillyard, *Shakespeare's History Plays*, 150 ff., 189 f. The quotation is from 3 *Henry VI*, V. ii. 11 ff.

[183] 2 *Henry IV*, IV. v. 234 ff.; *Henry V*, IV. i. 312 ff.   [184] See above, p. 201.

his arrival at Barkloughly Castle after his crossing of the seas from Ireland, Richard salutes the "Deere Earth" in an elaborate address which invests the Platform with poetic life. "Mock not my sencelesse Conjuration, Lords," he ends; "This Earth shall have a feeling . . ." The despairing King returns to this theme in a famous speech in the same scene:

> No matter where; of comfort no man speake:
> Let's talke of Graves, of Wormes, and Epitaphs.
> Make Dust our Paper, and with Raynie eyes
> Write Sorrow on the Bosome of the Earth.
> Let's chuse Executors, and talke of Wills:
> And yet not so; for what can we bequeath,
> Save our deposed bodies to the ground?
> Our Lands, our Lives, and all are *Bullingbrookes*,
> And nothing can we call our owne, but Death,
> And that small Modell of the barren Earth,
> Which serves as Paste, and Cover to our Bones:
> For Heavens [*read* Gods] sake let us sit upon the ground,
> And tell sad stories of the death of Kings . . .

The later speech gains an extra force from the elaborate atmospheric and emotional painting of the former. In the next scene Bolingbroke, claiming the restoration of his lands, utters his purpose thus:

> If not, Ile use th'advantage of my Power,
> And lay the Summers dust with showers of blood,
> Rayn'd from the wounds of slaughter'd Englishmen:
> The which, how farre off from the mind of *Bullingbrooke*
> It is, such Crimson Tempest should bedrench
> The fresh greene Lap of faire King *Richards* Land,
> My stooping dutie tenderly shall shew.
> Goe signifie as much, while here we march
> Upon the Grassie Carpet of this Plaine . . .

The same insistence on the land and the grass of pasture appears in Richard's reply:

> Tell *Bullingbrooke*, for yond me thinkes he is,
> That every stride he makes upon my Land,
> Is dangerous Treason: He is come to ope
> The purple Testament of bleeding Warre;
> But ere the Crowne he lookes for, live in peace,
> Ten thousand bloody crownes of Mothers Sonnes
> Shall ill become the flower of Englands face,
> Change the complexion of her Maid-pale Peace
> To Scarlet Indignation, and bedew
> Her Pastors Grasse with faithfull English Blood , . .

and the theme underlies the strained conceits of his resigned offer to
give

> my large Kingdome, for a little Grave,
> A little, little Grave, an obscure Grave.
> Or Ile be buryed in the Kings high-way,
> Some way of Common Trade, where Subjects feet
> May howrely trample on their Soveraignes Head:
> For on my heart they tread now, whilest I live;
> And buryed once, why not upon my Head?
> *Aumerle*, thou weep'st (my tender-hearted Cousin)
> Wee'le make foule Weather with despised Teares:
> Our sighes, and they, shall lodge the Summer Corne,
> And make a Dearth in this revolting Land.
> Or shall we play the Wantons with our Woes,
> And make some prettie Match, with shedding Teares?
> As thus: to drop them still upon one place,
> Till they have fretted us a payre of Graves,
> Within the Earth: and therein lay'd, there lyes
> Two Kinsmen, digg'd their Graves with weeping Eyes?

The theme is echoed later in the Queen's words, as she waits to
watch her husband's passing to prison:

> Here let us rest, if this rebellious Earth
> Have any resting for her true Kings Queene . . .

and in the King's dying speech, when he expresses the sin of regicide
which is to dwell lifelong in the conscience of the usurper:

> *Exton*, thy fierce hand,
> Hath with the Kings blood, stain'd the Kings own land.[185]

How much of this notion Shakespeare derived from his models I do
not know: the elaborate repetition of the theme shows that it was
often present in his mind as he planned his play. More certainly his
own was a theme which recurs in 1 *Henry IV*, and which circulates
round the words "honour", "plumes", "favours". It is stated
emphatically in Prince Hal's recantation before his father, when he
declares that he will

> in the closing of some glorious day,
> Be bold to tell you, that I am your Sonne,
> When I will weare a Garment all of Blood,
> And staine my favours in a bloody Maske:
> Which washt away, shall scowre my shame with it.
> And that shall be the day, when ere it lights,

---

[185] *Richard II*, III. ii. 6 ff., 144 ff.; III. iii. 42 ff., 91 ff., 153 ff.; V. i. 5 f.; V. v,
10 f.

> That this same Child of Honor and Renowne,
> This gallant *Hotspur*, this all-praysed Knight,
> And your unthought-of *Harry* chance to meet:
> For every Honor sitting on his Helme,
> Would they were multitudes, and on my head
> My shames redoubled. For the time will come,
> That I shall make this Northerne Youth exchange
> His glorious Deedes for my Indignities . . .

It receives vigorous reinforcement in Vernon's answer to Hotspur's question about "The nimble-footed Mad-Cap, Prince of Wales": Vernon had seen Hal and his comrades

> All furnisht, all in Armes,
> All plum'd like Estridges, that with the Winde
> Bayted like Eagles, having lately bath'd,
> Glittering in Golden Coates, like Images,
> As full of spirit as the Moneth of May,
> And gorgeous as the Sunne at Mid-summer,
> Wanton as youthfull Goates, wilde as young bulls.

In the following scene, when we see the Prince and Westmoreland on their way to the war, no doubt the company's wardrobe was well ransacked for the means to live up to Vernon's description. The theme is reflected in two distorting mirrors, first carly in the play by Hotspur with his impulsive ambition

> To plucke bright Honor from the pale-fac'd Moone—

and secondly on the eve of battle itself by Falstaff's celebrated "Catechisme". But it comes to a dramatic fruition in the chivalrous gesture of Prince Hal as he kneels by the dead body of his rival Harry, and covers his face with the plumes from his own helmet:

> If thou wer't sensible of curtesie,
> I should not make so great a shew of Zeale.
> But let my favours hide thy mangled face,
> And even in thy behalfe, Ile thanke my selfe
> For doing these fayre Rites of Tendernesse.[186]

This theme, it seems to me, is deliberately imposed by the poet upon his material, not (as earlier) taken from the material, or from the stock interpretations of the historians. It is devised, in the manner of a *leit-motif*, to create an emphatic and pervasive impression in the mind of the audience: its effect is a poetical one, made by the words,

---

[186] 1 *Henry IV*, III. ii. 133 ff.; IV. i. 95 ff.; IV. ii. 54; I. iii. 202; V. i. 128 ff.; V. iv. 94 ff. See Dover Wilson, *The Fortunes of Falstaff*, 66, and the reference on his p. 137 to an article by H. Hartman. See above, p. 59.

which invest the no doubt familiar plumes of the company's wardrobe with a new dramatic force.

The practice, though it perhaps arises naturally out of the habitual patterned interpretations of the historians, is not confined to the histories. In the same year as *Richard II*, *A Midsummer Night's Dream* shows in a still more striking way how the repetition of themes and images can invest the stage with atmosphere. The theme of moonlight, for instance, is established by constant repetition, right from the opening speech of the play, and well before there is any suggestion of the elopement to the wood.[187] The woodland imagery rises naturally from the subject, but it is thick-sown, to transform the Platform into a wood. We can catch the poet seeking his opportunity when Titania, winding Bottom in her arms, says

> So doth the woodbine, the sweet Honisuckle,
> Gently entwist; the female Ivy so
> Enrings the barky fingers of the Elme.[188]

She is describing her own doting embrace, but she is also keeping us conscious of the wood. Did Shakespeare about this year of 1595–6 become more fully aware of the poetical weapon of theme-repetition, or can we detect it already the year before in *Romeo and Juliet's* leit-motif of "the stars"? It is in the following year that *The Merchant of Venice* shows us, as we have seen, the pervasive Venetian colour sustained by Solanio and Salarino. In *Julius Caesar* the "Capitoll" exemplifies the force of a single word in reiteration to evoke drama, and the latter half of the play is dominated by the theme of "*Caesars* Spirit ranging for Revenge".

Hamlet introduces the highly-organised technique of a prevailing tissue of imagery.[189] Hamlet's urgent plea to his mother after the Ghost's visitation to her closet—

> mother for love of grace,
> Lay not that flattering unction to your soule
> That not your trespasse but my madnesse speakes,
> It will but skin and filme the ulcerous place
> Whiles ranck corruption mining all within
> Infects unseene, confesse your selfe to heaven,
> Repent what's past, avoyd what is to come,
> And doe not spread the compost on the weedes
> To make them rancker—[190]

---

[187] See my *Moonlight at the Globe*, 27, and note 1.
[188] *A Midsummer Night's Dream*, IV. i. 48 ff.
[189] The reader is referred to Caroline Spurgeon's *Shakespeare's Imagery* for a classification and analysis of the poet's images.
[190] *Hamlet*, III. iv. 144 ff.

contains two of the commonest themes that run through the play—
on the one hand, foul disease, the imposthume, sores and boils,
diseases desperate grown; on the other, the unweeded garden that
grows to seed, possessed merely by things rank and gross in nature.
The poet interprets his story through this prevalent imagery, and the
whole drama of that something rotten in the State of Denmark—the
disjointed time which Hamlet is born to set right—is coloured by it.

But it is not till the great tragic period that this method is per-
fected. *Othello* shows it fully developed and it is worth collecting some
of the main examples of its use. We can distinguish two forms—the
leit-motifs often contained in a single word or phrase, and the
pervasive imagery, in which images drawn from the same range of
ideas are built up into a structure of cumulative dramatic force.
The "Capitoll" of *Julius Caesar* is a *leit-motif*, the "disease" and
"weeds" of *Hamlet* are pervasive imagery. "Lieutenant" is one such
leit-motif in *Othello*. It is established as a motive in the drama in
Iago's opening tirade, when he tells Roderigo that Cassio whom he
despises has gained preferment over himself:

> He (in good time) must his Lieutenant be,
> And I (blesse the marke) his Mooreships Auntient.
> (I. i. 32 f.)

The invidious distinction between the lieutenant and the ensign is
kept before our notice. In the torchlit encounter in the streets
Othello recognises Cassio as "my Lieutenant", and Cassio addresses
Iago as "Aunciant" (I. ii. 34, 49). When later at Cyprus Iago has
managed to "fasten but one Cup upon" Cassio, he humours his
drunkenness with repetition of the title

> It's true, good Lieutenant.

and (when Cassio hopes "to be saved")

> And so do I too Lieutenant.

There is a stroke of irony in Cassio's quarrelsome retort:

> I: (but by your leave) not before me. The Lieutenant is to be saved
> before the Ancient.
>
> (II. iii. 109 ff.)

When Iago's contriving has lost Cassio his reputation and his office,
and yet persuades Cassio that he is his good friend in adversity, the
leit-motif returns with shrewd effect at their parting: "good night
Lieutenant, I must to the Watch." "Good night, honest *Iago*" (II.
iii. 342 f.). Here there is a counterpoint with another *motif*—that of

the "honest" Iago. The "lieutenant" *motif* reaches its ultimate climax at the terrible end of the temptation-scene, when Othello, bent on destroying both Cassio and Desdemona, says to Iago:

> Now art thou my Lieutenant.

and his tormentor with grim irony replies—

> I am your owne for ever.
>   (III. iii. 479 f.)

The word "honest" is of course another example. It would be tedious to quote every instance of its use (it is constantly applied to Iago), but we may note its sinister introduction, when Brabantio yields his daughter to Othello with the words

> Looke to her (Moore) if thou hast eies to see:
> She ha's deceiv'd her Father, and may thee . . .

and Othello replies

> My life upon her faith. Honest *Iago*,
> My *Desdemona* must I leave to thee . . .
>   (I. iii. 294 ff.)

We have seen above the irony of Cassio's use of the adjective. Desdemona, pleading with her lord for Cassio's reinstatement, says:

> For if he be not one, that truly loves you,
> That erres In Ignorance, and not in Cunning,
> I have no Judgement in an honest face.
>   (III. iii. 48 ff.)

How little her judgment is, we see later by her implicit trust in Iago's honesty. As Iago begins to sow the seeds of suspicion in Othello's mind, he draws from his victim the information that Cassio helped him in his wooing of Desdemona.

> *Iago.* I did not thinke he had bin acquainted with hir.
> *Oth.* O yes, and went betweene us very oft.
> *Iago.* Indeed?
> *Oth.* Indeed? I indeed. Discern'st thou ought in that?
>   Is he not honest?
> *Iago.* Honest, my Lord?
> *Oth.* Honest? I, Honest.
> *Iago.* My Lord, for ought I know.
>   (III. iii. 99 ff.)

It is not long before Othello is moved to say

> I do not thinke but *Desdemona's* honest.
>   (III. iii. 225)

The climax to which Shakespeare is building this word is the moment when, after Desdemona's death, Othello tells Aemilia that her husband knew it all. "My Husband?" she says over and over again in bewildered horror, till at last the Moor cries

> What needs this itterance, Woman?
> I say, thy Husband . . .

and as she persists in her question—

> He, Woman;
> I say thy Husband: Do'st understand the word?
> My Friend, thy Husband; honest, honest *Iago*.
> (V. ii. 148 ff.)

The "Handkerchiefe" is another such *motif*, with its climax in the scene where Desdemona's plea for Cassio makes a counterpoint of the simplest terms:

> Pray you let *Cassio* be receiv'd againe.
> *Oth.* Fetch me the Handkerchiefe,
>   My minde mis-gives.
> *Des.* Come, come: you'l never meete a more sufficient man.
> *Oth.* The Handkerchiefe.
> *Des.* A man that all his time
>   Hath founded his good Fortunes on your love;
>   Shar'd dangers with you.
> *Oth.* The Handkerchiefe.
> *Des.* Insooth, you are too blame.
> (III. iv. 88 ff.)

The pervasive imagery is perhaps harder to define, but in this play it is largely concerned with the background of mysterious romance and chivalry against which Othello's person stands in relief. Without it the story might seem merely a sensational melodrama, a newspaper "tragedy". It is best described in the poet's own words. Othello is already "sketched in" before his first entry: in this respect he is noticeably different from his predecessor on the tragic stage, who is only referred to almost casually at the end of the first scene as "yong *Hamlet*". Here we have Iago's bitter discussion of him, with its reiteration of "the Moore", "his Mooreship"; the "bumbast Circumstance, Horribly stufft with Epithites of warre"; mention of Rhodes and Cyprus and "others grounds Christen'd, and Heathen"; Roderigo's "the Thicks-lips"; Iago's more obscene descriptions to Brabantio; and the mention of his importance to the State as General in the prospective Cyprus wars. All this is given us

I

before Burbadge's appearance on the Platform. Soon after his arrival he tells us

> I fetch my life and being,
> From Men of Royall Seige.
>
> > (I. ii. 21 ff.)

Brabantio's suggestion that his daughter has been enchanted with foul charms, bound in chains of magic, helps to hint at the mysterious background of Othello's past. So too, of course, does the round, unvarnished tale that refutes the charge—

> the Storie of my life,
> From yeare to yeare: the Battaile, Sieges, Fortune,
> That I have past.
> I ran it through, even from my boyish daies,
> To th'very moment that he bad me tell it.
> Wherein I spoke of most disastrous chances:
> Of moving Accidents by Flood and Field,
> Of haire-breadth scapes i'th'imminent deadly breach;
> Of being taken by the Insolent Foe,
> And sold to slavery. Of my redemption thence,
> And portance in my Travellours historie.
> Wherein of Antais vast, and Desarts idle,
> Rough Quarries, Rocks, Hills, whose head touch heaven,
> It was my hint to speake. Such was my Processe,
> And of the Canibals that each other eate,
> The *Antropophague*, and men whose heads
> Grew beneath their shoulders.
>
> > (I. iii. 129 ff.)

Already, before this, he has told us

> since these Armes of mine, had seven yeares pith,
> Till now, some nine Moones wasted, they have us'd
> Their dearest action, in the Tented Field:
> And little of this great world can I speake,
> More then pertaines to Feats of Broiles, and Battaile.
>
> > (I. iii. 83ff.)

There follow such echoes as

> The Tirant Custome, most Grave Senators,
> Hath made the flinty and Steele Couch of Warre
> My thrice-driven bed of Downe . . .
>
> > (I. iii. 230 ff.)

and

> 'tis the Soldiers life,
> To have their Balmy slumbers wak'd with strife.
>
> > (II. iii. 259 f.)

Prominent in the series must be the famous "farewell" speech:

> Oh now, for ever
> Farewell the Tranquill minde; farewell Content;
> Farewell the plumed Troopes, and the bigge Warres,
> That makes Ambition, Vertue! Oh farewell;
> Farewell the neighing Steed, and the shrill Trumpe,
> The spirit-stirring Drum, th'Eare-piercing Fife,
> The Royall Banner, and all Qualitie,
> Pride, Pompe, and Circumstance of glorious Warre:
> And O you mortall Engines, whose rude throates
> Th'immortall Joves dread Clamours, counterfet,
> Farewell: *Othello's* Occupation's gone.
>
> (III. iii. 348 ff.)

and the "Sacred-vow" of revenge—

> Like to the Ponticke Sea,
> Whose Icie Current, and compulsive course,
> Nev'r keepes retyring ebbe, but keepes due on
> To the Proponticke, and the Hellespont:
> Even so my bloody thoughts, with violent pace
> Shall nev'r looke backe, nev'r ebbe to humble Love,
> Till that a capeable, and wide Revenge
> Swallow them up.
>
> (III. iii. 454 ff.)

With its heartrending irony, Desdemona's answer to Aemilia's question "Is he not jealious?" reminds us once again of the romance of his distant upbringing:

> Who, he? I thinke the Sun where he was borne,
> Drew all such humors from him.
>
> (III. iv. 30 ff.)

The theatrical trick of the handkerchief is touched with poetry so that it too becomes part of the romantic and mysterious background. We hear of the Egyptian Charmer who gave it to Othello's mother: the story of its potency in love raises it from a stage-trick to material of tragic import:

> There's Magicke in the web of it:
> A Sybill that had numbred in the world
> The Sun to course, two hundred compasses,
> In her Prophetticke furie sow'd the Worke:
> The Wormes were hallowed, that did breede the Silke,
> And it was dyde in Mummey, which the Skilfull
> Conserv'd of Maidens hearts.
>
> (III. iv. 70 ff.)

Iago's affected surprise at hearing of Othello's "strange un-
quietnesse"—

> Can he be angry? I have seene the Cannon
> When it hath blowne his Rankes into the Ayre,
> And like the Divell from his very Arme
> Puff't his owne Brother: And is he angry?
> Something of moment then:
>
> (III. iv. 133 ff.)

looks forward to Lodovico's comment on Othello's striking his wife—

> Is this the Nature
> Whom Passion could not shake? Whose solid vertue
> The shot of Accident, nor dart of Chance
> Could neither graze, nor pierce?
>
> (IV. i. 276 ff.)

In the last scene, left alone with the dead bodies of Desdemona and
Aemilia, Othello hunts for and finds "a Sword of Spaine, the Ice
brookes temper"; with this in hand he compels Gratiano to look in
on him:

> Behold, I have a weapon:
> A better never did it selfe sustaine
> Upon a Soldiers Thigh. I have seene the day,
> That with this little Arme, and this good Sword,
> I have made my way through more impediments
> Then twenty times your stop. But (oh vaine boast)
> Who can controll his Fate? 'Tis not so now.
> Be not affraid, though you do see me weapon'd:
> Heere is my journies end, heere is my butt
> And verie Sea-marke of my utmost Saile.
> Do you go backe dismaid? 'Tis a lost feare:
> Man but a Rush against *Othello's* brest,
> And he retires.
>
> (V. ii. 258 ff.)

Then the final speech—

> Soft you; a word or two before you goe—
>
> (V. ii. 337 ff.)

with its variety of outlandish colour (the Indian who threw a pearl
away richer than all his tribe; the Arabian trees dropping their
medicinable gum; the turbaned Turk in Aleppo) brings home
the background imagery full circle, and makes his death-stroke
seem indeed the last page in "the Storie of my life", the last of his
"most disastrous chances", the "journies end. . . . And verie Sea-
marke of my utmost Saile".

If we turn to *King Lear* we find *leit-motifs* akin to *Othello's*: the "hundred Knights" are like the "handkerchief"; "dotage" like "honest Iago"; "plainnesse" couples Cordelia's sincerity with Kent's. But the pervasive imagery is more subtle and more potent even that that of the earlier play. It circulates not round the principal person like the background imagery of Othello, but round an idea inherent in the play's story, or rather more exactly round the single *word* "nature" and its overtones—natural, unnatural, monster, bastard—and a strangely wider sense of the word including the nature of man and the nature of the universe. It is perhaps best to list the main instances of this pervasive imagery and ask the reader to draw his own conclusions.[191]

Lear asks his daughters which loves him most—

> That we, our largest bountie may extend
> Where Nature doth with merit challenge.
>> (I. i. 54 f.)

After Cordelia's disgrace, he speaks of her as

> a wretch whom Nature is asham'd
> Almost t' acknowledge hers.
>> (I. i. 215 f.)

France, astonished, asks how Cordelia could

> Commit a thing so monstrous, to dismantle
> So many folds of favour: sure her offence
> Must be of such unnaturall degree,
> That monsters it . . .
>> (I. i. 220 ff.)

Edmund's soliloquy at the beginning of the second scene has a new interpretation of the word "Nature", whom he invokes as his "Goddesse", to whose law his services are bound. His spirited advocacy of bastardy ("Now Gods, stand up for Bastards") certainly belongs to the pervasive train of thought (I. ii. 1 ff.). Gloucester, hearing of Edgar's supposed treachery, calls him "unnaturall" and says "He cannot bee such a Monster". His superstitious interpretation of the late eclipses in the sun and moon speaks of the King's tyranny to Cordelia as falling "from byas of Nature" (I. ii. 84, 105, 115 ff.). Enraged by Goneril, Lear calls her "Degenerate Bastard",

---

[191] Since this chapter was written, my attention has been drawn to John F. Danby's *Shakespeare's Doctrine of Nature (A Study of King Lear)*, published in 1949. The reader is referred to this book as containing a close and full analysis of the contrasted meanings of the word "nature" in this play, set in their historical perspective of contemporary thought.

and takes the imagery a step further when already the truth begins
to break in upon him:

> O most small fault,
> How ugly did'st thou in *Cordelia* shew?
> Which like an Engine, wrencht my frame of Nature
> From the fixt place . . .
>
> (I. iv. 290 ff.)

His terrible curse upon Goneril is addressed to Nature:

> Heare, Nature, heare deere Goddesse, heare:
> Suspend thy purpose, if thou did'st intend
> To make this Creature fruitfull . . .

and he proceeds

> If she must teeme
> Create her childe of Spleene, that it may live
> And be a thwart disnatur'd torment to her.
>
> (I. iv. 299 ff.)

Alone with the Fool, waiting for his horses, he mutters

> I will forget my Nature, so kind a Father?

and the cry is wrung from him

> To tak't againe perforce; Monster Ingratitude!
>
> (I. v. 36, 44)

Edmund, still deceiving his father, speaks of Edgar's "unnaturall
purpose", and Gloucester, thanking him, calls him "Loyall and
naturall Boy" (II. i. 52, 86). Later Cornwall praising the villain says
"Natures of such deepe trust, we shall much need"(II. i. 117). In a
comic vein, the disguised Kent says to Oswald "you cowardly
Rascall, nature disclaimes in thee: a Taylor made thee" (II. ii. 58).
Lear, exasperated by the refusal of Cornwall and Regan to see him,
yet tries to find excuses for the discourtesy—

> may be he is not well,
> Infirmity doth still neglect all office,
> Whereto our health is bound, we are not our selves,
> When Nature being opprest, commands the mind
> To suffer with the body . . .
>
> (II. iv. 106 ff.)

Regan, excusing her sister's treatment of their father, says

> O Sir, you are old,
> Nature in you stands on the very Verge
> Of his confine . . .
>
> (II. iv. 148 ff.)

Lear, drawing an invidious distinction between the two sisters, says
to Regan

> Thy tender-hefted Nature shall not give
> Thee o're to harshnesse . . .

and adds

> Thou better know'st
> The Offices of Nature, bond of Childhood,
> Effects of Curtesie, dues of Gratitude . . .
>   (II. iv. 174 ff.)

The sense shifts, though the word persists, in Lear's outburst before
he rushes forth into the storm:

> O reason not the need: our basest Beggers
> Are in the poorest thing superfluous,
> Allow not Nature, more then Nature needs:
> Mans life is cheape as Beastes. Thou art a Lady;
> If onely to go warme were gorgeous,
> Why Nature needs not what thou gorgeous wear'st,
> Which scarcely keepes thee warme, but for true need:
> You Heavens, give me that patience, patience I need . . .
>   (II. iv. 267 ff.)

The former sense returns in his almost incoherent cry

> No you unnaturall Hags,
> I will have such revenges on you both,
> That all the world shall——
>   (II. iv. 281 ff.)

Out in the storm, Lear bids the thunder

> Cracke Natures moulds, all germaines spill at once
> That makes ingratefull Man.
>   (III. ii. 8 f.)

Kent, characteristically nearer to earth, says of the weather

> Mans Nature cannot carry
> Th'affliction, nor the feare.
>   (III. ii. 48 f.)

Gloucester privately to Edmund disapproves of the "unnaturall
dealing" of Lear's daughters, and Edmund hypocritically agrees:
"Most savage and unnaturall" (III. iii). Kent repeats his former
view, as he tries to persuade Lear to shelter in the hovel:

> Here is the place my Lord, good my Lord enter,
> The tirrany of the open night's too rough
> For Nature to endure.
>   (III. iv. 1 ff.)

It is the thought of his unnatural daughters ("Filial ingratitude")
that leads Lear towards madness—

> O that way madnesse lies, let me shun that:
> No more of that.
>
> > (III. iv. 21 f.)

So as he contemplates the naked Bedlamite beggar, who is Edgar in
disguise, he cries

> nothing could have subdu'd Nature
> To such a lownesse, but his unkind Daughters.
>
> > (III. iv. 69 f.)

"Pelicane Daughters" he calls them, thinking of the young birds
that drink their parent's blood. The Nature of Man is visibly
symbolised in the naked Edgar. Lear, fascinated by the sight, says
"Is man no more then this? . . . Thou art the thing it selfe; unaccommodated man, is no more but such a poore, bare, forked
Animall as thou art" (III. iv. 105 ff.). Gloucester utters a kindred
theme as he tells the King "Our flesh and blood, my Lord, is growne
so vilde, that it doth hate what gets it" (III. iv. 149 f.). Edmund,
the hypocrite, pretends a dilemma as he says to Cornwall "How my
Lord, I may be censured, that Nature thus gives way to Loyaltie,
something feares mee to thinke of "(III. v. 3 ff.). Nature would
lead him to side with his father. loyalty gives him the excuse to
traffic with reigning authority. In the heartrending scene where
Lear fancies himself to be arraigning Goneril and Regan before his
bench of justices, he penetrates near to the core of this theme with
the words "Then let them Anatomize *Regan*: See what breeds about
her heart. Is there any cause in Nature that makes these hard-
hearts" (III. vi. 80 ff.). When Lear at last finds rest, Kent tells us
that "Oppressed nature sleepes", and regrets the immediate need to
disturb him again (III. vi. 106). Gloucester, deprived of his eyes,
calls upon Edmund for revenge. It is the unnatural Edmund who is
implored to

> enkindle all the sparkes of Nature
> To quit this horrid acte . . .
>
> > (III. vii. 86 f.)

and we should not miss the comment of the servant on Regan
(omitted in the Folio): "If she live long, & in the end meet the old
course of death, women will all turne monsters" (III. vii. 100 ff.).
Albany, for once speaking home truths to Goneril, states the moral
of her conduct:

> That nature which contemnes ith [*read* its] origin
> Cannot be bordered certaine in it selfe,
> She that her selfe will sliver and disbranch
> From her materiall sap, perforce must wither,
> And come to deadly use.
>
> (IV. ii. 32 ff.)

and declares his conviction—

> If that the heavens doe not their visible spirits
> Send quickly downe to tame this vild offences, it will come
> Humanity must perforce pray on it self like monsters
> of the deepe.
>
> (IV. ii. 46 ff.)

Cordelia, seeking the means to restore her father's "bereaved
Sense", is told that

> Our foster Nurse of Nature, is repose,
> The which he lackes . . .
>
> (IV. iv. 12 f.)

Here the anonymous speaker is using the familiar word in the simple
sense in which Kent has more than once employed it. Lear in the
height of his madness, "Crown'd with ranke Fenitar, and furrow
weeds", declares "I am the King himselfe", and adds pertinently
"Nature's above Art, in that respect" (IV. vi. 87). His raving about
Adultery and Luxury discloses its relevance in the words "Let
Copulation thrive: For Glousters bastard Son was kinder to his
Father, Then my Daughters got 'tweene the lawfull sheets" (IV. vi.
117 f.). The fact that we know it is not true about Edmund—and
that Gloucester too, who hears him, at last knows the truth—adds
tragic irony to the King's disjointed moralising. Blind Gloucester,
who recognises the King in spite of his madness, cries

> O ruin'd peece of Nature, this great world
> Shall so weare out to naught.
>
> (IV. vi. 138 f.)

As Lear runs away from his pursuers, a Gentleman makes comment:

> Thou hast a Daughter
> Who redeemes Nature from the generall curse
> Which twaine have brought her to.
>
> (IV. vi. 210 ff.)

Cordelia, speaking of her father and again using in Kent's presence
his simpler meaning of the word, begs the kind Gods to "Cure this
great breach in his abused Nature" (IV. vii. 15). And there,

strangely enough, the imagery fades away. The sublime simplicity of Lear's waking and of the very end of the play makes no direct or implied reference to the pervading theme. One may say, perhaps, that it is immanent in the situation and that the poet knows when to leave it unstated. One may also perhaps confess that the winding-up of the sub-plot of the play is protracted and sometimes clumsy, and, with inspiration temporarily sagging, Shakespeare found that the material would not evolve to its end in his newly wrought medium. *Othello* is more satisfactory for the sustaining of the climax, and *Macbeth* (in the abbreviated form in which we have it) a close second. And of *King Lear* let it be said that the play, like the old King himself, is redeemed past criticism by the last seventy lines.

I have thought it worth while to risk wearying my reader's patience with such lengthy quotation, because there is no other way of stating the point that must here be made. It is not an easy point to make, because the explanation does not reveal itself in a logical statement; that, for instance, Shakespeare uses the word "nature" thirty or forty times in the one play. It is clear that he uses the word in several senses: but that does not invalidate the fact that the word is pervasive; and, moreover, it will have been seen that in some examples the different meanings of the word merge or pass into each other. What we must remember is that Shakespeare the poet was fascinated by words themselves, that he delighted in their ambiguity, that he was used to playing with their varied senses. And it seems to me impossible to escape the suggestion that he had this *word*—and its kindred of words—(in Miranda's phrase) "beating" in his mind as he conceived the play. The *word* is the thread on which the unity of the play is strung together. To achieve unity and continuity thus is a verbal, a strictly *poetic* device. It is Shakespeare's crowning discovery in his search for the means to express drama in poetry. That Aeschylus had made the same discovery two thousand years before him does not lessen Shakespeare's claim to original invention. For with the new conditions of the Elizabethan playhouse and the Elizabethan dramatic convention, the discovery had to be made afresh. It is perhaps still this side idolatry to declare that Shakespeare's medium with its vastly greater flexibility enabled him to surpass the masterpieces of his predecessor.

That there is a fundamental difference between these two great dramas (and their successors, *Macbeth* and *Antony and Cleopatra*), and the earlier plays of Shakespeare, perhaps no one will deny. The sharp, intimate, objective focus is changed for remote classical panorama. Burbadge and Heminges and Lowin have suffered a sea-change into something rich and strange. Burbadge's Othello and

Lear are individuals, but less personally known to us than his Hamlet; Heminges's Kent is recognisable at once as a man we honour and admire and grow to love, but his Polonius had independent life of a different kind. The independence has gone, and therein perhaps lies the clue: the new characters are not independent of the drama in which they take part; they are closer knit in its texture, they serve the whole conception of the dramatist, and the result is a closer unity in the drama itself. *Othello, Macbeth, Antony and Cleopatra* are homogeneous dramatic poems—and so is four-fifths of *King Lear*. Each story in itself is conceived poetically, and a unified work of art is the outcome. The change—can we doubt it?—was a deliberate choice on the part of the dramatist, and it was made, not without labour and misgiving and temporary frustration, in the years between *Hamlet* and *Othello*.

(x) *Withdrawal-and-Return*

The years 1602 to 1604 make a startling impression even on a casual glance at Chambers' chronological list.[192] For the previous ten years there is a steady average of two plays a year (with two instances of three in the twelvemonth): then a year in which *Troilus and Cressida* is all the output—a baffling, bitter play, pricking the bubble of legendary chivalry, a satire but not in the happy vein of *As You Like It*, which runs so easily into poetry. There is certainly much cunning poetry in the scene of the first meeting of the lovers, when Troilus stalks about Cressida's door

> Like a strange soule upon the Stigian bankes
> Staying for waftage . . .

and in her presence murmurs

> You have bereft me of all words Lady.

The words—eloquent words—follow, but the verse is uneasily mixed with prose in the opening of the duet, and the presence and comments of Pandarus, and the ironical hints of Cressida's fickleness, make the scene—however subtly interesting—an awkward theme for poetical expression. Still, Shakespeare takes his opportunity: the sincerity of Troilus and the feigning of Cressida (after all, poetry is feigning) make equally fine protestations in sonnet form—"As true as *Troylus* . . ." "As false as *Cressid*." [193] Ever and anon, too, the speeches of Ulysses and Hector and Troilus soar from eloquence

---

[192] See Appendix I, p. 318.
[193] *Troilus and Cressida*, III. ii. 9 f.; 55; 179 ff., 191 ff.

into poetry. There is poetical evocation of character, as we have seen, in Ulysses' portraits of Diomed and Cressida: and of atmosphere in Hector's modest pride as he gazes across the playhouse yard at the walls of Troy. But the bitter mood that pervades the play is of a kind to choke the spring of poetry. Moreover, there are plain indications that the poet is tired and in need of a rest. There are hackneyed repetitions of old gambits and old situations. Nestor's defiance of Hector recreates Shallow's more vivid bravado; Hector's encounter with Thersites in battle is but a faint echo of Falstaff's with the Douglas; the battle itself is a muddle, for there are too many celebrities, and nothing happens to any of them except Patroclus (whom we do not see) and Hector, whose killing has surprisingly little dramatic force. More striking still, as a sign of exhaustion in the poet, is the fact that Troilus, in his agony at discovering that Cressida is false, betakes himself to voluble conceits in the style of Shakespeare's immaturity.[194]

Next year there is a still more pronounced flagging of inspiration: it is generally agreed that *All's Well That Ends Well* is the feeblest play in the canon. It gives the impression of hack-work, with much repetition of old devices. But some of the speeches of Helena should make us pause before we catch at this rare opportunity of pronouncing against Shakespeare. Hear her speak in soliloquy of her secret love for Bertram:

> 'Twas prettie, though a plague
> To see him everie houre [*read* houre;] to sit and draw
> His arched browes, his hawking eie, his curles
> In our hearts table: heart too capeable
> Of everie line and tricke of his sweet favour.
> (I. i. 104 ff.)

The syntax of her next soliloquy is less remarkable, but the obscurity of thought is new in Shakespeare: how can the audience at first hearing take in her meaning?

> Our remedies oft in our selves do lye,
> Which we ascribe to heaven: the fated skye
> Gives us free scope, onely doth backward pull
> Our slow designes, when we our selves are dull.
> What power is it, which mounts my love so hye,

---

[194] *Troilus and Cressida*, I. iii. 296 ff.; V. iv. 28 ff.; V. ii. 144 ff., 160 ff. It should perhaps be mentioned that Baldwin declares that "the play was evidently not constructed originally for the Shakesperean company. The abnormal number of major parts suggests that the play may have been cast originally for the abnormally large Admiral's company" (T. W. Baldwin, *Organization and Personnel of the Shakesperean Company*, footnote to table opposite p. 229).

> That makes me see, and cannot feede mine eye?
> The mightiest space in fortune, Nature brings
> To joyne like, likes; and kisse like native things.
> Impossible be strange attempts to those
> That weigh their paines in sence, and do suppose
> What hath beene, cannot be. Who ever strove
> To shew her merit, that did misse her love?
>
> (I. i. 235 ff.)

It takes no great subtlety of ear to detect an originality of rhythm and diction in these lines later in the play:

> I do presume sir, that you are not falne
> From the report that goes upon your goodnesse,
> And therefore goaded with most sharpe occasions,
> Which lay nice manners by, I put you to
> The use of your owne vertues, for the which
> I shall continue thankefull.
>
> (V. i. 12 ff.)

We can indeed hear a faint prophetic echo of *The Tempest* in this speech. But the play shows an odd mixture of styles, the formal couplets of an earlier period are suddenly interrupted by the realistic vigour of the King's charge to Bertram:

> My Honor's at the stake, which to defeate
> I must produce my power. Heere, take her hand,
> Proud scornfull boy, unworthie this good gift,
> That dost in vile misprision shackle up
> My love, and her desert: that canst not dreame,
> We poizing us in her defective scale,
> Shall weigh thee to the beame: That wilt not know,
> It is in Us to plant thine Honour, where
> We please to have it grow.
>
> (II. iii. 156 ff.)

Later in the story, Helena's despairing letter to the Countess is couched in the exact shape of a sonnet (III. iv. 4 ff.). There is perhaps an attempt at a running theme in the contention between the arrogant assurance of youth, as exemplified in Bertram, and the mellow wisdom of age, in the persons of the *Old* Countess, *Old* Lafeu, and the King of France who speaks for the older generation in recalling the words of Bertram's dead father:

> Let me not live (quoth hee)
> After my flame lackes oyle, to be the snuffe
> Of yonger spirits, whose apprehensive senses
> All but new things disdaine . . .
>
> (I. ii. 58 ff.)

But the conception is tentative, and indeed the play never catches fire.

The total silence of the ensuing year is a logical sequel to this flagging of inspiration. It is usual to seek some external reason for this silence and for the following tragic period: personal misfortunes in the poet's life are hinted at rather than specified; or the tragic fall of Essex, which may indeed have touched Shakespeare as well as any other sensitive or intelligent person as a public calamity; and the consequent gloom which overcast the end of the old Queen's reign, together with the anxious uncertainty about the succession—all this may well have checked the optimism of animal spirits in a man nearing forty. But is it not more likely that an artist's inspiration may have come to a temporary halt owing to a reason connected with his art? Is it not probable that the restlessly experimental Shakespeare found himself after writing *Hamlet* at an impasse in the development of his poetic drama? And if after a couple of years of baffling struggle he emerges into a full-flowing inspiration of a new order from his past achievement, may we not justly borrow a phrase from Professor Toynbee and call the inexpressive years a period of "Withdrawal-and-Return". In his *Study of History*, Toynbee has drawn attention to a movement in the lives of the greatest men, whether saints, scholars or poets, to which he attaches this descriptive phrase.[195] It would not be surprising—it would be just what we should expect—to find that some such break occurred in Shakespeare's artistic development. Such a break, indeed, is admitted by all critics to be apparent after the great achievement of *Hamlet*. "After *Hamlet*," says Chambers, "came a group of plays which, to some readers at least, show Shakespeare in a rather uncomfortable mood: the bitter comedies of *All's Well* and *Measure for Measure*, and *Troilus and Cressida*, the comedy, if you will, but rather, as I think, the tragedy, of disillusionment with the world's ancient ideals of heroism and romance." [196] Granville-Barker hints at the fundamental change in a sentence of his lecture, "From *Henry V* to *Hamlet*", when he asks: "Did Shakespeare, when with *Henry V* he came to the end of all he could find to his purpose in the technique of the drama as his contemporaries and masters understood it, when, passing over that bridge which is *Julius Caesar*, he found in the working out of *Hamlet* the technique best suited to his genius, did he then and thereafter take the wrong road? . . . Frankly,

---

[195] Professor Arnold J. Toynbee, *A Study of History*, vol. iii, 248 ff. It is curious that after mentioning Dante as an example of a creative poet, Toynbee then gives Hamlet as an instance of a character from fiction: but he does not make allusion to Shakespeare himself.

[196] E. K. Chambers, *Shakesperian Gleanings*, 50.

I am for Shakespeare the playwright and Yes . . . But . . ." [197] The
scope of that excellent essay causes an arbitrary line to be drawn
after *Hamlet:* otherwise one might get a truer vision of the sequel,
where the technical problems raised by the poet had to be worked
out.

After the "withdrawal" the first play of the "return" continues in
one respect at least the tentative experimenting of *All's Well That
Ends Well.* The new obscure-conciseness of diction, which appeared
once or twice in that play, is already the order of the day in *Measure
for Measure.* Claudio, on his way to prison, asked by the outspoken
Lucio if his offence is that of getting Juliet with child, replies:

> Unhappely, even so.
> And the new Deputie, now for the Duke,
> Whether it be the fault and glimpse of newnes,
> Or whether that the body publique, be
> A horse whereon the Governor doth ride,
> Who newly in the Seate, that it may know
> He can command; lets it strait feele the spur:
> Whether the Tirranny be in his place,
> Or in his Eminence that fills it up
> I stagger in: But this new Governor
> Awakes me all the inrolled penalties
> Which have (like un-scowr'd Armor) hung by th'wall
> So long, that nineteene Zodiacks have gone round,
> And none of them beene worne; and for a name
> Now puts the drowsie and neglected Act
> Freshly on me: 'tis surely for a name.
>   (I. ii. 166 ff.)

One wonders what the Chamberlain's Men (now the King's Men)
made of this new style of speech? Whether they took to it, or whether
it needed some coaxing from the poet? It is a problem play: indeed,
Shakespeare states a double problem in the early scene between the
Duke and Friar Thomas; the Duke wants to see the effect of strict-
ness upon the lax state, but also the effect of power upon Angelo—
"hence shall we see If power change purpose: what our Seemers be"
(I. iii. 53 f.). The personal problem presents itself so forcibly in
Shakespeare's mind that he is carried away by it: Angelo and
Isabella possess him for three splendid acts. But the other problem,
the public problem, is intended to bind the play together, and the
Duke is meant to be the central figure: indeed, as it stands, his part
is more than twice as long as Angelo's. The play is broken-backed;
after Angelo has done his worst, there is nothing for him to do except

---

[197] Granville-Barker, *From Henry V to Hamlet,* 22.

await retribution. And the Duke's purpose wavers, perhaps because
Shakespeare found it essentially undramatic. The last act is ingenious,
but so long protracted that the ingenuity defeats its own ends. There
is what ought to be a great moment—Isabella (at Mariana's request)
pleading for Angelo, although she still thinks Claudio is dead—yet
even that moment does not come off as greatly as it should (V. i.
444 ff.). And in the sorting out of individual fortunes, comedy-wise,
we lose sight of the Duke's first purpose—to observe the government
of his state in detachment.

It is impossible to dismiss the impression that Shakespeare lost
interest and concentration half-way through his play. But it is a
magnificent failure: the first three acts lead logically on to the
splendours of the tragic period. Isabella's pleading introduces a new
philosophical note characteristic of the play: wisdom is distilled in
poetry when she speaks of

> man, proud man,
> Drest in a little briefe authoritie,
> Most ignorant of what he's most assur'd,
> (His glassie Essence) like an angry Ape
> Plaies such phantastique tricks before high heaven,
> As makes the Angels weepe;
>   (II. ii. 117 f.)

and warns Angelo that

> Authoritie, though it erre like others,
> Hath yet a kinde of medicine in it selfe
> That skins the vice o'th' top . . .
>   (II. ii. 134 ff.)

Ulysses is commonplace to this, so is even Brutus, and Hamlet does
not often go as deep. Whether it is as good drama depends, perhaps,
on the taste of the spectator, but in its later development in the great
tragedies, this depth of poetical insight carries all before it. The
whole drama of the relationship of Angelo and Isabella and Claudio
is worked out by poetical means. It is foolish to complain that
Isabella is inhuman or that Angelo is "a type": the dilemma
(poetically created and sustained) has vitality enough. It should be
realised that the spoken word sustains the tension by which the theme
rises to its tragic proportions. The spoken word is more important
than ever in Shakespeare's scheme. We in the audience must listen
ever more and more attentively, and the actor can rely less and less
upon miming to make his speech clear: his voice becomes his chief
instrument for this play, as for the great tragedies. That the Duke's
half of the play—the latter half—falls away from the tragic tension,

is due largely to the fact that his problem could not find expression,
as the personal problem did, in poetical terms.

Then in the same year comes the wholly triumphant *Othello*, with
its relentless compression, its unflagging tension, its poetical unity.
The full flavour of the new magic is already present in the opening
dialogue. Iago's speeches are an excellent example of the new
conciseness; as a good speaker delivers them, we get much more
than plain sense from them; they breed drama by poetical means:
one specimen must suffice here, for the scope of the present enquiry
will not admit of more than a hint of the extent of Shakespeare's
new-found power:

> Three Great-ones of the Cittie,
> (In personall suite to make me his Lieutenant)
> Off-capt to him: and by the faith of man
> I know my price, I am worth no worsse a place.
> But he (as loving his owne pride and purposes)
> Evades them, with a bumbast Circumstance,
> Horribly stufft with Epithites of warre,
> Non-suites my Mediators, For certes, saies he,
> I have already chose my Officer. And what was he?
> For-sooth, a great Arithmatician.
> One *Michaell Cassio*, a *Florentine*,
> (A fellow almost damn'd in a faire Wife)
> That never set a Squadron in the Field,
> Nor the devision of a Battaile knowes
> More then a Spinster. Unlesse the Bookish Theoricke:
> Wherein the Tongued Consuls can propose
> As Masterly as he. Meere pratle (without practise)
> Is all his Souldership. But he (Sir) had th'election;
> And I (of whom his eies had seene the proofe
> At Rhodes, at Ciprus, and on others grounds
> Christen'd, and Heathen) must be be-leed, and calm'd
> By Debitor, and Creditor. This Counter-caster,
> He (in good time) must his Lieutenant be,
> And I (blesse the marke) his Mooreships Auntient.[198]

It would need a long analysis to point out how much of the tragedy
is already latent in the fully-charged poetry of this one speech. And
analysis would hardly be so potent a proof as the speech itself. The
miracle is that this rich poetical content is sustained throughout the
whole play, and throughout most of *King Lear* and *Macbeth* and
Antony and Cleopatra, till the exhausted poet was forced to pause and
draw breath again. Yet we must not fail to realise, as a perusal of

---

[198] *Othello*, I. i. 8 ff.

the many examples from *Othello* and *King Lear* quoted in the course of my argument will show, that, in the full flood of his new-found mastery, Shakespeare still grounded his play in the playhouse for which he was writing; that his new-created style of poetic drama fitted the Globe as well as the old; and that for its full enjoyment it is still necessary to present it once again in the conditions of its first production.

(*xi*) *The Poetic Drama*

It is now time to summarise this chapter, in which an attempt has been made to show that Shakespeare's poetic drama springs from the playhouse for which he wrote it. His dramatic vision, such is the argument, was grounded in this playhouse: it was regulated to the capabilities and needs of the company of which he was a member: it helped to establish their tradition of acting, and (mutually) was helped by them in its own development. It was based on a substructure of objectivity—practical, of the playhouse, and modern, that is to say, Elizabethan. Moreover, Shakespeare's turn of mind was such as to revel in making opportunities out of the very limitations of his medium. He realised that his chief and sharpest weapon was the spoken word, and discovered that it could be used for all manner of purposes in his playhouse: to give life to properties and furniture, to the stage itself, its permanent features and its imagined environs; to create the circumstances of a scene, the illusion of neighbouring space, of up-and-down-hill, of dizzy height; and the atmosphere of a scene, sunrise, sunset, hot noon, storm, moonlight, darkness, and the timeless hour of the visitation of ghosts; and further not only to create the atmosphere, but also to comment on it, and prompt the reactions of the audience to it; to create character likewise—habitual character, both open and concealed, and momentary mood by the method of "close-up" description—and to comment on it and prompt the audience's reaction; and to create the action itself, and again comment and prompt the audience. He learnt, moreover, that with his poetical medium he could transcend the visible scene and use the same conventional Platform and Tiring-House as a vehicle for thoughts beyond the reaches of our souls.

We have seen cause to revise our opinion of Shakespeare's architectural powers, realising that much that seems diffuse and desultory in the theatre of to-day was part of the essential technique of his stagecraft in the conditions of his playhouse; that a producer must therefore consider, in the first place, what is the main design of each play and be careful of his cutting. We recognised an insistent relevance in most of the poet's construction, and examined his means of achieving continuity—the direct method, the method of alternation, the "rod-in-pickle" method; the power of rhythm to sustain the tension; the technique of pervasive motif, and the kindred device of pervasive imagery.

A large part of this equipment was already at Shakespeare's command by the time he wrote *Hamlet*. But we are led to realise that *Hamlet* is not the last word, and we postulate in the years immediately succeeding that play a period of "Withdrawal-and-Return" during which the poet discovered by anxious and laborious experiment new possibilities in his chosen medium. The ensuing period of the great tragedies throws still more emphasis upon the spoken word, with a new conciseness and pregnancy of expression, a highly organised texture of pervasive theme and imagery, admitting of counterpoint and rising to climaxes, and a still wider exploration of the transcendental.

Yet the new drama is still within the compass of the Wooden O, can still be most easily shown within the girdle of these walls; and the familiar images are there to remind us—the Cue and Prompter of *Othello*, the great stage of Fooles of *King Lear*, the poore Player of *Macbeth*. The argument of the preceding pages is of no avail if it does not justify the presumption that *Othello*, *King Lear* and *Macbeth* are all devised for and admirably adapted to this stage, and can therefore only achieve their full effect if played upon it in the tradition of the Chamberlain's Men. The proof of the pudding is in the eating, and the argument cannot be clinched unless and until we see the Globe rebuilt and the repertory recruited and trained once more.

The conjectural generalisation of the latter sections of this chapter lacks the tonic criticism which only practical experience in such a playhouse can give. It will therefore be a refreshment, perhaps to the reader no less than to the writer, to return from the general to the particular. The last chapter of the present investigation takes the form of some production notes on *Macbeth*. I choose this play not only because I have twice produced it in conditions approximating to those of the Globe, but also as a sustained example of Shakespeare's poetic drama in its full maturity of development.[199]

---

[199] Any contemplation of the sequel to the tragic period, when the acquisition of the Blackfriars Theatre alters the picture, is irrelevant to the present study.

6

MACBETH AT THE GLOBE

THE object of the following notes is not to provide an alternative commentary on the text of the play, but to supplement the many already in existence; nor is it intended to furnish a complete "acting edition", but rather to point out some of the differences from the normal practice of to-day which would arise from presenting the play in its original setting, and to apply the argument of the foregoing pages to a specific example. For this last reason, at the end of most of the notes appears an italicised reference to one or other section of the preceding chapters, so that a student of *Macbeth* (whether producer or player or of the audience), if he wishes confirmation of this or that point, may glance back to the fuller explanation above.

Our only prompt-book for *Macbeth* is the Folio text: it is not possible to discuss here the problem of the copy for that text—since there is no other available, we must use it and assume that it has been cut from the original normal length. There is support for the view that the cutting was done by Shakespeare himself: certainly the result (in spite of loose ends) remains a masterpiece of sustained tragic tension. Dr. Richard Flatter, in his *Shakespeare's Producing Hand* (page 94), expresses his belief that "the text of *Macbeth* is the only one of which we may assume with any measure of certainty that it shows no traces of 'editorial' interference", and speaks of it as "the only play from which the real yard-stick of Shakespeare's diction can be obtained". He devotes four chapters of his book to the play, and no producer can afford to ignore these chapters.

COSTUME. Substructure Elizabethan. A touch or two of tartan plaid over the Elizabethan styles will help to create the national atmosphere, but the kilt is an anachronism of the wrong kind, introducing a note of a later civilisation (than Shakespeare's). The play is no more Scottish than *The Merchant of Venice* is Venetian, less so than *Julius Caesar* is Roman, but more so than *A Midsummer Night's Dream* is Athenian. The weather and the scene-painting is north of the border, but the Porter is not another Jamy: he is pure Bankside.

And Macduff, for instance, has less feeling of Scotland than the Douglas of 1 *Henry IV*.

(Costume, pp. 53 ff.)

For casting, Baldwin gives us (among others):

Macbeth	Burbadge
Banquo	Lowin
Malcolm	Cundall
Ross	Heminges
Macduff	Sly
Duncan	Shakespeare
The Porter	Armin
The Old Man	Cowley
Lady Macbeth	Edmans

(The Repertory, pp. 156 ff.)

ACT I, *Scene i*

It would be difficult to imagine a better start, both for exposition of necessary information, and for atmospheric effect. The weird sisters preside over the opening of the play, rather than take part in it. Locality unspecified. Positioning: probably one at either end of the Tarras, the *first* witch being in the Music Gallery above—a triangular group in mid-air. They thus give the illusion at the end of the scene of parting with each other, R and L of Tarras, and into the Music Gallery curtains. The action of the play proper begins at once on the Platform below them.

(Scene-Rotation, pp. 31 ff.)

ACT I, *Scene ii*

. . . *meeting a bleeding Captaine.* The significant fact at once emphasised in Duncan's opening words: *What bloody man is that?* The description is an example of the "close-up" method.

(The Prompt Book, pp. 25 ff.)

7 The bleeding Captain's narrative shows the Messenger-Speech method: he does not speak in character, his gashes do not persistently cry for help, but he most powerfully evokes by speech and miming the battle itself, without which Macbeth would not have his stature (nor Banquo his). It is characteristic of the method that at the time of speaking the issue is still in doubt, so that in a sense the battle sways to and fro (stands doubtful) before our eyes. A similar effect can be seen in 1 *Henry IV* (I. i) where Westmoreland's description of Holmedon

is left in the air, for the King (*via* Sir Walter Blunt) to complete. It is also significant that the music-cue at the beginning of the scene is *Alarum*, indicating that the battle is still in progress, not *Flourish*.

(*Creation in Words—of the Action*, pp. 226 ff.)

The themes of "blood" and "darkness" and "sleep" are pervasive in this play. Bradley has collected many of the examples in his *Shakesperian Tragedy*, 333 ff.

(*Pervasive Theme*, pp. 249 ff.)

Heath Set in Study

49 Is it only accidental that the tenses at the beginning of Ross' recital are in the present? It is as if the battle itself were taking place *at this moment* before our eyes. The scene is not "a camp near Forres": it is unlocalised, and presents the action of the battle in poetic form. An interesting point suggests itself after contemplation of the bleeding Captain's and Ross' speeches: presumably this kind of unlocalised scene *must* take place *on the Platform*. The effect of playing on any of the other stages is to suggest (if not represent) a locality.

(*Creation in Words—of the Action*, pp. 226 ff.)
(*Locality and Unlocalisation*, pp. 103 ff.)

If the suggestion is right that the essentially unlocalised I. ii must be on the Platform, then we get the following rotation for Act I:

(*Scene-Rotation*, pp. 31 ff.)

Act I, *Scene iii*

The set in the Study will contain gaunt bushes, their shape
chosen to indicate that the wind is blowing strongly *towards* the

How farre is't call'd to Forres?

point of Macbeth's entry. The grave-trap will be open ready to
receive one of the disappearing sisters, and will perhaps be
disguised with a turf-bank or stone.

(*Furnishing and Properties*, pp. 38 ff.)

4 With masterly compression, the malignancy of witchcraft is
dramatised for us in the short story of the Master of the Tiger
(Messenger Speech method). First witch should mime for us
the rump-fed ronyon's munching, and perhaps also the voyage
in the sieve. No amount of make-up can create an equally
horrible effect.

(*Creation in Words—of the Action*, pp. 226 ff.)
(*Miming*, pp. 125 ff.)

32 *The weyward Sisters, hand in hand* . . . the rhythmical incantation
accompanies a ritual dance with which the three mark out in

the centre of the Platform a charmed circle for Macbeth to step into. *Peace, the Charme's wound up.* They retreat hastily to the perimeter outside the Stage-Post on the opposite side from the Door of Macbeth's entry.

(*Positioning*, pp. 131 ff.)

38 In the vast depth and width of the Platform it is possible to give an impression of the four distinct phases in the approach of the two generals to the expectant witches—*So foule and faire a day* . . . (spoken to Banquo, unaware that there is anyone in sight). *How farre is't call'd to Soris* [read Forres]? . . . (shouted through the fog at the distant figures). *Live you, or are you aught* . . . (spoken at close range). *Speake if you can* . . . (spoken by Macbeth, from the charmed circle which the witches have just made). While Macbeth moves almost at once into the circle, reacting from the spell with a shudder, Banquo's course is forward from the door round the perimeter, outside the Stage-Post opposite to that near which the sisters huddle.

(*Positioning*, pp. 131 ff.)

39 *What are these, So wither'd, and so wilde in their attyre.* . . . Banquo's description of the witches is the familiar "close-up" technique. The minute portraiture is part of the poet's character-drawing, and if the actor realises this he will give the lines their dramatic force, and not make the speech sound like a rather long winded version of Macbeth's impatient question, *what are you?* Further examples in this same scene (also in Heminges' part) are *Good Sir, why doe you start, and seeme to feare Things that doe sound so faire?* and *he seemes wrapt withall;* as likewise, after the entry of Ross and Angus, *Looke how our Partner's rapt.*

(*Creation in Words—of Character*, pp. 217 ff.)

78 *Witches vanish.* No difficulty at the Globe, with the grave-trap in the Study, and the two minor traps at the back of the Platform. Nor is it anyway hard to achieve a plausible illusion, without traps, in the distant Study: plenty of smoke, and Macbeth's stretched cloak does it. I imagine a serial departure, with Macbeth addressing each in turn: *Say from whence* . . . *or why* . . . *Speake, I charge you.*

116 *Glamys, and Thane of Cawdor* . . . *Thankes for your paines. Doe you not hope.* . . . In these five lines Macbeth takes up three separate positions: alone, then towards Ross and Angus, then privately to Banquo. Banquo, after his warning reply, retires to speak to

the others at the back of the Platform: Macbeth remains forward centre, in the middle of his audience. His isolation from the others is helped by Banquo's whispered comments *Looke how our Partner's rapt . . .* etc. Banquo, at *Worthy Macbeth . . .* comes forward to his colleague; then Macbeth crosses with his apology to Ross and Angus, but turns back again to Banquo (now forward) for the intimate exchange of the last five lines of the scene.

(Positioning, pp. 131 ff.)

ACT I, Scene iv

35 *Sonnes, Kinsmen, Thanes . . .* an example of the address to the whole playhouse over the heads of the stage-company: the audience are included among *you whose places are the nearest*, and are thereby taken up into the action of the play.

(Positioning, see especially p. 146; see also pp. 88 f.

48 *The Prince of Cumberland: that is a step . . .* a clear case of the normal soliloquising position, with another conversation upstage.

(Positioning, see especially p. 137)

The *incidents* of this scene are: (1) Cawdor's execution—unnecessary, but the ironical point of the juxtaposition of . . . *absolute Trust. O worthyest Cousin* is what Shakespeare is aiming at; (2) *The Prince of Cumberland;* (3) *my Wife.*

(The Architecture of the Play, see especially pp. 233 ff.)

ACT I, Scene v

After Macbeth's . . . *make joyfull The hearing of my Wife, with your approach*, the following scene begins with the instruction *Enter Macbeths Wife alone with a Letter.* You can almost see the train of thought forming in Shakespeare's mind.

(The Prompt Book, pp. 25 ff.)
(Continuity, pp. 241 ff.)

The furniture of the Chamber is a domestic Elizabethan interior—which may of course include pieces of an *earlier* date. The Chamber has to serve for such domestic scenes at Inverness, at the royal palace, at Macduff's castle, and finally at Dunsinane. There is no reason to make elaborate differentiation: the position of tables and chairs should merely suit the plotting of each scene. In this case, a table and chair are the only necessities: Lady Macbeth may well be discovered reading her letter at the table, rising to her feet perhaps on the words *haile King that shalt be.*

(*Furnishing and Properties*, pp. 38 ff.)

13, If it is true that Lady Macbeth speaks from the Chamber, it is
38 interesting that both her soliloquys in this scene are, unlike Macbeth's reflective broodings, addressed to *hearers* (absent or imaginary)—the first to her husband, the second to the *Spirits, that Tend on mortall thoughts . . . you murth'ring Ministers . . .* and to *thick Night.* This is in line with the fact that Prince Hal's "I

Haile King that shalt be

know you all . . ." is spoken from the Chamber, while Hamlet's reflective brooding is usually delivered from the Platform.

(*Positioning*, see especially pp. 140 ff.)

16 *Glamys thou art, and Cawdor, and shalt be What thou art promis'd:* the repetition of Glamys-Cawdor-King as a triple climax is a convenient dramatic symbol, a *leit-motif* of the same kind as the "Handkerchiefe" in *Othello.* She repeats it in this same scene when she greets her husband as *Great Glamys, worthy Cawdor, Greater then both, by the all-haile hereafter.* The *motif* begins with the salutation of the witches, and comes to a head in Macbeth's imagined cry of *Glamis hath murther'd Sleepe, and therefore Cawdor Shall sleepe no more: Macbeth shall sleepe no more* (II. ii. 43 f.).

(*Pervasive Theme*, pp. 249 ff.)

39 *The Raven himselfe is hoarse, That croakes the fatall entrance of Duncan Under my Battlements.* Up aloft on the Tarras, she points with a malignant gesture downwards to the Platform below her. We have not forgotten her words when, two minutes later, Duncan is entering the castle under this Tarras rail. The device sustains the continuity of dramatic tension.

(*Scene-Rotation*, pp. 31 ff.)
(*Continuity*, pp. 241 ff.)

42 *Unsex me here . . .* see note below on I. vii. 54 ff.

58 The lineation and punctuation of the Folio is worth reproducing here, as an example of the expressiveness of the prompt-book:

> . . . I feele now
> The future in the instant.
> > *Macb.* My dearest Love,
> *Duncan* comes here to Night.
> > *Lady.* And when goes hence?
> > *Macb.* To morrow, as he purposes.
> > *Lady.* O never,
> Shall Sunne that Morrow see.
> Your Face, my *Thane*, is as a Booke, where men . . .

The regular rhythm is suspended when Macbeth begins to speak: it is not resumed until the words *Your Face, my Thane.* . . . In a musical score the effect would be marked by a series of pauses. The Book-Keeper has his rhythm marked just as distinctly by various punctuation and lineation.

(*The Prompt Book*, pp. 25 ff.)

63 *Your Face, my Thane, is as a Booke, where men May reade strange matters.* . . . The continuity of much of the early part of the play is sustained by the insistent focus on Macbeth's mind, his thoughts, his conscience. This appears not only in the fact that many of his early utterances are in soliloquy or aside, but also in the *content* of the passage which begins *This supernaturall solliciting* . . . (where the theme is heavily underlined), and in Lady Macbeth's character-sketch: *yet doe I feare thy Nature . . .* and in her "close-up" of his brooding: *Your Face, my Thane . . .* The comment, after the previous pregnant exchange, would not be necessary under the strong lights of the modern theatre, or in the "close-up" focus of the cinema, where a significant frown would be enough. Here, her subsequent warning to *Looke like the time* adds dramatic plausibility.

(*Continuity*, pp. 241 ff.)
(*Creation in Words—of Character*, pp. 217 ff.)

66   *looke like th'innocent flower, But be the Serpent under't* . . . This turns
out to be an anticipatory poetical description of LadyMacbeth's
own behaviour in the following scene. Once again Shakespeare
seems to leave nothing to chance. Moreover, he strengthens
his continuity thus.

(*Creation in Words—of Character*, pp. 217 ff.)

ACT I, *Scene vi*

The King's three entries are quite logically differentiated in the
musical instructions—*Alarum*, for battle (I. ii), *Flourish*, for the
state occasion (I. iv), *Hoboyes*, for the more informal progress
(I. vi). In general, the musical score of this play is divided
between these three categories: the drums and trumpets for the
military contexts at beginning and end; the trumpets and
cornets for the state occasions; the *hoboyes* (or reed band) for the
informal scenes of journeying and banqueting. The reeds can
perhaps indicate an affinity with the bagpipes; otherwise the
music is best kept conventional, and in period, preserving the
triple distinction of mood suggested above.

(*Music*, pp. 62 ff.)

3   There is an obvious effect of dramatic irony in the atmospheric
description of the Castle with its *pleasant seat* and of the *Temple-
haunting Barlet* [read *Martlet*], which proves *By his loved Mansonry,
that the Heavens breath Smells wooingly here.* Note that Banquo's
contribution is not "in character"—not merely that there is no
hint of the nature-lover in his personality, but there is not even
any dramatic reason for stressing his serenity of mind at this
moment: both before and after this scene, he voices foreboding.
The words here are more important than the speaker—as not
infrequently in the poetic drama.

(*Creation in Words—of Atmosphere*, pp. 198 ff.)

10   There is a *leit-motif* in the words "host" and "hostess", which
will have been gently stressed by the poet himself, if he is playing the part of Duncan: *See, see, our honor'd Hostesse . . . Faire and
Noble Hostesse We are your guest to night . . . Conduct me to mine
Host . . . By your leave Hostesse.* The theme is repeated in Macbeth's following soliloquy: *Then, as his Host, Who should against
his Murtherer shut the doore, Not beare the knife my selfe* (I. vii. 14).
It is echoed again later when Banquo presents to Macbeth the
diamond with which Duncan greets his wife *By the name of most
kind Hostesse* (II. i. 16).

(*Pervasive Theme*, pp. 249 ff.)

ACT I, *Scene vii*

The Folio direction gives all that is necessary in Shakespeare's playhouse to change the scene from the approach to the castle to the interior. The insistent continuity of the plot demands here only that we should feel ourselves outside the banqueting-hall. This is done quite simply by the process of opening the Study curtains (to reveal a set which will afterwards serve for the scene of the murder and its discovery; see below, on II. ii. 1) and following the Prompt Book. *Ho-boyes. Torches. Enter a Sewer, and divers Servants with Dishes and Service over the Stage. Then enter Macbeth.* In fact, the comedy gang of the company

Dishes and Service over the Stage

make a brief appearance, one no doubt unpunctual, another caught tasting the dish he carries: there is a detailed model in the domestic staff of Capulet's household, Potpan and his fellows. They will form up for inspection by the Sewer, before marching into the banquet-hall: noises of merriment from inside the Tiring-House will become suddenly louder and more hilarious as they disappear, and will be hushed all at once as an unseen door bangs shut: Macbeth comes swiftly on to the Platform in the sudden silence.

(*Prompt Book*, pp. 25 ff.)
(*Effects*, pp. 69 ff.)

The locality of the scene is "outside the banquet-room"—nothing else, and we see here both the merits of an unlocalised stage, and Shakespeare's unerring sense of the relevant. The subject-matter of the scene is *the proposed murder:* Macbeth's soliloquy presents it—by speculation on the consequences, by considering its special wickedness in the circumstances, and by a highly poetical passage of transcending imagery depicting its full horror in the sight of heaven. He has no adequate spur, but Lady Macbeth comes to apply the goad of her over-whelming rhetoric. For this theme the ideal locality is outside the banquet-room, where the King-kinsman-guest is being entertained. The advantage of the unlocalised platform is shown by the passage later in the scene where Lady Macbeth takes us in imagination (for the first time in the play) to the death-chamber of Duncan (see below, on II. i. 16). The scene closes—in the last two lines—with a reminder of the banquet, no doubt accompanied by noises off. We simultaneously return from *horrible Imaginings* to the genial reality of the feast.

(*Locality and Unlocalisation,* pp. 103 ff.)
(*The Architecture of the Play,* pp. 232 ff.)

1 ff.   Macbeth's soliloquy dramatises the deed in advance, so that we feel the horror of it still more when it comes. It is brought within range of divine censure by the mention of time and the life to come, and still more forcibly by the transcendental images of the climax. The idea, so often expressed, that Macbeth is himself a poet contains, I think, a fallacy: it is true that he is represented as prone to brooding and musing and becoming "wrapt", as having a restless conscience which causes him to debate his murder before he commits it and to suffer torments afterwards: but the poet is Shakespeare himself who seeks to represent these inward struggles in terms of the poetic drama. In respect of poetical *expression* Macbeth is no different from Othello, Lear and Antony.

54   Lady Macbeth's lines about her Babe are a *dramatisation* of her unsexing. They bear as little relation to an actual child, as Othello's jealousy to an actual opportunity of adultery. Shakespeare wants Othello jealous, and he wants Lady Macbeth unnaturally unfeminine. It is vain speculation to draw inferences about Macbeth's family. The deliberate disclaimer of feminine nature, like her earlier prayer to be unsexed (I. v. 39), is in a sense a tragic parallel to the male disguises of the comedies. Shakespeare seizes the opportunity that his story

offers him of exploiting his material: the boy Edmans can play
this part without inhibition.

(Creation in Words—of Character, pp. 217 ff.)
(The Boy Actors, pp. 163 ff.)

78 *As we shall make our Griefes and Clamor rore, Upon his Death?* . . .
the anticipatory description helps in the plotting of the scene of
the discovery of Duncan's murder. This roaring is Macbeth's
style in the sequence which begins *Had I but dy'd an houre before
this chance* . . . (II. iii. 73 ff.)

(The Method in Practice, pp. 175 ff.)

Act II
Scene-Rotation as follows:
Scene i *Platform* alone: night-exterior painted immediately by the
torch and by the words of Banquo and Fleance.
 ii *Study* and *Platform:* the opening of the curtains indicates
that Lady Macbeth is *inside* the castle.
 iii *Study* and *Platform:* continuous from II. ii.
 iv *Platform* alone.

(Scene-Rotation, pp. 31 ff.)

Act II, *Scene i*
The darkness is drawn with a few swift strokes: it is a *dramatic*
darkness, made so by Banquo's yawning line *A heavie Summons
lyes like Lead upon me*, coupled with his unwillingness to sleep,
and the sinister prayer: *Mercifull Powers, restraine in me the
cursed thoughts That Nature gives way to in repose:* also by the
sudden alarm of *Give me my Sword*.

(Creation in Words—of Atmosphere, pp. 198 ff.)

16 It is part of Shakespeare's intention to keep constantly before
our mind's eye the apartment in which Duncan is sleeping: we
have already had a glimpse of it when Lady Macbeth outlined
her plan to her husband: *when Duncan is asleepe, (Whereto the
rather shall his dayes hard Journey Soundly invite him), his two
Chamberlaines* . . . *when in Swinish sleepe, Their drenched Natures
lyes as in a Death, What cannot you and I performe upon Th' un-
guarded Duncan?* (I. vii. 61 ff.). The vision accumulates in a
running series, and we have a reinforcement here in Banquo's
words: . . . *shut up in measurelesse content*. The unlocalised Platform helps us to visualise such pictures, which are painted in
the words.

(Locality and Unlocalisation, pp. 103 ff.)

33 The *Dagger of the Minde* is another skilful device of this magical
art of poetic drama. Requiring the most expert miming from
Burbadge, it is a poetical means of making us visualise the very
act of murder with its objective details (*The Handle toward my
Hand . . . And on thy Blade, and Dudgeon, Gouts of Blood*) much
more vividly than we could by merely seeing the actor plant
his property-dagger wide of his victim's ribs.

(*Creation in Words—of the Action*, pp. 226 ff.)

(*Miming*, pp. 125 ff.)

49 *Now o're the one halfe World . . .* the imagery of this passage takes
us right off the Platform to a hemisphere of night-prowling
villainy. We follow this best when we are not pinned down by
a suggestion of locality. It is the method of the white-screen
upon which the poet's images are projected in rapid succession
(see above, p. 108). The compactness is astonishing, as, for
instance, when *wicked Dreames* echo Banquo's prayer just
uttered (*restraine in me the cursed thoughts . . .*), and *The Curtain'd
sleepe* takes us back to Duncan's apartment: *Witchcraft* recalls
the weyard sisters: *the Wolfe, Whose howle's his Watch*, gives
Burbadge a chance to curdle our blood with vocal imitation of
the sinister night-cry: *Murther's stealthy pace* sets him prowling
round a Stage-Post, and *Tarquins ravishing sides* [read *strides*]
take him half-way to his foul purpose behind the Study
curtains. With the imperceptible cunning of genius, Shakespeare returns us to the Platform and the reality of Macbeth's
situation, in the words *Thou sowre* [read *sure*] *and firme-set Earth.*
. . . On the invitation of the bell, Burbadge disappears between
the Study curtains: his dagger visible behind his back, he goes
to his murder charged with all the force, both realistic and
transcendental, that poetry can raise.

(*Speech*, see especially pp. 113 f.)

(*Locality and Unlocalisation*, pp. 103 ff.)

Act II, *Scene ii*

I fancy that the Study curtains are opened at the beginning of
the scene, as soon as Macbeth has had time to leave the Study.
The effect is to carry us indoors. Lady Macbeth appears in the
Study and remains there for her opening words. Macbeth
perhaps steps on to the Tarras at the moment where his entry is
marked in the Folio (l. 9): he is in a panic-stricken and head-
long flight, with the imaginary voice still ringing in his ears
"Sleep no more". This is surely the explanation of his strange
cry *Who's there? what hoa?*—the last thing you would expect

from a murderer immediately after his crime. Meanwhile, of course, Lady Macbeth, in the Study, cannot see him on the Tarras. Macbeth reappears in the Study five lines later, and his previous momentary appearance makes clear both *his* words *Didst thou not heare a noyse?* and her *Did not you speake?*

(*Positioning*, pp. 131 ff.)

The Furniture of the Study at the beginning of II. ii is the same as for I. vii—interior, with a touch of primitive Scotland in the shape perhaps of antlers of a stag, and hunting spear. The habitual doorway of the Study would be visible, and through it the beginning of the flight of steps which leads up to Duncan's apartment. A burning candle by the doorway helps the illusion of deep midnight, and makes a dramatic point if it is extinguished by Lady Macbeth as she drags Macbeth away, with the words *be not lost So poorely in your thoughts.*

(*Furnishing and Properties*, pp. 38 ff.)

4 . . . *it was the Owle that shriek'd, The fatall Bell-man, which gives the stern'st good-night.* The poetic creation of atmosphere is turned, as so often, to dramatic use, in the sinister phrase *the stern'st good-night.* The topicality of the *fatall Bell-man* would hit home in 1606—now, of course, only among examination candidates!

(*Creation in Words—of Atmosphere*, pp. 198 ff.)
(*Objectivity of Vision*, pp. 189 ff.)

27f. The *two lodg'd together*, who cried *God blesse us* and *Amen* are surely Donalbaine and his companion (? Malcolm) *i'th' second Chamber*—not the grooms. I do not know whether the commentaries make this clear.

36 The voice that cried *Sleep no more* takes us right away from the visible scene into the conscience, the hurt mind, of the murderer himself. It is built on the image of Duncan *shut up in measurelesse content*, resembling Lady Macbeth's father—the picture of innocent sleep. But the force of the poetry piles on the idea of murdering sleep itself, so that, as the bloody instructions return to plague the inventor, *Macbeth shall sleepe no more.* The web of imagery, so close woven, is of the essence of this poetic drama. Sleep is one of the most pervasive strands in the pattern.

(*Pervasive Theme*, pp. 249 ff.)

A clear example of the contrast between the objective and the transcendental vision of Shakespeare lies in the speeches of Macbeth and his wife in this scene. She gives us a wonderfully

K

vivid objective picture (projected in advance also in I. vii) of
the circumstances of the murder, which we never actually see.
But Macbeth is all the time translating the scene into transcendent terms—*Glamis hath murther'd Sleepe; this my Hand will
rather The multitudinous Seas incarnadine; Wake Duncan with thy
knocking* (Bradley makes the point in his *Shakespearian Tragedy*,
355, 374). It is interesting to note that both are legitimate

Be not lost So poorely in your thoughts

effects of the poetic drama—both the objective atmospheric
painting of the Lady, and the transcendent interpretation of
her Thane.

         (*Transcending the Visible Scene*, pp. 229 ff.)

72 *be not lost So poorely in your thoughts*. The phrase is another
example of the "close-up" method of character-creation (see
on I. v. 60, above).

    (*Creation in Words—of Character*, see especially pp. 221 f.)

The whole scene (II. ii) between the guilty pair after the
murder is a perfect example of the sustained rhythm which is
Shakespeare's most powerful device for casting a spell upon his
audience. Performance of this scene must be based upon the

continuous rhythm of the verse, with its implied changes of
pace and tread, and its subtlety of pause and renewal of *tempo*.
Gesture, movement, and miming must flow from this rhythm:
any "business" that holds it up or distorts it should make the
producer cry *"Pox, leave thy damnable Faces, and begin."*

(Speech, see especially pp. 119 ff.)

Act II, *Scene iii*

The Devil-Portering scene is an excellent example of Shakespeare's objective method. Wanted: (*a*) someone to open the
gate at the south entry; (*b*) time for Macbeth to change his
clothes; (*c*) some temporary relief of the tension. The solution
presents itself in the person of Armin. Then follows the habitual
brilliant opportunism: the stock comic gambit of the drunken
servant develops into the ironical fantasy of the porter of Hell-
gate; and then by a sort of inversion the detail of the porter's
speech is objectively topical—the Farmer, the Equivocator, the
Taylor, all "music-hall" jokes. I can see no reason for thinking
this episode un-Shakespearian; on the contrary, it is characteristic, like the "little Yases" and the touch of mad Hamlet being
sent to England—" 'Twill not be seene in him, there the men
are as mad as he."

(Objectivity of Vision, pp. 189 ff.)
(Opportunity Snatched from Necessity, pp. 196 ff.)

The dialogue between Macduff and the Porter, neither edify-
ing nor very amusing (though no doubt helped by Armin's
playing), serves nevertheless a necessary purpose—of making
the night pass into early morning, an hour when Macduff
could reasonably *call timely on* the King. An interesting feature
of this passing night is the way that Lennox colours it in retro-
spect: the unruly night is nowhere indicated up to this point,
and it would be inappropriate to the oppressive silence of II. i
and II. ii to punctuate with storm noises. Perhaps the first
indications of boisterous weather would be given by the back-
stage men at the moment when the Porter opens the door to
Macduff and Lennox. For a parallel example of a storm
dramatically organised, see above, p. 70, where the effects in
Julius Caesar are considered. Lennox's descriptive speech (*The
Night ha's been unruly* . . .) gives the cue for Macbeth's ironical
'Twas a rough Night: it also serves as a *crescendo* leading up to
Macduff's *O horror, horror, horror;* and prepares us for the atmo-
spherics of II. iv, the dialogue between Ross and an Old Man.

(Effects, pp. 69 ff.)

56   *This is the Doore.* Presumably Macbeth indicates the permanent door in the Study, through which he himself ascended to Duncan's room. The main Doors of the Platform have each an identity at this moment: from one the Porter has emerged, as from the servants' quarters; the other leads from the gate at the south entry, through which Macduff and Lennox were admitted into the Castle.

(Plotting Entries, pp. 72 ff.)

70   Note that in the moment of rousing the house it is part of the technique of *poetic* drama to present us with the picture of the household asleep: that is the effect (and presumably the purpose) of such lines as . . . *Shake off this Downey sleepe, Deaths counterfeit, . . .* and *What's the Businesse? That such a hideous Trumpet calls to parley The sleepers of the House?*

(Creation in Words—of the Action, pp. 226 ff.)

87   The Alarum bell, as in the Cyprus-brawl of *Othello,* and again in the last act of this play, adds its note to the confusion of the scene, and frights the playhouse from its propriety.

(Effects, pp. 69 ff.)

108   Once again the adaptability of the unlocalised Platform is shown when Lennox and Macbeth present us with a further and still more graphic description of Duncan's chamber. Between them Cooke and Burbadge must evoke the scene, and Lady Macbeth's faint is all the more plausible if they succeed. Lennox's previous speech about the unruly night suggests that Cooke could be relied upon for this kind of graphic evocation. A later scene (III. vi) proves that he had other talents as well.

(Locality and Unlocalisation, pp. 103 ff.)

132   She *really* faints, of course. The strain of her visit to the death-chamber is a principal cause of her startling collapse and it will be noticed that it follows immediately upon Macbeth's circumstantial description of the scene of murder. Moreover, it is difficult to think of any device by which the boy-player could indicate pretence: we may at least think it likely that if Shakespeare had intended a sham faint, he would have made the fact somehow clear to the audience *in the spoken dialogue.* The irony of Lennox in III. vi hints at a possible method.

(Creation in Words—of the Action, pp. 226 ff.)
(Creation in Words—of Character, see especially pp. 222 ff.)

132 *Looke to the Lady: And when we have our naked Frailties hid . . . a*
fine wild scene with the Thanes in dishabille: the nightgowns
are, of course, not nightshirts, but rather the Elizabethan
equivalent of dressing-gowns: the servants half naked. The
fainting Lady is one focal point up-stage and surrounded by
Thanes and servants, so as not to distract from the whispered
conversation of Malcolm and Donalblain, right forward at the
centre of the octagon; Macbeth no doubt prominent on the
perimeter, outside one of the Stage-Posts, with a grim eye of
menace on the two princes. How much easier to plot at the
Globe than on a picture-stage!

(*Positioning*, pp. 131 ff.)

Looke to the Lady

ACT II, *Scene iv*

5 *Thou seest the Heavens, as troubled with mans Act, Threatens his*
bloody Stage: byth' Clock 'tis Day, And yet darke Night strangles the
travailing Lampe . . . There is an unnatural darkness instead of
daylight: Ross speaks of this as a sign of divine anger, and his
transcendental interpretation is expressed in the familiar
objective metaphor of the playhouse: no doubt Heminges
embraces with his gestures the canopy of "the Heavens" and
the Platform on which he stands.

(*Objectivity of Vision*, pp. 189 ff.)

The Platform is unlocalised, and though we are led to infer
from the Old Man's opening speech, which recalls Lennox's
description of the unruly night (II. iii. 36 ff.), that this is the

morning after the murder, the scene is in a sense timeless because the day is unnaturally turned to night. It seems therefore like a choric interlude, giving information about the "official view" of the murder, the sequel of Macbeth's succession, and (by the pregnant reticence of Macduff) the attitude of those *That would make good of bad*. Once again, the neutral Platform is the ideal setting for such a scene. (If there is to be an interval in the course of the play, the rhymed couplet of the Old Man's pious wish makes a good cadence, and the disclosure of the royal throne in the Study a sufficiently striking dramatic effect to recapture the interest of the audience.)

(*Locality and Unlocalisation*, pp. 103 ff.)
(*Continuity*, pp. 241 ff.)

ACT III

Scene-Rotation as follows:

Scene i *Study* and *Platform*: the Study contains the royal "state": it is in fact the stock throne-room set; seen with great effect for the first time in the play as Banquo says *Thou hast it now*.

ii *Chamber*: for it is Lady Macbeth's apartment, to which she invites the King for a few words. Macbeth's invocation of the night from aloft on the Tarras, and the immediate sequel of the murderers' stealthy appearance on the Platform, is a master-stroke of continuity only possible in the conditions of Shakespeare's playhouse.

iii *Platform*: the murderers will no doubt use the Stage-Posts for their ambush, hiding *in front* of them (in company with the audience).

iv *Study* and *Platform*. *Our Hostesse keepes her State*: i.e. she remains seated on the throne in the Study—it is in fact the same throne-room set as in III. i. *Banquet prepar'd* means the carrying of table and stools forward on to the Platform (see above, pp. 42 f.).

v It is usual to omit the Hecate scene as un-Shakespearian. Presumably, as it is in the Folio, it was at some period performed at the Globe: positioning difficult, perhaps Hecate on the Tarras, with witches below—the music appropriately comes from the gallery aloft *in a Foggy cloud*. The scene can hardly have belonged to Shakespeare's original conception: one reason for its insertion might have been the mechanical one of giving time to the stagehands for the change from throne-room to Witches' cave. In practice it should prove unnecessary, for the removal of the banquet after III. iv, which takes place in view of the audience, gives extra time also for scene-shifting operations in the curtained Study.

vi *Tarras:* Disregarding the Hecate scene, the Book-Keeper has to place this short dialogue between two scenes of Platform-cum-Study. The Tarras is convenient here, and the entry can be given a natural air if Lennox discovers a solitary piper entertaining the servants below as they finish their clearing of the banquet. The two Thanes will

Thou hast it now

seem to be in the musicians' gallery of the banquet-hall, and this supposition lends, perhaps, an extra point of emphatic gesture to the hope that *we may againe Give to our Tables meate, sleepe to our Nights: Free from our Feasts, and Banquets bloody Knives.* The speaker gesticulates to the Platform below him, which has just been the scene of a ghost-ridden banquet.

(*Scene-Rotation*, pp. 31 ff.)

ACT III, *Scene i*

The Study is furnished with the usual throne-room set familiar from the history plays: steps up to a dais on which stands the

"state" capable of accommodating both King and Queen;
carpets on steps and floor, tapestries hung all round on the
three walls; an overhanging canopy (see above, p. 39). The
first sight of the throne has a dramatic effect in this story of
usurpation comparable to that in *Richard III*, IV. ii.

(Furnishing and Properties, pp. 38 ff.)

1 The theme of the "second movement" is quickly stated—
Banquo, and in particular Banquo's issue—and (at least in the
extant form of the play) is worked out with insistent relevance
and continuity.

(The Architecture of the Play, pp. 232 ff.)

10 Bradley would have it that Shakespeare's characterisation of
Banquo makes him something like an accessory after the fact
(see *Shakesperian Tragedy*, 384 ff.). If he is right, then it looks as
if some important material has been omitted from our existing
version of the play. A study of the "close-up" method of
characterisation outlined above suggests that Shakespeare
would not normally have left the point ambiguous. If he had
wished to show Banquo as a double dealer, he would have
given us the hint on the lips of Banquo himself or some other
character. It may be, for instance, that some lines have dropped
out after the words . . . *And set me up in hope.*

(Creation in Words—of Character, see especially pp. 222 ff.)

11 *Senit sounded.* The usual sign of a big formal entry, with the
appropriate pomp and circumstance to indicate that Macbeth
and his Lady have achieved the object of their ambition.

(Music, see especially pp. 63 f.)

14 The dialogue between Macbeth and Banquo on the subject of
the *solemne Supper*, which culminates in Macbeth's words *Faile
not our Feast*, and Banquo's reply—*My Lord, I will not*—is a good
example of the "rod-in-pickle" method by which Shakespeare
suspends our interest and preserves the continuity.

(Continuity, see especially pp. 247 f.)

48 *To be thus, is nothing . . . Our feares in Banquo sticke deepe.* There
can be no better background for this soliloquy than the royal
"state" on which Macbeth sits in his King's robes, wearing his
fruitless crown, and grasping his barren sceptre. The setting is
more properly one of circumstance than of locality.

(Locality and Unlocalisation, pp. 103 ff.)

55   ... *and under him, My Genius is rebuk'd, as it is said Mark Anthonies was by Caesar.* We look over the poet's shoulder and see him turning the pages of his Plutarch, and dwelling on the theme of his next play—*Antony and Cleopatra.*

The soliloquy has a cumulative rhythm, with a great *crescendo* at the end. The last sentence should, I think, be pointed thus: "... come Fate into the *Lyst*"—i.e. rather than have Banquo's children succeed me, I'll *fight* against the witches' prophesied fate.

(*Speech,* pp. 111 ff.)

It is, I think, characteristic of the intensely concentrated relevance of Shakespeare's dramatic method that the question of the succession is not explored beyond its relation to Banquo and Fleance. As others have pointed out, Macbeth's own issue is left almost without comment: Lady Macbeth knows the love of an infant at the breast (I. vii. 54 ff.); Macduff perhaps speaks of Macbeth when he cries *He ha's no Children* (IV. iii. 211): more we are not told. See above, on I. vii. 54 ff.

(*The Architecture of the Play,* see especially pp. 240 f.)

74   In the scene of Macbeth's persuasion of the murderers, there is less than the usual objectivity: ... *it was he, in the times past, which held you so under fortune, Which you thought had been our innocent selfe* ... *How you were borne in hand, how crost* ... *whose heavie hand Hath bow'd you to the Grave, and begger'd Yours for ever—* what sort of circumstances do these phrases suggest? It looks as if Shakespeare decided that to give detailed substance to the complaints of the cut-throats would carry him and us too far from the main theme. But as it is, he has not been able to create the necessary effect briefly. His inspiration momentarily flagging, he falls back upon his technique: for the scene is carried along not only by the melodrama inherent in the situation but also by the rhetorical and rhythmical energy of Macbeth's speeches.

(*Speech,* see especially pp. 117 f.)

131   ... *for't must be done to Night, And something from the Pallace* ... *that darke houre* ... the anticipatory sketching of Banquo's murder helps to create the atmosphere of the murder-scene in advance, and is also a "rod-in-pickle" for the continuity.

(*Creation in Words—of Atmosphere,* pp. 198 ff.)
(*Continuity,* see especially pp. 247 ff.)

ACT III, *Scene ii*

The furniture of the Chamber, though representing what is actually a different room (the royal palace, not Inverness), need not differ from that in I. v. It is still an apartment private to Lady Macbeth. The "women's quarters" in the Elizabethan playhouse are habitually in the Chamber aloft.

(*Furnishing and Properties*, pp. 38 ff.)

The scene is a masterpiece. It preserves and indeed enhances the tension of expectation of Banquo's murder. It shows us Lady Macbeth's disillusion, and the unexpected but in the event obviously probable change of relationship between her and her husband, and the growing feverish energy of Macbeth (following on *Come Fate into the Lyst*, we now have *But let the frame of things dis-joynt . . . So shall I love, and so I pray be you . . . Then be thou jocund . . .* etc.). It is full, moreover, of the most powerfully dramatic poetry; especially the bloodcurdling invocation of night at the end. Imagine Burbadge speaking this from the Tarras rail in front of the Chamber, while the night gathers below on the Platform. Note how, once again, together with the atmosphere itself, the appropriate emotional reaction is suggested to us—most subtly this time—in the words *Come, seeling Night, Skarfe up the tender Eye of pittiful Day*. To *seel* is a technical term in falconry for the sewing up of the eyelids of a young hawk to make him used to the hood. Would Burbadge have illuminated the metaphor with a gesture, easily recognisable to his audience?

(*Creation in Words—of Atmosphere*, pp. 198 ff.)
(*Positioning*, pp. 131 ff.)

ACT III, *Scene iii*

Having invoked the night, Macbeth retires into the Chamber to escort his wife: he leaves his spell behind him, and the atmosphere is already half created for the Murtherers. The effect is almost of his presiding over the murder, and is comparable to Lady Macbeth's *fatall entrance of Duncan Under my Battlements* (I. v. 37 f.). The matter is clinched by the lines of the First Murderer, *The West yet glimmers . . .* etc. Once again our emotional reponse is prompted for us—*Now spurres the lated Traveller apace, To gayne the timely Inne*. We too want to get under cover, in case there are cut-throats on the prowl.

(*Continuity*, see especially p. 245)

The problem of the Third Murderer is unsolved, and it is not the kind of loose end that Shakespeare usually leaves; for most of his loose ends are such as would be overlooked in performance; here the point is emphasised in the dialogue. Something may be missing from our cut version of the play. But it is worth remarking that there is a purely mechanical reason why a third is necessary: if the scene is played on the Platform, Banquo's body must be carried off, and it takes two to carry him expeditiously; not only that, but the light struck from the hand of Fleance must also be removed before the change of locality to the ensuing banquet scene. One of the trio must pick up the light. The suggestion is sometimes made that Macbeth is himself the third murderer: but as he leaves the Chamber on the last line of the preceding scene, continuity and the "law of re-entry" make the suggestion impossible (see above, p. 75).

Unlike the earlier dialogue with the murderers, the scene of Banquo's murder itself is fully furnished with objective detail—the glimmering western sky, the sound of horses, the call for light, Banquo the last-comer *within the note of expectation*, the horses going about (with appropriate imitation off-stage), the usual walk to the palace gate, *It will be Rayne to Night*, and the savage, ironical retort, the striking out of the light, the escape of Fleance. Every detail is clear to the audience partly because in the daylight of the playhouse they can in fact see what is happening, partly because the words themselves present all the significant items. The graphic realism of the scene can be compared with the robbery on Gads Hill in 1 *Henry IV* and the attempt on Cassio's life in *Othello*.

> (*Creation in Words—of Atmosphere*,
> see especially pp. 203 ff., 208 ff.)

ACT III, *Scene iv*

The banquet-scene presents an interesting problem of positioning. Note the data: *Our selfe will mingle with Society . . . Our Hostesse keepes her State . . . Both sides are even: heere Ile sit i'th'mid'st. . . .* Besides, the murderer's appearance at the door has to be accommodated. The Study is furnished as in III. i, Lady Macbeth sitting alone upon the "state". The *Banquet* is *prepar'd* on the Platform, between the two Stage-Posts, Macbeth's place being central. Bright lights on the table and perhaps in brackets hooked on to the Stage-Posts help to dazzle the eyes of the audience when the Ghost appears. The whispered colloquy with the murderer will be on the perimeter

Never shake Thy goary lockes at me

outside one of the Stage-Posts. *Enter the Ghost of Banquo, and sits in Macbeths place:* this instruction of the Folio looks like a straightforward entry perhaps through one of the arrases at the side of the Study. Macbeth's speeches to the Ghost on both its appearances, and the interjections of Lady Macbeth are so long extended that it is difficult on a shallow stage to make them plausible: the difficulty largely disappears on the Globe Platform where there is room for manœuvring both in front of the banquet-table and up-stage between it and the Study.

(*Positioning*, pp. 131 ff.)

Though there is no cue in the Folio, Musicians on the Tarras (during the preparation of the Banquet and for the formal entry of the King and Queen and their guests) would give the impression of a musicians' gallery in the great hall of an Elizabethan house. For the necessarily lengthy process of preparation and removal of the banquet, some informal music is a help. Hoboyes—the reed band—rather than trumpets.

(*Music*, see especially pp. 64 f.)

Examples of the "close-up" method of description are plentiful in this scene: *never shake Thy goary lockes at me* (50). *Why do you make such faces?* (67) *Thou hast no speculation in those eyes Which thou dost glare with* (95) . . . *you can behold such sights, And keepe the naturall Rubie of your Cheekes, When mine is blanch'd with feare* (114).

Such description is often a clue to the actor whose part is being described, but the speaker too must give reality to the poetical characterisation.

(*Creation in Words—of Character*, see especially pp. 221 ff.)

122 The end of the scene, the *coda* between Macbeth and Lady Macbeth, shows the poet's technique at its busiest. It is full of pervasive themes—blood, darkness (the night at odds with morning), sleep—and there are two "rods-in-pickle" in the mention of Macduff's refusal and the projected visit to the Weird Sisters. It is strange that theatrical tradition presents both Macbeth and his wife as weary at this point: *she* is indeed exhausted, but he is already *possessed* with the diabolical energy which, though it alternates with heart-sickness, yet carries him through to the climax of the battlefield.

(*Continuity*, pp. 241 ff.)

The table, stools and lamps and the remains of the banquet must be removed at the end of the scene. The operation can be conducted without offence, with some mildly diverting business, by the comic gang of servants (on this occasion with their tails between their legs). It is after all a no more complicated manœuvre than the *Dishes and service* of I. vii, or the preparation of the banquet at the beginning of this scene. The comic business was probably "in the repertoire"—e.g. Capulet's servants (*Romeo and Juliet*, I. v. 1 ff.; IV. iv. 13 ff.) and Aufidius' (*Coriolanus*, IV, v. 1 ff.). It gives more time for the scene-change in the Study to the Witches' cave, getting the noisy business of shifting the throne-set over before the Lennox scene begins. A solitary piper on the Tarras can accompany the removal of the banquet, and when Lennox and his fellow lord appear on the Tarras they can dismiss the piper with a gesture.

(*Scene-Rotation*, pp. 31 ff.)

Act III, *Scene vi*

The scene (like II. iv) is narrative in effect. It implies, with a veiled but pungent irony, the gathering of suspicion and revolt. Young Cooke, graduating from female parts, which include Queen Margaret and Katharine the Shrew, needs more than ordinary skill of speech to make the most of Lennox (see above, on II. iii. 83 ff.). The theme of the sorrows of Scotland, predominant in the rest of the play, is clearly and forcibly enunciated by his partner. The prayer that *we may againe Give to our Tables meate, sleepe to our Nights* . . . comes appropriately

from the gallery above the recent ghost-ridden banquet. There
is a "rod-in-pickle", for we are led to expect Macduff's visit to
the English court, whence *a swift blessing May soone returne to this
our suffering Country.*

(*Continuity*, pp. 241 ff.)

ACT IV

Scene-Rotation as follows:

Scene i *Study* and *Platform:* The cauldron possibly in the grave-
trap, but more probably in the centre-trap on the Platform
(its appearance and descent concealed by the Weird
Sisters). The show of eight kings in the Study. Macbeth
and (later) Lennox enter by a stage-door, to detach them
from the cavern.

ii *Chamber:* A domestic scene, in Lady Macduff's apartments.

iii *Study* and *Platform:* Indication in Study of the English
court—perhaps an easily recognisable blazonry.

(*Scene-Rotation*, pp. 31 ff.)

ACT IV, *Scene i*

There need be no elaborate furniture in the Study for the
Witches' cavern. Dark curtains draped for a cave-mouth. The
cauldron in the centre-trap (with smoke rising round it) must
be wide enough to allow the apparitions to rise through it from
Hell below.

(*Furnishing and Properties*, pp. 38 ff.)

It seems that the Apparitions from the cauldron are plainly
visible to the audience, for except for the third who *weares upon
his Baby-brow, the round And top of Soveraignty* there is no "close-
up" description in the dialogue: for once we must rely upon
the stage-directions of the Folio. The show of eight kings, on
the other hand, is minutely described (in such a way, indeed,
as to suggest that the preceding stage-direction is wrong in
bringing Banquo on last of the procession). The contrast indicates the probability that whereas the Cauldron was on the
Platform, the Show was more remote in the Study.

(*Positioning*, pp. 131 ff.)
(*Creation in Words—of Character*, see especially pp. 221 ff.)

132 It seems possible that the vanishing of the Witches is done by
the simple expedient of drawing the Study curtains, and leaving
Macbeth outside, for his final colloquy with Lennox.

(*Positioning*, pp 131 ff.)

147   *The very firstlings of my heart shall be The firstlings of my hand . . .*
      This deed Ile do, before this purpose coole. And so straight on to the
      scene (in the Chamber) of Lady Macduff's murder. The swift
      continuity is a deliberate dramatic stroke.

                                             (*Continuity,* pp. 241 ff.)

ACT IV, *Scene ii*
      Enter Macduffes Wife, her Son and Rosse. The prompt-book
      reflects the words of the preceding speech . . . *give to th'edge
      o'th'Sword His Wife, his Babes . . .*

Upon his Baby-brow, the round And top of Soveraignty

The furniture will be different from Lady Macbeth's apartments, but the difference need not be stressed. This is a typical
Chamber scene, essentially (and in this case pathetically)
domestic: the tyrant's cruelty penetrates to the privacy of home
life. There is an obvious but effective stroke of irony in the
contrast between the beginning of the scene where Lady
Macduff is bitter against her husband, and speaks of him as a
traitor, and the climax when she stands up for him, and the
Boy in denying that he is a traitor meets his death.

                         (*Scene-Rotation,* see especially pp. 32 f.)

ACT IV, *Scene iii*
      The longest scene in the play, and seemingly out of proportion
      in the main architectural design. Is it possible that when the
      play was cut we lost material about Macduff and Malcolm

which would have put it into perspective? Shakespeare, for instance, never explicitly answers the question *Why in that rawnesse* he left *Wife, and Childe . . . Without leave-taking* (26). Nevertheless, in a larger design the scene cannot be called irrelevant, providing as it does a vivid picture of Scotland's distress under tyranny when even the good men must suspect each other. The public aspect of the story becomes increasingly important as the play proceeds. It is Malcolm's elaborate deception which seems to strike a false note. Shakespeare found it in Holinshed and set his hand to it, falling back, as even the greatest artists will do, when his material fails to inspire him, upon his long-learnt technique. If even Shakespeare's rhetorical skill cannot make Malcolm's lying and Macduff's credulity altogether plausible, yet it must be admitted that in practice, even on the modern stage, this dialogue usually holds the attention, and the fine climax of the scene sets the audience applauding the three actors, and sweeps on to the dénouement of Act V.

(*The Architecture of the Play*, pp. 232 ff.)

(*Speech*, see especially pp. 117 ff.)

139 The brief episode of the English Doctor's entrance is an example of Shakespeare's opportunism turned to a somewhat undignified end—flattery of King James. Nevertheless, we should not miss the fact that it also has a place in the poet's dramatic design. The theme of sickness and the need for healing pervades the last act of the play, and this is a striking enunciation of the *motif*.

(*Pervasive Theme*, pp. 249 ff.)

One must not forget as a reason for the length of this scene the practice of resting the chief actor (and his audience) round about the fourth act of a tragedy. *Othello* is the only one of Bradley's "big four" that does not follow this practice—and the only one that does not sag a little at this point; the best-constructed, therefore (but perhaps Burbadge would not agree!)

(*The Architecture of the Play*, pp. 232 ff.)

203 An interesting example of the "close-up" method is Malcolm's description of Macduff's silent reception of the news: *What man, ne're pull your hat upon your browes: Give sorrow words; the griefe that do's not speake, Whispers the o're fraught heart, and bids it breake.* A stoical silence without comment is not permissible in Shakespeare's technique. His handling of Brutus' stoicism has been remarked above.

(*Creation in Words—of Character*, see especially pp. 224 f.)

Act V
  Scene-Rotation as follows:
  Scene i *Chamber.*
      ii *Platform.*
     iii *Chamber.*
      iv *Platform.*
       v *Tarras* and *Chamber.*
      vi *Platform.*
     vii *Study—Platform.*
    viii *Study—Platform.*

(*Scene-Rotation,* pp. 31 ff.)

Act V, *Scene i*
  The furnishing of the Chamber again needs no special
differentiation: the mere fact of the scene's being in the
Chamber gives it the touch of domestic intimacy which suits
its particular pathos. A table is necessary, for Lady Macbeth to
put the taper on; she needs both hands for her miming.
Perhaps the writing materials of the Gentlewoman's description could be indicated. What is meant by *unlocke her Closset?*
A little desk?

(*Furnishing and Properties,* pp. 38 ff.)

It is by now a commonplace to say that Shakespeare can create
darkness out of daylight. In this scene we notice also the
familiar method of an anticipatory description, so that by the
time Lady Macbeth enters, we understand at once that she is
asleep (with *A great perturbation in Nature*) and imagine her
carrying out the actions described by the Gentlewoman before
her appearance. The Gentlewoman's sinister refusal to report
what her mistress has *said,* keys us up to tense expectation of
her words. There is also the "close-up" of her appearance and
actions after she enters—*You see her eyes are open . . . I but their
sense are shut . . . Looke how she rubbes her hands . . . thus washing
her hands.*
  (*Creation in Words—of Character,* see especially pp. 221 ff.)

The words of the sleepwalker are an elaborate development of
the mimed "Messenger Speech" method. For Lady Macbeth,
in the intervals of washing her hands, is re-enacting scenes
which we have witnessed and others which we have not. The
player—if he were a Ruth Draper of a boy—could recall to us
previous moments of his own and Burbadge's performances,

with the words *no more o' that: you marre all with this starting* and *Wash your hands, put on your Night-Gowne* and *To bed, to bed: there's Knocking at the gate: Come, come, come, come, give me your hand*—and could also suggest other moments which we can imagine and infer but have not seen, with *One: Two:* (the clock? or the bell which tells Macbeth that his drink is ready?) *Why then 'tis time to doo't,* and . . . *who would have thought the olde man to have had so much blood in him* (which recalls *My Hands are of your colour* . . . and the previous visit to Duncan's apartment, *Had he not resembled My Father as he slept, I had don't*). The player must remind us of these earlier moments in the play, must light up for us all these close-woven strands in the poet's tapestry. It is an effect of the *poetic drama*, and can only be made through the voice and miming. The passive childish whimper of the traditional sleepwalking scene makes nothing of this most powerful and strenuous poetical evocation.

> (*Miming*, pp. 125 ff.)
> (*Creation in Words—of the Action*, pp. 126 ff.)

The Doctor and the Gentlewoman *stand close* on the extreme edge of the Tarras (possibly even in one of the Window-Stages). Perhaps they enter with a light, and extinguish it as Lady Macbeth appears: there is atmospheric force in the sight of smoke blowing off their extinguished candle, as the other light focuses attention on the Chamber.

> (*Positioning*, pp. 131 ff.)
> (*Effects*, pp. 69 ff.)

ACT V, *Scene ii*

The climax of the play, on the battlefield, is—as we have now learnt to expect—no anti-climax in the Globe playhouse, such as it inevitably is on the picture-stage. The pattern of the sequence is admirably adapted to the multiple stage, for Macbeth is on the defensive at Dunsinane, and so is quite logically penned in the upper stages, while the attackers move ever nearer to him on the Platform level. In this way the sleepwalking scene is an admirable prelude to the battle-sequence, for both in V. iii and V. v the haunting presence of the sick Queen is prominent. This is an additional reason for placing the sleepwalking scene in the Chamber, which therefore becomes associated with the sickness of Lady Macbeth. Inevitably for the climax Macbeth sallies forth from the castle to fight his enemies on the Platform. The sequence is made doubly easy for the audience to understand by the prophecies of the Witches' apparitions. We expect the gathering of the attackers at Birnam, we know Macbeth is in Dunsinane, we have been told that Macduff is Macbeth's great danger.

(*Battle Sequences*, pp. 83 ff.)

Producer and actors should not fail to notice (otherwise the audience will miss it too) the very cunning texture woven from the themes of sickness and healing. They are of course strongly prominent in the sleepwalking scene. In V. ii Malcolm is spoken of as *the Med'cine of the sickly Weale* (27). In V. iii Macbeth passes from the contemplation of the Queen's *minde diseas'd* (and his own?) to the equally desperate *If thou could'st Doctor, cast The Water of my Land, finde her Disease, And purge it to a sound and pristine Health* (50) . . .

(*Pervasive Theme*, pp. 249 ff.)

The Scottish and the English soldiers will presumably be differentiated in uniform. At present, all Scottish.

(*Costume*, pp. 53 ff.)

Drum and Colours. We are shown the Scots at home marching to meet the English powre, under Malcolm, Seyward and *the good Macduff*. The scene is informative and suggestive of mood—the speeches (as in the opening of I. vi and in III. vi) more important than the speakers. *Neere Byrnan wood Shall we well meet them* (5). We have a hint of the "match-card" technique (see above, pp. 88 f.)—Donalbain not there, but emphasis laid on Seywards Sonne (9), who has his moment of glory in the sequel. Macbeth, we hear, fortifies Dunsinane (12). There is an anticipatory description of Macbeth's frame of mind—*Some say hee's mad: Others, that lesser hate him, Do call it valiant Fury* . . . (13). Shakespeare does not pronounce judgment, but leaves us to interpret what we see and hear in the following scenes.

(*Battle Sequences*, pp. 83 ff.)

ACT V, *Scene iii*

The elements of Macbeth's decline are distilled in terms of poetic drama. The static themes of desperate confidence in the witches, disillusioned ambition, and uneasiness about his wife's breakdown, are woven together with the dynamic material of *Reports* such as that of the *cream-fac'd Loone*, and the purposeless putting on and shaking off of his armour. The veiled censure of the Doctor's speeches makes an admirable foil.

11 We have a vivid "close-up" of the panic-stricken servant in
    Macbeth's abuse—*cream fac'd Loone; that Goose-looke; Go pricke
    thy face, and over-red thy feare Thou lilly-liver'd Boy; those Linnen
    cheekes of thine; Whay-face.*
        (*Creation in Words—of Character*, see especially pp. 221 ff.)

ACT V, *Scene iv*
    Still Malcolm's marching drum: the English uniforms mingle
    with the Scottish: we are at *The wood of Birnane* (4), and orders
    are given for the famous stratagem.
                              (*Battle Sequences*, pp. 83 ff.)

ACT V, *Scene v*
    As Malcolm's drum fades away, *diminuendo*, it is answered by
    the new note of Macbeth's drum *crescendo* (see above, p. 65,
    where the lines of Faulconbridge in *King John* are quoted which
    describe such a rivalry of drums). Macbeth, Seyton and the
    soldiers are now all in their armour and appear on the Tarras:
    the *Banners on the outward walls* (1) would perhaps be displayed
    in the Window-Stages—to be lowered at the appropriate
    moment, when the attackers enter the Castle. The curtains of
    the Chamber are perhaps half drawn, and the *Cry within of
    Women* (7) would be heard from the Chamber, which we now
    associate with the sick Queen.
                              (*Battle Sequences*, pp. 83 ff.)

 9 *I have almost forgot the taste of Feares . . . I have supt full with
    horrors . . .* Macbeth's lines as he waits to hear the reason for the
    cry, create for us in the audience the appropriate thrill of
    horror—though he is denying it to his disillusioned self. The
    denial also paves the way for what would otherwise seem an
    inadequate comment—*She should have dy'de heereafter.* The
    method is the same as when Cordelia tells us *beforehand* that in
    answer to her father's question she will "Love, and be silent".
    Shakespeare does not leave us guessing: the drama is *complete*
    in the words. *There would have been a time for such a word:* Quiller-
    Couch (*Shakespeare's Workmanship*, 50) stresses *There*, and I
    agree with him that this was probably Shakespeare's pointing.
        (*Creation in Words—of Atmosphere*, see especially pp. 215 ff.)
        (*Creation in Words—of Character*, see especially p. 223 ff.)

19 *To morrow, and to morrow, and to morrow . . .* Here is again one of
    those passages which carry us right away from any visible
    scene or set of circumstances. It is interesting that precisely

here, Shakespeare once again thinks of the Player and the Stage as an image of Man upon The Earth. Macbeth's gesture to illustrate the *poore Player, That struts and frets his houre upon the Stage*, points downward to the Platform beneath him: but the effect is enhanced, of course, by the fact that Burbadge at this moment steps, as it were, out of his part and lets us remember that he is himself *a poore Player* . . .

> (*Transcending the Visible Scene*, pp. 229 ff.)
> (*Objectivity of Vision*, pp. 189 ff.)
> (*Opportunity Snatched from Necessity*, pp. 196 ff.)

46 *Arme, Arme, and out* . . . The death of his wife and the news of Birnam Wood coming to Dunsinane combine to drive Macbeth out into the field. The Alarum bell, used for the second time in the play, makes a stirring contribution to the gathering climax.

ACT V, *Scene vi*

The Platform is suddenly filled with the foliage of Birnam Wood—a dramatic spectacle—and the throwing down of the *leavy Skreenes* helps to quicken the pace.

Seyward and his son and the English soldiers go out by one door, the Scottish by the other.

9 As in other battles (e.g. Shrewsbury Field in 1 *Henry IV*) the ceremonial trumpets give the signal, *Those clamorous Harbingers of Blood, & Death*. We proceed straight to the direction *Alarums continued* (? i.e. "prolonged").

> (*Music*, see especially pp. 65 f.)

ACT V, *Scene vii*

At this point, it seems likely that the Study curtains were thrown open to reveal the gate of Macbeth's castle, with perhaps a portcullis hanging under the Tarras. Macbeth himself stands at bay before the gates.

> (*Scene-Rotation*, pp. 31 ff.)

1 *They have tied me to a stake, I cannot flye, But Beare-like I must fight the course.* There is a touch of objectivity in Macbeth's metaphor. Though the Globe was not used for bear-baiting, other playhouses were, and it would not be hard for the audience to make the imaginative comparison with what to them was a familiar sight in a familiar setting. Macduff's mockery—*Wee'l*

have thee, as our rarer Monsters are Painted upon a pole, and under-
writ, Heere may you see the Tyrant (54 ff.)—is a similar effect.

(Objectivity of Vision, pp. 189 ff.)

The battle itself follows the simple Homeric structure. Young
Seyward, singled out in V. vi. 2—*You (worthy Unkle) Shall with
my Cosin your right Noble Sonne Leade our first Battell*—is the
Patroclus. His body is removed, for we hear later that he has
been *brought off the field* (V. vii. 73): presumably, therefore,
there are some *excursions* as well as *alarums*, either at line 13 or
line 23, or at the end of this scene.

(Battle Sequences, see especially pp. 91 f.)

14 *That way the noise is . . . There thou should'st be, By this great clatter,
one of greatest note Seemes bruited.* The backstage gang are kept
busy, but the Book-Keeper working with the prompt-book,
would no doubt see that they worked with discretion. The
words must always be audible, or the shape of the play's
climax is marred.

(Effects, pp. 69 ff.)

24 *This way my Lord, the Castles gently rendred.* The formal entry into
the Castle, after surrender, is made, of course, through the
gates visible in the Study. Victorious soldiers no doubt appear
in the window-stages and dip the tyrant's Banners, planting
those of Malcolm and Seyward on the Tarras. Macbeth's next
entry and that of Macduff would probably be made through
the two stage-doors on to the Platform.

(Plotting Entries, pp. 72 ff.)
(Battle Sequences, pp. 83 ff.)

30 Macbeth's diabolical energy, his *valiant fury,* continues to his
last line: Burbadge would make the welkin ring indeed with
the grandeur of his end. The rhythmical climax of his final
speech is unmistakable: the actor who misses it, mars all.

(Speech, see especially pp. 119 ff.)

63 The Folio's *Enter Fighting, and Macbeth slaine,* seems not to
chime with Malcolm's statement that *Macduffe is missing.* It
seems like a later alteration of the original ending. It is difficult
to see how the decapitation could have been made plausible.
Retreat, and Flourish. This is the normal end of a battle sequence,
and the contrasted trumpet calls would no doubt be easily
recognisable to the audience.

(Battle Sequences, pp. 83 ff.)
(Music, see especially pp. 65 f.)

Th'Usurpers cursed head

68 The brief dialogue between Seyward and Rosse is beautifully written. Rosse has already done something of the same kind in breaking bad news to Macduff (IV. iii. 172 ff.). It seems to have been one of Heminges' accomplishments: he had played Exeter in *Henry V* and described the affecting deaths of Suffolk and York (*Henry V*, IV. vi. 7 ff.). It was he, too, who had just played Kent in *King Lear*.

(*The Repertory*, see especially pp. 157 f.)

84 No squeamishness, I think, in the portrayal of *Th'Usurpers cursed head*, which would be the most prominent feature of the end of the play; fixed on a pole, perhaps, and lashed to the

middle of the Tarras rail, like the familiar sight of traitors' heads on London Bridge.

(Furnishing and Properties, pp. 38 ff.)

The finale a fully crowded scene. Malcolm central, with Macduff and Siward near him: the Thanes grouped by the two Stage-Posts; some soldiers round the perimeter, others on the Tarras with Macbeth's head and the banners. The departure is processional through the Castle gates, to the accompaniment of a *Flourish*. The tyrant's head remains when all others have withdrawn into the Tiring-House.

(Positioning, pp. 131 ff.)

EPILOGUE

Till the Globe is Rebuilt

THIS, then, is the contention. The wonderful detail of Shakespeare's stagecraft is waiting still to be revealed: it has not been seen in practice since his own day. More than that, the broad architectural design of his plays is habitually obscured, because we have not understood the nature of his poetic drama. That poetic drama was designed for, and evolved from, the unique conditions of performance in the Elizabethan theatre. Shakespeare's genius consisted not only in the creation of pure poetry and in the deeply sensitive understanding of the human heart, but also in transforming his theatre by poetical means into a whole world of the imagination. He was a practical man of the theatre, as few poets have been; he was a poet of genius, as few dramatists have been; and he found ready for his art the perfect vehicle for poetic drama, in the Globe Playhouse.

Is the case then proven, that if we want to experience the whole genius of Shakespeare, we must reconstruct the conditions of performance at the Globe? We must rebuild the Globe, in London certainly, in Stratford too, perhaps, and wherever an audience will meet to support a Shakespearian repertory. Rebuild the Globe! At the moment of writing, the slogan shrivels on the paper before the ink is dry. We cannot be adventurous with bricks and mortar in the spirit of the Chamberlain's Men shouldering the timbers of their theatre. The Muses come late on the list for a building permit. Nevertheless, a palatial concert-hall already rises on Bankside, and the project of a National Theatre is to-day much canvassed. The recovery of the national dramatist would certainly not cost as much as either.

What can be done meanwhile? Little, perhaps, in the present conditions, by the theatre of West End London—inextricably committed to the picture-stage and to the practice of long "runs" with hand-to-mouth recruiting and small chance of a continuous tradition of acting. More by repertories—whether professional or amateur—and by universities and schools where the tradition if not continuous can be hereditary. The Maddermarket Theatre at Norwich, for many years a solitary prophetic voice, shows the power of such a tradition of repertory. News comes over the Atlantic of a series of

Elizabethan performances of Shakespeare at Illinois University, the staging based upon the scene-rotations of John Cranford Adams, each production drawing larger audiences than its predecessor. Since 1941 there has been a series of performances in the semicircular Speech Room at Harrow School, where it is possible to reproduce the dimensions and central position of the Platform in a building no larger and no less intimate than Shakespeare's Globe. Every now and then letters come through the post telling of producers, at schools and elsewhere, who have tried or who want to try a similar experiment. The belief grows—and it is a simple faith—that the best way of producing Shakespeare's plays is his own. It seems possible that in time the body of opinion will grow so strong as to create the demand for a full-scale professional undertaking on these lines. More power, therefore, in the interim, to all those who will help to create the demand.

It must, of course, be a matter of improvisation and makeshift, of making the best of existing circumstances. One needs sometimes to be Napoleonic in ignoring precedent—turning one's back on a convenient and well equipped picture-stage ready at hand, and choosing instead a bare hall with a wide floor to manœuvre on. I came across an octagonal cattle-ring in the Border country which could (without further ado) have housed a performance of *Macbeth*. But we cannot always be lucky enough to find an octagonal or circular building. Perhaps it will be helpful to recapitulate the conditions which are most necessary.

First, an auditorium which is not too big: the Globe was only 84 feet in outside diameter, and the sense of crowded intimacy is extremely important.

Secondly, a broad and deep Platform, jutting out right into the middle of the audience: this is the main acting arena: it cannot be concealed from view: it is unlocalised, but can take its locality from the dialogue or from the setting of the inset. If possible, two pillars towards the front, which will help in the grouping and in other ways.

Thirdly, at the back of this Platform the Tiring-House can be represented by curtains: there must be a clear and spacious entry at each end of the curtain to represent the Globe stage-doors. Between the two doors an inset should be available, which can be hidden or exposed by parting the curtains: this represents the Globe Study.

Fourthly, any of the other features of the Globe Tiring-House that can be imitated—the Tarras, the Chamber, the Window-Stages— will help the scene-rotation. So, too, the trap-doors—especially that in the main platform, which gives access to Hell. But in practice it is

A new model of the Globe Playhouse made by John Cranford Adams for exhibition in the Folger Library, Washington

possible to do without these features, their need being supplied by other makeshift devices. The important thing here is to achieve that swift-running continuous action—the long rhythm of the play—which was so skilfully contrived by Shakespeare on the multiple stage of the Globe with its seven acting areas.

Fifthly, it is essential that the performance should be in steady daylight—or if that is not available, in a steady light representing daylight. No lighting effects, as we know them, except such as can be achieved by the use of torch, candle or fire. This requires faith—but it works triumphantly, even in such plays as *A Midsummer Night's Dream* and *Macbeth*—and some bravery too; for it is half the battle to have the audience sitting in the same light as the players; the actor's courage will be rewarded by the astonishing intimacy thus created between himself and his audience.

Sixthly, music should be used only for an explicit dramatic purpose: no overtures and incidental music: the indications are mostly given by Shakespeare or his colleagues in the Quartos or the Folio (which should for all purposes be used as Prompt Book). A fairly safe test is that the music should always be heard by the actors on the stage (or by some of them), never treated as incidental music, as a private comment passed from the orchestra to the audience. It should be in period—that is to say, Elizabethan—and this is no hardship, for the choice is wide and varied. But let it be remembered at the same time that Shakespeare is much inclined to experiment, to improvise and to be opportunist, both in style of music, and in instrumentation. Modern idiom, and modern harmony, and modern instrumentation should be avoided, since there is nothing that more quickly strikes irrelevant overtones than a musical anachronism. But one need not be pedantic in this matter: modern strings and modern wind can imitate the older style.

Seventhly, the costume likewise should avoid a post-Elizabethan style. The substructure should be Elizabethan—indeed, in many plays the whole wardrobe will be Elizabethan—but on top of this, one should superimpose the *Elizabethan's idea* of a Roman, a Scotsman, a fairy or a monster. Both in costume and furniture, one should remember to see the story through Elizabethan spectacles. The result is to make the characters fully alive instead of archaistic. The Babington-plot conspirators in *Julius Caesar* are an excellent case in point.

Eighthly, the repertory company should be trained as a team, in the acting tradition of the Chamberlain's Men. The choice of personnel should be made with some consideration for the "lines" of the Chamberlain's Men—we must have a Burbadge, a Pope-Lowin, a Kemp or an Armin, a Heminges, and so forth. We must have three or four boy-actors with the necessary skill or aptitude. The whole company should be trained especially to manage the great subtleties and the wide range of Shakespeare's speech: this should be their *first* accomplishment. Then they should be expert mimes, able (in the manner of the *Compagnie des Quinze*) to make us see more with the mind than we can with the eye. They should learn the special opportunities of the deep-perspective grouping on the Globe stage. They should understand the special quality of Shakespeare's characterisation—they should in fact learn to play their part in the drama, and to play it through Shakespeare's own medium, the medium of the spoken word.

These are the essentials, and granted these, there is still plenty of latitude for the creative imagination of the modern producer: only he must by implication subordinate his own imagination to that of Shakespeare himself. To follow his lead is, as I know by experience, an exhilarating adventure. Stand in imagination—since you cannot in reality—upon the Globe Platform, and ask yourself what did he do—what did the Chamberlain's Men do—at this point or that? The answer is almost always there, stated or implied in the text of the play, and the search, if not easy, is an absorbing and rewarding one.

I have a vivid picture in my mind of the poet pacing that Platform sometimes of a morning, when the playhouse was empty, and planning to himself what next he will transform it to; how next he will give to airy nothing a local habitation and a name. I am sure that he thought continually in terms of this theatre and understood how to use it as no one else has since, and learnt how wonderfully expressive a medium it could be for poetic drama—how much more expressive than our flat picture-stage can ever be. And I am sure that he thought of it as an excellent little world in which he and his fellow-players could "hold the mirror up to nature". I am not *so* sure, but I like to believe, that with his fondness for the double-meaning, he put his tongue lovingly into his cheek as he penned, at Stratford, at a distance from his old friends and colleagues in London, Prospero's familiar lines:

> The Clowd-capt Towres, the gorgeous Pallaces,
> The solemne Temples, the great Globe it selfe,
> Yea, all which it inherit, shall dissolve,
> And like this insubstantiall Pageant faded
> Leave not a racke behinde . . .

The great Globe itself dissolved in 1644, and though three hundred years of general acclamation have since passed, we have never seen the full splendour of the art we profess to admire. The Globe has not been rebuilt—not yet. When it is, if it is, I have little doubt that some of to-day's poets will be quick to delight in it, to walk with the freedom of Shakespeare himself, to feel themselves as broad and general as the casing air, whereas hitherto they have been cabined, cribbed, confined, bound in to the oppression of the proscenium arch.

APPENDIX I

E. K. Chambers' conjectural chronology of the plays is as follows (*William Shakespeare*, Vol. I, 270, 271):

1590–1   *2 Henry VI. 3 Henry VI.*
1591–2   *1 Henry VI.*
1592–3   *Richard III. Comedy of Errors.*
1593–4   *Titus Andronicus. Taming of the Shrew.*
1594–5   *Two Gentlemen of Verona. Love's Labour's Lost. Romeo and Juliet.*
1595–6   *Richard II. A Midsummer Night's Dream.*
1596–7   *King John. The Merchant of Venice.*
1597–8   *1 Henry IV. 2 Henry IV.*
1598–9   *Much Ado About Nothing. Henry V.*
1599–1600   *Julius Caesar. As You Like It. Twelfth Night.*
1600–1   *Hamlet.[1] Merry Wives of Windsor.*
1601–2   *Troilus and Cressida.*
1602–3   *All's Well That Ends Well.*
1603–4   ——
1604–5   *Measure for Measure. Othello.*
1605–6   *King Lear. Macbeth.*
1606–7   *Antony and Cleopatra.*
1607–8   *Coriolanus. Timon of Athens.*
1608–9   *Pericles.*
1609–10   *Cymbeline.*
1610–11   *The Winter's Tale.*
1611–12   *The Tempest.*
1612–13   *Henry VIII. Two Noble Kinsmen.*

---

[1] In his *Shakesperian Gleanings* (p. 68) Chambers revises the ascription of *Hamlet* and puts it in 1601.

APPENDIX II

Twelfth Night shows how it is possible to devise a neat scheme of scene-rotation for a neatly-constructed play. I suggest the following plan:

I. i (Orsino): *Chamber*. I. ii (Viola and Sea-Captain): *Platform*. I. iii (Toby-Maria-Andrew): *Study* and *Platform*. I. iv (at Orsino's): *Chamber*. I. v (Olivia-Viola-Malvolio): *Study* and *Platform*.

II. i (Antonio-Sebastian): *Platform*. II. ii (Viola-Malvolio in Street): *Platform*. II. iii (drinking scene): *Study* and *Platform*. (with centre-trap open for cellar). II. iv (at Orsino's): *Chamber*. II. v (Box tree): *Study* and *Platform*.

III. i (Viola-Feste-Toby-Olivia): *Study* and *Platform*. III. ii (Toby, etc.): *Study* and *Platform*. III. iii (Sebastian-Antonio): *Platform*. III. iv (cross-garters, duel, arrest): *Study* and *Platform*.

IV. i (Sebastian-and-Olivia): *Platform* and *Study*. IV. ii (Sir Topas): *Platform* (with wicket, and bay-window above). IV. iii (Sebastian-Olivia): *Platform* (other door).

V. i *Study* and *Platform* (at Olivia's; "if you will let your Lady know I am here to speak with her . . ." (45) and "Heere at my house" (331)).

Thus the Duke's scenes (the static scenes, with a minimum of movement) are all in the *Chamber* (until he visits Olivia at the end), and the *Study* needs but two sets: Olivia's apartment (I. iii and v; II. iii); garden-set (II. v.; III. i, ii, iv; IV. i; V. i). An interval after II. iv makes easy the transformation of the Study from Olivia's apartment to the garden-set.

APPENDIX III

A selection from T. W. Baldwin's conjectural cast-lists is given below. For the complete lists the reader is referred to *Organization and Personnel of the Shakespearean Company*. Baldwin's chronology differs (especially in the early years) from that of Chambers, which I have adopted as representative of the orthodox view. The asterisks indicate those characters whose casting is based on external evidence; (w) after the date means "winter" and (s) "summer".

	Richard III	*A Midsummer Night's Dream*	*King John*	*Richard II*
	1593 (w)	1594 (s)	1595 (s)	1595 (w)
PHILLIPS	Edward IV	Theseus	King Philip	Bolingbroke
BURBADGE	*Richard III	Demetrius	John	Richard II
POPE	Buckingham	Quince	Philip	Mowbray
LOWIN				
BRYANE	Stanley	Philostrate	Pandulph	Gaunt
CUNDALL	Richmond	Lysander	Salisbury	Northumber-land
OSTLER				
HEMINGES	Hastings	Egeus	Hubert	York
SLY		Flute	Lewis	Harry Percy
UNDERWOOD				
SHAKESPEARE				
KEMP		Bottom		
ARMIN				
COWLEY			Robert	
PALLANT	Clarence			
BELT				
COOKE	Margaret	Helena		
TOOLEY	Elizabeth	Puck		
GOFFE	Anne	Oberon	Constance	Queen
ECCLESTON	Duchess of Y.	Hermia	Q. Elinor	D. Gloucester
GILBURNE	Prince Edward	Titania	Arthur	D. of York
NED SHAKE-SPEARE	York	Hippolyta	L. Faulcon-bridge	
WILSON				
CROSSE				
EDMANS				
RICE				
SANDS				
ROBINSON				

	1 *Henry IV* 1596 (s)	2 *Henry IV* 1596 (w)	*The Merchant of Venice* 1597 (s)	*Romeo and Juliet* 1598 (s)
PHILLIPS	Henry IV	Henry IV	Gratiano	Benvolio
BURBADGE	Hal	Hal	Bassanio	Romeo
POPE	Falstaff	Falstaff	Shylock	Mercutio
LOWIN				
BRYANE	Worcester	Scroop	Morocco	
CUNDALL	Northumber- land	Northumber- land	Antonio	F. Laurence
OSTLER				
HEMINGES	Glendower	Chief Justice	Salarino	Capulet
SLY	Hotspur	Lancaster	Lorenzo	Tybalt
UNDERWOOD				
SHAKESPEARE			Duke	Escalus
KEMP		Shallow	Launcelot	*Peter, etc.
ARMIN				
COWLEY		Silence	Gobbo	Sampson
PALLANT				
BELT				
COOKE				
TOOLEY				
GOFFE	L. Mortimer	L. Northumb.	Portia	Juliet
ECCLESTON	Mrs. Quickly	*Mrs. Quickly	Nerissa	Nurse
GILBURNE	L. Percy	L. Percy	Jessica	L. Capulet
NED SHAKE- SPEARE	Francis	Doll		L. Montague
WILSON				
CROSSE				
EDMANS				
RICE				
SANDS				
ROBINSON				

L

	Much Ado About Nothing 1598 (w)	*Henry V* 1599 (s)	*Julius Caesar* 1599 (w)	*As You Like It* 1600 (s)
PHILLIPS	Don John	Constable	Cassius	Frederick
BURBADGE	Claudio	Henry V	Brutus	Orlando
POPE	Benedick	Fluellen	Casca	Jaques
LOWIN				
BRYANE				
CUNDALL	Don Pedro	Canterbury	Antony	Oliver
OSTLER				
HEMINGES	Leonato	Exeter	Caesar	Duke Sr.
SLY	Borachio	Dauphin	Octavius	Silvius
UNDERWOOD				
SHAKESPEARE	F. Francis	Charles	? Poet Cinna ? Cicero	*Adam
KEMP	*Dogberry			
ARMIN				Touchstone
COWLEY	*Verges			William
PALLANT				
BELT				
COOKE				
TOOLEY				
GOFFE				
ECCLESTON	Beatrice			
GILBURNE	Hero	Katherine	Portia	Celia
NED SHAKE-SPEARE	Margaret	Alice	Calphurnia	Rosalind
WILSON	Balthazar	Isabel	Lucius	Phebe
CROSSE	Ursula	Mrs. Quickly		Audrey
EDMANS				
RICE				
SANDS				
ROBINSON				

	Twelfth Night 1600 (w)	Hamlet 1603 (s)	The Merry Wives of Windsor 1603 (w)	Othello 1604 (s)
PHILLIPS	Malvolio			
BURBADGE	Orsino	*Hamlet	Ford	*Othello
POPE	Toby			
LOWIN		Claudius	Falstaff	Iago
BRYANE				
CUNDALL	Antonio	Horatio	Page	Cassio
OSTLER				
HEMINGES	Fabian	Polonius	Host	Brabantio
SLY	Sebastian	Laertes	Fenton	Roderigo
UNDERWOOD				
SHAKESPEARE	Sea-Captain	*Ghost		Duke
KEMP				
ARMIN	Feste	1st G. D.	Evans	Clown
COWLEY	Aguecheek	Osric	Slender	
PALLANT				
BELT				
COOKE		Rosencrantz	Caius	Lodovico
TOOLEY				
GOFFE				
ECCLESTON				
GILBURNE	Olivia	Fortinbras		
NED SHAKE-SPEARE	Viola			
WILSON		Ophelia	Mrs. Page	Desdemona
CROSSE	Maria	Gertrude	Fairy Queen Mrs. Quickly	Emilia
EDMANS			Mrs. Ford	Bianca
RICE			Wm. Page	
SANDS			Anne Page	
ROBINSON				

	Measure for Measure 1604 (w)	King Lear 1605 (w)	Macbeth 1606 (s)	Antony and Cleopatra 1606 (w)
PHILLIPS				
BURBADGE	Angelo	*Lear	Macbeth	Antony
POPE				
LOWIN	Lucio	Gloucester	Banquo	Enobarbus
BRYANE				
CUNDALL	Duke	Edgar	Malcolm	Caesar
OSTLER				
HEMINGES	Escalus	Kent	Ross	Pompey
SLY	Claudio	Edmund	Macduff	Menas
UNDERWOOD				
SHAKESPEARE	Peter		Duncan	Lepidus
KEMP				
ARMIN	Pompey	Fool	Porter	Clown
COWLEY	Elbow	Oswald	Old Man	
PALLANT				
BELT				
COOKE	Provost	Cornwall	Lennox	
GOFFE		Albany		
TOOLEY				
ECCLESTON				
GILBURNE		?King of F.	?Siward	?Agrippa
NED SHAKE-SPEARE				
WILSON	Isabella	Goneril		
CROSSE	Overdone			
EDMANS		Regan	L. Macbeth	Cleopatra
RICE	Juliet		Hecate	Charmian
SANDS	Mariana	Cordelia	L. Macduff	Octavia
ROBINSON			Son	

GENERAL INDEX

INDEX OF CHARACTERS

(For characters in *Macbeth*, see also pp. 276–312)

INDEX OF PASSAGES

The following Index is a select list of those passages on which my comments may perhaps be helpful to producers: